Cameroon

THE BRADT TRAVEL GUIDE

Ben West

Bradt Travel Guides Ltd, UK
The Globe Pequot Press Inc, USA

First published in 2004 by Bradt Travel Guides Ltd,
19 High Street, Chalfont St Peter, Bucks SL9 9QE, England
www.bradtguides.com
Published in the USA by The Globe Pequot Press Inc, 246 Goose Lane,
PO Box 480, Guilford, Connecticut 06437-0480

British Library Cataloguing in Publication Data
A catalogue record for this book is available from the British Library

ISBN-10: 1 84162 078 5
ISBN-13: 978 184162 078 7

Photographs
Front cover: Goliath frog (Daniel Heuclin/NHPA)
Text: Keith Barnes (KB), Brian Cruickshank (BC), Troy Inman (TI), Janusz Konarski (JK),
Rowena Quantrill (RQ), Toby Quantrill (TQ), Andrew Pape-Salmon (APS)

Illustrations Annabel Milne
Maps Alan Whitaker

Typeset from the author's disc by Wakewing, High Wycombe
Printed and bound in Italy by Legoprint SpA

Author

Ben West has written on a wide variety of subjects for many newspapers and magazines, including the *Guardian*, the *Independent*, the *Daily Telegraph*, *The Times*, the *Daily Mail*, the *Evening Standard* and *Readers' Digest*. Travel writing has taken him to more than 20 countries, including five in Africa, and his first trip to Cameroon netted him four tropical diseases. He was chief property correspondent of the *Daily Express* and the *Sunday Express* from 1999 to 2001, at which time penning one-too-many features on the joys of bungalow living became too much. His books *London for Free* (1996), *Fun for a Fiver in London* (2002) and *Fun for a Fiver in Amsterdam* (2002) were published by Pan Books, and *Buying a Home: The Virgin Guide* was published by Virgin Books in 2003. He has written a short film, *Gertrude*, featuring Prunella Scales, which was filmed in 2004.

PUBLISHER'S FOREWORD
Hilary Bradt

The first Bradt travel guide was written in 1974 by George and Hilary Bradt on a river barge floating down a tributary of the Amazon. In the 1980s and '90s the focus shifted away from hiking to broader-based guides to new destinations – usually the first to be published on these places. In the 21st century Bradt continues to publish these ground-breaking guides, along with others to established holiday destinations, incorporating in-depth information on culture and natural history alongside the nuts and bolts of where to stay and what to see.

Bradt authors support responsible travel, with advice not only on minimum impact but also on how to give something back through local charities. Thus a true synergy is achieved between the traveller and local communities.

*   *   *

When I published *Backpacker's Africa: West* in 1988 I was particularly taken by the Cameroon chapter. Here was a country that had the best hiking in West Africa and also some of the finest wildlife reserves. Such a combination sounded irresistible! Then we could only give Cameroon 15 pages; it is exciting to be able to do it justice in a full-length book.

Contents

CAMEROON PROVINCES

Acknowledgements

I would most like to thank my wife, Bryony, for her great patience and tolerance of my obsession with Cameroon. I would also like to thank my children, Josh, Jerusha and Jethro, for stoically managing to listen again and again to my accounts of various African wonders, tropical diseases and sub-Saharan frustrations.

There are a couple of people I would very much like to thank for introducing me to the country in the first place, helping with research and being of great assistance while I was there, but I cannot mention them by name for reasons too complicated to mention here. They know who they are.

I would particularly like to thank J and Geeta Ravikumar. Not only were they so welcoming in Cameroon, but they were remarkably helpful and generous when it was needed. Thank you also to Hester Brown and Arun Muttreja, who introduced me to them.

The excellent contributions by Keith Barnes and Christian Boix concerning birding in Cameroon must of course receive prominent acknowledgement, as should further information kindly provided by Colin Workman and Andrew Pape-Salmon. Brian Cruickshank's information and suggestions have been very helpful.

Lastly I would like to thank my editor at Bradt Travel Guides, Tricia Hayne, as well as Adrian Phillips, Selena Dickson, Hilary Bradt and everyone else at Bradt for their patience and support on this project.

FEEDBACK REQUEST

Although I have attempted to be as up to date and accurate as possible, it is in the nature of guidebooks that things change. The African continent in particular is always in a state of change. If you have any comments or new information or a story to share – however lengthy or brief – I would greatly appreciate your assistance in updating the next edition. Any help will be acknowledged in the guide. If you would like to help, please email ben@benwest.info or write to me care of Bradt Travel Guides Ltd (Cameroon guide).

Preface

My first visit to Cameroon was my first contact with Africa, leading to a fascination with the continent that remains unabated. In 1986 I joined a friend who was visiting his father, who lived in the Cameroonian capital, Yaoundé.

I was instantly captivated by the country, not least due to its diversity, and the great contrasts to the way of life I knew. That first trip was certainly eventful. After an excursion to the north of the country I returned to Britain with two types of malaria, blackwater fever and another tropical illness, filariasis. My friend ended up in a Yaoundé hospital, also having contracted malaria and dysentery.

Despite this, the strong force Africa seems to take hold on many people applied with us, and both of us have returned to Africa a number of times.

Inexplicably, Cameroon seldom features on travellers' plans despite the huge wealth of cultural and geographical treasures it possesses. To non-travellers it also remains a little-known country, and indeed the impressive performance of its football team from 1990 onwards, the Lake Nyos tragedy of 1986 (where volcanic toxic gas claimed hundreds of Cameroonian lives) and celebrated *makossa* musician Manu Dibango are about the only things many people can associate with it.

Much of the year, and during the rainy season especially, there are indeed very few travellers (as most people like to call themselves) or tourists (as others call most travellers). In September, for example, in many areas you may only see one tourist a week, if that.

To enjoy it most, accept that life in Cameroon, as in the whole of Africa, runs at a slower pace than most of us are probably used to. Patience is a massive virtue here. Cameroonians do not pay as much attention to time and punctuality as the typical Westerner, as they feel that one need not be enslaved by a clock. So slow down, and you'll take it all in and enjoy it so much more.

Introduction

Cameroon is often described as being 'the melting pot of Africa' or 'Africa in miniature' or 'Africa in microcosm'. This is because it encompasses much from elsewhere on the continent, from every type of African people to every form of landscape.

The contrasts are spectacular: in geography (from lush rainforest in the south to the near-desert of the north); in climate (the coastal city of Douala has on average about ten times as much rainfall in July than the nearby capital, Yaoundé); in the peoples (there are over 275 ethnic groups in Cameroon); in language (Cameroon is officially bilingual, but around 160 African dialects are spoken); and religion (there's a Catholic and Protestant south and Muslim north, with a good dose of traditional African religions thrown in).

Touristically, the country is so attractive it is perplexing that it is so little known or visited. Blending magnificent scenery – from the arid plains in the north to verdant mountains in the south – and impressive national parks with an exceptional richness of culture, Cameroon can offer the whole African gamut from 'pygmy' hunting camps deep in the rainforest in the south to Arabic-speaking trading towns in the near-desert of the north, as well as the colourful ancient tribal kingdoms and striking mountain scenery in the Ring Road region near Bamenda in the Western Highlands. In this region the town of Foumban has a market, a royal palace and museum to explore.

Cameroon also has many gloriously unspoilt, empty, relaxing beaches. Kribi, a popular resort in the south, has beautiful white beaches, while Limbé, northwest of Douala, has black volcanic ones. Limbé is also an ideal starting point for climbing Mount Cameroon, West Africa's highest peak but still a relatively easy hike, best started from the mountainside town of Buéa.

To the northwest, the country is equally beautiful, with further volcanic peaks covered by bamboo forest rising to over 2,000m (6,500ft), and with picturesque waterfalls and villages scattered over the lower slopes. This region boasts Korup National Park, which has adequate facilities to allow visitors to explore spectacular rainforest.

Cameroon's two biggest towns, Yaoundé, the capital, and the port of Douala, both boast luxury hotels, a good range of restaurants, as well as nightclubs and vibrant markets.

Cameroon has a large number of lakes, including crater lakes created by volcanic activity. The largest include Lake Barombi at Kumba, Lake Baleng near Bafoussam, lakes Tison and Mbalang around Ngaoundéré, the twin lakes of Manenguba and lakes Oku, Nyos and Wum in the northwest.

There are also lakes formed from basins such as gigantic Lake Chad and Lake Fiango, and also tectonic lakes, formed by large depressions caused by tectonic movements in the earth's crust. These include Lake Ejagani near Mamfé, Lake Ossa near Edea and Lake Dissoni near Kumba.

In addition, there are lagoons made from the accumulation of sand on the Wouri and Ndian basins, and artificial lakes at Edea and Songloulou on the Sanaga River, at Lagdo on the Bénoué River, at Mape on the Mbam River, at Mbakaou on the Djerem and at Bamendjin on the Noun.

Highlights for a visitor also include Waza National Park, with its abundance of wildlife, the mountains and pretty villages around laid-back Islamic-influenced Maroua, with its tree-lined streets, and Mora's colourful Sunday market.

As well as fabulous beaches, much of southeast Cameroon is made up of virgin forest that is home to abundant wildlife, including lowland gorillas and so-called pygmies. This region has the lowest density of services and lowest quality roads in the country and therefore is the most challenging to travel through.

Wherever you are in Cameroon – and even if you are not particularly religious – do not miss the Sunday-morning church services. The atmosphere and music are excellent. One word of warning: the services will probably not start on time and may last well into the afternoon. It is acceptable to excuse yourself quietly if you need to be somewhere else, but this may be a little tricky if you are placed at the front of the church in a place of honour.

Spellings

There is wide variety and inconsistency of spellings in Cameroon, and those in this book are randomly chosen. In some cases French spellings are adopted, in others those that are more easily recognisable to English speakers. In no case, however, do I expect you to confuse one name or word for an entirely different and unconnected one.

Part One

General Information

CAMEROON AT A GLANCE
Location West coast of Africa
Size 475,440km² (183,639 square miles)
Capital Yaoundé
Population 15.5 million
Time GMT + 1. No daylight saving time.
Currency CFA franc
Electricity 220V
Official language English
Religion Islam (90%), Christianity (10%)

Background Information

FACTS AND FIGURES
Republic of Cameroon/République du Cameroun

The country is often referred to as 'Cameroon', 'Cameroun', and 'The Cameroons'. Cameroon is the English spelling, while Cameroun is the French one. The Cameroons is an obsolete expression dating from the time when the country was split into separate British and French territories. The name is derived from *camarões*, the Portuguese word for prawns, which were found in great quantities in the Wouri River by the first European explorers.

Location

Situated on the west coast of Africa, running north to south from the Sahara Desert to the Atlantic Ocean, Cameroon is bounded by the Gulf of Guinea, Nigeria, Chad, the Central African Republic, the Republic of Congo, Gabon and Equatorial Guinea.

Like most African countries, Cameroon was created by Europeans drawing arbitrary lines on a map. These boundaries did not coincide with any pre-existing geographic or cultural divisions.

Size

Cameroon covers an area totalling 475,440km² (183,638 square miles), which makes it larger than California and about twice the size of the UK. It comprises 469,440km² of land and 6,000km² of water, and has a coastline of 402km.

Elevation extremes

Lowest point Atlantic Ocean (0m)
Highest point Mount Fako (4,095m)

Capital

The capital of Cameroon, and home of the government, is Yaoundé, a city set in a lush region in the centre of the south of the country at an altitude of about 750m. Built upon seven hills, it is more relaxed than Cameroon's largest city, the economic and industrial capital Douala.

Population

A 1999 estimate of Cameroon's population settled upon just under 15.5 million with about 50% living in rural areas. However, migration from rural areas to the cities is increasing all the time.

Yaoundé is estimated to have a population of around 1.1 million, Douala 1.5 million, Garoua 290,000, Maroua 200,000, Bafoussam 140,000, Bamenda 220,000, Nkongsamba 110,000 and Ngaoundéré approximately 100,000.

Nearly a third of the population lives in Littoral and Central provinces, not least because they contain the two largest cities in the country, Yaoundé and Douala.

3

About 11,000 Europeans (predominantly French) and 1,200 Americans live in the country, including around 150 Peace Corps volunteers stationed throughout. There are also sizeable immigrant populations of Nigerians, Chadians, Congolese and Senegalese.

The regions have distinct societies – from the Muslim traders and pastoralists in the north, to the farmers and craftspeople of the west and the forest peoples of the south.

Life expectancy, age structures and mortality rates
Infant mortality rate 76.88 deaths per 1,000 live births
Life expectancy at birth Total population 54.59 years; male: 53.76 years; female: 55.44 years
Fertility rate 4.8 children born per woman
Age structure 0–14 years: 42.37%, 15–64 years: 54.28%, 65 years and over: 3.35%
Population growth rate 2.41%
Birth rate 36.12 births per 1,000 population
Death rate 11.99 deaths per 1,000 population
(All the above 2001 estimates.)
Adult prevalence rate of HIV/AIDS 7.73% (1999 estimate)

Land use
Arable land 13%
Permanent crops 2%
Permanent pastures 4%
Forests and woodland 78%
Other 3%
Irrigated land 210km^2

Natural hazards
Recent volcanic activity with release of poisonous gases at Lake Nyos.

Ports, harbours and waterways
Cameroon's main ports and harbours are Bonaberi, Douala, Garoua, Kribi and Tiko. Cameroon has 2,090km of waterways.

Provinces and districts
Cameroon is divided into ten administrative provinces. These are, with both their English and French names and with their capitals in brackets:

Adamawa/Adamaoua (Ngaoundéré)
Centre/Centre (Yaoundé)
East/Est (Bertoua)
Extreme North/Extrème Nord (Maroua)
Littoral/Littoral (Douala)
North/Nord (Garoua)
Northwest/Nord-Ouest (Bamenda)
West/Ouest (Bafoussam)
South/Sud (Ebolowa)
Southwest/Sud-Ouest (Buéa)

Education
Cameroon does well compared with its neighbours as far as education goes. Education is compulsory between the ages of six and 14, attendance is more than 70%, literacy is around 63% and nearly 90% of children receive primary education.

Literacy
Of those aged 15 and over, 63.4% of the population can read and write according to a 1995 estimate.

Legal system
The legal system is based upon the French civil law system, with a common law influence. Traditional courts are still very important in domestic, property and probate law. Tribal laws and customs are recognised in the formal court system when they do not conflict with national law. Traditional kingdoms and organisations also exercise other functions of government, while traditional rulers receive a government allowance.

Time
The time in Cameroon is one hour ahead of Greenwich Mean Time; consequently, when it is noon in Cameroon it is 11.00 in London, 06.00 in New York, noon in Paris and 21.00 in Sydney. Cameroon does not observe daylight saving time.

Opening times
Government offices and banks are generally open from 07.30 to 15.30 from Monday to Friday, and shops and businesses vary from around 08.00–15.00 daily, or 09.00–12.30 and 15.30–19.30, or 08.00–12.00 and 14.30–17.30. Pharmacies tend to open from 08.00–20.00, markets from approximately 07.00–18.00, and post offices from Monday to Friday 08.00–15.30 and Saturday 08.00–13.00.

Currency
Cameroon's currency is the Central African economic zone's (Communauté Financière Africaine/the African Financial Community) CFA franc. In this book, £1 = CFA933 and US$1 = CFA529 based on exchange rates in late 2003.

Electricity
The electricity supply is 220V and plugs are usually of the European two-pin type, although the British three-pin variety may be occasionally found in anglophone regions.

Weights and measures
The metric system is used.

GEOGRAPHY
Cameroon has an extremely diverse terrain, but its variety should come as no surprise in a country which encompasses the edges of the Sahara in the north to more than 20 million hectares of dense equatorial rainforest in the south and east, with every African landscape in between, including dry grassy plains, volcanic ranges punctuated by crater lakes, rocky mountainous tracts and savanna.

It possesses four distinct geographical regions. To the west and the northwest are rolling hills and volcanic mountains draped in lush vegetation fed by heavy rainfall; the low coastal plains of the south are blanketed with thick equatorial rainforest extending to the Sanaga River; in central Cameroon, this rainforest yields to the vast, sparsely vegetated Adamaoua Plateau; and extending northwards from this plateau to Lake Chad at the most northerly point of the country are the northern plains, where savanna contrasts strikingly with unusual rock formations in the Mandara Mountains.

Much of the south of the country is a low-lying coastal plain dominated by dense, rain-fed lowland forest (or rainforest) where trees can grow as high as 50m, their upper branches forming a canopy preventing light from reaching the forest floor. This prevents many plants from flourishing in such regions, apart from vines and other epiphytes.

At the centre of the country is a dissected plateau, the Adamaoua, averaging 1,300m above sea level, which does much to separate the north from the south of the country.

As a striking contrast to the rough vegetation of the south, the landscape of north Cameroon is characterised by a semi-arid region dotted with rocky escarpments. The region begins with the huge grassy plains of the Adamaoua Plateau, extending further to the north between Maroua and Kousséri into extensive dry flat plains, spotted with patches of grain plants on the border of the Sahel.

About 150 million years ago, when South America pulled away from Africa, the rifting caused volcanic activity in West Africa, notably in the Highlands of Cameroon, which comprise the Rumpi Hills, Mount Kupé and the Bamenda Highlands, and which extend into Nigeria's Obodu Plateau. A series of volcanic mountains lead from Bioko Island (part of Equatorial Guinea) along a volcanic intrusion that roughly follows the Nigerian border. The mountain chain extends inland as far as the Adamawa Plateau and the wild, unfertile Mandara Mountains in the north of the country. The biggest is the active volcano Mount Cameroon, at 4,095m (13,353ft) the highest peak in West Africa and the sixth-highest in Africa. There are a number of volcanic crater lakes in this area.

CLIMATE

This part of the world is often assumed to be constantly very hot. A glance at a climate chart would show that this belief is something of a myth.

The climate of Cameroon varies greatly with the terrain, ranging from tropical along the coast to semi-arid and hot in the northern plains and the Sahel region, which boasts a seven-month dry season.

The great variations in rainfall from one region to the next are astonishing – from hardly enough rain to support agriculture in the extreme north to over 5m per annum in the southwest.

Debundscha, near Limbé in the southwest, is the second-wettest region in the world, after Mawsynvan in Maghalaya State, India.

The south

Generally, the south has a dry season from approximately November to February, light rains from March to May and a rainy season from June to October. Humidity rises greatly in the south in July and August.

Great disruption can be experienced during the rainy season, with roads and tracks washed away. Many towns, including Douala, which is warm and humid all year round, become overrun by floods (not surprising, considering that the average rainfall in July is around 75cm compared with 5cm in January). Mamfé especially can be difficult to reach. The temperature is highest from March to May (around 30°C/86°F in Yaoundé) and stays around a minimum (in the night) of 19°C/66°F and a maximum (in the day) of around 28°C/82°F in Yaoundé throughout the year, while in Douala the minimum temperature hovers around 23°, the maximum nearer 28°.

The north

Northern Cameroon has a long, less dramatic rainy season from around May or June to September (peaking at around 32cm rainfall in August compared with no rainfall from November to March) and, although travel is easier than in the south, the national parks are generally closed from May to December. The temperature in Kousséri ranges from a minimum of 14° (in the night) from December to February to 23° and upwards from April to June, with a maximum (in the day) of 33° from December to February and a blistering 42°C/104°F from March to May.

HISTORY

Since as long ago as around 8000BC, Cameroon has received countless human migrations and become home to a very varied range of cultural, tribal, linguistic and cultural groups, such as Puels from the coast of Guinea, Fulani and Arab people from western Sudan, and Bantus from the Republic of Congo.

The earliest inhabitants of the country were likely to have been the Bakas and other ethno-linguistic groups of short stature (commonly but incorrectly known as 'pygmies'), some of whom still inhabit the forests of the South and East provinces. They were forced into the forests by Bantu-speaking peoples originating from the Cameroonian Western Highlands, the Sahel and the Nigerian Plateau in around 200BC.

While Bantu peoples settled in the south and east of the country, the north became inhabited by a combination of Arabic, Hamitic and Negroid peoples. In the north of the country, around the Chad basin, a series of important African civilisations originated, including the Kanem, Bornou and Sao peoples, the last having migrated from the Nile valley. Sao archaeological finds from this period include jewellery, terracotta and bronze sculptures, and coins.

At the start of the 15th century the Fulani, a pastoral, nomadic Islamic people, started migrating from the western Sahel and by the end of the 16th century had a strong presence in the north of the country.

Portuguese explorers, led by Fernando Po, arrived on Cameroon's coast in 1472 and became the first Europeans to sail up the estuary of the Wouri River, which Po dubbed the Rio dos Camarões (River of Prawns) because of the high number of giant prawns it contained, and which later gave the country its name.

The Portuguese set up sugar plantations and began a 400-year slave and goods trade with local chiefs (especially around Douala, Limbé and Bonaberi), which would later also involve the British, Dutch, French and Germans. The chiefs also traded ivory against European goods. Despite Cameroon's new relationship with these countries, there would be no attempt made to colonise the country until the 19th century.

As the coastal region grew in influence, it overtook that of powers in the north such as the Bornou empire, which extended as far as the Adamawa region in the 16th century.

Between the late 1770s and early 1800s, the Fulani defeated much of what is now northern Cameroon, conquering or displacing its largely non-Muslim inhabitants. A slave trade developed here also.

Increasingly during the first half of the 19th century, British missionaries established a presence in Cameroon (starting with the Baptist Missionary Society of London's first station in Cameroon at Bimbia in 1844) and protested against the slave trade. American Presbyterians also sent missionaries, and the result was not only the Christianisation of the country but the introduction of European culture and education.

Significant European settlement and conquest of the interior then followed, especially from the late 1870s, when supplies of the malaria suppressant, quinine, became plentiful. At this time feudal northern Cameroon was under the control of the Fulani empire in Sokoto (Nigeria), while in the south trade in slaves switched to so-called legitimate trade in things like gold and ivory between the coastal chiefs and German, French and British trading companies. In return they received European manufactured items such as cloth, metals, firearms and alcohol.

At this time the whole continent was being transformed by the influx of European powers, known as the Scramble for Africa. In 1880, around 90% of Africa was ruled by Africans. Twenty years later, European powers had seized almost all of the continent.

The chiefs located around Douala became increasingly concerned that tradesmen in the interior of the country would deal directly with the Europeans, sidestepping them, and therefore pressed for British guarantees that would have led to the creation of a protectorate. Queen Victoria delayed doing anything about the issue and when at last she sent an envoy to solve the matter in 1884 Germany had already signed a treaty with Douala and Bamiléké chiefs in which they gave their sovereignty to Germany to receive trade advantages.

Cameroon as a political unit was thus created, replacing numerous states, chiefdoms and political entities; each had its own history, culture, economy and governments.

All of present-day Cameroon and sections of several of its neighbours became the German colony of Kamerun, with a capital at Buéa which later switched to Yaoundé.

From 1885 Baron von Soden, the first governor of the colony, concentrated on putting down rebellions in the interior of the country. The German intention was initially to establish an increased presence inland before British or French officials and traders did so. There were serious conflicts, especially with the Bafut, Bulu and Kpe.

A decade later von Soden's replacement, von Puttkamer, built the country's first railway line using forced labour. German rule brought further infrastructure of practical value like public buildings, roads, and other engineering projects. But German rule was harsh: at one plantation a fifth of the labourers died in a single year from overwork. In 1899 German forces attacked the Adamawa region and conquered Tibati. At this time the population of Kamerun stood at around 2,650,000, including around 150 European missionaries and 50,000 African Christians.

World War I stopped German expansion. Soon after the war began, British, Belgian and French colonial troops, made up principally of Africans, invaded Cameroon and in 1916 forced the Germans to leave.

In 1919 a League of Nations mandate divided the colony between Britain and France, with a British administrative zone, which took up 20% of the land, divided into Northern and Southern Cameroons, and a French one taking up the remaining 80%.

France ruled from Yaoundé while Britain's territory, a strip bordering Nigeria from the sea to Lake Chad, was governed from Lagos in Nigeria. In 1922 the League of Nations formally conferred mandates on Britain and France for their respective administrative zones.

In 1946 the French and British mandates were renewed as United Nations trusteeships and on the whole the British territory was still governed from Nigeria. Two groups began to emerge in the British sector, one wanting reunification with French Cameroon, the other wanting to merge with Nigeria.

The exportation of products like cocoa, timber and palm oil increased greatly in the years after the war, but the French imposed taxes and used forced labour to build roads, plantations and other facilities, which caused resentment to build up in the country.

The French authorities faced increasing calls for reunification and anti-British/French political parties formed and grew in strength, including the Union of Cameroonian Peoples (UPC), based largely among the Bamiléké and Bassa ethnic groups, and French-educated Fulani northerner Ahmadou Ahidjo's Bloc Democratique Camerounais.

The UPC demanded unification of the two Cameroons and independence from France. With these demands not met, in 1955 the UPC began an armed struggle for independence in French Cameroon. This rebellion, which caused thousands of deaths and much damage, continued with a weakening intensity, even after independence.

In 1958 Ahidjo formed a new, more conservative party, l'Union Camerounaise, and French Cameroon was granted self-government with Ahidjo as prime minister. French Cameroon achieved independence on January 1 1960 as the Republic of Cameroon.

In 1961, following a UN-sponsored referendum, the largely Christian (British) Southern Cameroon joined the Republic of Cameroon to become the Federal Republic of Cameroon, while the largely Muslim Northern Cameroon voted to join Nigeria.

At this time Cameroon – with its multi-ethnic and multi-religious population impatient for development and change – was weary of its chequered colonial past. It was increasingly disillusioned by a weak economy heavily reliant on a few exports, little industrial production and an undeveloped infrastructure. Cameroon seemed to be a typical African nation ripe for a period of significant political, social and economic problems. Yet it soon established a stable footing, avoiding debt, diversifying its economy, avoiding political instability and working towards producing enough food to feed its people.

The formerly French and British sectors each continued to maintain substantial autonomy. During 1961–63 there was large-scale unrest, believed to have been orchestrated by the UPC. Ahidjo quelled this with the help of French forces. He then outlawed all political parties but his own in 1966, and successfully suppressed the UPC rebellion, censoring the press, imprisoning thousands of political opponents and capturing the last important rebel leader in 1970.

In 1972, following a national referendum, a new constitution replaced the federation with a unitary state and the country was renamed the United Republic of Cameroon, to the great consternation of anglophone Cameroon. Economically Cameroon was growing stronger at this time, successfully exploiting its copious natural resources such as coffee, cocoa and oil. Ahidjo resisted borrowing heavily and instead concentrated on developing the agricultural and industrial sectors and invested in health, education and roads. School enrolment reached 70%, the country became self-sufficient in food, and exported a growing range of commodities.

Despite such successes, Ahidjo resigned as president in 1982 and allowed his prime minister Paul Biya, from the Bulu-Beti ethnic group in the south, to succeed him. Yet a year later Ahidjo went into exile after Biya accused him of masterminding a coup against the government. Biya also dismissed the prime minister and several of his cabinet because of this. Biya was elected to his first full term as president and changed the name of the country to the Republic of Cameroon.

In 1984 members of the Presidential guard, who had originally been appointed by Ahidjo and who remained loyal to him, initiated a revolt in the capital and three days of fighting ensued that may have caused as many as a thousand deaths. Biya had the rebels tried and some executed.

In 1985 Biya announced that there would be no legal opposition to the ruling party, which he renamed the Rassemblement Démocratique du Peuple Camerounais (RDPC).

In 1986 Cameroon was international news when it experienced its worst-ever natural disaster, a discharge of toxic underwater volcanic gases from Lake Nyos, a crater lake in the North West Province. More than 2,000 people were killed. Cameroon also received international recognition after the national football team did exceptionally well in the 1990 World Cup, defeating Cup holders Argentina in the first game. They were defeated by England in the quarter-finals.

As the economy remained buoyant when compared with Cameroon's neighbours', elections were held in 1988 giving Biya more than 99% of the vote, helped no doubt by him being the only presidential candidate.

The early 1990s were characterised by episodes of unrest and growing discontent from certain elements of the population. A pro-democracy demonstration with 35,000 participants in Bamenda in 1990 resulted in six deaths and many injured when troops intervened. Anglophone regions increasingly felt neglected by the francophone majority and groups like Amnesty International questioned Cameroon's record on political detentions and torture.

Opposition parties increasingly demanded a multi-party political system but instead their meetings were banned, the independent press and media were restricted, and seven out of the ten provinces were put under military rule. It took a five-month strike in 1991 that greatly disrupted the cities and industry for the ban on opposition meetings to be lifted, for political prisoners to be released, and for a multi-party presidential election to be set for the next year. The election saw Biya re-elected after he exerted control on the media and instigated other anti-democratic measures. Demonstrations followed, a state of emergency was declared in the west of the country and detainment, torture and deaths of demonstrators, political opponents and journalists brought international attention as a national debt crisis loomed.

Clashes between Cameroon and Nigeria broke out from 1993 over border disputes, chiefly the oil-rich Bakassi Peninsula, and hostilities in 1996 led to Cameroon and Nigeria agreeing to UN mediation over the peninsula. The situation eased two years later when both countries exchanged more than 200 prisoners of war. Some observers see the dispute as a political red flag to be waved to direct public attention away from internal problems, rather than being caused by the economic greed of either country over still unconfirmed oil in the area.

International support for Cameroon slowly grew again and in 1995 it joined the Commonwealth, while maintaining a close relationship with France. In 1997 Biya's party, the RDPC, won a majority of seats in parliament amid further allegations of irregularities, and Biya was re-elected president despite the election being boycotted by the main opposition parties.

In both 1998 and 1999 Cameroon was classed as the most corrupt country in the world by Berlin-based research organisation Transparency International. The Roman Catholic Church in Cameroon denounced corruption in the country in 2000, saying that it had permeated all levels of society.

The economy improved at this time and in 2000 the World Bank approved funding for a massive oil and pipeline project stretching from the oilfields of southern Chad through Cameroon to Kribi on the coast, despite strong criticism from environmental and human rights activists. It is hoped the pipeline will generate US$50 million annually for the country, as well as many jobs.

Concerns for the country's environment remain high, and in 2001 Global Forest Watch reported that 80% of the country's indigenous forests had been allocated for logging.

The same year saw a growing tension between the Biya government and separatists lobbying on behalf of the country's five million English-speakers in the west of the country. Unrest reached serious levels in 2002 and opposition to Biya was also concentrated in the north among the Muslim communities. At the time of writing, he is expected to announce the next election in October 2004, and to again sweep the board with the opposition being in disarray.

As well as the continuation of periodic unrest, the country also has formidable social problems to overcome, including continuing corruption, unpaid public sector salaries, a poor health and education infrastructure and rising violent crime.

POLITICS

Politically the country is relatively stable by African standards, yet increasing demands for a more democratic system and the restoration of human rights has led to regular discontent, including waves of strikes and violence in all sections of the country.

President Paul Biya has been chief of state since November 6 1982, as head of the Rassemblement Démocratique du Peuple Camerounais (RDPC), which was the only political party until opposition parties were permitted by law in 1990.

The president is elected by popular vote for a seven-year term and an election was last held on October 12 1997. The head of government is Prime Minister Peter Mafany Musonge, who has held the post since September 19 1996.

The cabinet and prime minister are appointed by the president. He appoints and dismisses judges, ratifies treaties, leads the armed forces and has considerable authority in other areas. The president appoints the governors of Cameroon's ten provinces and his government can reorganise electoral districts in ways that would benefit itself.

People have the right to vote from the age of 21. Since Cameroon has had a multi-party system, elections have been dogged by allegations of vote-rigging by Biya's party, which holds the overwhelming majority in the 180-member national assembly. The chief opposition party is the Social Democratic Front (SDF), which is predominantly anglophone.

One dominant ongoing problem the country has endured for many years is the clash between the anglophone and francophone regions. Many in the minority, English-speaking population advocate restoration of the decentralised federal structure which consisted of separate anglophone and francophone regions that was in place until unification in 1972. Some anglophone groups advocate secession of the two English-speaking provinces. The government is opposed to both of these proposals.

Other problems include Cameroon's conflict with Nigeria over the Bakassi Peninsula, and opposition to government plans to privatise public enterprises and reduce the number of civil servants. A dysfunctional judicial system also hampers development, as does personal political rivalry between Biya and the leader of Gabon, President El Hadj Omar Bongo. Cameroon and Gabon represent more than half of Central Africa's population and commerce. But because of the rivalry, advances such as the development of positive initiatives like a workable economic community, a viable customs union, a securities exchange and a single market have been held back.

ECONOMY

Compared with most Western industrial nations, which typically have per-capita gross national products (GNPs) of at least US$20,000, Cameroon is poor. Yet compared with its neighbours, Cameroon's economy is buoyant. According to the World Bank, the per-capita GNP currently hovers around US$580–650, which compared with West Africa's and the world's poorest country, Sierra Leone, with a per-capita GNP of under US$140, is very good.

Cameroon is helped by its varied natural resources, which include petroleum and timber. There are also sizeable but unexploited deposits of iron ore, bauxite, copper, chromium, uranium and other metals.

Agriculture, mainly subsistence and small-scale farming, is the country's principal economic activity, employing about 80% of the population. The main agricultural products are cocoa (of which Cameroon is one of the world's largest producers), robusta and arabica coffee, bananas, cotton, palm oil, wood, tobacco and rubber. Hydro-electricity covers almost all of Cameroon's energy needs, so that oil and gas are largely treated as export products.

Yet Cameroon faces many of the serious problems facing other underdeveloped countries, including a top-heavy civil service and a generally unfavourable climate for business enterprise. International oil and cocoa prices have considerable impact upon the economy. Widespread poverty exists, with about half the population living below the poverty line, and significant social problems persist, as does widespread corruption at all levels of society. Unemployment, the infant mortality rate and population growth remain high.

In the 1990s the government opened up much of the economy to competition. France and the Netherlands are the major export markets, followed by Germany, the USA and fellow members of the Central African Customs and Economic Union, of which Cameroon is a member.

From 1990 the government embarked upon IMF and World Bank programmes intended to encourage trade and business investment, improve efficiency in agriculture, and recapitalise the nation's banks. Yet coffee and cocoa prices dropped in the early 1990s, while less and less was being manufactured and much was being imported.

A major setback occurred in January 1994 when the currency was massively devalued. Overnight it went from CFA100 to CFA50, equalling one French franc. It was the main reason around 20,000 French expatriates in 1994 were reduced to 5,000 in 1995.

The year 1997 saw the initiation of a government, IMF and World Bank economic reform programme aimed to reduce government control over the economy and stimulate more private-sector investment and growth. In 1997, 1998 and 1999, the country's economy grew at a 4–5% annual rate, while the government reduced its spending.

Low world prices for cocoa and coffee in 1999 again threatened the economy, while banana exporters faced increased competition from Latin American producers.

Banks that had become insolvent following the devaluation crisis had been closed by the end of the decade and the government privatised all state-owned banks. Today, Cameroon has nine banks, the majority owned by foreign banking companies. The government has also been privatising large state-owned companies such as utilities and those in the food sector.

Work

The minimum wage is currently CFA23,514 per month (approximately £25/US$44). To give an idea of typical wages, domestic staff working for an expatriate would expect to earn CFA27,000–81,000 (£28–86/US$50–150) per month depending upon qualifications, duties and hours worked. A 54-hour week with one day off is the official workweek in Cameroon. The minimum age for the employment of children is 14 years.

The law prohibits forced or compulsory labour, yet it occurs in practice. For example, prison inmates can be contracted out to private employers or used as communal labour for municipal projects. In rural regions it is not uncommon for children to work from an early age on family farms, and relatives often employ rural youths, especially girls, as domestic helpers. Many urban street vendors in the country are less than 14 years of age. Cameroon has also been known in the past to be a source, destination and transit point for trafficked children.

PEOPLE

Cameroon is very diverse culturally, and contains more than 275 ethno-linguistic groups. The ethnic distinctions include the Bantoid-speaking inhabitants of the kingdoms of the Western Highlands, the hunting and gathering 'pygmies' of the southern forests, and the Muslim sultanates and non-Muslim people of the north.

According to the US Department of State, the population is made up of Cameroon Western Highlanders (including Bamiléké and Bamoun) (31%); Equatorial Bantu (19%); Kirdi (11%); Fulani (10%); Northwestern Bantu (8%); Eastern Nigritic (7%); other African (13%); and non-African (less than 1%).

The population can roughly be separated into groups occupying the south, west and north.

Peoples of the south
The 'pygmies'
The first settlers in Cameroon were the so-called 'pygmies', who have one of the oldest cultures on Earth. They have long fascinated Western academics and theologians because so many of their legends correspond with Old Testament stories. Their complex pattern of nomadic life, established over thousands of years, is threatened more than ever by outside influences like politics and commerce, and those who remain live increasingly sedentary lives.

The incorrect term 'pygmy' has long been used to identify such people of short stature living in Central African rainforests. These people would never call themselves pygmies as they believe the word is based on roots that show a great ignorance and misunderstanding of them. It could imply that there is something wrong or laughable about their size. These people instead see themselves as members of their own very distinct ethnic groups.

In Cameroon they are predominantly from the Baka ethnic grouping and to a lesser extent the Bakola, Bagyeli, Bofi and Medzan groups, living in the dense forests of the south and southeast. Bantu farmers commonly associate closely with them. They still practise their traditional hunting and gathering way of life, trading resources of the forest with neighbouring farming villages for cultivated foods and other goods. This can be a fair exchange but is increasingly less so as the forest peoples lose more and more control of the forest and its resources.

Being forest dwellers, they know the forest, its plants and animals intimately. They live by hunting animals such as pigs, antelopes and monkeys, as well as fishing and gathering yams, berries and other edible plants. They see the forest as a generous god who provides for all their needs.

According to Survival International, there are now about 250,000 of these forest peoples living in Central Africa (ie: the Democratic Republic of Congo, the Republic of Congo, Cameroon, Gabon, Central African Republic, Rwanda, Burundi and Uganda).

The southeastern rainforests of Cameroon where many of these people live are pretty impenetrable and you need plenty of time and determination to meet them there. But if you visit Kribi, where the beach leads directly into rainforest, there is a good chance of meeting some; they may be found hollowing out a canoe by the shore or scaling the trees for avocados.

Conservation organisations such as the Worldwide Fund for Nature (WWF) encourage the needs of these forest peoples being met. For example, in the Lobéké National Park, Bakas were recently granted access to some forest areas so that they could participate in shrimp fishing, harvesting and the gathering of mangoes, honey and other non-timber forest products.

The Baka are largely nomadic, often moving from one area to another. Their traditional festivity to celebrate their forest spirit, Jengi, and to enshrine young men into their secret society is still widely celebrated. Jengi celebrations used to involve the killing of an elephant, but this is no longer the case.

Bantu-speaking groups
The Bantu-speaking groups, such as the Bassa, Douala, Bakweiri, Batanga, Malimba, Mbos and Bakoko, generally spread from the Adamawa range to settle along the northwest coastal region from the 15th century onwards, to be followed in the 19th century by the Ewondo, Bulu, Yezum, Ntumu, Fang, Eton and others, who settled around Yaoundé and the equatorial region.

Peoples of the west
A semi-Bantu population became established from the 16th century onwards in the west of the country, including the Tikar and the Bamoun – who are both now settled in the chiefdoms of the Grassfields, and who now dominate in the northwest – and the Bamiléké, a mixture of peoples from all directions and now the country's biggest and most economically dominant ethnic group.

The Tikar
This is a British designation encompassing a number of ethnic groups. Having largely migrated from Nigeria, they generally occupy the Mbam and Bamenda regions.

The Bamoun
Famous for their royal dynasty, which goes back to 1394, this ethnic group are centred around Foumban and are known for their wood carvings and other artwork.

The Bamiléké
Population density is greatest in the south and southwest of the country, and most widespread in this region are the Bamiléké. They are spread around Yaoundé and Bafoussam, and Douala especially. In their rural homelands in the southwest, they have around 75 political units governed by *chefferies* (chiefs), and secret societies within these organisations keep their many traditional rituals alive. The Bamiléké retain the skulls of their dead ancestors in order to continue to pay homage to their spirits. Known for being good farmers, their traditional homes are made from a variety of local materials, including sun-baked soil bricks.

Peoples of the north
The Fulani
The Fulani (or Fula, Foulbé or Peul) tend to be tall, thin and lightly built people with aquiline noses, oval faces and a light complexion. Dominant in the north and northwest, they are an Islamic population that has been settling across the savanna of West Africa for centuries but that first arrived in Cameroon in the 19th century. Originally nomadic *(bororo* or *wodaabe)* cattle herders, many are now settled farmers and merchants. Those that remain cattle herders see cattle as central to their lives, and the health of their cattle is often seen as a bigger priority than their own.

The nomadic Fulani have an initiation ceremony involving boys being lashed with sticks, which scars them, against a backdrop of drumming. Their homes differ depending on the region: in the Mandara Mountains in the northwest they live in hamlets of thatched huts, while around Pouss, in the northeast, their huts are made completely from dried mud.

The Kirdi
Even further north, in the Mandara Mountains of the northwest, can be found Kirdi (the word comes from 'pagan' from the Fulani), known as 'mountain peoples'. They are made up of Chadic- and Adamawa-speaking peoples such as the Fali, Kapsiki, Mafa, Massa, Mousgoum, Mofou, Matakam, Toupouris, Guidar, Bata, Fata and Podoko, whose main occupation is farming. Looked at from afar, their cliffside villages around the Mora, Mokolo, Tourou and Mabas regions almost look like a hobbit community, with their round homes with pointed roofs, which are covered with grass.

The Kirdi are non-Muslim peoples, instead retaining their traditional religious beliefs. They were originally driven by the Fulani into the inhospitable and isolated rocky areas near the Nigerian border. Life expectancy for them is generally under 30 years.

The Choa
Even further north, around Lake Chad, are the semi-nomadic Choa, of Arabic origin. The Choa arrived in Cameroon around 300 years ago from Sudan.

The Kotoko
Also living in the Lake Chad region, and relying on subsistence farming and fishing, the Kotoko are descendants of the Sao peoples, one of the earliest cultures to populate Cameroon.

Marriage
The current marriage rate for 15–19-year-old girls in Cameroon is 41%, which compares to 72% in Mali and 26% in Ivory Coast.

Especially in more rural areas, a young girl often does not have a say as to whether, or to whom, she will marry. Instead, both sets of parents make such decisions. The girl may also be subordinate in important decisions, such as when to have children and how many to have.

A dowry of some kind is usually very important. When a couple gets married in villages in northwest Cameroon, for example, the bridegroom is expected to present bushmeat to his in-laws as part of his dowry. In Batibo, where the bulk of Cameroon's palm wine is produced, suitors wishing to marry a girl from the region must provide a mandatory ten litres of palm wine. The bride shares this with the groom to demonstrate that they will share everything as married partners. Her suitor is also required to give his future in-laws other goods, such as beer, salt and oil.

LANGUAGE

Cameroon's official languages are English and French. Arabic is also widely spoken, particularly in the north. French is by far the most prevalent, with English spoken by around 20% of the population. The staffs of the major hotels and restaurants are predominantly bilingual (although this is not always true in francophone areas). Spanish and German are also very occasionally spoken.

West Africa is the most linguistically intricate region in the world and Cameroon alone has more than 275 African languages and dialects still spoken, including Fulfulde (the language of the Fulani), Douala (language of the Douala people) and Ewondo (the dialect of a Beti clan near Yaoundé). Broadly speaking, the south of the country speaks semi-Bantu, Ewondo and Fang, while the north speaks Adamwala, Fulani and Chadic. Other African languages commonly spoken are Bamiléké, Bamoun and Arabic.

Around 10% of the country relies upon pidgin English, spread around half the provinces of the country, but primarily in the west, near Nigeria.

If you log on to www.ethnologue.com it has details (including region, alternative language names and classification) of 279 living languages, three second languages without mother-tongue speakers, and four extinct languages in the country.

The east–west linguistic division

Superimposed upon the north–south divisions of the country – the large geographical and climatical differences as well as the religious ones (a largely Muslim north and Christian south) – is an east–west division resulting from European colonialism.

After World War I the westernmost region of Cameroon became controlled by the British, while the larger central and eastern portion came under the rule of the French. Consequently, Cameroonians are divided linguistically into English and French speakers, with francophones dominating both because they are a numerical majority and because the most important centres, Douala and Yaoundé, are French-speaking.

RELIGION

Estimates of the population percentage observing traditional animist African beliefs (the base of most traditional religions in Africa, where there is the belief in and worship of a spirit in all natural things) stand at about 40%, with the remainder made up of around 40% Christian and 20% Muslim. Yet such statistics are misleading as they fail to take into account the overlapping of Christianity with pre-colonial beliefs.

Many Cameroonians are Christian and yet follow traditional beliefs, such as taking part in a traditional dance at a funeral or wedding. Also, the above statistic for Christianity relates mainly to those practising rather than simply professing their religion, a proportion far higher than that in many Western countries.

Particularly strong observance of traditional African beliefs comes from the 'pygmy' communities of the southern rainforests. They typically believe in a forest spirit, where the forest is seen as a mother, father and guardian. There is also a sizeable community of non-Muslim animists, known as Kirdi, in the north.

Witchcraft and superstition

Traditional beliefs are still very much alive and well throughout many of the more rural parts of Cameroon.

In early 2001, for example, an average of ten people a week were dying in the town of Baba in northwest Cameroon. Although reports in the press attributed the deaths to meningitis, most people in the town believed the cause to be witches and wizards.

The traditional ruler, Fon Fuekemshi II, decided to suspend all funerals in the town in an attempt to reduce the high death rate. He believed that the disease was being spread when large numbers of people gathered to pay their respects to the dead.

The villagers hired a 'witch hunter' from a nearby village but he was soon expelled by local officials when local people started refusing to attend hospital on his instructions. One report claimed that people took dead bodies to him to be resurrected after rumours spread that he had made a dead man speak and reveal his killer.

ARTS AND CULTURE
Traditional festivals

Annual festivals provide an occasion for carnivals and colourful dances. In much of the country, there are ceremonies and feasting because of births, deaths, sowing the seeds and harvesting as well as commemorating ancestors. Many of these festivities feature colourful, musical ceremonies.

They include the **Ngondo** Festival of the Sawa, the coastal dwellers of Cameroon from Limbé to Kribi, with the Wouri River being the focal point of the festival in Douala. The ritual and feast, held in the first week of each December, celebrates the unity of the Sawa peoples and their ancestors, who are believed to live in the waters. The festival, beginning on the banks of the River Wouri, features traditional dances, choral music, handicraft exhibitions, a canoe parade and race, a carnival, and the collection of the ancestors' message by a diver, from the bottom of the river, contained in a calabash.

Originally organised to resolve land disputes, the **Ngouon** Festival of the Bamouns takes place once every two years in Foumban and features horse parades.

The **Nyem-Nyem** annual festival in the Adamaoua, centred around Ngaoundéré, traces the heroic resistance of the people against German penetration into their land. Each January traditional festivities are held around caves on the top of Mount Djim, about halfway between Tignere and Tibati, near Galim, about 65km from Tignere.

The **Medumba Festival** in Bangangte is held every two years, usually in July, to promote both the Medumba language and the artworks of the 13 villages in the locality.

Arts and crafts

The arts and crafts of Cameroon reflect the great ethnic diversity of its peoples. Ancestral traditions form the basis for most art forms, with wood sculpture prominent. Each ethnic group typically translates wooden decorative panels, furniture and doors into a multitude of expressions in wood.

Some crafts, such as weaving baskets, embroidering cloth, batik works, the painting and carving of calabashes and bas relief sculpture, show the presence of art in the daily lives of Cameroonians.

The peoples of the Western Highlands are known for their bronzework and brasswork and wooden sculptures embroidered with glass beads. The regions around Bafoussam, Foumban and Bamenda in the west are renowned for their masks, embroidered costumes, miniature figures, thrones, pipes and statues made from earthenware, bronze or wood.

Because of the high quality of the clay in the region, villages near Bamenda, such as Bali and around Foumban, have a rich tradition of producing ceramics. Masks (usually depicting animals) and woodcarvings are also in abundance here.

Detailed figurative artworks and distinctive, long tobacco pipes made from brass and bronze are also to be seen in Tikar areas north and east of Foumban.

Bamum beadwork is renowned. Cowrie shells (*mbuum*) were traditionally used as money and today *mbuum* remains the Bamum word for money. When the Bamum Kingdom enlarged at the beginning of the 19th century, beads were very rare and small glass beads were brought from Nigeria and the coast. The Bamum started a tradition of producing royal costume decorated with beads.

In the northern provinces cloth-weaving, leather goods and decorative brasswork are prevalent. Fulani women wear large copol amber beads, which are opalescent rather than transparent. Such beads are increasingly rare and are highly valuable.

Maroua and nearby villages in the north are known for their colourful markets where embroidered tablecloths, bracelets, swords, mats and other decorative objects are available.

Dance

The huge number of ethnic groups in Cameroon provide more than 200 distinctive dances. Local festivals and public holidays offer excellent opportunities to experience Cameroon's lively dance traditions.

In the south, there are Bafia or Bikutsi ballets and other dances led by the *mvet* (or zither) player, a bard and epic poet. In the west, Bamiléké dancers wearing picturesque costumes display striking masks.

In 2000 an overtly sexual dance from neighbouring Ivory Coast, *mapouka*, performed either naked or with few clothes in public places, was banned in southwest Cameroon, on the grounds that it was causing public immorality. The dance features a woman bending almost double while a man supports her waist from behind.

Traditional and folk music

The huge number of ethnic groups in Cameroon provide a wide variety of musical types. Local festivals and public holidays offer a good opportunity to experience Cameroon's lively music traditions.

In the north of the country, the Toupouri people perform the *gourna*, where dancers form a circle and carry long sticks vertically. The Bamiléké perform war dances including the Lali, protecting the village against invaders, and the Tso, where the dancers wear panther skins. The *motio* dance, in the southwest, features the slaughtering of a goat in one blow of a blade, to signify the bravery and strength of the men.

The folk music of the south of the country is particularly varied, with mainly drum- and xylophone-based compositions of the Bakweiri, Bamoun, Beti and Bamiléké, often performed accompanying masked dancers.

The rare bird, the Bannerman's turaco, is important to the culture of the Kom people, from the highlands of the northwest. They use its feathers to decorate their traditional costumes, called *chindohs*. The turaco's song is mimicked using a *njang*, which is similar to a xylophone. When there is a death in the village, *njang* music is played for three days continuously.

A greater variety of instruments are played in the south by the Fang, Eton, Bulu and Mvele, including a small xylophone called the *mendzan*, zithers, lutes and the *ngkul*, a traditional drum.

Traditional music of the Baka peoples ('pygmies') of the rainforest typically consists of instrumentally simple music made from drums, rattles and chants that can be divided into either long, percussive dirges or earthy, polyphonic a cappella chants.

An audio CD that is available showcasing the music of the Baka is *The Baka Forest People: Heart Of The Forest* (Hannibal 2002) performed by Baka pygmies in the rainforests of Cameroon.

Other musical styles

Cameroon's best-known musician by far has to be saxophonist, pianist and singer **Manu Dibango**, who has done much to promote the infectious, slick *makossa* dance rhythm of Cameroon and who can be considered an African international superstar. Makossa evolved from the 1930s and originated from the Douala region. Fusing soul and high-life, it was influenced by Congolese dance music and today greatly uses the electric guitar. You are often likely to hear makossa blaring out of clubs and discos.

Born Emmanuel Dibango N'Djocke in 1933 in Douala, Dibango's father was of the Yabassi people, his mother of the Douala. Dibango has always felt that he is a divided man, being born of two antagonistic ethnic groups.

His training and career began when he was just 15, when his parents sent him to Paris. Here he met **Francis Bebey** (who died in 2001), another African expatriate and another of Cameroon's most successful musicians, who played a wide range of instruments and styles including traditional Cameroonian music, jazz, pop, classical guitar and makossa. *Nandolo/With Love – Works 1963–1994* (Original Music) is one of over 20 of his very varied albums.

Both Dibango and Bebey explored the Calais jazz scene together and started a band, learning how to play the instruments as they went along. Bebey explained 12-bar blues to Manu, who studied classical piano before taking up the saxophone in 1954.

Dibango's albums include *Afrijazzy* and *Mboa'Su*, while his album *Wakafrika* features a Nigerian juju guitarist (King Sunny Ade) and Dibango's jazzy saxophone performing a tune by Benin composer Wally Badarou.

Makossa was further popularised by **Moni Bile** in the 1980s, whose albums include *Amour and Esperance* (Sonodisc, France 2001).

The mid-1980s also saw the emergence of **Sam Fan Thomas**, who has enjoyed considerable success with a lighter form of makossa, *makassi*, giving the sound an even more commercial bent. Albums include *The Best of Sam Fan Thomas* (TJR, France 1995).

Petit-Pays became Cameroon's most popular makossa band, taking off in the late 1980s, since when they have had several big hits. Albums consist of dance music influenced by makossa, sokous, the more slow and sensual zouk and sometimes a little touch of salsa.

Bikutsi, the war music of the Beti people, is another popular dance music, and which is typically sung in Ewonde. In the late 1980s a group called **Les Têtes Brulées** briefly enjoyed international attention with their quick-rhythmed Bikutsi music style.

Henri Dikongue's recording, *C'est La Vie* (Tinder 1998), integrates Afro-Parisian, Latin, Caribbean and other styles.

Les Nubians are French-Cameroonian sisters Helene and Celia Faussart. Their album *Princesses Nubiennes* (Virgin 2002) is a mix of hip hop, r&b and soul mixed with the rhythms of Africa.

Cameroonian artiste **Wes** has recorded *Welenga*, which combines traditional instruments, synthesisers and rock guitars into a style that touches both the Western pop charts and the Bantou villages of his upbringing.

Specialist music shops
Britain
Stern's 74–75 Warren St, London W1T 5PF; tel: 020 7387 5550

France
Afric' Antilles Music 3 Rue des Plantes, 75014, Paris; tel: 01 45 42 43 52

North America
Africassette Music PO Box 24941, Detroit, MI 48224; tel: www.africassette.com

Cinema
One of Cameroon's earliest film-makers was **Jean-Paul Ngassa**, noted for his *Aventures en France* (1962) and *La Grande Case Bamilékée* (1965).

Producer and director **Daniel Kamwa** later found success with a prize-winning short film, *Boubou Cravatte* (1972), which he followed with the very successful *Pousse Pousse* (1977), dealing with the clash between tradition and modern city living, and then *Notre Fille* (1980).

One of Cameroon's most widely recognised cinematographers is **Jean Pierre Dikongue-Pipa**, who produced *Muno Moto* (1975), *Prix de la Liberté* (1978) and *Badiaga* (1983).

Another emerging talent at that time was **Arthur Si Batar**, whose debut feature, *Les Cooperants* (1978), focused on the common theme of city and village life.

One of musician Francis Bebey's novels, *Les Trois Petits Cireurs*, was successfully made into a film by **Louis Balthazar Amadangoleda** in 1985.

Claire Denis's film, *Chocolat* (1988), was an international success and is about a young white girl (pointedly named France) growing up in the Cameroons and learning the ways of colonialism.

Jean-Marie Teno examines political regimes since independence in his documentary, *Afrique, Je te Plummerai* (1992) and his feature film, *Clando* (1996).

Quartier Mozart (1992), directed by **Jean-Pierre Bekolo**, is a lively, modern film dealing with a girl given magical powers that allow her to transform into a male.

Natural History

Because of its outstanding geographical and climatic features, Cameroon has some of Africa's richest and most varied fauna and flora, boasting more than a thousand species of tree alone. Not only does the country offer some of the best wildlife reserves in West Africa, but there are plenty of opportunities to view birds and mammals in all of Africa's natural habitats, including desert, swamp, woodland, rainforest and savanna. That said, game is far more difficult to see than in East Africa.

The remarkable biodiversity of the country is coupled with a high number of animals and plants that are endemic to their localities. More than 40 plant species are thought to be unique to Mount Cameroon, for example, as are numerous birds. The mountain is also home to a rich variety of monkeys and forest elephants.

Rarities found in the rainforests of the southwest include chimpanzees, red-capped mangabeys and the drill, one of the rarest primates in Africa, which can also be found on Equatorial Guinea's Bioko Island and in southeastern Nigeria. Rainforest areas are also home to elephants, gorillas and buffaloes, although the thick vegetation can make it very difficult to spot them.

Forested regions are home to colourful spiders, ants and termites, and large centipedes and millipedes. Many types of butterfly are also prevalent, especially in lowland forest areas.

RESERVES, NATIONAL PARKS AND CONSERVATION AREAS

Hunting, overgrazing, deforestation and human population pressure mean that in many areas Cameroon's reserves are the best bet by far for seeing the biggest range of wildlife. Even then, the animals can be secretive and solitary, and in the rainforest areas the lack of infrastructure for visitors and the dense vegetation can make viewing difficult. A great variety of birds, on the other hand, are widespread.

The game parks of northern Cameroon may not have the diversity and density of animals found in East and southern Africa, but can nevertheless guarantee some spectacular wildlife.

Waza National Park, in the far north of the country wedged between the borders of Chad and Nigeria, is Cameroon's most visited national park, not only because it is most geared to visitors both in terms of infrastructure and facilities like accommodation, guides and transport, but because it contains some of West and Central Africa's most impressive wildlife. Its forest and huge expanse of grassy and wet plains contain a good variety of wildlife, including lion, hippopotamus, monkey, giraffe, buffalo, herds of elephant and a wide range of birdlife. You are least likely to see lion, buffalo and hippos and more likely to view red-fronted gazelle and kob.

Korup National Park, in the southwest of the country and bordering Nigeria, is the most accessible of Cameroon's protected tropical rainforest areas. It contains an exceptional variety of flora and fauna. Although reasonably geared to visitors, access to the park can be difficult in the rainy season.

To the north of Korup National Park, and in reality a continuation of Korup, is the **Ejagham Forest Reserve**. Around both Korup and Ejagham are spread the sizeable **Banyang Mbo Wildlife Sanctuary** near Nguti, as well as three more forest reserves, the **Mawne River**, **Nta-ali** and **Rumpi Hills**, the last's terrain peaking with the 1,769m Mount Rata.

Three parks lie in a row roughly between Garoua and Ngaoundéré – **Faro Reserve**, and **Bénoué** and **Bouba Ndjida national parks**. A combination of hunting and poaching in this region means that Waza, further north, is a better bet for observing wildlife, although Faro's forested savanna, hills and mountains, and the Guinea woodlands of Bénoué and Bouba Ndjida, on the banks of the Mayo Lidi River, all have a good range of animals to search out.

Kalamaloué National Reserve, by Chad just outside Kousséri in the extreme north, is small, yet offers opportunities for viewing wildlife, including antelope, giraffe, monkey and warthog. Some elephants also cross the reserve.

Bafut-Nguemba Forest Reserve is easily reached from Bamenda but unfortunately has been substantially destroyed by overfarming and logging. Despite that, it is rich in birdlife.

The remote **Dja Reserve**, southeast of Yaoundé, is difficult to get to and has virtually no facilities. Declared a World Heritage Site by UNESCO for its outstanding natural significance, it shelters many hundreds of species of plant, bird, mammal and other wildlife. Dja is one of the few remaining gorilla sanctuaries in the world and is also home to significant numbers of 'pygmies' and other traditional forest dwellers.

Between Douala and Kribi is the **Douala-Edea Reserve**, bordered on its northern edge by the Sanaga River and on its western edge by the Atlantic Ocean. It features a wide variety of fauna, flora and habitats.

Campo-Ma'an National Park, bordering Equatorial Guinea and the coast near Kribi, is a virtually unmanaged patch of rainforest and has few facilities for visitors, although there is basic accommodation and guides are available.

Nki and **Boumba-Bek forest reserves** and **Lobéké National Park** in the southeastern corner of Cameroon lie within the thick and extensive Congo basin rainforest. Reaching them involves a lot of time, planning, persistence and patience, and the wildlife can be very difficult to see because of the dense vegetation. Although rich in wildlife and home to a significant 'pygmy' population, this region has suffered considerably from logging and poaching, notably within Lobéké (the most accessible of the three) and to some extent Boumba-Bek. Much of Nki, on the other hand, remains unexplored and is devoid of human habitation.

Cameroon is scattered with further small reserves, notably the **De Bafia Reserve** near the beaches of Sanaga and the town of Monatele, north of Yaoundé; the 1,700ha **Mozogo-Gokoro Reserve** north of Maroua; the **Kalfou Reserve**, east of Maroua; and the very sizeable **Pangare Djerem Reserve** (also called the Mbam and Djerem National Park), southeast of Tibati. But unless you have a particular or specialist interest in wildlife or are spending a great deal of time in the country, those most easily accessible, best geared to visitors and with the most and easily seen animals should be focused upon, such as the very contrasting Waza and Korup national parks.

ECOLOGICAL THREATS AND CONSERVATION

Conservation of the natural world, especially in Africa, remains more urgent than ever before. For example, in 2003 only 23,000 lions remained in Africa compared with 230,000 some 20 years before, and many of those that have survived harbour feline Aids and bovine tuberculosis. According to wildlife experts, this means that the lion in Cameroon is frighteningly close to extinction. When you add the unprecedented variety of other flora and fauna that are fast depleting and disappearing, it paints a particularly sad picture for the natural world. The greatest threat to biodiversity in Cameroon comes from deforestation. Poaching is another major threat to biodiversity in the country.

Deforestation

According to the World Resources Institute, more than 80% of the Earth's natural forests have already been destroyed, and as much as 90% of West Africa's coastal rainforests have disappeared since 1900.

As well as providing wildlife habitats – 70% of the Earth's land animals and plants live in forests – rainforests also help generate rainfall in drought-prone countries elsewhere. Studies have found that destruction of rainforests in Cameroon may have caused droughts in the interior of Africa. This is in addition to the catastrophic global effects, such as the increase in global warming.

Logging has led to vast areas of the forest being cleared through unsustainable methods, and timber exploitation in the country tripled in the early 1990s, triggered somewhat by the devaluation of the local currency, the CFA franc. Currency devaluations effectively halved the cost of hauling 800-year-old trees through the hundreds of miles of forest to the parquet-flooring and furniture markets of Europe and Japan.

Also, logging was boosted by a sharp fall in prices of agricultural products such as cocoa and coffee that beforehand were a big part of the national economy. In Cameroon, wood production soared 50% between 1992 and 1997, the last years for which figures are available. It is little surprise when logging currently creates a US$60-million-a-year revenue for the Cameroonian government.

The wood is exported mainly to Europe and almost all of it is known to have been felled illegally, with little or no monitoring of the logging industry. The scale of destruction in the Congo basin, for example, is now thought to be so serious and rapid that up to 20% of the forest could be lost within 15 years, with potential implications for climate control, flooding and loss of plant species.

A recent report by Global Witness, an official monitor of the Cameroon government, found that almost all companies working in the country had been acting illegally. Some were working in protected areas, while others were falsely declaring how much timber they were taking and bribing officials.

The logging roads facilitate access to sensitive areas by poachers. Illegal logging has caused great damage as thousands of protected tree species have been cut down. Logging (along with mining) also threatens the way of life of the so-called 'pygmy' peoples of the forest, like the Baka and the Kola.

In a survey conducted in 1993, nearly 70% of respondents from Lobéké in southeastern Cameroon considered that the timber companies had an overwhelmingly negative impact on the forest and its people, despite some short-term economic benefit. The most critical problem is the easy access to forested areas: as timber companies open new roads in search of exploitable trees, vast tracts of previously unreachable forest become accessible.

There are encouraging signs though. In 2002, for example, the US, France, Germany, Japan and the EC, working with the World Bank, international conservation groups and giant logging companies, pledged to invest up to US$100m into trying to save the forests of the Congo basin.

Poaching and hunting

Bushmeat is the main source of protein for many impoverished villagers in Cameroon's forests, as well as a delicacy for rich city dwellers. Hunting is further promoted because it is also financially attractive: hunters can easily earn CFA550,000/£600/US$1,000 a year, much more than most Cameroonians. A collapse in the price of cash crops like coffee and cocoa in recent years has also made sales of bushmeat of increasing importance to local people.

Experts increasingly believe that numerous animals might be exterminated within a decade if commercial bushmeat hunting is not stopped. Though habitat loss is often seen as the main cause of wildlife extinction, commercial bushmeat hunting has become the most immediate threat.

Though the selling of bushmeat is illegal, it is widely practised. At a central Yaoundé market, for example, without much difficulty you could find fresh snake, monkey, pangolin and lizard, and even elephant and gorilla. There are only about 125,000 common chimpanzees left in Central Africa's rainforests, and thousands are shot every year.

At the same time, elephant hunting for the ivory trade has hit an all-time high as tons of ivory are shipped out by expatriate workers. Many opportunists have also turned to poaching after being encouraged by rumours of rich mineral deposits in the southeastern rainforests.

Even the smallest small-scale farmer can think killing predators like lion or leopard is of personal benefit, despite the fact that more and more species are reaching the brink of extinction. A study in the Laikipia region of Kenya in 2003 found that on average a lion attacks livestock worth £200 a year, equivalent to one cow or three sheep. With better husbandry, such as using a night guard or installing strong fencing and gates, losses would plummet, but using poison and bullets is always a cheaper option.

Poaching remains a considerable threat to animal species populations in the reserves. Some of the hunting is done for subsistence by local inhabitants, some to provide meat for timber-company employees, but widescale commercialised hunting is carried out mostly by outsiders to cash in on the booming bushmeat trade. The indigenous population has noted a decline in the densities of animals suitable for bushmeat, necessitating longer forays into the forest for their traditional subsistence activities.

Bushmeat markets thrive in many rainforest regions, especially in the logging towns. Animals are also taken to feed the exotic animals trade in gorillas, chimpanzees and grey parrots, for example. Exotic skins and other trophy items (from bongo and leopard, for instance) are also in demand.

The savannas of the north have also not escaped the effect of hunting. At one time this region supported a large and diverse ungulate community, but almost a century of habitat loss and uncontrolled over-hunting with modern firearms and vehicles have decimated animal populations.

Much bushmeat hunting is carried out using wire snares, especially for forest antelopes; .458 calibre guns are used for hunting of elephants. Also, several European-based safari companies operate in the forests, usually from December to June, catering to wealthy foreign clients interested in hunting trophy animals. Some of these companies have been operating in Cameroon for more than 20 years. They receive government permission to hunt, but have no clearly defined concessions.

Local people are typically upset with the hunting companies, which have apparently never consulted with local chiefs or the population in general. Some are even known to intimidate local residents by burning their hunting camps and

BIRD CONSERVATION IN CAMEROON: IMPORTANT BIRD AREAS (IBAS)
Keith Barnes

The IBA programme aims to identify and protect a network of sites throughout the world that are critical for naturally occurring bird populations.

What are IBAs?
Put simply, IBAs are sites, either protected or unprotected, that are vital for the conservation of the world's birds. Because IBAs target specific suites of birds, normally threatened, rare or range-restricted, they often double as some of the finest birding destinations on the continent, particularly for those birders seeking more elusive species. Korup National Park, Ngoundaba Ranch, the Bakossi Mountains, Mount Cameroon and Dja Faunal Reserve are all IBAs. What makes them IBAs is that they are well-defined sites with boundaries – it is possible to demarcate and conserve them – and they each hold one or more of a particular set of special birds worthy of conservation attention. Also, because IBAs are selected using identical and standardised criteria, an IBA in Cameroon is the same as an IBA in Liberia, Malawi, Iraq or England; as a result they form a global conservation currency. Cameroon holds 33 IBAs that support an excellent cross-section of the country's threatened and unique avifauna. Often these sites double as key birdwatching areas, with ecotourism-based initiatives alongside them.

How are IBAs protected?
Selecting IBAs according to the criteria is probably the easiest part of the process. The publication of the directories documenting the sites is only a beginning. The directories serve to highlight certain areas requiring additional conservation attention, as an alarming proportion of the sites fall outside the official protected area network. The most difficult job is to get people to sit up and listen. The members of the BirdLife Partnership have been most influential in this regard, liaising with government officials, international conservation bodies and key global decision-makers to further the ends of the programme.

Cameroon's national IBA programme stands to benefit from concerned individuals taking an interest in their local IBAs, as volunteers or custodians.

If you would like to become involved, please contact the Cameroon Ornithological Club or the BirdLife International Secretariat, Wellbrooke Court, Girton Road, Cambridge CB3 0NA, UK; fax: +44 1223 277200; email: birdlife@birdlife.org.uk; web: www.birdlife.net for more information.

possessions, and have even directly threatened to shoot people found in the forest. There are also instances where professional hunters take many more animals than they officially report, often burying those not considered trophy specimens.

'Pygmies' still use traditional hunting techniques such as the use of bows and poisoned arrows, especially for primate hunting, but recent increased instability in neighbouring countries has led to a wide circulation of firearms and ammunition, and an increasing number of Baka pygmies being used by local big-game hunters.

Fortunately, there are some encouraging signs. In 2003 Nigeria and Cameroon announced plans to create a cross-border park to protect rare birds and endangered chimpanzees threatened by the bushmeat trade. The park would encompass the mountain forests, savanna and grasslands of the Gashaka Gumti National Park in eastern Nigeria and Tchabal-Mbabo in Cameroon. The area hosts 28 bird species unique to the massif, including 13 found only in the mountain chain. The area is also home to endangered chimpanzees found only in eastern Nigeria and western Cameroon, and the endangered African wild dog.

In May 2003 the Cameroonian authorities announced that any restaurant owner caught serving meat from endangered animals could face up to three years in prison and a fine of more than US$16,000, which should further discourage the bushmeat trade.

In December of the same year international conservation group WWF and Traffic, a group that monitors the trade in endangered species, 'named and shamed' Nigeria, Senegal and Ivory Coast for allegedly sustaining the illegal ivory trade. Having largely destroyed their own elephant populations, the three countries were found to have been importing and selling tonnes of ivory poached in nearby countries, including Cameroon. Poachers, using machine guns, can easily kill a herd in a day.

The Worldwide Fund for Nature, which has an office in the Bastos district of Yaoundé (tel: 221 62 67; web: www.wwfcameroon.org), is working with the Cameroonian government to increase protected areas of the forest, discourage logging and poaching, and support the continuing traditional lifestyles of the communities living in the forest.

The Lobéké, Boumba-Bek and Nki forest reserves have become national parks in recent years, with the increased environmental protection this brings. Increased protection of the wilder regions of Cameroon cannot come soon enough.

WILDLIFE
Mammals
Elephants

Cameroon has a number of the most distinctive large mammals of the continent.

Both forest (*Loxodonta africana cyclotis*) and savanna (*Loxodonta africana africana*) African elephant (the latter having larger bodies, ears and tusks, and less hair) are present in Cameroon, in Waza and Bénoué national parks in the north, Korup and Faro national parks in the west, and, most noticeably, the reserves and numerous other sites in the southeast of the country. Indeed, Lobéké, Boumba-Bek and Nki, with their extensive swampland and forest vegetation, are important elephant habitats and have an elephant population estimated at nearly 10,000. Elephant also pass through the Kalamaloué Reserve, near Lake Chad in the far north.

Unfortunately, elephant hunting remains a significant problem in the country, especially in the southeast where logging roads have opened up far more forest in recent years, providing easy access to bushmeat poachers.

Rhinoceros

The north of Cameroon contains the most northerly surviving population of the endangered black rhinoceros (*Diceros bicornis*) in Africa, notably in Bénoué and Bouba Ndjida national parks. It has a striking hooked upper lip. Like the white rhinoceros, the black rhinoceros is actually grey in colour.

Hippopotamus
The common hippopotamus (*Hippopotamus amphibius*) is found in the southwest of the country and in the north in lakes and waterways. It spends much of the day under water, to emerge at night to graze. The mangroves of the coastal regions by the Nigerian border and either side of Douala also provide habitat for isolated populations of pygmy hippopotamus (*Hexaprotodon liberiensis heslopi*).

Buffalo
Cameroon has sizeable populations of the African buffalo (*Syncerus caffer*). This species is unpredictably aggressive and it is best not to approach on foot. Particularly adaptable to different habitats, it lives both in the forests and savanna regions. The red forest buffalo (*Syncerus caffer nanus*) lives in small herds in the forests of the south, while the savanna variety (*Syncerus caffer caffer*) of the north tends to live in large herds. The former is somewhat smaller.

Antelope
The savanna and woodland regions in the north of the country contain the biggest species of antelope. These include Lord Derby's eland (*Taurotragus derbianus*), which is also known as the giant eland; this is misleading as, although it has larger horns than the common eland (*Taurotragus oryx*), it is a lighter animal. Cameroon is now the only country where Lord Derby's eland remains common.

Other species prevalent in the north include the handsome roan antelope (*Hippotragus equinus*), which has a light, red-brown coat; the large, robust, shaggy-coated waterbuck (*Kobus ellipsiprymnus*) and the Buffon's kob (*Kobus kob kob*), which is similar to but smaller than the Uganda kob (*Kobus kob thomasi*), absent in Cameroon.

The large and ungainly-looking hartebeest (*Alcelaphus buselaphus*), the gazelle-like oribi (*Ourebia ourebi*) and the red-fronted gazelle (*Gazella rufifrons*), with deep-reddish-brown upperparts and white underparts, are also present.

Now restricted to tiny pockets in northern Cameroon are the hartebeest-like korrigum (*Damaliscus lunatus korrigum*) and, more widespread, the similar-looking tiang (*Damaliscus lunatus tiang*).

Around Korup and the forest regions straddling the Nigerian border, elephants create paths used by a variety of antelope species such as the secretive bushbuck (*Tragelaphus scriptus*), the most widely distributed of the African tragelaphines.

The forests east and southeast of Yaoundé provide a suitable habitat for larger forest antelopes such as the semi-aquatic sitatunga (*Tragelaphus spekei*), which is similar in appearance to its near-relation the bushbuck, and the bongo (*Tragelaphus euryceros*). When under threat, bongos hold their spiral horns against the backs of their necks as they run, to prevent them from tangling in vegetation.

The Mandara Mountains in the north of the country harbour a population of the endangered western subspecies of mountain reedbuck (*Redunca fulvorufula adamauae*), a grey-brown antelope with crescent-shaped horns.

Over-hunting in the extreme north of the country has greatly reduced numbers of such species as the scimitar-horned oryx (*Oryx dammah*), dama gazelle (*Gazella dama*), dorcas gazelle (*Gazella dorcas*) and red-fronted gazelle (*Gazella rufifrons*). A subspecies of the common hartebeest, the bubal hartebeest (*Alcelaphus busephalus buselaphus*), is now extinct.

Eight types of duiker, a group of about 16 small antelope species, are commonly found in Cameroon. The common, grey or bush duiker (*Sylvicapra grimmia*) and red-flanked duiker (*Cephalophus rufilatis*) are found in the savanna regions in the centre and north of the country, the white-bellied (*Cephalophus leucogaster*), Peters' (*Cephalophus callipygus*), Weyns' (*Cephalophus weynsi*) and black-fronted duikers (*Cephalophus nigrifrons*) in the south and east, while the bay (*Cephalophus dorsalis*), the blue (*Cephalophus monticola*) and the yellow-backed (*Cephalophus silvicultor*) duiker are found everywhere but the north. All but the common (grey) duiker are forest-dwelling. Duikers are distinguished by having arched backs, skulking habits and tufts of hair between the ears, and the forest-dwellers have a stocky, squat appearance.

Giraffe

Typically living in herds of between five and 15, there used to be good-sized populations of northern savanna giraffe (*Giraffa camelopardus congoensis*) in the north of the country, but now these are generally absent outside protected areas such as Waza, Bénoué and Kalamaloué, and even here they are still significantly threatened by poaching.

Gorillas

Cameroon is one of the few countries where coastal/lowland gorillas (*Gorilla gorilla*) still exist in the wild. Growing up to 1.8m high and weighing up to 210kg, they actually thrive in a disturbed environment, whether it be caused by volcanic disturbance, landslides, fires or tree-felling, as such instability contributes to generating the growth of the low-level herbs they need. Primarily vegetarian, much of their diet consists of plants like bamboo, wild celery, galium vines and lobelias.

The vast Congo basin rainforest, of which the southeast of Cameroon is part, is one of the richest areas in the world for primates, and possibly contains more gorillas than any other area. Here, the vast tracts of lowland forest harbour thousands of western lowland gorillas (*Gorilla gorilla gorilla*), smaller than either mountain or eastern lowland species, with around 5,000 believed to be in Lobéké National Park alone.

The montane forests in the Cross River region around the chain of mountains that roughly follow the border with Nigeria contain an isolated population of an endangered endemic subspecies of lowland gorilla (*Gorilla gorilla diehli*). In 2000 there were estimated to be between 150 and 200 individuals, making this subspecies of gorilla one of the most endangered primates by far.

Southern Cameroon is one of the few remaining gorilla sanctuaries left in the world, although widespread logging, bushmeat hunting and agricultural expansion increasingly threaten the region.

Viewing gorillas in the wild in Cameroon invariably involves persistence and perseverance, but is well worth the effort: they share many attributes with humans, living in groups with the male acting as family head and the female cuddling her offspring.

Chimpanzees

Though not as common as gorillas, chimpanzees (*Pan troglodytes*), the closest relation to humans of all animals, are widely present throughout the forested areas of southern Cameroon, and especially where human disturbance is minimal or non-existent. Chimpanzees have been found at Mount Cameroon, Korup National Park, Bwombi-Mwo Forest Reserve and Mount Kupé, as well as the Douala-Edea and Campo reserves. In southeastern Cameroon a small number of chimpanzees are present near Yokadouma. They are present in greater numbers in the evergreen forest of Dja, and Lobéké, Boumba-Bek and Nki in the southeast.

Chimps are hunted for their meat throughout Cameroon and their habitats are increasingly threatened by human activities like timber extraction, the pet trade and laboratory testing.

In the Nigerian border region the forests of the mountains support the endangered chimpanzee subspecies, *Pan troglodytes vellerosus*.

Monkeys, drills and guenons

Around 20 species of monkey are found in Cameroon, including the crested, the red-capped and the grey-cheeked mangabey in the south, the vervet (green) monkey, found everywhere but the south, the mona monkey in the southwest, including mounts Cameroon and Kupé, and the endangered red-eared guenon, also in the southwest, by the Nigerian border.

The lowland forests in the vicinity of the Nigerian border, the Cross and Sanaga rivers and Mount Cameroon play a key role in the conservation of primates. The strictly endemic, hill-loving Preuss's red colobus monkey (*Procolobus pennanti preussi*) and the shy, near-endemic red-eared monkey (*Cercopithecus erythrotis*), which has a red tail, a red spot on the nose and red-tipped ears, are present here.

The crowned guenon (*Cercopithecus pogonias*), a slim and graceful monkey that sits upright while sleeping in the trees, is also present here, as is the highly endangered drill (*Mandrillus leucophaeus*), which differs from other monkeys because of the male's large size and short tail. This region is also the habitat of the black colobus monkey (*Colobus satanas*).

The mangroves of the coastal regions by the Nigerian border and around the coast at Douala provide a suitable habitat for both the near-endemic Sclater's monkey (*Cercopithecus sclateri*) and the talapoin monkey (*Miopithecus talapoin*).

North of Yaoundé as far as Ngaoundéré can be found the patas monkey (*Cercopithicus patas*), a slender, light reddish-brown monkey with a black stripe above the eyes, distinguished for being one of the few ground-dwelling primates. Feeding on grass, fruit, insects and new shoots, these monkeys can run at speeds of up to 35 miles (55km) per hour.

The savanna olive baboon (*Papio anubis*) is present in the centre and north, including Waza, while the baboon-like mandrill is found in the south.

Otters and civets

Both the smallest of the sub-Saharan otters, the spotted-necked otter (*Lutra maculicollis*), and the largest African otter, the Cape clawless otter (*Aonyx capensis*), are present throughout the country. The Congo clawless otter (*Aonyx congica*), very similar to the Cape clawless otter, is found in the southeast.

The long and sleek, nocturnal grey-brown tree civet (*Nandinia binotata*) can be found in the forests of the south, while the more adaptable, heavier and longer African civet (*Civettictis civetta*) is present throughout the country. All are largely crepuscular, difficult to see, and a spotlight would be needed to search for them.

Genet and linsang

Several genet species – with their long, slender bodies, long tails and short legs – are present in Cameroon, although only the experienced observer would find it easy to identify them to species level. The large-spotted genet (*Genetta tigrina*) is generally found north of Ngaoundéré and south of Maroua, while the servaline genet (*Genetta servalina*) can be found in the tropical forests of the south, from west to east. The thinly distributed panther genet (*Genetta maculata*) is found at Korup and in the forests of the west of the country. The African linsang (*Poiana richardsoni*), a genet-like species found in the rainforests of the southeast of Cameroon, is also present here.

Mongoose

Various species of mongoose also inhabit Cameroon. These include the long-nosed mongoose (*Herpestes naso*) and the black-footed mongoose (*Bdeogale nigripes*), both found only in the forested areas of the south. Conversely, the slender mongoose (*Galerella sanguinea*), the white-tailed mongoose (*Ichneumia albicauda*) and the large grey mongoose (*Herpestes ichneumon*) only inhabit the centre and north, with the water (marsh) mongoose (*Atilax paludinosus*), similar to an otter, found in well-watered habitats throughout the country. The flat-headed cusimanse (*Crossarchus platycephalus*), a species of small mongoose about which little is known, is also present in the lowland forests of the southwest.

Jackal, wild dog, polecat, weasel, fox and hyena

The nocturnal side-striped jackal (*Canis adustus*) inhabits well-watered and wooded pockets of the north, as does the wild dog (*Lycaon pictus*). The striped polecat (*Ictonyx striatus*) and the Libyan striped weasel (*Poecilictis libyca*) are found in the extreme north only. The heavily built spotted hyena (*Crocuta crocuta*), the best-known of the hyenas, and the striped hyena (*Hyaena hyaena*) are both present in low densities in the extreme north. The pale fox (*Vulpes pallida*) exists in the very extreme north.

Cats

The sighting of big cats is generally a rarity in Cameroon. Lions (*Panthera leo*) are present in the centre and north, but outside protected areas such as Waza, Bouba Ndjida and Bénoué national parks, their numbers have declined dramatically. The cheetah (*Acinonyx jubatus*) populates the north, but numbers have dropped significantly in recent years. More encouragingly, the leopard (*Panthera pardus*) is found all over the country. Caracals (*Caracal caracal*), with their distinctive long tufts of hair at the tips of their pointed ears, servals (*Leptailurus serval*) and African wild cats (*Felis silvestris*) are to be found in northern areas, while golden cats (*Felis aurata*) are domiciled in the tropical forests of the south, east and west.

Hedgehog, hare, squirrel and porcupine

The white-bellied hedgehog (*Atelerix albiventris*) is restricted to the centre and north of Cameroon, while the almost-grey cape hare (*Lepus capensis*) is found in the extreme north only. The centre, west and north of the country support the western ground squirrel (*Xerus erythropus*), which sports white side stripes. The North African porcupine (*Hystrix cristata*) is present throughout the country. The African brush-tailed porcupine (*Atherurus africanus*), on the other hand, is found in the south and southwest only. The long, black and white banded quills of these porcupines lie flat unless the animal is threatened, when they become raised and allow the animal to appear far larger than it really is. Porcupine is sought-after bushmeat and often lines roadsides.

Hogs

Several kinds of hog live in the country: the warthog (*Phacochoerus africanus*), which Lydekker unkindly descibed in 1908 as being an 'incarnation of hideous dreams'; the bushpig-like red river hog (*Potamochoerus porcus*); and the giant forest hog (*Hylochoerus meinertzhageni*), which lives up to its name, being Africa's largest pig species and ranging from about 1.5m to 2.5m in length and 130–240kg in weight.

Hyraxes and aardvarks

The stout and diurnal, guinea pig-like rock hyrax (*Procavia capensis*) is found in the north, while the nocturnal tree hyrax (*Dendrohydrax dorsalis*) is found in the forests of both the west and south. The unmistakable insectivore the aardvark (*Orycteropus afer*), with its elongated pig-like snout, is found everywhere but in the south, although it's seldom seen because of its nocturnal lifestyle.

Galagos

Of the galago species, the bushbaby (*Galago senegalensis*), is most often seen; identification is aided by its distinctive big round eyes, highly mobile ears and long fluffy tail. It is found north of the centre of the country. In the south the grey-furred Allen's galago (*Galago alleni*) is found, as is the western needle-clawed galago (*Galago elegantulus*), which sports red-hued dorsal fur and a white-tipped tail.

Pangolins

Three rare species of the striking, scaly pangolin are found in Cameroon, the giant ground pangolin (*Manis gigantea*) throughout the country, and the smaller long-tailed tree pangolin (*Manis tetradactyla*) and white-bellied tree pangolin (*Manis tricspis*) in the lowland forests of the south. They scour the forest floor for termites and ants, and when frightened they curl into a ball, so that their tough scales can act as a deterrent against predators.

Insects
Butterflies and moths

While the majority of Cameroon's many thousands of species of invertebrate life are overlooked by most visitors, butterflies and moths (order *Lepidoptera*), which worldwide constitute around 1% of all named insects, seldom fail to capture the attention of those visiting Cameroon.

This is not surprising considering their comparatively large size and bright colours, and the wide variety of species prevalent. More than a thousand species of butterfly inhabit Cameroon, compared to just 56 in the UK. That represents more than a quarter of the total number of species found in tropical Africa.

The forests of the Nigeria–Cameroon border region are especially rich in butterflies, including the striking creamy white *Charaxes superbus* and powerful *Charaxes acraeoides*. In all, around 950 species are present in this region, more than in any other forest in Africa. Of these, around 100 species are found nowhere else. The area around Mount Cameroon and the forests of the southeast of the country are also particularly important regions for butterflies, including the endemic *Charaxes musakensis*.

Amphibians and reptiles
Frogs and toads

Cameroon's frogs are of all sizes, including the goliath frog, which at 0.3m long (over 0.6m with legs extended) is the biggest frog in the world. It was allowed to evolve because of the perennial wetness of the region. As heavy as a domestic cat, it feels like a balloon filled with wet sand if you hold it. Found only along isolated rainforest rivers in Cameroon and Equatorial Guinea, this is just one of many species threatened by logging and by locals slaying it for its exotic, sweet meat.

The species richness of amphibians and reptiles is particularly high in the rainforests of the southeast. Here there are two endemic clawed frog species, *Xeropus boumbaensis* and *Xeropus pygmaeus*. The Mount Cameroon region harbours one strictly endemic toad, *Werneria preussi*, with the four-digit toad (*Didynamipus sjotstedti*), Tandy's smalltongue toad (*Werneria tandyi*) and the frog, *Athroleptis bivittatus,* all being near-endemics. Around the Korup region on the border with Nigeria, the amphibian fauna is very diverse and endemic species include the Dizangue reed frog (*Hyperolius bopeleti*), Schneider's banana frog (*Afrixalus schneideri*) and Werner's river frog (*Phrynobatrachus werneri*). The savanna and grasslands north of Yaoundé and Ngaoundéré yield such endemic amphibians as the Bouda River frog (*Phrynobatrachus scapularis*) and the Bamiléké Plateau frog (*Rana longipes*).

Turtles and manatees

If you are lucky, turtles can be seen on the coast, with the females laying their many eggs on the beaches. The mangroves of the coastal regions situated by the Nigerian border and either side of Douala provide a habitat to the threatened West African manatee (*Trichechus senegalensis*) and the soft-skinned turtle (*Trionyx triunguis*). In the summer, several species of marine turtle appear. These include the green (*Chelonia mydas*), leatherback (*Dermochelys coricea*), loggerhead (*Caretta caretta*) and hawksbill turtle (*Eretomychelys imbricata*).

Lizards

Lizards are plentiful in many areas, with chameleons and geckos a common sight. Of more than 170 species of reptiles and amphibians in Korup, the forest chameleon (*Chamaeleo camurunensis*) and two worm lizards (*Cynisca schaeferi* and *C. gansi*) are endemic. In the forested areas south and southeast of Yaoundé, endemics include the Cameroon stumptail chameleon (*Rhampholeon spectrum*), the grey chameleon (*Chameleo chapini*) and the crested chameleon (*Chameleo cristatus*). There are also endemic skinks (small, long-tailed lizards), such as Fuhn's five-toed skink (*Leptosiaphos fuhni*) and Peter's lidless skink (*Panaspis breviceps*). The Mandara

BIRDING: RECOMMENDED EQUIPMENT
Optical equipment
Binoculars that are sealed and waterproof are the most essential piece of equipment. Those who have been thrifty when buying binoculars will soon realise that they have wasted their time and money, because once they fill with water or mist, they become useless. In the rainforest 8x32 magnification is normally the safest bet as it tends to gather more light, and pinning down the bird in your viewfinder is therefore easier. In open areas (eg: savanna) 10x40s are more useful as the image is larger. Telescopes can be useful, particularly in the savannas, or when watching waterbirds on an open lake. In the rainforest a telescope is a personal preference, but in my experience their use is limited and they are cumbersome to carry. Finally, if you use glasses, be warned: most birding is done watching straight into the canopy which means that invariably your glasses will steam up and you will end up seeing very little when the frantic flock moves past. Contact lenses are good, but if you can't use them be sure to have several cleaning devices handy to demist your glasses and binoculars (binos in birder parlance).

Raingear
The only thing worse than your binoculars being filled with water is you being soaking wet. Be sure to get waterproof and sturdy boots, ponchos and waterproof trousers. Boots also double as protective ant-swarm gear, and ponchos make excellent makeshift hides. Peak or broad-rimmed hats keep rainwater out of your eyes and binoculars.

Sound gear
Seeing much in the rainforest often depends on your ability to recognise, follow, locate and reproduce bird sounds. These days, mini-disk (MD)

Mountains in the north of the country are home to a couple of endemic reptile species, the Mount Lefo chameleon (*Chamaeleo wiedersheimi*) and the African wall gecko (*Tarentola ephippiata*).

Crocodiles
The Nile crocodile (*Crocodylus niloticus*), which grows to about 6m in length, is the most widespread species present in waterways both throughout the country, and notably around the Mount Cameroon area and the mangroves of the coastal regions by the Nigerian border and around Douala. The nocturnal Dwarf crocodile (*Osteolaemus tetraspis*) lives in the rivers and streams of the rainforests to the south of the country; the smallest of African crocodiles, it grows up to 2m in length.

Snakes
Snakes, both venomous and harmless, are also common in Cameroon, though they can be difficult to spot, and thankfully most fear humans and hurry away.

The Gaboon viper (*Bitis gabonica*), the largest viper in Africa, growing to almost 2m in length, is present in the rainforests of the south and notably in the Mount Cameroon region. It has the largest fangs (up to 5cm) of any venomous snake worldwide. In the densely forested areas south and southeast of Yaoundé, Grant's African ground snake (*Gonionotophis grantii*) and Zenker's worm snake (*Typhlops*

recorders, with an attached amplified speaker are the norm. For bird recording, I recommend the Sony TC-D5 Pro II analogue cassette deck and Sennheiser MKH-70 RF-condenser microphone with Sennheiser blimp windscreen, pistol grip/shockmount and power supply. For more information on bird vocalisation recording in the tropics, see Nick Athanas's informative article 'Making sense of the sounds: learning tropical bird vocalizations' at www.thebirdindex.com. West Africa has a superb set of bird sounds in the form of Claude Chappuis's *African Bird Sounds* CDs available from Wildsounds (web: www.wildsounds.co.uk).

Watches
Watches with both compass and altimeter can be extremely useful. Birders are known to wander off the path of forest trails and a compass could be invaluable in helping you find your way home. Some birds in the Cameroon Highlands are specific to certain altitudinal bands and here the altimeter can be useful in helping you find your most-sought-after quarry.

Global Positioning System (GPS)
Definitely becoming more relevant, both in terms of being able to describe exactly where you saw a sought-after species and allowing you to wander freely into the field in the knowledge that you will be able to find your way back to where you came from. But beware of thick rainforest canopies such as at Korup National Park, where acquiring a satellite signal may be tricky at times.

Flashlights
A Maglite is useful, both as a torch and to be able to spot owls, nightjars and roosting birds at night.

zenkeri) are present. In the savanna and grasslands north of Yaoundé the strictly endemic Sudan beaked snake (*Rhinotyphlops sudanensis*) is present.

Birds
Cameroon's diversity of habitats supports over 900 bird species in about 75 families, with seven endemic species, 20 speciality species and 18 endangered species. Eight of the ten families endemic to mainland Africa are present in the country. In a two-week trip you could expect to see around 250–300 species. Some birders manage far more in a longer trip taking in more areas.

For the greatest success, research the region thoroughly before the trip. The website www.wildsounds.co.uk has a selection of CDs and cassettes of bird calls. The online natural history, environment and science bookstore, www.nhbs.com, can help you select field guides, while www.birdingpal.com may be able to help with finding an experienced local bird guide.

The coastal lowlands on the outskirts of Douala make a good start to a birding holiday, and on the mangroves and mudflats of the Wouri River, off the Limbé road, you may see such birds as the black tern, white-fronted plover, grey parrot, purple heron, black heron, little egret, western reef egret, intermediate egret, carmelite sunbird, hartlaub's duck and great egret. Moving west from Douala, Limbé is a good spot for searching out the western reef egret, western bluebill and carmelite sunbird.

FINDING GREY-NECKED ROCKFOWL: CAMEROON'S COVERT CATAPULT
Christian Boix

Cameroon is probably the best place in the world to see grey-necked rockfowl, which along with the yellow-necked rockfowl of Upper Guinea is a member of the family Picathartidae, arguably the most difficult family of birds to see in the world. The rockfowl has been an avian oddity since its discovery in Cameroon in 1899. The poor beast has suffered a century of chronic taxonomic identity crises, being initially described as a crow (*Corvidae*), later as a starling (*Sturnidae*) and not long ago as a flycatcher (*Muscicapidae*), with some workers considering its closest relatives to be babblers (*Timaliidae*) and others thrushes (*Turdidae*). Recent DNA and anatomical work supports a 'crow-like' ancestry, but others suggest that another African oddity, the South Africa rockjumpers (*Chaetops*), are more likely cousins. Such confusion stems from the fact that rockfowls are probably remnants of an archaic avian lineage. Fortunately, both species of rockfowl presently enjoy some phylogenetic stability by being placed within a separate family.

The grey-necked rockfowl is a medium-sized bird (200–250g) with a strong broad tail (c180mm long) to balance its weight on vines, stems and branches. A pair of long, muscular, silver-grey legs are responsible for its rapid catapulting motion and are used as powerful leaf-litter rakes for foraging. Despite an apparent reluctance to fly, the bird is endowed with enough wing load both for take off and sustained flight. Its large black bill gives it the appearance of a crow and is a powerful tool used to forage along the forest floor. However, what never fails to mesmerise the observer is its tri-coloured, bald, bulbous head with a double-lobed blue-grey fore-crown and bulging crimson nape, separated on either side by a sinister-looking triangular black mask. The underparts, including throat and belly, are soft lemon-yellow with a grey wash on the throat and upper chest. The bird's primaries form a distinct black band that separates the yellow underparts from the slate-grey upperparts. The combination of its equivocal past and its unusual appearance make it arguably the most sought-after bird in Africa.

The rockfowl is also lightning fast, its fluid motion almost shadowless, bounding silently in Gollum-like fashion through the forest undergrowth leaving only a trail of quivering stems and vines for the ill-prepared birder. They generally occur in groups of three to five birds scouring the forest floor and undergrowth in search of insects, earthworms, millipedes, centipedes, frogs and lizards.

Rockfowls are restricted to the lushest Guinea–Congolian primary and secondary rainforests of West Africa. The grey-necked rockfowl is found mainly in the lowland rainforests of Cameroon, Gabon, Nigeria and Bioko. Within Cameroon, colonies have been found at Korup National Park, Dja Reserve and Campo Reserve. There are even rumours of a small colony on the outskirts of Yaoundé. Colonies are generally small (two to five nests) with the exception of

In a recent article in *Travel Africa*, Keith Betton, vice-chairman of the African Bird Club, cited Mount Kupé as second in the top-ten birding sites in Africa.

Birding Cameroon
Keith Barnes

Rainforest birding in West Africa can be slow and frustrating. Most species occur at low densities, others are frequently heard and rarely seen, and many of those that

a very large colony at Dja Reserve that is blessed with 47 nests, of which at least 20 are believed to be active! Nests are made of mud, and are like a very large swallow's nest.

From a conservation perspective, the rockfowl's bizarre nature and reluctance to take to the wing have been its downfall. It is sought after for local cuisine, zoos, museums and the bird trade, resulting in it being considered globally threatened by BirdLife International. Unfortunately, the Cameroon birds are not protected by folklore, as are its congeners in Sierra Leone, where their presence around rocks (preferred burial places of many forest tribes) have earned them a mythical respect from all worshipping visitors. Although law in Cameroon protects the rockfowl, hunting, the bird trade, conversion of forest into farmland and logging operations are challenging its survival.

Where to find a rockfowl
By far the most reliable site to see grey-necked Picathartes in Cameroon is in Korup National Park. Chief Adolf at the WWF office in Mundemba will be able to help arrange such trips. Other breeding sites in Cameroon include the rocks around Mount Kupé, although it is seldom seen there anymore. The onset of the wet season is the best time to find them (March–May).

Tips to see rockfowl
To say that Rockfowl loathe surprises is a gross understatement. The bird is extremely skittish and any sudden movement or noise will result in it beating a rapid retreat. However, they can be fairly bold, curious and confident around breeding sites if the observer behaves cautiously, silently and respectfully.

- Do not wear any material that may rustle such as nylon or plastic.
- Avoid brightly coloured garments: choose dark and sombre clothing.
- Avoid hanging or dangling items off your clothes, belt, binoculars, etc, especially if they are shiny, noisy or may get caught in the vegetation.
- Wear good walking shoes and walk cautiously.
- Pre-empt your next step and move, avoiding snapping twigs and branches to push out of the way. Bear in mind that getting to the rock/cave is no assurance of success. How silently you get there may be!
- Before your final approach, rest and drink. Coughing, sneezing and throat clearing are likely to alert the birds to your presence and result in disappointment.
- As you are likely to be sitting for a long time, choose your favourite sitting position.
- Once you have bagged the 'beast', please remember that the dome is no place to celebrate! Retreat as silently as you arrived; respect the bird, the silence and the moment.

show up may do so once only. When species do show themselves, it is often fleetingly and generally in poor light. But for those who are persistent and patient, the rewards are endless, and when a rockfowl finally leaps into view, the frustration vanishes – the rainforest offers the most exotic and sought-after species in Africa, from blue cuckooshrikes to ant-thrushes and alethes. It is all well worth the persistence. Birding the savanna is much easier and much more productive in short time-spells; the weather and conditions are also more conducive to seeing more birds. Many of the larger and more spectacular species Africa is renowned for are absent or exceptionally rare in West Africa. However, what West Africa lacks in quantity it more than makes up for in quality; in fact the region probably holds more desirable bird species than any other part of Africa.

Despite being the richest country in West Africa for birds, ornithologically speaking Cameroon remains little known. It is probably the most accessible country in West-Central Africa with many exceptionally exciting and interesting bird species. Cameroon supports 915 bird species if you include the golden nightjar discovered recently by Ian Sinclair et al (April 2003). Of these, 704 are resident and 218 are seasonal migrants (145 from the Palaearctic and 73 intra-African). Seven species are endemic to Cameroon.

Key birds

There is no doubt that Cameroon's potential popularity as a birding destination is bolstered by it containing some of Africa's – and indeed the world's – most highly desirable bird species. The grey-necked rockfowl (Picathartes) is chief among these (see box on finding rockfowl, pages 36–7). Along with the rockfowl, the Mount Kupé bush shrike, Arabian bustard and Egyptian plover were all included in *Birdwatch* magazine's 2003 poll of the world's 50 most desirable birds. Other highly sought-after specialities include quail plover, stone partridge, violet turaco, Sudan golden sparrow and scissor-tailed kite in the northern savannas, and grey pratincole, bare-cheeked trogon, and grey-sided and red-sided broadbills in the forested southwest. Alongside these rare and spectacular species, well-represented members of the avifauna include hornbills, turacos, kingfishers, illadopsis and bee-eaters in the forests, and seed-eaters, cisticolas, raptors and starlings in the northern woodlands and semi-desert.

Access

Although occasionally frustrating, Cameroon is a well-connected country with a road and air network that can (and usually does) get one from A to B very effectively. Regular flights connect the two main birding zones in the north (Maroua–Garoua) and south (Yaoundé–Douala) of the country and the roads in the north are good year-round. In the south, it is best to avoid the rainy season between May and August when the roads become mudpaths and places such as Korup are virtually inaccessible. For most of the year, however, although the roads are poor, most sites can be visited.

Timing

March and early April are the optimal times to visit Cameroon for birding. This is before the heavy rains come, when many birds in the south are actively setting up territories and many of the seasonal migrants are still present in the far north.

Major birding biomes/habitats

The diversity of habitats in Cameroon is staggering and is replicated nowhere else in West Africa. Far north Cameroon comprises the sparse, thorn-dominated woodlands and grasslands of the Sahel biome. This biome extends from just north of Bénoué to Lake Chad. There are many species characteristic of this dry woodland-grassland mosaic, although these are shared with many other West African nations. To the south, Cameroon is covered by Guinea savanna, which is a broad-leaved woodland. The third major habitat is Afromontane forest. Within Cameroon, this habitat is found on Mount Cameroon, Mount Kupé and in the Bamenda-Banso Highlands. According to BirdLife International, two vital Endemic Bird Areas (EBA) form a major part of Cameroon: the first is the

Above Manengouba Lake,
Southwest Province (RQ)

Left Chutes de Tello,
Adamawa Province (RQ)

Above Cattle fording the river near
Chutes de Tello, Adamawa Province (RQ)

Below Sport fishing in Kribi (APS)

Cameroon Mountains (EBA 086). This holds some 29 restricted-range endemics that are confined to Cameroon and a small portion of Nigeria (Obodu Plateau); undoubtedly, Cameroon remains the country of choice to see these, and many other birds. The remainder of the country comprises lowland Guinea–Congo forest, home to the Cameroon and Gabon lowlands (EBA 085), which has six bird species found nowhere else in the world, including the rare grey-necked rockfowl.

Independent birding
Although possible, independent birders need to plan well and expect a few surprises en route. The best area for independent birders is Mount Kupé, where transport, accommodation, good guides and sound advice are all available from the WWF office at Nyasoso.

Birding tours
Tropical Birding runs commercial birding tours to Cameroon (tel: +27 82 400 3400; fax: +27 556 4124; email: info@tropicalbirding.com; web: www.tropicalbirding.com). Both set-departure trips in March and April, as well as customised trips for small groups in search of mega-specials such as grey-necked rockfowl and Mount Kupé bush shrike, are available.

Further ornithological information
Cameroon Ornithological Club BP 3055; Messa, Yaoundé; email: coc@iccnet.cam
The African Bird Club BirdLife International, Wellbrook Court, Girton Rd, Cambridge CB3 0NA; web: www.africanbirdclub.org. The leading organisation concerning the conservation and study of African birds. It provides biannual newsletters and other benefits. Membership currently costs £12 per year.
West African Ornithological Society 1 Fishers Heron, East Mills, Fordingbridge, Hants SP6 2JR. Has regular bulletins.

Trip reports are available from the Foreign Birdwatching Reports and Information Service (5 Stanway Close, Lackpole, Worcester WR4 9XL, tel: 01905 454541). The Dutch Birding Travel Report Service (PO Box 737, 9700 AS Groningen, The Netherlands; tel: 315 014 5925; www.worldtwitch.com) also has very informative reports on Cameroonian birding tours, most in search of rare birds.

Some relevant field guides for birding are listed in *Appendix 2*.

Online updated versions of the site guides that appear in the relevant sections of this book, and trip reports and recent information about birding Cameroon may be found at www.tropicalbirding.com and www.thebirdinginn.com

When you return from your trip, be sure to sign up for a free account and create your own Cameroon checklist and submit your valuable data to the WOBAP (World Bird Atlas Project) at www.thebirdindex.com.

Practical Information

TOURIST INFORMATION
Cameroon
Ministry of Tourism (Ministère du Tourisme) BP 266; Bd Rudolf Manga Bell, Yaoundé; tel: 223 29 36; email: mintour@camnet.cm; web: www.camnet.cm/mintour/tourisme/. This is the Cameroon phone number. International dialling and calling from abroad are explained on page 91.

Europe
Tourism Information Bureau for Europe 26 Rue de Longchamps, 75016 Paris, France; tel: 01 45 05 96 48; email: office@cameroun-infotourisme.com; web: www.cameroun-infotourisme.com

WHEN TO VISIT
From a climatic point of view, the best time to visit is during the cooler, drier months between November and February. December and January are ideal, although dust from the *harmattan* wind that blows sand south from the Sahara from around November to March can turn the skies a sandy grey and greatly restrict visibility. This can cause flights to be delayed or cancelled, and can spoil views and gives photographs an overcast look.

The rainy season, which is generally from May to November, but which is usually worst from July to October, can make roads almost impassable and travel very difficult in many regions.

TOUR OPERATORS AND TRAVEL AGENTS
General
Organised tours can make a lot of sense, especially as in Cameroon many interesting places can be difficult to reach by public transport, or even with your own vehicle. The following tour operators offer itineraries that include Cameroon.

UK
African Trails 3 Conway Av, Preston PR1 9TR; tel: 01772 330 907; web: africantrails.co.uk. North to south 22- or 29-week tours of Africa pass through Cameroon. There are agents for the company in Australia, New Zealand, Austria, Belgium, Denmark, Germany, Kenya, Canada and the USA.
Dragoman Camp Green, Kenton Rd, Debenham, Stowmarket IP14 6LA; tel: 01728 861133; web: www.dragoman.com. Sister company of Encounter Overland, also offering several overland trips that visit Cameroon.
Earthwatch 267 Banbury Rd, Oxford, OX2 7HT; tel: 01865 318831; email: info@earthwatch.org.uk; web: www.earthwatch.org/europe. The Earthwatch Institute engages people worldwide in scientific field research and education to promote the understanding and action necessary for a sustainable environment. It currently offers

Cameroon rainforest tours (£840) documenting rare and endemic plants in protected forest areas, preparing plant specimens and cataloguing findings. Earthwatch has offices worldwide.
Encounter Overland Camp Green, Kenton Rd, Debenham, Stowmarket IP14 6LA; tel: 01728 862222; web: www.encounter-overland.co.uk. British-based company offering several overland trips passing through Cameroon.
truckafrica.com Wissett Pl, Norwich Rd, Halesworth, Suffolk IP19 8HY; tel: 01509 881509; web: www.truckafrica.com. Part one of the Transafrican Expedition goes through the north of Cameroon, visiting Rhoumsiki and Waza. The tour from Morocco to Tanzania in October costs £2,400 plus £595 kitty, including travel and accommodation, working out at £148 per week.

US

Access Africa Suite 1105, 82 Wall St, New York, NY 1005; tel: 212 722 8250; web: www.accessafrica.com. Access Africa offers various West African tours including Cameroon visits, as well as other services such as visa processing, hotel reservations and car rental. The ten-day US$1,600 Nigeria/Cameroon trip, for example, includes a round-trip transatlantic airfare, accommodation in Douala, Yaoundé and Lagos with sightseeing tours, and flights from Lagos to Douala and Douala to Yaoundé. An eight-day Cameroon package at US$1,600 covers Limbé, Mount Cameroon, the Kribi region, Foumban and Waza National Park.
Africa Desk 123 Danbury Rd, New Milford, CT 06776; tel: 860 354 9341; email: info@africadesk.com; web: africadesk.com. Africa Desk's 15-day Cameroon Rainforest Adventure features equatorial rainforest trekking and camping, learning about rainforest mammal, bird and plant life, and making visits to beaches and pygmy villages. The US$4,689 cost includes the airfare from the USA (New York), transport, a guide, fees, tolls and taxes, hotels, camping and meals.
Bicycle Africa 4887 Columbia Dr South, Seattle, WA 98108-1919; tel: 206 767 0848; web: www.ibike.org. Bicycle Africa specialises in ecotourism bike holidays for small groups. There are currently two tours in Cameroon, a 15-day 570km/340-mile bicycle tour of the west (US$1,090 plus airfare), and a 15-day 480km/220-mile tour of the north (US$1,490 plus airfare).
DreamWeaver Travel 1185 River Dr, River Falls, WI 54022; tel: 715 425 1037; web: www.dreamweavertravel.net. DreamWeaver Travel organises 'ecologically and culturally appropriate' trips to Cameroon usually in October and December, and also builds trips around other dates and offers custom trips for individuals. Visits cover anything from southeastern Cameroon's equatorial rainforest and meetings with Baka 'pygmies' to northern Cameroon's arid moonscape and nomadic culture.
Turtle Tours Box 1147, Carefree, AZ 85377; tel: 480 488 3688; email: turtletours@ earthlink.net; web: www.turtletours.com. Offers custom-made tours of Cameroon.

Specialist

These agents can organise flights to and from Cameroon and may be able to help with overland tours and advice. It is also worth trying online booking agents/discounters like www.lastminute.com, www.cheapflights.com and www.priceline.co.uk in the UK; www.cheaptickets.com and www.priceline.com in the US; and www.travelshop.com.au in Australia.

UK

Africa Travel Centre 21 Leigh St, London WC1H 9QX; tel: 020 7387 1211 or 0845 4501525; web: www.africatravel.co.uk
African Travel Specialists 229 Old Kent Rd, London SE1 5LU; tel: 0870 345 5454
Bridge the World 45–47 Chalk Farm Rd, London NW1 8AJ; tel: 0870 814 4400; web: www.bridgetheworld.com

Flightbookers 178 Tottenham Court Rd, London W1P 9LF; tel: 020 7757 2000; web: www.ebookers.com
Global Village 57– 59 Leather La, London EC1N 7TJ; tel: 0870 442 4848; web: www.gvillage.co.uk
STA Travel 86 Old Brompton Rd, London SW7 3LQ; tel: 020 7361 6161/6262; web: www.statravel.co.uk
Student Travel Centre 24 Rupert St, London W1D 6DQ; tel: 020 7437 6370; web: www.student-travel-centre.com
Trailfinders 194 Kensington High St, London W8 7RG; tel: 020 7938 3366/3939; web: www.trailfinders.com

France
Capital Tours 54 Rue du Brave Rondeau, 17000 La Rochelle; tel: 05 46 68 24 58
Club Aventure 18 Rue Seguiler, 75006 Paris; tel: 01 44 32 09 30
Go Voyages 14 Rue Clery, 75002 Paris; tel: 01 53 40 44 00
Nouvelles Frontieres 87 Bd de Grenelle, 75015 Paris; tel: 01 45 68 70 00
Vie Sauvage 24 Rue Vignon, 75009 Paris; tel: 01 44 51 08 00

South Africa
Tropical Birding 17 Toucan Tropics, Bloubergrise, 7441, CapeTown; tel: 82 400 3400; email: tropicalbirding@telkomsa.net; web: www.tropicalbirding.com

USA
These agents can organise discount flights and overland tours and advice.

Air Hitch Web: www.airhitch.org. Offers a rather long-winded system offering discounted tickets from the US to Europe, currently from US$167 one-way.
Cortez Travel Tel: 800 854 1029). Can arrange flights on Cam Air.
Nomad Travel Bazaar 127 Harmon Cove Towers, Secaucus, NJ 07094; tel: 201 770 0120; web: www.travelbazaar.com.
Travel Cuts 124 MacDougal St, New York, NY 10012; tel: 212 674 2887; web: www.travelcuts.com. Specialises in budget and student travel.

In Cameroon
The following local operators can generally organise such things as tours, internal and international flights, car rental and hotel bookings, and can often help in other ways, such as changing currency. Tours tend to be pricey.

Yaoundé
Cameroon Tours and Safaris (CAMTOURS) BP 1198; tel: 220 50 70; email: camtours@iccnet.cm. Situated at Rond-point Nlongkak, about 3km from the centre, CAMTOURS specialises in birdwatching and safari tours, the latter concentrating on the most popular national parks, Waza, Korup and Bénoué. Tours are also organised to rainforest sanctuaries, and there are cultural tours of the grasslands region as well as beach vacations to Kribi and Limbé. Car and minibus rentals can also be organised.
Safar Tours BP 11852; Hilton Hotel, Bd du 20 Mai; tel: 222 87 06/223 36 46; email: info@safartours.com; web: www.safartours.com. Books domestic/international air tickets and organises tours.

Other tour operators and travel agents in Yaoundé:

Cameroon Travel Center BP 6977; 139 Rue Joseph Omgba Nsi, Quartier Elig-Essono; tel: 222 62 21

Camvoyages BP 606; Av de l'Indépendance; tel: 223 22 12
Inter Tour Route Mvog-Mbià; tel: 223 97 62
Inter Voyages BP 127; 71 Rue Valéry Giscard d'Estaing; tel: 223 10 05/222 03 01
Jully Voyages BP 6064; 385 Rue Mvog-Fouda Ada, Quartier Elig-Essono; tel: 222 14 48
Moabi Voyages BP 2374; 1061 Av de l'Indépendance; tel: 222 87 37
MTA (Mouwayoue Travel Agency) BP 3176; 272 Av J F Kennedy, Centre Ville; tel: 223 97 65/223 44 44

Douala

Ebene Voyages BP 446; tel: 342 29 85; mobile: 999 66 31; email: ebene.voyages@camnet.cm. This highly recommended, established tour operator is based in the Bali neighbourhood of Douala. Ebene offers personalised tours including trekking, canoeing and travel by railway, taxi and 4WD minibus. In the north, tours often cover the Mandara Mountains and Lake Chad, while in the southeast there are trips to see the Baka pygmies and Dja Reserve. In the west, trips are organised to Mount Cameroon, crater lakes and various chiefdoms. Prices start at about ∈ 1,600 each for a group of eight people for 15 days.
Globe Travel BP 4855; Rue Joss, Bonanjo; tel: 343 12 79. Excursions that can be arranged include visits to Mount Cameroon, Foumban, the villages of the Mandara Mountains in the north and 'xy' villages in the southeast rainforests. Other services include car rental, hotel and flight reservations.
Jet Cam Tour BP 5300; junction of Bd de la Liberté and Rue Galliéni, Akwa, by Residence La Falaise; tel: 343 30 78. Changes money, books flights and arranges tours.
Prestige Tours Cameroon BP 1766; tel: 342 11 64. Prestige can help with such things as flight bookings and car hire, as well as organising tours.
Souad Travel Agency BP 4200; Bd de la Liberté, by Hotel Parfait Garden; tel: 342 65 50. Arranges excursions throughout Cameroon.
Trans Africa Tours BP 15435; tel: 342 90 04. Offers various excursions as well as car rental, air ticket reservation, etc.

Others in Douala include:

Cameroon Rev'Tour Tel: 342 10 05/774 94 46
Cameroun Horizon BP 3237; off Pl du Gouvernement; tel: 342 94 24; email: camhoriz@camnet.cm
Delmas Voyages BP 263; Rue Kitchener; tel: 342 11 84
Jully Voyages BP 1868; Rue Boué de Lapeyrère, Akwa; tel: 342 32 09

Bafoussam

Tandel Voyages Sarl BP 994; Rue Entrée de la Ville, Ndiengdam; tel: 344 65 81
MTA (Mouwayoue Travel Agency) BP 1240; Bd Pachoin Adolphe-Tamdja; tel: 344 49 21

Ngaoundéré

Alto Agence de Tourisme by the Grand Marché; tel: 225 11 29. Various half-day and day trips including horseriding.

Garoua

Cameroon Safari Agency BP 1050; Bd Dr Jamot, town centre; tel: 227 23 26; mobile: 997 92 40; email: camsafagency@yahoo.fr

Maroua

Fagus Voyages BP 352; tel: 986 18 71; web: www.fagusvoyages.com. Organises safaris in Boubandjida, Waza and Bénoué reserves, fishing trips in lakes and rivers, and hiking and trekking in the Mandara and Atlantika mountains. Also offers car hire.

Jean-Remy Zra Teri BP 507; tel: 229 26 23
Transcontinental Travels Tel: 229 24 49

ENTRY REQUIREMENTS AND RED TAPE
Passport
All visitors to Cameroon require a full ten-year passport, which should remain valid at least six months beyond the end of the trip.

Foreigners are required to carry their passport (or an officially certified photocopy) with them at all times while in the country, and will be asked to produce this at the various roadside checkpoints.

It is a good idea to have photocopies made of the title and visa pages of your passport, as well as the page showing your arrival date in Cameroon, and to get these certified, so that you can safeguard against loss or confiscation while in the country, and so that you can keep your passport in a safe place.

Main police stations in Cameroon can certify the photocopies for free if you provide them with your passport, visa and a CFA500 (95c/53p) fiscal stamp *(timbre)* purchased from the Ministry of Finance (Minefi), which has an office in all of the bigger towns.

Yellow-fever certificate
All visitors require a yellow-fever certificate, which becomes valid ten days after the vaccine is administered and lasts for ten years.

Cholera certificate
Although the cholera jab is not considered to be very effective, the certificate may be requested by officials, especially if there is a cholera epidemic in the region or, more probably, they are seeking a bribe. Many travel clinics are happy to provide a certificate misleadingly stating that you *haven't* had the jab, but which tends to do the trick at borders.

Return ticket
If you arrive by air, this is required for entry into the country.

Visa
Apart from nationals of the Central African Republic, Republic of Congo, Mali and Nigeria arriving for a stay not exceeding 90 days, all passport holders must have a tourist visa issued by a Cameroonian high commission or embassy, unless there is no representation in the country of departure. In West Africa there are Cameroonian embassies or consulates in Dakar, Lagos, Abidjan and Calabar, but these offices may refuse to issue a visa.

Passengers in transit and continuing their journey out of Cameroon on the first or same aircraft within 24 hours, and who are holding onward tickets and not leaving the airport, do not require a visa.

Obtaining a visa is an example of how haggling and vague bureaucracy can affect all areas of African life. Strictly speaking, visitors without a visa may be required to leave Cameroon on the next available flight, particularly if they are coming from a country where there is a Cameroonian embassy. Unofficially, visas may be available at the airports at Douala and Yaoundé.

For passengers arriving from countries without Cameroonian diplomatic representation, airport visas are usually available.

Visas can take more than three weeks to obtain by post or two or three days if applied for and collected in person. In the UK tourist visas currently cost £33.25

(about US$60) and in theory this is for a three-month visa, although when I last applied, the high commission in London would only grant one-month visas costing the same amount.

Be aware that documents required can vary and therefore applying for a visa can take several visits and can be far more time-consuming than you would at first assume. Ask whether you can submit photocopies of documents like air tickets, travellers' cheques or bank statements, rather than the originals. I have submitted original bank statements in the past and did not get these returned, much to the consternation of my accountant.

Required documents to be submitted are a passport valid for at least six months, two completed application forms (available from the high commission or embassy), two passport-sized photographs and the visa application fee.

You would need to show a return or continuation air ticket (or possibly a receipt with flight details from a tour operator) and proof of means of subsistence (for example a bank statement, but failing that travellers' cheques or a credit card statement should normally suffice) unless a tour operator or travel agency is organising the trip.

Last time I applied for a visa, because I was travelling independently I was asked also to provide a letter of invitation from my host or contact in Cameroon. From London this seemed a bit of a time-consuming, logistical headache to say the least, so I politely remonstrated and the official then said proof of a hotel reservation would do. There are numerous websites that allow you to book a Douala or Yaoundé hotel for a night for this purpose so that you can print out a reservation, which you can cancel at a later stage at no cost, if required.

Visas are valid from the date you are entering Cameroon, not from date of issue, but must be activated within a month of issue. A visa only represents permission to apply to enter and does not guarantee entry into Cameroon. You can be refused entry, for example for not having a yellow-fever certificate or for having only a one-way ticket.

Visas can be extended, which is easiest to do in Yaoundé, although it's also often possible in the regional capitals. Apart from the mandatory visa you need to enter Cameroon, it is generally best to obtain any further visas you may need before you leave home rather than in Cameroon.

Visa service companies
Visa service agents such as Corporate Visa Services (tel: 020 7336 0101; web: www.visa4travel.com) in the UK and Travisa (tel: 202 463 6166 or 1-800 222 2589; web: www.travisa.com) in North America can obtain a visa on your behalf for a fee. Currently Corporate Visa Services charge a £45 fee on top of a £39.22 consulate fee for a one-month visa, and quote two days for processing once accepted by the embassy, while Travisa charge a US$39 fee and US$70.22 for a one-month visa and have a three-day turnaround.

Sufficient funds
When you enter the country, you may have to convince immigration officials that you have what they consider to be sufficient funds for your time in Cameroon.

Travel insurance
In this part of the world a good travel insurance policy covering possible medical complications, including an emergency flight home, is essential, with coverage of theft and loss a bonus. Shop around, as policies can vary widely in price, and check the small print. 'Dangerous activities', which could even include trekking, may be

excluded. Bear in mind that you may have to pay for medical treatment on the spot and claim later, so keep all documentation.

EMBASSIES, CONSULATES AND DIPLOMATIC MISSIONS
Abroad

Australia 65 Bingara Rd, Beecroft, NSW 2119; tel: 02 9876 4544; web: www.cameroon.consul.com

Belgium Av Brughmann 131–133, 1060 Brussels; tel: 02 345 1870

Canada 170 Clemow Av, Ottawa, Ontario K1S 2B4; tel: 613 236 1522/865 16 64; web: www.haut-commissariat-cameroun-ottawa.ca

Central African Republic BP 935, Av de la France, Bangui; tel: 61 16 87

Chad Rue des Poids Lourds, N'djamena; tel: 51 28 94

Republic of Congo BP 2136, Rue General Bayardelle, Brazzaville; tel: 83 34 84

Ethiopia Bole Rd, Addis Ababa; tel: 44 81 16

France 73 Rue d'Auteuil, 75016 Paris; tel: 01 47 43 98 33

Gabon BP 14001, Bd Leon Mba, Libreville; tel: 73 29 10

Germany 532 Bad Godesberg, Rheinallee 76, Bonn 53; tel: 0228 356 038

Italy 282 Corso Vittorio Emmanuelle, 00186 Rome; tel: 654 71 50

Ivory Coast (Côte d'Ivoire) Immeuble le General, Rue Botreau-Roussel; tel: 20 21 33 31

Netherlands Amalistraat 14, The Hague; tel: 70 346 97 15; web: www.cameroon-embassy.nl

Switzerland 6 Rue Dunant, Geneva; tel: 022 736 2022

UK 84 Holland Pk, London W11 3SB; tel: 020 7727 0771

USA 2349 Massachusetts Av NW, Washington, DC 20008; tel: 202 265 8790

In Cameroon
Yaoundé

Canada BP 572; Stamatiades Bldg, Av de l'Indépendance; tel: 223 23 11/223 02 03

Central African Republic BP 396; off Rue Albert Ateba Ebe; tel: 22 51 55

Chad BP 506; Rue Joseph Mballa Eloumden, Bastos, Yaoundé; tel: 221 06 24

Republic of Congo Rue 1815, Bastos; tel: 221 24 58

Democratic Republic of Congo BP 632; Bd de l'URSS, Bastos; tel: 220 51 03

Equatorial Guinea BP 277; Rue 1805, Bastos; tel: 221 08 04

France BP 1631; Plateau Atemengue, Av de France, near Pl de la Réunification; tel: 223 40 13/222 17 76

Gabon BP 4130; Rue 1816, off Bd de l'URSS, Bastos; tel: 220 29 66

Germany Av de Gaulle; tel: 221 00 56

Ivory Coast (Côte d'Ivoire) BP 11357; Rue 1805, Bastos, Yaoundé, tel: 221 74 59/221 74 59

Liberia BP 1185; Bd de l'URSS, Bastos; tel: 221 54 57

Nigeria BP 448; off Av Monseigneur Vogt; tel: 222 34 55

UK BP 547; British High Commission, Av Winston Churchill; tel: 222 07 96/222 05 45; web: www.britcam.org

USA PO Box 817; Rue de Nachtigal; tel: 223 05 12; web: www.usembassy.state.gov/yaoundé

Douala

Benin Bepanda College Maturite, Bepanda; tel: 340 13 41/340 21 53

Canada BP 2373; 1726 Av de Gaulle, Bonanjo; tel: 342 31 05/342 31 03

Central African Republic Rue Castelnau, Akwa; tel: 343 45 47.

China Tel: 342 62 76

Democratic Republic of Congo BP 690; 70 Rue Sylvanie, Akwa; tel: 343 20 29
Denmark Tel: 342 64 64
Equatorial Guinea BP 5544; Rue Tokoto, Bonapriso; tel: 342 96 09
France BP 869; Av des Cocotiers, Bonanjo; tel: 342 62 50
Greece Tel: 342 81 09
Italy Tel: 342 95 37
Nigeria BP 1553; Bd de la Liberté, Akwa; tel: 343 21 68
Norway Tel: 342 52 69
Senegal Galerie MAM, Bonanjo; tel: 342 28 63
Spain Tel: 342 72 40
Sweden Tel: 342 52 69
Switzerland Tel: 342 21 70
Togo BP 828; 490 Rue Dika Mpondo, Akwa; tel: 342 11 87
Tunisia Tel: 342 70 37
UK BP 1784; British Consulate, 3rd Floor, Standard Chartered Bank Bldg, Bd de la Liberté, Akwa; tel: 342 36 12/342 21 77
USA BP 4006; Immeuble Flatters, off Av de Gaulle, Bonanjo; tel: 342 03 03

GETTING THERE AND AWAY
By air
Yaoundé or Douala?
Almost all visitors to Cameroon fly to Douala, which for many years has been Cameroon's principal international airport. Yet several airlines also fly to Yaoundé and landing here to an extent avoids the bigger crowds and more chaotic reception you will invariably receive at Douala.

Although Yaoundé is further east than Douala, you can get to most of the key tourism areas in the south and west almost as easily. Yaoundé is also more convenient for the north, as you can hop off the plane on to the train to Ngaoundéré, and it will also save hassle if you are visiting the rainforests of the east.

Prearrange and relax
Because arrival at Douala airport can feel rather hectic, or even a bit hostile if you're an unseasoned traveller in Africa, and because reliable onward transport can be difficult to secure, it is a good idea to prearrange being picked up. Your hotel may offer this service, as could an established tour operator, such as Ebene Voyages (tel: 342 29 85; mobile: 999 66 31; email: ebene.voyages@camnet.cm), which could also prearrange some activities for the start of your time in Cameroon. A few days lazing on the beach at Kribi, or at a laid-back little Cameroonian beach community like nearby Ebodje, before commencing touring or trekking, is a great antidote to a punishing schedule of long-haul flights, visa applications and the rest.

Flights to Cameroon
Flights to Cameroon from Europe (either to Yaoundé, or far more frequently, to Douala) are currently available via Paris, Brussels, Amsterdam, Zurich or London. The Air France flight from Paris to Douala, for example, takes about six hours, and the connecting flight to London takes around 50 minutes.

There are currently no direct flights to Cameroon from North America, so visitors have to make a connection in Europe.

At the time of writing, a return trip from London to Douala or Yaoundé typically costs from £525 to £850 including taxes, or up to £3,000 first class. January to April is generally the cheapest time of year for flights. With the recent demise of Air Afrique, those listed below are current carriers, all with connections from London, although Air France and KLM have agreed to merge on September 16 2004, subject to regulatory approval, which would obviously reduce choice:

Air France Tel: 0845 0845 111; web: www.airfrance.com/uk. Flies from London to Douala (daily) and Yaoundé (three times a week) via Paris.

Cameroon Airlines Tel: London: 020 833 0386, Paris: 01 43 12 30 12. Flies from London (on an Air France flight) to Paris Charles de Gaulle Airport and then to Yaoundé and Douala several times a week. At the time of writing all Cameroon Airlines websites were out of date and should be ignored.

Ethiopian Airlines Tel: 020 8987 7000; web: www.flyethiopian.com. Flies from London to Douala via Addis Ababa twice a week, and although it often offers the cheapest fares, you typically have to spend a day in Addis Ababa on the outward journey and a night on the way back (although accommodation is usually provided free on the return).

Kenya Airways Tel: 01784 888222; web: www.kenya-airways.com. Flies to Douala from London via Nairobi and is generally one of the cheapest airlines for the route, but the stopover in Nairobi often makes the journey one of the longest.

KLM Royal Dutch Airlines Tel: 0870 243 0541; web: www.klm.com. Flies to Douala and Yaoundé via Amsterdam with connecting London flights.

SN Brussels Airlines (previously Sabena) Tel: 0870 735 2345; web: www.brusselsairlines.com. Flies twice a week to Douala and once a week to Yaoundé via Brussels with connecting London flights.

Swiss International Airlines Tel: 0845 601 0956; web: www.swiss.com. Flies to Douala twice weekly and Yaoundé once weekly via Zurich, again with connecting London flights.

LONG-HAUL FLIGHTS

There is growing evidence, albeit circumstantial, that long-haul air travel increases the risk of developing deep vein thrombosis (DVT). This condition is potentially life threatening, but it should be stressed that the danger to the average traveller is slight.

Certain risk factors specific to air travel have been identified. These include immobility, compression of the veins at the back of the knee by the edge of the seat, the decreased air pressure and slightly reduced oxygen in the cabin, and dehydration. Consuming alcohol may exacerbate the situation by increasing fluid loss and encouraging immobility.

In theory everyone is at risk, but those at highest risk are shown below:

* Passengers on journeys of longer than eight hours' duration
* People over 40
* People with heart disease
* People with cancer
* People with clotting disorders
* People who have had recent surgery, especially on the legs
* Women on the pill or other oestrogen therapy
* Pregnant women
* People who are very tall (over 6ft/1.8m) or short (under 5ft/1.5m)

A deep vein thrombosis is a clot of blood that forms in the leg veins. Symptoms include swelling and pain in the calf or thigh. The skin may feel hot to touch and becomes discoloured (light blue-red). A DVT is not dangerous in itself, but if a

Flights from Cameroon to other destinations in Africa

Cameroon Airlines currently flies to **Johannesburg, Kinshasa, Ndjamena, Lagos, Abidjan, Cotonou, Ouagadougou, Bamako, Dakar, Bangui, Malabo, Libreville** and **Brazzaville**, although destinations are regularly subject to change.

Air Gabon flies from Douala to **Libreville**; Equato Guineana de Aviacion has regular flights to **Malabo** from Douala; Kenya Airways flies from Douala and Yaoundé to **Nairobi**.

In the past Nigerian Airways has operated flights to **Lagos** from Douala, although at the time of going to press these had been suspended.

Airline offices in Cameroon

Yaoundé

Air France BP 14335; 528 Rue de Nachtigal; tel: 223 43 78; web: www.airfrance.com/cm
Cameroon Airlines Av Monseigneur Vogt; tel: 223 03 04/223 40 01
Kenya Airways Nsimalen Airport; tel: 223 36 02
SN Brussels Airlines BP 13812; Av Foch; tel: 223 47 29/223 47 35; web:
www.brusselsairlines.com
Swiss International Airlines BP 14710; Av Foch; tel: 222 97 37/223 94 52, airport 222 97 30; web: www.swiss.com

Douala

Air France BP 4076; 1 Pl du Gouvernement, Bonanjo; tel: 342 15 55, airport: 342 28 78; web: www.airfrance.com/cm
Air Gabon BP 371; off Av de Gaulle; tel: 342 49 43

clot breaks down then it may travel to the lungs (pulmonary embolus). Symptoms of a pulmonary embolus (PE) include chest pain, shortness of breath and coughing up small amounts of blood.

Symptoms of a DVT rarely occur during the flight, and typically occur within three days of arrival, although symptoms of a DVT or PE have been reported up to two weeks later. Anyone who suspects that they have these symptoms should see a doctor immediately as anticoagulation (blood thinning) treatment can be given.

Prevention of DVT

General measures to reduce the risk of thrombosis are shown below. This advice also applies to long train or bus journeys.

- While waiting to board the plane, try to walk around rather than sit
- During the flight drink plenty of water (at least two small glasses every hour)
- Avoid excessive tea, coffee and alcohol consumption
- Perform gentle leg-stretching exercises, such as pointing the toes up and down
- Move around the cabin when practicable

If you fit into the high-risk category (see opposite) ask your doctor if it is safe to travel. Additional protective measures such as graded compression stockings, aspirin or low molecular weight heparin can be given. No matter how tall you are, where possible request a seat with extra legroom.

Cameroon Airlines BP 4092; 3 Av de Gaulle, Bonanjo; tel: 342 32 22/342 01 11, Hotel Akwa Palace; tel: 342 26 01; airport tel: 342 25 25
Equato Guineana de Aviacion BP 11673; represented by Hila Hotel; tel: 342 15 86/996 46 66
Kenya Airways Rue de Trieste, Bonanjo; tel: 342 96 91
Nigeria Airways BP 1126; 17 Bd de la Liberté, Akwa; tel: 342 73 21
SN Brussels Airlines BP 2074; 100 Av de Gaulle, Bonapriso; tel: 342 05 15; web: www.brusselsairlines.com
Swiss International Airlines BP 2959; Av de Gaulle, Bonanjo; tel: 342 29 29, airport 342 10 40; web: www.swiss.com

Airports

Yaoundé Nsimalen International Airport BP 13615; tel: 223 17 44/223 06 11
Douala International Airport BP 3131; tel: 342 36 30
Garoua International Airport BP 987; tel: 227 23 46
Maroua-salak Airport BP 271; tel: 229 19 49
Ngaoundéré Airport BP 279; tel: 225 11 57
Bertoua Airport Tel: 224 14 86

By land
Border crossings

Ensure all your paperwork is completely in order to satisfy customs and immigration staff. Accept that, especially at quiet borders, there may be a considerable wait. An official may have to be summoned from his home or another location before you can get the required stamp to proceed, and the matter may not be treated with the same degree of urgency as you would like. Borders may close in the afternoon, evening, on national holidays, at weekends and, in Muslim areas, on Fridays. If there is a wait, don't get impatient or lose your temper with border officials, which could make matters worse, but instead make the most of your time, for example by reading up on your destination or writing a letter.

The principal border crossings are Kousséri for Chad; Banki or Ekok for Nigeria; Ambam to Bitam for Gabon; Campo or Ebebiyin for Equatorial Guinea; Garoua-Boulai or Kenzou, near Gamboula, for the Central African Republic; and Ouesso for the Republic of Congo.

Overland from Nigeria

The two most popular routes from Nigeria lead to Mora in the north of Cameroon and Mamfé in the west of the country.

If you take the northern route, a good road takes you from Maiduguri to Bama and then to the border post at Banki. This takes about 90 minutes by minibus. Taxis and minibuses are available on the Cameroon side to take you across the plains to Mora and Maroua, the latter taking around 90 minutes and typically costing CFA2000 (£2.15/US$3.80).

If you take the western route, you can take a three-hour bush taxi from Calabar to Ikom and then one from Ikom to the Nigerian border village of Mfum, which is 25km. Here you go through Nigerian customs and red tape and continue towards Ekok, walking across the bridge over the Cross River and up a hill to the Cameroonian border post at Ekok. The border post closes at 19.00. You have a choice then of taking a 60km taxi ride from Ekok to Mamfé through the mountains, or you can go by *pirogue* (canoe) from Ekok down the Cross River to reach Mamfé. An alternative *pirogue* route takes you from Calabar to Mamfé.

If you are travelling to Nigeria, Nigerian visas currently cost CFA30,000–40,000 (£32–42/US$56–75) depending on nationality and are available from the Nigerian embassy in Yaoundé or consulates in Douala and Buea.

Overland from Chad

A relatively new bridge links Ndjamena, Chad's capital, with Kousséri in Cameroon. You can take an inexpensive taxi or motorcycle taxi from Ndjamena or Nguele to the Cameroonian side of the bridge. Minibuses operate from Kousséri to Maroua and the CFA4500 (£4.82/US$8.50) journey, which is very beautiful, takes around four hours. There have been some incidents involving armed bandits along this route in recent years and the minibus to/from Maroua may have an armed escort. Check the security situation locally. The border closes at 17.00.

You can also enter Cameroon from Lere and Bongor in southern Chad, the latter by canoe over the Logone River.

If you are going to Chad, one-month visas to Chad currently cost CFA35,000 (£37/US$66) and are available from the Chad embassy in Yaoundé.

Overland from the Central African Republic

The Cameroonian border post at Batouri can be reached from Berberati and Gamboula in the Central African Republic, while the border point at Garoua Boulai is reached from Bouar. There are some buses or you can hitch a lift on a truck. From Garoua Boulai you can head north for Ngaoundal via Meidougou, a 270km journey, where you can catch the Yaoundé–Ngaoundéré train, or take a minibus for Bertoua (93km from Batouri, 255km from Garoua Boulai), where you can take a 90km taxi trip to Belabo train station. There is also at least one bus daily from Garoua Boulai to Ngaoundéré, which takes around ten hours.

A one-month visa for visiting the Central African Republic is CFA35,000 (£37/US$66), available from the Central African Republic embassy in Yaoundé.

Overland from Equatorial Guinea

The main road from Bata in Equatorial Guinea becomes rougher at Micomeseng and leads to the main Cameroon entry point (as well as one for Gabon) at Ebebiyin. The Ntem River is crossed by ferry. The road continues to Ambam, where it meets the main road to Ebolowa.

Alternatively, taking the coastal route, take the track from Bata to Elende on the border with Cameroon, where you can take a boat to Ipono, just south of Campo. Bear in mind that there is no accommodation on either side of the border. At Campo you can get a minibus for the 90km journey to the coastal beach town of Kribi, which takes about four hours and costs CFA1,500 (£1.60/US$2.83).

Visas for Equatorial Guinea are CFA36,000 (£38/US$67), valid for a month, and are available from the embassy in Yaoundé and the consulate in Douala.

Overland from the Republic of Congo

At the time of going to press the border with the Republic of Congo was closed. When it is not, entering Cameroon from the Republic of Congo is time-consuming and strenuous. You need to head for Ouesso. Barges for Ouesso leave Brazzaville infrequently and you may be waiting for a week or two. At Ouesso you can take a minibus to the border where a *pirogue* transports you over the Ngoko River to the village of Kika. You then need to hitch eastwards as far as the town of Moloundou where, during the dry season, you can take the 212km route to

Yokadouma by bus, which takes about eight hours and costs CFA5,000 (£5.35/US$9.45).

Visas for visiting the Republic of Congo are valid for three months and available from the Republic of Congo embassy in Yaoundé.

Overland from Gabon

You can enter Cameroon by taking the main road from Libreville to Oyem, continuing to Bitam for the exit formalities, and heading for Ambam in Cameroon, where you get your entry stamp. At Kye Ossi a ferry takes you across the Ntem River. Both the 90km journey by minibus from Ambam to Ebolowa and the 170km trip from Ebolowa to Yaoundé take about three hours.

Visas for visiting Gabon cost CFA40,000 (£42/US$75) and last a month.

By sea
From the UK

Grimaldi Line sails from Tilbury, near London, and several other European ports, and stops at a number of major ports in West Africa, including Douala. Strand Voyages (Charing Cross Shopping Concourse, Strand, London WC2N 4HZ; tel: 020 7836 6363) and Freighter World Cruises (180 South Lake Avenue No 335, Pasadena, CA 91101, USA; tel: 626 449 3106) can both provide further details.

From Nigeria

It is possible to take a boat from Calcemco Beach just north of Caabar in Nigeria, or alternatively from Oron, south of Calabar, which goes to Limbé and Idenao in Cameroon. A passenger speedboat costs anything from CFA20,000 to CFA40,000 (€21–42/US$37–74) and takes around four hours. Cargo boats are another option but these are not recommended as they are often unsafe.

There are also boats from Ikang in Nigeria that go to Mundemba in Cameroon.

If you are considering arriving by boat, check the current security situation as you pass the Bakassi Peninsula, which is under dispute by Nigeria and Cameroon and which has been subject to serious unrest in recent years.

Visas currently cost CFA30,000–40,000 (£32–42/US$56–75) depending on nationality and are available from the embassy in Yaoundé or consulates in Douala and Buéa.

From Equatorial Guinea

There are sometimes boats connecting Douala, Limbé and Ngueme, a village near Limbé, with Malabo on Bioco Island (Equatorial Guinea). Enquire at the shipping offices around Limbé and Douala's port.

Visas for Equatorial Guinea are available from the embassy in Yaoundé or the consulate in Douala and are currently CFA36,000 (£38/US$67).

HEALTH
With assistance from Dr Felicity Nicholson

Although there are a number of serious diseases that can be contracted in Cameroon, there is a lot you can do to greatly lessen the chance of trouble. With luck, the most you'll suffer from is a cold caught on the aeroplane, sunburn, or short-term travellers' diarrhoea, which is often associated more with the change of environment than anything specific.

Health insurance

Ensure that you have adequate health insurance before setting off. Check that it covers such things as ambulances, emergency airlifts and flights home, plus any activities – like trekking or climbing – that you might participate in during your stay.

Preparations

Preparations to ensure a healthy trip to Cameroon require checks on your immunisation status. Be up to date on immunisations and don't skimp on any, especially tetanus (ten-yearly) and diphtheria (also ten-yearly). Polio is also important: cases of polio (immunisations again ten-yearly) were reported in early 2004 in Cameroon, previously a polio-free country. Meningococcus, rabies and hepatitis A jabs are also recommended, and immunisation against yellow fever is mandatory as a condition of entry for those over one year of age. A yellow-fever vaccination provides protection for ten years.

The hepatitis A vaccine (Havrix Monodose or Avaxim) comprises two injections given about a year apart. The course costs about £100, but protects for ten years. It is now felt that the vaccine can be used even close to the time of departure, and it has replaced the old-fashioned gamma globulin.

The newer typhoid vaccines (eg: Typhim Vi) last for three years and are about 85% effective. They should be encouraged unless the traveller is leaving within a few days for a trip of a week or less, in which case the vaccine would not be effective in time.

A meningitis vaccine (containing strains ACW and Y) is also recommended, especially for trips of more than four weeks (see *Meningitis*, page 60), or for shorter trips if you are working closely with the local population.

Immunisation against cholera is no longer recommended for Cameroon as the vaccine offers little protection and has a number of potential side effects. Even so, it can be beneficial to have a stamp for it on a vaccination certificate as occasionally immigration officials may ask for it. If asked when giving other vaccinations, many travel clinics are happy to provide a certificate misleadingly stating that you *haven't* had the jab, which tends to do the trick at borders.

Vaccinations for rabies are advised for travellers visiting more remote areas (see *Rabies*, pages 62–3). A hepatitis B vaccination should be considered for longer trips (two months or more) or for those working with children or in situations where contact with blood is likely. Three injections are needed for the best protection and can be given over a four-week period if time is short. Longer schedules give more sustained protection and are therefore preferred if time allows. A BCG vaccination against tuberculosis (TB) is also advised for trips of two months or more.

Ideally you should visit your own doctor or a specialist travel clinic (see pages 64–6) to discuss your requirements about eight weeks before you plan to travel, especially as some vaccinations require more than one injection, and some should not be given together.

Protection from the sun

Give some thought to packing suncream. The incidence of skin cancer is rocketing as Caucasians are travelling more and spending more time exposed to the sun. Keep out of the sun during the middle of the day and, if you must be exposed to the sun, build up gradually from 20 minutes per day. Be especially careful of sun reflected off water and wear a T-shirt and lots of waterproof SPF15 suncream when swimming; snorkelling often leads to scorched backs of the thighs so wear Bermuda shorts. Sun exposure ages the skin and makes people prematurely wrinkly; cover up with long, loose clothes and wear a hat when you can. The glare and the dust can be hard on the eyes, too, so pack UV-protecting sunglasses and, perhaps, a soothing eyebath or eyedrops.

Malaria in Cameroon

Taking adequate precautions against malaria and being vigilant over possible symptoms is vital in this part of the world. Along with road accidents, it poses the greatest threat to travellers by far.

I should know: the first time I visited Cameroon, for three weeks, I came back with four tropical diseases, including two types of malaria that developed into blackwater fever, which I assure you is not a memento one would ever want.

Not only that, but my companion on the trip also contracted malaria, and a Peace Corps volunteer based in Yaoundé died from the disease while we were there.

Malaria is spread by the *Anopheles* mosquito, which is most often found near still water (even small puddles can become a mosquito hothouse) and marshes. The malaria parasite is commonest at low altitudes, and at mid-altitude it is largely seasonal, with the risk of transmission highest during the rainy season.

Moist, low-lying places such as coastal regions, rivers, streams and other waterways represent high-risk areas throughout the year, especially during the rainy season.

Malaria prophylaxis is essential throughout Cameroon, which is in a region with very virulent strains of the disease. Even if you are visiting supposedly low-risk areas, you should assume, as in the whole of Central and West Africa, that you will be exposed to malaria and should take precautions. This cannot be stressed highly enough: while malaria may be present in many other parts of the world, but doesn't necessarily pose a great problem, it is particularly widespread in Cameroon. Not only that, but Cameroon harbours the most dangerous form, *plasmodium falciparum* (or cerebral malaria), which can kill within 24 hours of the first symptoms.

A lot of dangerous misinformation occurs about malaria, from health columns in national newspapers recommending that travellers ditch their malaria pills for homoeopathy (yes, I've read such dangerous advice), to people convinced they retain immunity from the disease even though they haven't visited Africa in years. Tour operators and travel agents often play down the dangers so as not to scare people off booking a holiday. Add the lack of training and experience many Western doctors have concerning tropical disease (my malaria symptoms became so much worse because for a week my doctor believed I had influenza rather than malaria, despite having just come back from West Africa) and you have a potentially serious situation.

As well as taking the recommended anti-malarials before, during and after your trip, it is important to protect yourself from mosquito bites by using insect repellent regularly and by using a mosquito net. Be aware that no prophylactic is 100% protective (when I contracted malaria I had been taking the anti-malarial drugs meticulously) but that those on prophylactics who are unlucky enough to catch malaria are less likely to get into serious trouble.

Taking malaria prophylactics correctly and taking steps to avoid mosquito bites does not guarantee that you will not contract a strain of the disease that is resistant to the drugs. Untreated, malaria can be fatal, and therefore if you display any possible malaria symptoms even a year after visiting Cameroon (although the disease typically takes around two weeks to incubate) you need to see a doctor to establish whether you have the disease. If you are in Africa at such a time, don't be put off by the thought of African hospitals. Their experience of treating malaria is a great advantage, and the alternative to hospitalisation could be far worse.

Malaria symptoms can include any combination of flu-like aches and pains, rapid rises in temperature, a sense of disorientation, headache, nausea and diarrhoea.

The blood test for malaria is quick and simple. Even if it shows that you do not have the disease, you should have a retest two or three days later if the symptoms remain, as the parasite does not always show up on tests, especially if the degree of infection is low or anti-malarials have hidden the infection.

Also, if you test negative, you may have another infection, such as typhoid, which might also require speedy attention.

Malaria can cause you to go from feeling perfectly healthy to having a high fever very swiftly. If you are in a rural area far from a doctor, clinic or hospital, self-diagnosis and self-treatment until you can get appropriate help easily outweighs the risks of treating yourself for malaria unnecessarily. Unless you are staying near cities and main towns, it is well worth considering including a malaria treatment kit, which is often available from tropical disease clinics.

Opinions vary as to the most effective treatment regimes, but quinine/doxycycline is popular, safe and effective. Quinine and Fansidar is an alternative if doxycycline is unavailable or unsuitable, although there have been concerns about the side effects of Fansidar in recent years. Malarone is also increasingly popular as a treatment for malaria, as it can be very effective against the more dangerous types of malaria and has relatively few side effects. Another drug, Halfan, should not be used as it is dangerous, especially if Lariam has been your prophylactic. However, you should always consult with an expert in travel medicine if you are planning to take self-treatment with you, regardless of whether or not you are also planning to take prophylactic medication.

Malaria prevention

There is no vaccine against malaria (*le paludisme* in French), but there are other ways to avoid it; since most of Africa is very high risk for malaria, and Cameroon has the most dangerous strain of the disease (*plasmodium falciparum*) as well as an ever-changing list of malaria prophylactics, travellers must plan their malaria protection very thoroughly. Seek current advice on the best antimalarials to take.

If mefloquine (Lariam) is suggested, start this two-and-a-half weeks (three doses) before departure to check that it suits you; stop it immediately if it seems to cause depression or anxiety, visual or hearing disturbances, severe headaches, fits or changes in heart rhythm. Side effects such as nightmares or dizziness are not medical reasons for stopping unless they are sufficiently debilitating or annoying. Anyone who is pregnant, who has suffered fits in the past, has been treated for depression or psychiatric problems, has diabetes controlled by oral therapy or who is epileptic (or who has suffered fits in the past) or has a close blood relative who is epileptic, should avoid mefloquine.

Malarone (proguanil and atovaquone) is a new drug that is almost as effective as mefloquine. It has the advantage of having few side effects and need only be started one day before arrival and continued for one week after returning. However, it is expensive and because of this tends to be reserved for shorter trips, although a licence has been granted for up to three months' use. Paediatric Malarone is now available for children under 40kg. The number of paediatric tablets required is calculated by weight. Malarone may not be suitable for all travellers, so advice should be taken from a doctor.

The antibiotic doxycycline (100mg daily) is a viable alternative when either mefloquine or Malarone are not considered suitable for whatever reason. Like

Malarone, it can be started one day before arrival. Unlike mefloquine, it may also be used in travellers with epilepsy, although certain anti-epileptic medication may make it less effective. Users must be warned about the possibility of allergic skin reactions developing in sunlight which can occur in about 1-3% of people. The drug should be stopped if this happens. Women using an oral contraceptive should use an additional method of protection for the first four weeks when using doxycycline. It is also unsuitable in pregnancy or for children under 12 years.

Chloroquine and proguanil are no longer considered to be very effective for Cameroon. However, they may still be recommended if no other regime is suitable.

All prophylactic agents should be taken with or after the evening meal, washed down with plenty of fluid and, with the exception of Malarone (see above), continued for four weeks after leaving.

Travellers to remote parts would probably be wise to carry a course of treatment to cure malaria. Experts differ on the costs and benefits of self-treatment, but agree that it leads to over-treatment and to many people taking drugs they do not need; yet treatment may save your life. Current kits include quinine sulphate and doxycycline for those who have been taking Malarone as a prophylactic, or the doxycycline substituted for Malarone for those who have been taking doxycycline as a prophylactic. The drug Fansidar is commonly used in Cameroon (three tablets) as emergency back-up treatment but is not recommended by doctors in the UK because there are potential serious side effects, and there is resistance to the drug in Cameroon anyway. If you do need to resort to using a self-treatment kit, advice from a doctor should still be sought without delay, even if the symptoms disappear.

Discuss your trip with a specialist to determine your particular needs and risks, and be sure you understand when and how to take the cure. If you are somewhere remote in a malarial region you probably have to assume that any high fever (over 38°C/104°F) for more than a few hours is due to malaria (regardless of any other symptoms) and should seek treatment. Diagnosing malaria is not easy, which is why consulting a doctor is sensible: there are other dangerous causes of fever in Africa, which require different treatments. However, testing kits are now available in the UK from some travel clinics and pharmacies for diagnosing falciparum malaria, the most serious form of the disease. So consider taking a testing kit with you if your trip includes visiting remote, inaccessible regions.

Presently quinine and doxycycline, Malarone, or quinine and Fansidar are the favoured regimes, but check for up-to-date advice on the current recommended treatment. And remember malaria may occur anything from seven days into the trip to up to one year after leaving Africa.

The risk of malaria above 1,800m is low. It is unwise to travel in malarial parts of Africa while pregnant or with young children: the risk of malaria in many parts is considerable and these travellers are likely to succumb rapidly to the disease.

In addition to antimalarial medicines, it is important to avoid mosquito bites, particularly between dusk and dawn. Pack a DEET-based insect repellent, such as Repel (roll-ons or sticks are the least messy preparations for travelling).

You also need either a permethrin-impregnated mosquito or bed net or a permethrin spray so that you can 'treat' bednets in hotels. Permethrin treatment makes even very tatty nets protective and prevents mosquitoes from biting you through the impregnated net when you roll against it; it also deters other biters. Many hotels in Cameroon do not have insect screens. The electric plug-in insecticide vapourisers work well. Don't forget a plug adaptor. Air conditioning helps discourage mosquitoes, as does using a knock-down fly spray at night.

QUICK TICK REMOVAL

African ticks are not the prolific disease transmitters that they are in the Americas, but they may spread Lyme disease, tick-bite fever and a few rarities. Tick-bite fever is a non-serious, flu-like illness, but it's still worth avoiding. If you get the tick off whole and promptly the chances of disease transmission are reduced to a minimum. Manoeuvre your finger and thumb so that you can pinch the tick's mouthparts, as close to your skin as possible, and slowly and steadily pull away at right angles to your skin. This often hurts. Jerking or twisting will increase the chances of damaging the tick, which in turn increases the chances of disease transmission, as well as leaving the mouthparts behind. Once the tick is off, dowse the little wound with alcohol (local spirit, whisky or similar are excellent) or iodine. An area of spreading redness around the bite site, or a rash or fever coming on a few days or more after the bite, should stimulate a trip to a doctor.

Taking garlic capsules or vitamin B tablets is thought by many to help discourage mosquitoes.

Wear long sleeves, long trousers, light-coloured clothing, shoes, socks and insect repellent in the evenings. Avoid aftershave or perfumes. Putting on long clothes at dusk means you can reduce the amount of repellent you need to put on your skin, but be aware that malaria mosquitoes hunt at ankle level and will bite through socks, so apply repellent under socks too. Travel clinics usually sell a good range of nets, treatment kits and repellents.

Insect bites

It is crucial to avoid mosquito bites between dusk and dawn; as the sun is going down, don long clothes and apply repellent on any exposed flesh. This will protect you from malaria, elephantiasis and a range of nasty insect-borne viruses.

Otherwise retire to an air-conditioned room, burn mosquito coils or sleep under a fan. Coils and fans reduce rather than eliminate bites. During the day it is wise to wear long, loose (preferably 100% cotton) clothes if you are pushing through scrubby country; this will keep ticks off and also tsetse flies and day-biting Aedes mosquitoes which may spread dengue and yellow fever. Tsetse flies hurt when they bite and are attracted to dark colours; locals will advise on where they are a problem and where they transmit sleeping sickness.

Minute pestilential biting blackflies spread river blindness in some parts of Africa between 190° north and 170° south; the disease is caught close to fast-flowing rivers since flies breed there and the larvae live in rapids. The flies bite during the day but long trousers tucked into socks will help keep them off. Citronella-based natural repellents do not work against them.

Mosquitoes and many other insects are attracted to light. If you are camping, never put a lamp near the opening of your tent, or you will have a swarm of biters waiting to join you when you retire. In hotel rooms, be aware that the longer your light is on, the greater the number of insects will be sharing your accommodation.

Tumbu flies or putsi are a problem where the climate is hot and humid. The adult fly lays her eggs on the soil or on drying laundry, and when the eggs come in contact with human flesh (when you put on clothes or lie on a bed) they hatch and bury themselves under the skin. Here they form a crop of 'boils' that each hatch a grub after about eight days, when the inflammation will settle down. In putsi areas

TREATING TRAVELLERS' DIARRHOEA

It is dehydration that makes you feel awful during a bout of diarrhoea and the most important part of treatment is drinking lots of clear fluids. Sachets of oral rehydration salts give the perfect biochemical mix to replace what you are losing but other recipes taste nicer. Any dilute mixture of sugar and salt in water will do you good. Try Coke or orange squash with a three-finger pinch of salt added to each glass (if you are salt-depleted you won't taste the salt). Otherwise make a solution of a four-finger scoop of sugar with a three-finger pinch of salt in a glass of water. Or add eight level teaspoons of sugar (18g) and one level teaspoon of salt (3g) to one litre (five cups) of safe water. A squeeze of lemon or orange juice improves the taste and adds potassium, which is also lost in diarrhoea. Drink two large glasses after every bowel action, and more if you are thirsty. These solutions are still absorbed well if you are vomiting, but you will need to take sips at a time. If you are not eating you need to drink three litres a day plus whatever is pouring into the toilet. If you feel like eating, take a bland, high-carbohydrate diet. Heavy greasy foods will probably give you cramps.

If the diarrhoea is bad, or you are passing blood or slime, or you have a fever, you will almost certainly need antibiotics in addition to fluid replacement. A single dose of ciprofloxacin (500mg) repeated after 12 hours may be appropriate. If the diarrhoea is greasy and bulky and is accompanied by sulphurous (eggy) burps, the likely cause is giardia (or giardiasis). This is best treated with tinidazole (four x 500mg in one dose, repeated seven days later if symptoms persist).

Persistent diarrhoea can also indicate amoebic dysentery, also treatable by tinidazole or metronidazole, but you should seek medical advice if you suspect these conditions.

either dry your clothes and sheets within a screened house, dry them in direct sunshine until they are crisp, or iron them.

Jiggers or sandfleas are another flesh-feaster. They latch on if you walk barefoot in contaminated places, and set up home under the skin of the foot, usually at the side of a toenail where they cause a painful, boil-like swelling. They need picking out by a local expert; if the distended flea bursts during eviction the wound should be dowsed in spirit, alcohol or kerosene, otherwise more jiggers will infest you.

Other diseases

Even more reason to discourage bites are the numerous other diseases that can be contracted from insect bites. For example, **leishmaniasis**, which can cause disfigurement and damage to internal organs, is caused by sandfly bites. **Sleeping sickness**, which can be fatal, is caused by the bite of the tsetse fly.

Filariasis

This is another disease I added to my personal tropical disease collection and in my case the symptoms did not appear for a whole year after visiting Cameroon. Curiously little-known, although very prevalent in Africa, there are different types, causing fever, pain, swellings, rashes and even blindness. I got loa loa, where parasitic worms cause swellings on the arms and legs. Prompt medical advice should be sought if filariasis is suspected.

Dengue fever

This mosquito-borne disease may mimic malaria but there is no prophylactic medication available to deal with it. The mosquitoes that carry this virus bite during the daytime, so it is worth applying repellent if you see any mosquitoes around. Symptoms include strong headaches, rashes, excruciating joint and muscle pains, and high fever. Dengue fever lasts only for a week or so and is not usually fatal. Complete rest and paracetamol are the usual treatment; plenty of fluids also help. Some patients are given an intravenous drip to prevent dehydration. It is especially important to protect yourself if you have had dengue fever before, since a second infection with a different strain can result in the potentially fatal dengue haemorrhagic fever.

Bilharzia or schistosomiasis

with thanks to Dr Vaughan Southgate of the Natural History Museum, London

Bilharzia or schistosomiasis is a disease that commonly afflicts the rural poor of the tropics. Infected travellers and expatriates generally suffer fewer problems because symptoms will encourage them to seek prompt treatment and they are also exposed to fewer parasites. However, it is still an unpleasant problem that is worth avoiding.

The parasites digest their way through your skin when you wade, bathe or even shower in infested fresh water. Unfortunately, many African lakes, rivers and irrigation canals carry a risk of bilharzia.

The most risky shores will be close to places where infected people use water, wash clothes, etc. Winds disperse the cercariae, though, so they can be blown some distance, perhaps up to 200m from where they entered the water. Scuba-diving off a boat into deep offshore water, then, should be a low-risk activity, but showering in lake water or paddling along a reedy lake shore near a village is risky.

Although the absence of early symptoms does not necessarily mean there is no infection, infected people usually notice symptoms two or more weeks after parasite penetration. Travellers and expatriates will probably experience a fever and often a wheezy cough; local residents do not usually have symptoms. There is now a very good blood test which, if done six weeks or more after likely exposure, will determine whether you need treatment. Since bilharzia can be a nasty illness, avoidance is better than waiting to be cured and it is wise to avoid bathing in high-risk areas.

Avoiding bilharzia

- If you are bathing, swimming, paddling or wading in fresh water that you think may carry a bilharzia risk, try get out of the water within ten minutes.
- Dry off thoroughly with a towel; rub vigorously.
- Avoid bathing or paddling on shores within 200m of villages or places where people use the water a great deal, especially reedy shores or where there is lots of water-weed.
- If your bathing water comes from a risky source, try to ensure that the water is taken from the lake in the early morning and stored snail-free, otherwise it should be filtered, or Dettol or Cresol added.
- Bathing early in the morning is safer than bathing in the last half of the day.
- Covering yourself with DEET insect repellent before swimming will protect you.
- If you think that you have been exposed to bilharzia parasites, arrange a screening blood test (your GP can do this) MORE than six weeks after your last possible contact with suspect water.

Meningitis

This is a particularly nasty disease as it can kill within hours of the first symptoms appearing. The telltale symptoms are a combination of a blinding headache (light sensitivity), a blotchy rash and a high fever. Immunisation protects against the most serious bacterial form of meningitis and the tetravalent vaccine ACWY is recommended for West and Central Africa. Other forms of meningitis exist (usually viral) but there are no vaccines for these. Local papers normally report localised outbreaks. A severe headache and fever should make you seek a doctor immediately. There are also other causes of headache and fever, one of which is typhoid, which can occur in travellers to Cameroon. Seek prompt medical help if such symptoms appear.

Asthma, sinus and respiratory problems

Dust and smoke can be a problem in the dry season, so take asthma and sinus medication if a sufferer.

Common medical problems

Travellers' diarrhoea

Travelling in Cameroon carries a risk of getting a dose of travellers' diarrhoea; perhaps as many as half of all visitors will suffer, and the newer you are to travel, the more likely you are to get it. By taking precautions against travellers' diarrhoea you will also help to avoid typhoid, cholera, hepatitis, dysentery, worms, etc. Travellers' diarrhoea and the other faecal-oral diseases come from getting other peoples' faeces in your mouth. This most often happens from cooks not washing their hands after a trip to the toilet, but even if the restaurant cook does not understand basic hygiene you will be safe if your food has been properly cooked and arrives piping hot. The maxim to remind you what you can safely eat is:

PEEL IT, BOIL IT, COOK IT OR FORGET IT.

This means that fruit you have washed and peeled yourself, and hot foods, should be safe, but raw foods, cold cooked foods, salads, fruit salads that have been prepared by others, ice-cream and ice are all risky. And foods kept lukewarm in hotel buffets are often dangerous. If you are struck, see the box on page 58 for treatment.

Water sterilisation

It is much rarer to get sick from drinking contaminated water, but it happens, so try to drink from safe sources.

Water should have been brought to the boil (even at altitude it only needs to be brought to the boil), or passed through a good bacteriological filter or purified with iodine; chlorine tablets (eg: Puritabs) are also adequate although less effective (they do not kill all parasites, such as giardia and amoebic cysts) and also they taste nastier. As a rule, mineral water is safer than contaminated tap water. Bottled water is readily available throughout the country: ensure the top is sealed. It is more expensive than beer, so try and buy it in a supermarket.

Tap water in Yaoundé and Douala is not considered safe to drink because although the water is chemically treated, the poor condition of water transport pipes and interruptions in service encourage contamination.

Intestinal worms

These parasites may enter through your skin (eg: hookworm) or be ingested in food such as undercooked meat (eg: tapeworm). Infestations may take a long time to show up and can cause later health problems, so it is worth considering being tested for parasites on your return home.

Milk
Avoid milk unless it has been pasteurised or boiled: it can harbour tuberculosis, brucellosis, typhoid and dysentery.

Food and health
Much Cameroonian cooking involves a sauce or topping with freshly killed meat, chicken or fish, or fresh vegetables, which have been thoroughly boiled or sautéd at a high heat. Dishes are usually served over a carbohydrate like rice, millet, corn or a tuber that has been boiled.

While many seasoned travellers eat thoroughly cooked meat in this region without problems, think twice if you have any doubts concerning hygiene or preparation. Harmful bacteria are obviously much more likely to have been destroyed if the meat has been cooked in front of you rather than reheated after sitting around all day.

Skin infections
Any mosquito bite or small nick in the skin gives an opportunity for bacteria to foil the body's usually excellent defences; it will surprise many travellers how quickly skin infections start in warm humid climates, and it is essential to clean and cover even the slightest wound. Creams are not as effective as a good drying antiseptic such as dilute iodine, potassium permanganate (a few crystals in half a cup of water) or crystal (or gentian) violet. One of these should be available in main towns. If the wound starts to throb, or becomes red and the redness starts to spread, or the wound oozes, and especially if you develop a fever, antibiotics will probably be needed: flucloxacillin (250mg four times a day) or Augmentin (250-500mg three times a day). For those allergic to penicillin, erythromycin (500mg twice a day) for five days should help. See a doctor if the symptoms do not start to improve in 48 hours.

Fungal infections also get a hold easily in hot moist climates, so wear 100% cotton socks and underwear and shower frequently. An itchy rash in the groin or flaking between the toes is likely to be a fungal infection. This needs treatment with an antifungal cream such as Canesten (clotrimazole); if this is not available try Whitfield's ointment (compound benzoic acid ointment) or crystal violet (although this will turn you purple!).

Eye problems
Bacterial conjunctivitis (pink eye) is a common infection in Africa; people who wear contact lenses are most prone to this irritating problem. The eyes feel sore and gritty and they will often be stuck together in the mornings. They will need treatment with antibiotic drops or ointment. Lesser eye irritation should settle with bathing in salt water and keeping the eyes shaded. If an insect flies into your eye, extract it with great care, ensuring you do not crush or damage it, otherwise you may get a nastily inflamed eye from toxins secreted by the creature.

Prickly heat
A fine pimply rash on the trunk is likely to be heat rash; cool showers, dabbing dry, and talc will help. Treat the problem by slowing down to a relaxed schedule, wearing only loose, baggy, 100% cotton clothes and sleeping naked under a fan; if it's bad you may need to check into an air-conditioned hotel room for a while.

Heatstroke

Here the body temperature rises to dangerous, even fatal, levels (39°C/102°F–41°C/106°F). A feeling of being unwell is followed by little or no sweating, severe headaches, confusion and delirium. The patient needs to be fanned and taken away from the sun while their clothing is removed and replaced by a wet towel or sheet, and hospitalisation arranged.

Hypothermia

Cameroon's mountains, especially, can become very cold at night. The symptoms of hypothermia, where the body temperature lowers to dangerous levels, include tiredness, numb skin, dizziness, shivering, slurred speech and irrationality. To avoid potentially fatal severe hypothermia, patients need to come out of the cold, have their clothes, if wet, replaced by warm, dry ones and be given high-energy food and hot drinks.

Altitude sickness

Cameroon has a number of mountainous areas and lack of oxygen at high altitudes (over 2,500m) can cause problems. It is worth remembering that while most people can travel up to 3,000m (9,843ft) in a short period, and can cope with 4,500m (14,764ft) after spending a night at 3,000m, going straight to 4,500m (a little more than Mount Cameroon) can be dangerous. About 50% of people attempting to reach this altitude can suffer headache, lethargy, loss of appetite and difficulty sleeping. Resting at the same altitude for a day or two should suffice, but if symptoms become severe (including turning blue, a dry cough leading to coughing up pink mucus, breathlessness, vomiting, drowsiness, confusion and unconsciousness) the person should immediately descend at least 500m. Symptoms can appear within the first 24 hours but can take as much as three weeks to become apparent.

Altitude difficulties can be discouraged by ascending slowly, using maximum sunblock, not over-exerting oneself, eating lightly, drinking plenty of fluids (at least 3-4 litres over 24 hours), but avoiding alcohol, and keeping warm when the sun goes down. Consider taking an altimeter if you will be climbing in Cameroon.

Safe sex

Travel is a time when many enjoy sexual adventures, especially when alcohol reduces inhibitions. Remember that the risks of sexually transmitted infection are high, whether you sleep with fellow travellers or locals. About 40% of HIV infections in British heterosexuals are acquired abroad. Currently in Cameroon over 19,000 Aids cases have been reported and it is estimated that over 920,000 people are living with the condition. Use condoms or femidoms – it is always best to buy these before you go; spermicide pessaries help reduce the risk of transmission. If you notice any genital ulcers or discharge, get treatment promptly since these increase the risk of acquiring HIV.

Rabies

Rabies is carried by all mammals (beware the village dogs and small monkeys that are used to being fed in the parks) and can be passed on to man through a bite, scratch or a lick of an open wound. You must always assume any animal is rabid (unless personally known to you) and seek medical help as soon as possible. In the interim, scrub the wound with soap and bottled/boiled water, then pour on a strong iodine or alcohol solution. This helps stop the rabies virus entering the body and will guard against wound infections, including tetanus.

If you intend to have contact with animals and/or are likely to be more than 24 hours away from medical help, then pre-exposure vaccination is advised. Ideally three doses should be taken over four weeks. Contrary to popular belief, these vaccinations are relatively painless!

If you are exposed as described, treatment should be given as soon as possible, but it is never too late to seek help as the incubation period for rabies can be very long. Those who have not been immunised will need a full course of injections together with rabies immunoglobulin (RIG), but this product is expensive (around US$800) and may be hard to come by – another reason why pre-exposure vaccination should be encouraged in travellers who are planning to visit more remote areas!

Tell the doctor if you have had the pre-exposure vaccine, as this will change the treatment you receive. And remember that there is no cure for rabies, and that death from rabies is probably one of the worst ways to go!

Marine dangers

Before assuming a beach is safe for swimming, always ask local advice. It is always better to err on the side of caution if no sensible advice is forthcoming, since there is always a possibility of being swept away by strong currents or undertows that cannot be detected until you are actually in the water.

Snorkellers and divers should wear something on their feet to avoid treading on coral reefs, and should never touch the reefs with their bare hands – coral itself can give nasty cuts, and there is a danger of touching a venomous creature camouflaged against the reef. On beaches, never walk barefoot on exposed coral. Even on sandy beaches, people who walk barefoot risk getting coral, urchin spines or venomous fish spines in their feet.

If you do tread on a venomous fish, soak the foot in hot (but not scalding) water until some time after the pain subsides; this may be for 20–30 minutes in all. Take the foot out of the water to top up; otherwise you may scald it. If the pain returns, re-immerse the foot. Once the venom has been heat-inactivated, get a doctor to check and remove any bits of fish spine in the wound.

Snakes

Snakes rarely attack unless provoked, and bites in travellers are unusual. You are less likely to get bitten if you wear stout shoes and long trousers when in the bush. Most snakes are harmless and even venomous species will dispense venom in only about half of their bites. If bitten, then, you are unlikely to have received venom; keeping this fact in mind may help you to stay calm. Many so-called first-aid techniques do more harm than good: cutting into the wound is harmful; tourniquets are dangerous; suction and electrical inactivation devices do not work. The only treatment is antivenom. In the event of a bite which you fear may have been from a venomous snake:

- Try to keep calm – it is likely that no venom has been dispensed.
- Prevent movement of the bitten limb by applying a splint.
- Keep the bitten limb BELOW heart height to slow the spread of any venom.
- If you have a crêpe bandage, bind up as much of the bitten limb as you can, but release the bandage every half-hour.
- Evacuate to a hospital which has antivenom.

And remember:

NEVER give aspirin; you may offer paracetamol, which is safe.
NEVER cut or suck the wound.

DO NOT apply ice packs.
DO NOT apply potassium permanganate.

If the offending snake can be captured without risk of someone else being bitten, take it to show the doctor – but beware since even a decapitated head is able to bite.

Medical facilities

Hospitals, clinics, surgeries, dentists and pharmacies are listed in the relevant chapters of *Part Two: The Guide*. The overwhelming majority are in Douala and Yaoundé. Unlike in the UK, pharmacies in Cameroon can dispense many drugs such as antibiotics and antimalarials without a prescription.

Commonly required medicines such as broad-spectrum antibiotics are widely available throughout the region, as are malaria cures and prophylactics. Quinine and doxycycline, or quinine and Fansidar, are best bought in advance – in fact it's advisable to carry all malaria-related tablets on you, and only to rely on their availability locally if you need to restock your supplies.

Private clinics, hospitals and pharmacies can be found in most large towns. A high standard of dental treatment is available in both Douala and Yaoundé, and the best hospitals are in Yaoundé. Clinics elsewhere in the country, however, are often lacking in equipment and medicines and may have a low standard of cleanliness. The patient is generally expected to supply his or her own food and drink while in hospital. Treatment costs, consultation fees and laboratory tests are similar to those in most Western countries.

In Cameroon, in all likelihood you will need to speak French with the doctors except in the anglophone west of the country.

If you are visiting the rainforest, the basic precautions for the whole country are even more vital, ie: ensure all immunisations and vaccinations are up to date, take precautions for malaria, use a mosquito net and insect repellent, and carry a good first-aid kit. In the rainforest you will need clothing that covers your arms and legs, as well as high-topped boots because of the risk of snake bites. If a leech attaches itself to you, do not pull it off as the bite is more likely to become infected. Instead use salt or a lit cigarette to make it fall off.

If you are on any medication prior to departure, or you have specific needs relating to a known medical condition (for instance, if you are allergic to bee stings or you are prone to attacks of asthma), then you are strongly advised to bring any related drugs and devices with you. It is a good idea to carry a prescription or letter from your doctor indicating that you can legally use the medication, to avoid potential problems from officials.

Travel clinics and health information

A full list of current travel clinic websites worldwide is available on www.istm.org/. For other journey preparation information, consult www.tripprep.com. Information about various medications may be found on www.emedicine.com/wild/topiclist.htm.

UK

Berkeley Travel Clinic 32 Berkeley St, London W1J 8EL (near Green Park tube station); tel: 020 7629 6233

British Airways Travel Clinic and Immunisation Service There are two BA clinics in London, both on tel: 0845 600 2236; web: www.britishairways.com/travel/HEALTHCLININTRO. Appointments only at 101 Cheapside; or walk-in service Mon–Sat at 213 Piccadilly. Apart from providing inoculations and malaria prevention, they sell a variety of health-related goods.

PERSONAL FIRST-AID KIT

A kit could contain:

- A good drying antiseptic, eg: iodine or potassium permanganate (rather than an antiseptic cream)
- A few small wound dressings and plasters/Band-Aids
- Suncream
- Insect repellent; malaria tablets; impregnated bednet
- Aspirin or paracetamol (acetaminophen in the USA)
- Prochlorperazine or metachlopramide for nausea and vomiting
- Antihistamine for allergies, insect bites or stings and motion sickness
- Emergency dental repair kit
- Broad-spectrum antibiotics if off the beaten track, for any unexpected infection
- Water purification tablets or iodine
- Calamine lotion, aloe vera or sting-relief spray for insect bites, stings and sunburn
- Antifungal cream or powder (eg: Canesten)
- Diarrhoea treatment for mild cases (eg: Imodium/Loperamide or diphenoxylate) and ciprofloxacin or norfloxacin antibiotic, 500mg x 2 (or co-trimoxazole for children and pregnant women) for severe diarrhoea
- Tinidazole (500mg x 8) for giardia or amoebic dysentery
- Antibiotic eye drops, for sore, 'gritty', stuck-together eyes (conjunctivitis)
- Scissors and a pair of fine-pointed tweezers (to remove hairy caterpillar hairs, thorns, splinters, coral, etc)
- Sterile medical kit – a sealed medical kit with syringes, needles, etc
- Condoms or femidoms
- A malaria treatment kit if travelling off the beaten track
- Thermometer (although mercury thermometers are banned by airlines)
- A record of your blood group
- Consider joining the Blood Care Foundation (tel: 01403 262652; web: www.bloodcare.org.uk), which provides reliable emergency blood transfusion cover worldwide.

The Travel Clinic, Cambridge 48a Mill Rd, Cambridge CB1 2AS; tel: 01223 367362; fax: 01223 368021; email: enquiries@travelcliniccambridge.co.uk; web: www.travelcliniccambridge.co.uk. Open 12.00–19.00 Tue–Fri, 10.00–16.00 Sat.

Edinburgh Travel Clinic Regional Infectious Diseases Unit, Ward 41 OPD, Western General Hospital, Crewe Rd South, Edinburgh EH4 2UX; tel: 0131 537 2822. Travel helpline open 09.00–12.00 weekdays. Provides inoculations and anti-malarial prophylaxis and advises on travel-related health risks.

Fleet Street Travel Clinic 29 Fleet St, London EC4Y 1AA; tel: 020 7353 5678; web: www.fleetstreet.com. Injections, travel products and latest advice.

Hospital for Tropical Diseases Travel Clinic Mortimer Market Centre, 2nd Floor, Capper St (off Tottenham Court Rd), London WC1E 6AU; tel: 020 7388 9600; web: www.thehtd.org. Offers consultations and advice, and is able to provide all necessary drugs and vaccines for travellers. Runs a healthline (09061 337733) for country-specific information and health hazards. Also stocks nets, water-purification equipment and personal protection measures.

MASTA (Medical Advisory Service for Travellers Abroad), at the London School of Hygiene and Tropical Medicine, Keppel St, London WC1 7HT; tel: 09068 224100. This is a premium-line number, charged at 60p per minute. For a fee, they will provide an individually tailored health brief, with up-to-date information on how to stay healthy, inoculations and what to bring.
MASTA pre-travel clinics Tel: 01276 685040. Call for the nearest; there are currently 30 in Britain. In addition to providing travel advice, they also sell malaria prophylaxis memory cards, treatment kits, bednets and net treatment kits.
NHS travel website, www.fitfortravel.scot.nhs.uk, provides country-by-country advice on immunisation and malaria, plus details of recent developments, and a list of relevant health organisations.
Nomad Travel Store 3–4 Wellington Terr, Turnpike La, London N8 0PX; tel: 020 8889 7014; fax: 020 8889 9528; email: sales@nomadtravel.co.uk; web: www.nomadtravel.co.uk. Also at 40 Bernard St, London WC1N 1LJ; tel: 020 7833 4114; fax: 020 7833 4470 and 43 Queens Rd, Bristol BS8 1QH; tel: 0117 922 6567; fax: 0117 922 7789. As well as dispensing health advice, Nomad stocks mosquito nets and other anti-bug devices, and an excellent range of adventure travel gear.
Thames Medical 157 Waterloo Rd, London SE1 8US; tel: 020 7902 9000. Competitively priced, one-stop travel health service. All profits go to their affiliated company, InterHealth, which provides health care for overseas workers on Christian projects.
Trailfinders Immunisation Centre 194 Kensington High St, London W8 7RG; tel: 020 7938 3999. No appointment needed. Open Mon–Sat.
Travelpharm The Travelpharm website, www.travelpharm.com, offers up-to-date guidance on travel-related health and has a range of medications available through their online mini-pharmacy.

Irish Republic
Tropical Medical Bureau Grafton Street Medical Centre, Grafton Bldgs, 34 Grafton St, Dublin 2; tel: 1 671 9200. Has a useful website specific to tropical destinations: www.tmb.ie.

USA
Centers for Disease Control 1600 Clifton Rd, Atlanta, GA 30333; tel: 888 232 3228 (toll free and available 24 hours) or 800 311 3435; fax: 888 232 3299; web: www.cdc.gov/travel. The central source of travel information in the USA. Each summer they publish the invaluable *Health Information for International Travel,* available from the Division of Quarantine at the above address.
Connaught Laboratories PO Box 187, Swiftwater, PA 18370; tel: 800 822 2463. They will send a free list of specialist tropical-medicine physicians in your state.
IAMAT (International Association for Medical Assistance to Travelers) 417 Center St, Lewiston, NY 14092; tel: 716 754 4883; email: info@iamat.org; web: www.iamat.org. A non-profit organisation that provides lists of English-speaking doctors abroad.

Canada
IAMAT (International Association for Medical Assistance to Travelers) Suite 1, 1287 St Clair Av W, Toronto, Ontario M6E 1B8; tel: 416 652 0137; web: www.iamat.org
TMVC (Travel Doctors Group) Sulphur Springs Rd, Ancaster, Ontario; tel: 905 648 1112; web: www.tmvc.com.au

Australia, New Zealand, Thailand
TMVC Tel: 1300 65 88 44; web: www.tmvc.com.au. Twenty-two clinics in Australia, New Zealand and Thailand, including:

Auckland Canterbury Arcade, 170 Queen St, Auckland; tel: 9 373 3531
Brisbane Dr Deborah Mills, Qantas Domestic Bldg, 6th floor, 247 Adelaide St, Brisbane, QLD 4000; tel: 7 3221 9066; fax: 7 3321 7076
Melbourne Dr Sonny Lau, 393 Little Bourke St, 2nd floor, Melbourne, VIC 3000; tel: 3 9602 5788; fax: 3 9670 8394
Sydney Dr Mandy Hu, Dymocks Bldg, 7th Floor, 428 George St, Sydney, NSW 2000; tel: 2 221 7133; fax: 2 221 8401
IAMAT PO Box 5049, Christchurch 5, New Zealand; web: www.iamat.org

South Africa
SAA-Netcare Travel Clinics PO Box 786692, Sandton 2146; fax: 011 883 6152; web: www.travelclinic.co.za or www.malaria.co.za. Clinics throughout South Africa.
TMVC 113 D F Malan Dr, Roosevelt Pk, Johannesburg; tel: 011 888 7488; web: www.tmvc.com.au. Consult the website for details of clinics in South Africa.

Switzerland
IAMAT 57 Voirets, 1212 Grand Lancy, Geneva; web: www.iamat.org

SAFETY
I was once in conversation with the pilot of a small plane in Botswana while we were dipping and diving, doing the loop the loop and flying just above the elephants and trees of the stunning Okavango Delta. It was certainly a white-knuckle ride as impressive as one you would find at a state-of-the-art leisure park, and it was unfortunate that I was aware that he was barely sober after a heavy drinking session the night before.

A Zimbabwean, he told me of how he used to carry a gun to school during the Rhodesian war, and how various snakes and spiders had nearly claimed his life over the years. I said his life sounded incredibly dangerous, that he was lucky still to be alive.

He then said: 'Tell me again, you live in a house next to five lanes of traffic?'

At that time I lived on one of the busiest roads in London, so wide it was almost a motorway. He said my life in Britain sounded fraught with danger and indeed this week (as I write) a 13-year-old schoolboy was stabbed outside my London house.

Often, even when things seem to be as dangerous as things get, in reality the danger is negligible. I know a man who was living in Yaoundé during a coup attempt during the late 1980s. Gunfire was all around him for several days yet he just stayed at home and read a book. The danger soon subsided.

Certainly, Africa has armed robbers and maniacs, but there's more chance of being shot or robbed on holiday in many parts of America. Indeed, considering the extreme poverty so many people are forced to endure in Africa, it is surprising the crime levels are not far higher.

The first bit of standard advice to travellers is to use a money belt, but I would strongly advise against this. Muggers know that travellers routinely use these belts to put all their money, credit cards and documents in, and target them accordingly.

This belief was confirmed to me most forcefully when I was last in Douala. My companion was mugged at knifepoint by five men. The first thing they did was rip up his shirt in search of a money belt. When they failed to find one, they frisked him and left empty-handed. His money was stashed away in an elastic bandage around his lower leg. Strangely, the experience was not unduly alarming, because it was so slickly done and over in seconds, but it could have been a very different story if he had offered any resistance.

Obviously, it is wise not to flaunt any signs of wealth such as cash, jewellery or a camera, especially in urban areas where the threat of crime is greatest. Take taxis at night in the bigger towns and cities, rather than walk. Avoid going on the beaches alone. There should be no problems from fellow passengers or the driver when taking public transport.

In the unlikely event that you are mugged or carjacked, offer no resistance and hand over what is requested. Not only is there far more chance of escaping unhurt, but a wallet full of travellers' cheques is never worth as much as your life.

Don't expect miracles from the police if you are robbed: they may do little or nothing to help, and may even request a payment to stamp an insurance form. In smaller communities or more rural areas it can be a good idea to offer a reward to entice locals to help.

Women travellers

Sub-Saharan Africa is often seen by women travellers as a very safe place to visit, especially in rural areas. The exception to this – for all travellers, both male and female – is the cities, mainly at night. There may be a degree of flirting and even a direct proposition or two along the way, especially if you have a penchant for bars and nightclubs, but it's usually nothing a bit of humour or a firm refusal can't diffuse. Women travelling alone may occasionally be asked the whereabouts of their husband, and it can be simplest to invent one and maybe flaunt a fake wedding ring. Carry photos of your family to haul out if need be.

Cameroonians tend to dress conservatively, and to minimise hassle women travellers should do so too, especially in northern Cameroon, which is largely Muslim. A long skirt or trousers are better than a pair of skimpy shorts and a revealing top. Sunglasses are useful for avoiding eye contact.

Government travel advice

Like many people, I used to think that the travel advice concerning developing countries dished out by Western countries was unnecessarily negative and alarmist – until I found out the hard way that it can be very accurate. Several of the potential problems that can occur in Cameroon and that are highlighted in current government travel advice pages have recently happened to me, my travelling companions or expatriates or residents of Cameroon I have met. This is said not to encourage paranoia – dwelling on these aspects does not really allow you to enjoy your trip – but to encourage readers to take the advice seriously. Fortunately most visitors to Cameroon have no such troubles and Cameroonians in general are very hospitable and friendly.

Current travel advice issued by the British, American and Australian governments notes that visitors should avoid the border areas with the Central African Republic, and with Nigeria in the region of the Bakassi Peninsula, as the demarcation of the disputed border here is not yet settled. The border with the Republic of Congo is closed.

There are occasional reports of carjackings and robberies, particularly in and around Douala, Yaoundé, Kribi and the Adamawa, the Northern, and the Extreme North provinces. These are often armed attacks. Four-wheel-drive vehicles are particular targets. Travel in convoy if possible and avoid travelling at night.

Most African crime, though, takes place in cities. You are far more likely to be robbed in bustling, downtown Douala or Yaoundé than when camping in the bush. In Yaoundé, the isolated and poorer areas, particularly the Briquetterie, Mokolo and Mvog-Ada neighbourhoods, should be avoided. Robberies and muggings, often at knifepoint, are common after dark in Douala and Yaoundé, so travel at such times should be by car. You should also not walk around Ngaoundéré or Bafoussam at night.

Consider recruiting a local guide to accompany you around potentially risky areas. Your hotel should be able to find someone reliable.

Petty theft, pickpocketing and bag snatching are quite common in busy areas like markets, buses and train stations.

Identification (a certified copy of your passport) should be carried at all times, as failure to do so can lead to detention by the police. It's a good idea to photocopy documents. Even better, take digital pictures of things like your ticket, passport and insurance and then email them to an email account like Yahoo or Hotmail where you can retrieve them if required.

WHAT TO TAKE

Some suggestions:

- Pocket French dictionary/phrasebook
- Small gifts like pencil sets, Biros and calculators often come in handy
- Lightweight, easily erected mosquito net – essential to help avoid malaria
- Extra passport photos for photographic permits, visa extensions, etc
- Insect repellents
- Water purifing tablets/water filter
- Dental floss: as well as cleaning your teeth with it, it can double as string or can be used to secure a mosquito net, or as thread for clothes repairs
- Sewing kit
- Disposable razors
- Tampons
- Contraceptives
- Binoculars
- First-aid kit
- Alarm clock
- Map distance measurer
- Torch (flashlight) and spare bulb and batteries useful during electricity cuts
- Small towel for cheaper hotels that have none
- Earplugs (for noisy hotels)
- Calculator (for working out exchange rates)
- Padlock (for hotel doors without a lock and for securing luggage)
- Compass
- A hand-held Global Positioning System (GPS) unit, costing from about £100/US$175, is a consideration if you will be in remote areas
- Waterproof bag (to protect your luggage if you take boat trips)
- Plastic bags
- Plastic rain poncho/lightweight windproof/waterproof jacket, which can double as a ground mat and is easier than carrying an umbrella.
- Hat
- Penknife or Swiss Army Knife
- Short-wave radio for listening to local broadcasts or BBC World Service, etc
- Sheet sleeping bag/sleeping sheet/travel liner (for cheap hotels with unappealing or non-existent bedding)
- Compressible sleeping bag
- Novels – for those interminable waits at roadblocks and bus stations

MONEY
Currency
Cameroon's currency, along with most of the francophone countries in West Africa, is the Central African economic zone's (Communauté Financière Africaine or the African Financial Community) CFA franc, guaranteed by the French Treasury. To complicate things, there is also a West African CFA (used by Burkina Faso, Senegal, Guinea Bissau, Côte d'Ivoire, Togo, Benin, Mali and the Comoro Islands) which although identical in value cannot be used in Cameroon.

There are no limits on the importation of currency. Any amount of CFA francs can be exported to other Central African CFA countries (Gabon, Equatorial Guinea, the Republic of Congo, Central African Republic, Chad) but only a maximum of CFA25,000 can be exported from the Central African CFA zone.

Currency is available in CFA10,000, CFA5,000, CFA2,000, CFA1,000 and CFA500 notes, and 500, 100, 50, 25 10 and CFA5 coins.

Exchange rates for the prices in this book (2004):
£1 = CFA933
€1 = CFA656
US$1 = CFA529

Credit cards, travellers' cheques, cash and exchanging money
Those used to the convenience of using travellers' cheques, credit cards, debit cards and obtaining cash from hole-in-the-wall machines will get quite a shock in Cameroon. Changing money here can be a very frustrating experience. It is important to plan ahead, especially outside Douala and Yaoundé, as opportunities to obtain cash easily and inexpensively can be rare.

While some banks are open on Saturdays, this does not include foreign exchange services. Banks are typically open from 07.30 to 15.00 or 15.30 from Monday to Friday, and outside Douala and Yaoundé they may run out of money.

The moral arguments of using the black market aside, changing money through the black market is not really an option as it is in many African countries because the CFA is easily converted and pegged to the euro.

Travellers' cheques
It is common for banks, even in Douala and Yaoundé, not to accept travellers' cheques, and when they do they are likely to request to see your purchasing receipt, offer poor exchange rates and charge a very high commission.

Euro travellers' cheques are the most widely used but service can be slow, especially outside Douala and Yaoundé. Commission rates for foreign currencies start at around 2%, although exchange rates, especially for less common currencies, can be 25% below the official exchange rates, and a commission of around 20% is not uncommon on US dollars or sterling.

I gave up on bringing travellers' cheques to the country after spending a fruitless afternoon in Douala trying unsuccessfully to change some euro travellers' cheques, despite visiting virtually every bank in the city. Even if a bank takes euro travellers' cheques, it is likely that it will only accept ones issued by a certain bank, rather than all banks – and invariably not from the issuer of your cheques.

Credit cards
Although credit and debit cards can be used for a few more expensive hotels and restaurants, and occasionally for tourist services such as tours, car rentals and

flights, it is best to assume that you will not be able to use them. The high incidence of credit card fraud in Africa means that even organisations like Air France will not accept credit cards in their Cameroon offices.

If you do find that you can make use of a credit card, a 2–15% commission may be charged. It is seldom possible to draw cash against credit cards at banks or hotels. If you are able to, you will almost certainly need to use your PIN number.

ATMs

Automated teller machines (ATMs), or hole-in-the-wall cashpoint machines, are few and far between. The only ones I've been able to track down in Cameroon to date are at three SGBC Bank branches: at Rue Joss, Bonanjo, Douala; on Avenue de Gaulle, Yaoundé; and off Rue Centrale in Garoua. And even then, when I tried the one in Douala it ate my card.

Cash

It is advisable to ensure that you have more than enough hard currency in cash to cover all of your expected expenses. Exchange rates for cash are much more favourable than for travellers' cheques or credit cards. Euros are the best currency to travel with, followed by dollars and then sterling. But be aware that you are likely to have great difficulty changing dollars, sterling or other currencies other than euros outside Douala or Yaoundé, and especially in the north.

Banks – although not all branches – with a foreign exchange service include Crédit Lyonnais, Société Générale de Banque au Cameroun (SGBC), Amity, Standard Chartered Bank and Banque International du Cameroun pour l'Epargne et le Crédit (BICEC). The first three are perhaps most geared up for changing money, and the first two can also provide Western Union international money transfers. As you are likely to be carrying a significant amount of cash, store it in different places. Storing some with an elastic bandage on your lower leg (assuming it is covered!) is safer than using a money belt.

International money transfers

Cities and most bigger towns in Cameroon have at least one Western Union office that can wire money from abroad. Thankfully the transfer of money from abroad now takes only a few minutes rather than several days, as it used to do, and the person abroad wiring you the money can do so by telephone, giving their credit card details. Unfortunately, the service is expensive. For example, the Western Union service charge to send £200/US$352 from the UK to Cameroon by credit card is currently around £25/US$44, for £300/US$528 it's £32/US$56, and for £400/US$704 it's £39/US$68. The service charge using a debit card instead of a credit card is approximately 15% less. The exchange rate on the amount received in CFA is also several per cent less favourable than if money is changed from euros to CFA at a bank in Cameroon.

You can also have money wired from your own bank at home, but this is usually slow and more complicated.

Western Union Tel: (UK) 0800 833 833, (US and Canada) 1-800 325 6000, (Australia): 1800 501 500, (Republic of Ireland) 1800 395 395; web: www.westernunion.com

BUDGETING

You can live both extremely cheaply and at great cost in Cameroon. While road transport, simple hotels and market food can cost a fraction of what a Westerner is used to, conversely, international-standard hotels, car rental and top restaurants can cost far more. Public transport increases in cost the more remote and difficult the route, and can be higher during the rainy season, but is generally a bargain.

Although Douala and Yaoundé have the most expensive hotels by far, they also have some of the cheapest, and it is in the more remote areas, especially in the north, where budget-priced accommodation can be hard to come by, and the standard of accommodation for the money you are paying plunges.

Generally, locally produced items like food and drink and transport are cheap, while imported items can cost twice what they do in the West. Reckon on around CFA470 (50p/88c) for a litre of petrol, CFA375 (40p/70c) for a 50cl bottle of beer, and around CFA500 (53p/94c) for a 66cl bottle of beer in a bar. A packet of cigarettes varies from CFA300 (32p/56c) for local concoctions like 'Business Class', CFA500 (53p/94c) for Lambert and Butler, CFA1,000 (£1.07/US$1.89) for Benson and Hedges and CFA1,500 (£1.60/US$2.83) for Dunhill.

A city taxi ride is around CFA1,000 (£1.07/US$1.89), a night in a simple hotel under CFA10,000 (£10/US$18), a night in an air-conditioned one around CFA15,000 (£16/US$29), and comfortable hotels with extras like television or a pool cost from CFA30,000 (£32/US$58). Hiring a car and driver for the day will cost from CFA45,000 (£48/US$87), or double if you use one of the international agencies. Food from street vendors and simple cafés is easily obtainable for around CFA4,000 (£4.20/US$7.56) per day.

MAPS, BOOKS AND GENERAL INFORMATION

The Cameroonian Embassy and Cameroon Airlines may be able to provide a small amount of tourist information on the country.

Buy a good map before you leave home as these can be difficult to obtain. International Travel Maps (ITMB Publishing) publishes a good one, with a scale of 1:1,480,000, and Macmillan publishes another (1:1,500,00), both with place-name indexes and city plans of Yaoundé and Douala. The Macmillan map has much better maps of Douala and Yaoundé, and on the national map indicates more touristic sites.

There is also a full-colour sheet map published by Institut Geographique National (IGN), and an international road map from Freytag & Berndt Maps with a place-name index in several languages. The scale for both is 1:1,150,000. The former is not particularly detailed.

All the maps have considerable strengths and weaknesses and omissions, and if you are planning to go off the beaten track or travel extensively rurally, it may be worth buying two or three national maps and pooling their information.

In Cameroon, other maps are available at the Centre Géographique National, Avenue Monseigneur Vogt; tel: 222 29 21/222 34 65. It has national, regional and city maps, and publishes the national one for the Institut Géographique National, mentioned above.

Specialist map and travel bookshops
Britain
Africa Book Centre 38 King St, London WC2E 8JT; tel: 020 7240 6649. Well-stocked bookshop located within the Africa Centre in Covent Garden.
African Books Collective Jam Factory, 27 Park End St, Oxford OX1 1HU; tel: 01865 726686; web: www.africanbookscollective.com. Publications from many African publishers.
Blackwell's Map and Travel Shop 50 Broad St, Oxford OX1 3BQ; tel: 01865 793550
Daunt Books 83 Marylebone High St, W1M 4AL; tel: 020 7224 2295. Devoted to travel.
La Page French Bookshop 7 Harrington Rd, London SW7; tel: 020 7589 5991. For francophone publications about Cameroon.

Stanfords 12–14 Long Acre, London WC2E 9LP; tel: 020 7836 1321. Multi-storey travel bookshop emporium.
The Travel Bookshop 13–15 Blenheim Crescent, London W11 2EE; tel: 020 7229 5260; web: www.thetravelbookshop.co.uk

Republic of Ireland
Eason's 40 O'Connell St, Dublin 1; tel: 01 858 3881; web: www.eason.ie

France
L'Harmattan 16 Rue des Ecoles, 5e, Paris. A great choice of African books published in French.

North America
The Complete Traveler Bookstore 199 Madison Av, New York, NY 10019
Globe Corner Bookstore 28 Church St, Cambridge, MA 02138; tel: 1-800 358 6013; web: www.globecorner.com.
The Literate Traveller 8306 Wilshire Bd, Suite 591, Beverly Hills, Los Angeles, CA 90211; tel: 1-800 850 2665; web: www.literatetraveller.com.

GETTING AROUND
Possibly the easiest and cheapest way of getting around the country is to use buses to take you to the main centres. Once you are dropped off in the town or city by these buses, you can then use taxis, share-taxis or minivans for shorter, more localised trips. These can be ludicrously cramped and the cheaper the service, the more likely it is that you may have to wait a few hours for the vehicle to fill up.

An exception to this rule would be travelling between Yaoundé in the south and Ngaoundéré in the north, which is far quicker, easier and more comfortable by train.

The buses are cheap and generally efficient, and some routes, such as the route passing the verdant swathes of forest from Douala to Yaoundé, have operators that offer luxury, air-conditioned buses with drinks and snacks on board and a whole seat for each passenger. Even this option is comparatively cheap.

Share-taxis on set routes to other towns and within the city or town itself are very cheap, and even if you have a taxi to yourself in town it is good value. For optimum flexibility you could consider hiring a taxi for the day.

Flying is by far the most expensive way of getting around and can be subject to delays, and car rental is another expensive option.

Travel around Cameroon can be taxing at the best of times, and can be well nigh impossible in some areas during the rainy season. Even so, main cities and towns enjoy a comparatively good network of tarmac roads.

At times you may be subjected to incessant and seemingly inexplicable delays, cancellations and roadblocks.

By air
Cameroon Airlines (CAMAIR), the national carrier, operates a regular domestic air service between Douala, Yaoundé, Ngaoundéré, Bafoussam, Bertoua, Garoua and Maroua. There are sometimes also flights to Batouri, Kribi, Dschang, Mamfé, Bali and Koutaba.

Douala/Yaoundé flights are daily and cost around CFA30,000 (£32/US$56); Yaoundé/Garoua flights are thrice-weekly and CFA68,000 (£72/US$128); Yaoundé/Bafoussam, twice-weekly, CFA21,000 (£22/US$39); Yaoundé/Maroua, thrice-weekly, CFA85,000 (£91/US$160). Douala/Ngaoundéré, four times weekly, is CFA61,000 (£65/US$115); Douala/Bertoua, thrice-weekly, CFA50,000 (£53/US$94). All prices are one-way.

Be prepared for delays, cancellations and overbooking of internal flights. Check the day before flying that the flight is still scheduled and re-confirm on the day. Arrive at the airport early to improve your chances of receiving a boarding pass. The *harmattan* wind can cause visibility problems at Ngaoundéré and Maroua and therefore delays.

There are no runway lights at Ngoundéré airport and if the flight there leaves late, you may not be able to land, stranding you elsewhere.

Air travel times from Yaoundé are approximately 50 minutes to Bafoussam; 70 minutes to Bamenda; 30 minutes to Douala; 50 minutes to Dschang; 150 minutes to Garoua; 90 minutes to Koutaba; 45 minutes to Kribi; 60 minutes to Mamfé; 230 minutes to Maroua; and 160 minutes to Ngaoundéré.

Cameroon imposes a domestic airport departure tax of CFA500 (53p/95c) on domestic flights.

Douala airport

Like the airports of other large African cities, Douala's international airport can be quite chaotic, with the excessive heat and porters, hustlers and taxi drivers all touting for business.

When you arrive you will invariably have to work through this procedure: inspection of hand luggage, health (yellow-fever certificate) check, filling out an immigration card, passport control, handing in completed disembarkation card, showing return ticket if requested, getting health slip stamped, a baggage hall check.

When you exit from customs you hand in your baggage-registration slips from your ticket before being allowed to take away your luggage and show your passport. The officials here are very strict on seeing that the luggage slips stuck to your ticket match those on your luggage, no doubt as a bribe opportunity should you have misplaced them. In that event your luggage is likely to be 'impounded' so that you are forced to enter into discussions to retrieve them. Again, either pay up or insist on a receipt.

At the baggage-claim area you are likely to be approached by a number of young men offering to help with your luggage and to 'assist' you through customs. Do not take up the offers. The only official porters wear lime-green porters' jackets that have a number stencilled on the back. Even using one of these official porters will probably lead to you being passed around to other 'helpers' who will often request ridiculous sums just to drag your luggage a few metres. Therefore, do not allow these extra men to help. A normal tip is CFA2,000 (£2.14/$3.78), to be paid directly to the porter.

This introduction to the country may convey the impression that your stay will be full of hassles, but in general Cameroonians are a proud and dignified people and – except at the airport and around the tourist hotels – you should experience few problems. A simple '*non, merci*' usually makes unwanted advances disappear. This is not true, however, at the airport where they know you are likely to be tired, disorientated and on edge. Act like you know what you're doing (even if you don't) and you'll get through it.

It is best to have a car to pick you up at the airport to lessen the hassles. Shuttle buses (*navettes*) will be waiting in the parking lot by the entrance to the airport. The better hotels, like the Ibis and the Hotel Akwa, will pick you up at the airport at no charge as long as you are staying there. Arrange in advance for them to meet you as you leave customs.

Expect to pay around CFA3,500 (£3.75/$6.61) for a taxi from the airport for the 10km/6-mile journey to the centre of Douala.

Connecting flights to Yaoundé

If you have checked your baggage through to Yaoundé, you now collect it and go through customs. For connecting flights, enter the domestic flights section of the building. Baggage is checked in at the far end of the hall where you will receive a boarding card if you do not already have one. The departure lounge is down on the lower ground floor. Facilities include a duty-free shop, bar, post office, bank, shops and a buffet/restaurant.

Onward flights to Yaoundé can be unreliable and overbooked and a boarding card is not a guarantee of a seat or of departure. It is often quicker and more reliable to drive or take a bus from Douala to Yaoundé (allow three hours).

If you miss a connecting flight through delays in the arrival of your flight from Europe, the carrier airline should arrange hotel accommodation in Douala and onward transport free of charge. See ground staff of the airline on arrival to obtain the necessary vouchers.

Yaoundé (Nsimalen) airport

Arrival procedures are the same as for Douala. Nsimalen airport is about 25km (15.5 miles) from the centre of Yaoundé. There is no public transport system and the 20-minute taxi ride costs approximately CFA4,500 (£4.82/US$8.50). The Hilton and Mount Fébé hotels also operate a hotel express bus service.

Departure procedures: reconfirming your ticket

Confirm your onward or return flight as soon as possible after arrival. There is a departure tax of CFA10,000 (£10.71/US$18.90) for international flights. It is payable in CFA, euros or US dollars.

Air safari

If you are fortunate enough to have the funds to finance a private air tour of Cameroon, or need to charter a flight to an unusual destination in the country, there follows a list of Cameroon's towns with civil airport facilities. Most of the runways are unpaved. Abong-M'Bang, Akonolinga, Ambam, Bafia, Bafoussam, Bali, Bamenda, Banyo, Batouri, Bertoua, Betare-Oya, Dimako, Dizangue, Djoum, Douala, Dschang, Ebolowa, Eseka, Foumban (alternative name Koutaba), Garoua, Kribi, M'bakaou, M'bandjock, Mamfé, Maroua (two), Mokolo, Moloundou, N'gaoundéré, N'kongsamba, Nanga-Eboko, Ngaoundal, Nguti, Tibati, Tiko, Waza, Yaoundé (two).

By road
Car

Driving around Cameroon is not for the novice. Of the country's 37,000km of roads, only about 15% are paved. Broken bridges, pot-holes, general decay and overturned vehicles may close roads (especially the smaller dirt roads) temporarily. During the rainy season many roads are washed away or are passable only with 4WD vehicles.

In the cities driving is something of a free-for-all, a sort of military campaign, with cars, trucks, bikes and motorbikes going in all directions, especially at junctions. Strangely, it all seems to work most of the time. In theory, Cameroonians drive on the right.

On many roads, as well as hazards like pot-holes and ditches, road and traffic signs are infrequent, while livestock and pedestrians regularly create dangers. Some Cameroonian pedestrians have an unnerving habit of standing in the middle of a road with their arms outstretched to force cars to stop, in an attempt to hitch a lift. Many drivers drive too fast, drive when overtired, and overtake on blind bends.

Although the bad condition of roads can be a safety concern, the best roads, such as the main road from Douala to Yaoundé, can be a concern for the opposite reason – they're in such good condition that they actually encourage speeding. The Douala–Yaoundé road, for example, has a bad safety record and the Douala–Limbé road is often strewn with accidents.

Good roads connect Cameroon's other southern cities and both Yaoundé and Douala are easily accessible from Bamenda, Foumban and Bafoussam, and from Cameroon's two main seaside towns of Kribi and Limbé.

But many roads are not in such good condition. In places the road between Ekok and Mamfé, for example, is no more than a mound of red mud, about five feet wide, the sides sloping steeply down into the forest on either side of the road. In the rainy season this surface becomes very slippery when wet.

Travel in the east of the country is hampered by dense rainforest and a lack of paved roads, and in the south, south of Yaoundé, the network is mainly made up of tracks and dirt roads, apart from paved roads to Ebolowa, Kribi and Sangmélima.

A paved 510km road from Ngaoundéré to Maltam connects the three major northern cities of Ngaoundéré, Garoua and Maroua, but they are cut off from the south by long stretches of unpaved road. Roads around the Adamawa Plateau are particularly problematic. It is easier to take the train, which can transport vehicles, although this costs around CFA100,000 (£107/US$189).

Gangs of armed carjackers have also been a problem in recent years, especially in the Adamawa and northern provinces, and the golden rule here, if you are unlucky enough to be stopped by one, is to offer absolutely no resistance and simply give them your valuables (and vehicle if they want it). These gangs tend to target the more expensive vehicles like top-of-the-range 4WDs rather than clapped-out bangers.

Along with malaria, road safety is likely to be your biggest safety concern. Early morning is the safest time to be on the roads, with drivers most refreshed and least likely to be drunk, and travelling after dark is not to be recommended at all. Apart from the lack of visibility, you will have pot-holes and other hazards to contend with; both wild and domestic animals often spend the night by the roadside and maybe even on the road itself.

On the positive side, the roads in rural areas (which make up the majority of Cameroon) have very little traffic. Since many rural roads are dirt it is a courtesy to drive slowly through villages. You won't hit any people or animals and will also kick up as little dust as possible.

Road travel times from Yaoundé are approximately 3 hours 30 minutes to Bafoussam; 4 hours 30 minutes to Bamenda; 3 hours to Douala; 20 hours to Garoua; 24 hours to Maroua and 12 hours to Ngaoundéré.

In Cameroon there is little point in trying to deduce journey times from looking at maps. Even if the road is good and there is little traffic, long delays can be caused by police and military roadblocks.

Roadblocks

Police and military roadblocks are a frequent factor of travelling by road and are often situated on the edge of towns. They can be anything from a piece of rope or a plank of wood studded with nails, to a wooden barrier or a row of oil drums. To deal with roadblocks, ensure you have all your required documents to hand and remain polite and courteous, however rude and obstreperous the police you encounter may be.

Foreigners are allowed to carry a certified photocopy of the first five pages of their passport, which safeguards having your passport confiscated along the way. Main police stations can certify the photocopies if you provide them with your passport, visa and a CFA500 (53p/94c) fiscal stamp purchased from the Ministry of Finance.

Road accidents
If you are a motorist involved in a road accident, by law you are not permitted to move your vehicle until the police have inspected the scene and given the go-ahead. This can mean lengthy traffic delays for everyone else.

Before setting off
Before setting off on a journey, especially to areas off the beaten track, check the vehicle thoroughly, including the spare tyre, battery, water and engine, and be sure there are enough tools to at least change a wheel. You should carry jerrycans of water and fuel at all times, as well as all the required documents.

Car rental
You can cover a lot of ground by taking your own vehicle, but fuel, insurance and maintenance tend to make this option expensive, while security and breakdowns can be a real headache.

Car hire is most commonly available in Douala, Yaoundé, Bafoussam, Ngaoundéré, Maroua and Garoua. Saloon cars with the international agencies typically cost from around CFA20,000 (£21/US$37) per day plus further charges per kilometre (around CFA250/26p/47c), plus insurance and taxes, plus petrol. If you plan to leave the surfaced roads, you may be required to take a 4WD vehicle, and costs can be very high, typically around CFA50,000 (£53/US$94) per day with further charges per kilometre (around CFA350/37p/66c), plus insurance and 18.7% taxes, plus petrol. There is usually a deposit to be paid of at least CFA500,000 (£530/US$940). You may also be required to hire a driver if you are hiring an expensive car or leaving the main routes.

Considering all this, it is likely to be cheaper to hire a taxi on a daily basis. Generally speaking, rented cars cannot be driven into neighbouring countries, and the minimum age for renting a car is 21. Cars drive on the right.

Foreign licences and International Driving Permits are not valid in Cameroon, but a Cameroonian licence is usually obtainable within 24 hours upon production of the foreign licence and payment of the prescribed fee.

International car rental agencies operate in Cameroon through local licensed offices and there are various local companies, which are generally cheaper. Car hire can also be arranged through the better hotels and tour operators.

International car rental companies that operate in Cameroon include:

Avis Tel: UK: 0870 606 0100, Canada: 1-800 272 5871, Republic of Ireland: 01 605 7500; web: www.avis.com
Europcar Tel: UK: 0845 722 2525, Republic of Ireland: 01 614 2800; web: www.europcar.co.uk
Hertz Tel: UK: 0870 844 8844, Canada: 1-800 263 0600, Republic of Ireland: 01 660 2255; web: www.hertz.com

In Cameroon you can find rental companies at the following addresses:

Douala
Auto Joss BP 1265; 20 Rue Monoprix, near Score Supermarket, Bonapriso; tel: 342 86 19; email: autojoss@cyberix.cm. A Nissan Sunny is CFA22,000 (£23/US$41) per day plus

CFA200 (21p/37c) per kilometre, with insurance CFA6750 (£7.23/US$12.75) per day plus 18.7% taxes.
Avis Hotel Akwa Palace, Bd de la Liberté, Akwa; tel: 342 03 47. A small 4WD is CFA40,000 (£42/US$75) per day plus CFA285 (30p/53c) per kilometre plus CFA9,500 (£10/US$18) insurance per day. A larger 4WD such as a Landcruiser is CFA58,000 (£62/US$109) per day plus CFA350 (37p/66c) per kilometre plus CFA11,800 (£12/US$22) insurance per day. A driver is obligatory for the latter, at around CFA15,000 (£16/US$28) per day.
Avis Douala Airport; tel: 330 02 01
Europcar Rue Njonjo; tel: 343 21 26
Auto Rent Tel: 342 40 46
Auvergne Auto Tel: 342 94 55
Sam Auto Tel: 343 03 31

Yaoundé
Avis Route de Douala; tel: 230 22 85/230 20 88
Avis Hilton Hotel; tel: 223 36 46
Europcar Near Cameroon Airlines office, off Av Vogt; tel: 223 08 11
Jully Voyages Av Mvog-Fouda Ada, near the train station; tel: 222 39 47
Eurovoyages Rue Narvick; tel: 222 66 10
Auvergne Auto Bd du 20 Mai; tel: 222 57 06
Hertz near the centre, on the road to the airport; tel: 230 41 88
ADA c/o Safar Tours, Hilton Hotel, Bd du 20 Mai; tel: 222 87 03

Bafoussam
Avis BP 1045; Route de Foumban; tel: 344 13 71

Ngaoundéré
Vina Voyages Av Ahidjo; tel: 225 25 25

Garoua
Avis Near the port; tel: 227 12 98
Auto Location Rue Ahmadou Ahidjo; tel: 227 20 38
Lasal Voyages Rue des Banques; tel: 227 21 37/227 12 98

Buses, minibuses and share-taxis
Buses, minibuses and share-taxis cover most of Cameroon's towns and vary from super-efficient, air-conditioned minibuses with waitress service that ply popular routes like Yaoundé to Douala, to cheaper, but relatively safe buses and inexpensive, licensed minibuses. Unregulated, overcrowded vehicles, including minibuses, seated vans and oversized saloon cars, cover the widest range of destinations.

A vehicle due to leave at 08.00 may not leave until noon, and the driver may wait an hour just to get a last passenger. Typically there are innumerable stops for passengers, police roadblocks and, in the north, praying. At stops you are likely to be offered things like fruit, brochettes and boiled eggs by locals. As accidents are quite frequent, travel at night should be avoided when possible.

Embarkation systems can be puzzling, or even alarming, but generally are no cause for concern. Your luggage may be spirited away the moment you agree to buy a ticket, for example, and you are left to wait luggageless for a couple of hours until it miraculously appears again and the vehicle is on its way. Centrale Voyages, for instance, sells you a ticket, writes your name on it and then keeps it while your luggage is taken from you by porters in green coats. Despite having no luggage and no ticket, when the bus is ready to leave the passengers' names are read out and given their tickets back so that they can board the bus.

Popular routes, such as Douala to Limbé or Douala to Kribi, will have a large choice of carriers, and it can seem quite alarming when you get stormed by about 20 men eager to sell you a ticket. Even more alarming, though, can be a cramped ride at breakneck speed: very generally, the less you pay, the less attention is paid to safety.

If you are in a bus, minibus or share-taxi and want to complain about dangerous driving, it is often better to say you feel nauseous rather than simply ask the driver to slow down, as he will generally be more concerned to keep vomit off the seats than avoid an accident.

Agency buses

Private, agency-run *(agences de voyage)* long-distance coaches and buses (or *car, grand car, 'big bus'*) and minibuses to many destinations operate in the absence of a national bus network. They include Guaranti Express, Centrale Voyages, Alliance Voyages and Binam, and are generally very good value.

The buses usually run from outside the agency's office. Finding out destinations, timetables (which frequently change) and where a particular bus departs from can be a challenging business. The easiest way is to ask at your hotel which agency is recommended for your destination. Taxi drivers generally know all of the agencies and the destinations they offer.

Regular bus services run between main towns and cities like Yaoundé, Douala, Limbé, Kribi, Bafoussam and Bamenda, and in the north, Ngaoundéré, Garoua and Maroua. There are no bus services across the Adamawa Plateau from Yaoundé to Ngaoundéré, where the train service is the best option.

Share-taxis and minibus taxis

Share-taxis, or bush taxis *(taxi brousse* in French), are a very common way to get around and are commonly saloon cars (often Peugeot 504s and 505s seating seven passengers), less comfortable minibuses *(minicars)* seating around 12–20 passengers, and station wagons and covered pick-ups *(baches)* with benches down the sides seating 15 or 16 and crammed in to the point of discomfort.

The advantage is that they are licensed passenger vehicles, so their low rates and routes are fixed by the government. They can be found at the town or city's bus, bush taxi/motor parks *(gare routière, autogare)*, although many towns have several of these, which complicates things. They almost always leave when full rather than run to a timetable, and are likely to pick up further passengers along the way even though they are not registered for extra passengers.

Often there is a choice of operators. If more than one is competing for the route, usually the one that is most full will leave first, whatever the touts claim. The best seats are behind the driver, or near a window, and on the side with most shade. The place not to be is in the row of seats directly beside the sliding door as it will be musical chairs the whole way, and any passengers picked up on the way will invariably have to cram themselves in here.

You can buy two seats for more comfort, or even charter the whole vehicle by multiplying the price of each seat by the number available. Luggage is generally charged at about 10% of the fare per item.

Clandos

Clandos are similar to share-taxis and minibus taxis except that they are unregistered, but they tend to cover destinations the agencies and registered share-taxis do not. They're also not as well maintained and can be even more overcrowded. They can be found at the town or city's taxi or motor parks or touting for business near agency offices.

Taxis
Taxis are available in most of the towns and cities and the official hire rate is CFA2300 (£2.46/US$4.34) per hour from 06.00 to 22.00 and CFA2,800 (£3/US$5.29) per hour from 22.00 to 06.00.

In urban areas many taxis operate as share-taxis where you flag the taxi down, tell the driver where you want to go, and if this is on the route he is already taking with his other passengers, you jump in. Agree the price before doing so. In urban areas the fare is generally set at CFA150 (16p/28c; I know, crazy) per drop within the town from 06.00 to 22.00 and CFA175 (18p/33c) from 22.00 to 06.00.

For longer journeys, taxis are considerably cheaper than in the West, but far more expensive than other options by road. For example, Douala to Limbé by taxi is likely to cost in the region of CFA25,000 (£26.79/US$47.25), compared with around CFA1,000 (£1.07/US$1.89) by minibus. Drink-driving can be a problem. Ensure your driver is sober.

Motorcycle taxis
In northern towns and increasingly in the south are moto taxis (motorbikes) taking one or two passengers on the back on short journeys. The fare is generally CFA100 (11p/18c) per trip during the day and double at night, although it is common for the rider to try it on and ask for more. This means of transport is popular and cheap, but safety is more of an issue and it is probably better to pay a little extra for a conventional taxi or share-taxi.

Hiring a taxi instead of car rental
Hiring a taxi by the day can be a better bet than car rental. Not only is it likely to be cheaper but if it breaks down it is not your problem. Also, a knowledgeable driver may show you things you would have otherwise missed.

But a hired taxi is more likely to break down than a rental car. Therefore, have a good look at the condition of the vehicle before hiring. Is there a spare tyre? Are the tyres bald? Are the lights and windscreen intact?

Before hiring, agree all aspects of the hire with the driver, such as the driver's bed and board and whether petrol is included in the price.

Hitching
In some rural regions, especially in the southeast of the country, where your only option may be a logging truck, hitchhiking may be the only way of getting around unless you have your own hire car or motorbike. Even so, it is not completely safe and therefore cannot be recommended. If you do hitchhike, don't do it alone and take advice from other hitchers and reliable locals beforehand.

Waving down a vehicle is a common way of travelling in Cameroon, but you are usually expected to pay, unless an expat, aid worker, volunteer, tourist or missionary picks you up. This is understandable, as roads may be in poor condition and public transport may be non-existent, rare or infrequent, and therefore any traffic can be seen as potential 'public transport'. If you cannot pay anything, say so at the outset.

Vehicles with markings for international aid and relief agencies can be a good bet, so look out for markings for organisations like Unesco.

Cycling

Cycling can be an excellent way of exploring as you can discover areas inaccessible by car or motorbike. If you need a rest from riding, bikes can be strapped to the top of a bus or minibus.

Cycling is best avoided in urban areas and is best done in the early morning and late afternoon. Food and water needs should be planned carefully in advance as there may not be many opportunities to restock.

Staff at hotels and bicycle repair stands should be able to find you a bike to hire. Mountain bikes are most suitable in this region but are often not available so consider bringing your own. Check with your airline whether you have to dismantle it for the flight and whether there is an extra charge. Carry ample spares, including a puncture repair kit, inner tubes and a spare tyre, plus a chain tool, spare brake and gear cables, and spare spokes for longer journeys.

By rail

Cameroon has a total of 1,104km of railway tracks and there are services from:

Douala to Yaoundé
Yaoundé to Ngaoundéré via Belabo
Douala to Mbanga
Mbanga to Kumba
Ngoumou to Mbalmayo

The 622km Yaoundé to Ngaoundéré service is by far the most popular and most useful for travellers and is a daily overnight service in each direction. It is scheduled to take around 12 hours but can sometimes take over 30. But it is a good bet as it covers an area, the Adamawa Plateau, where road travel can be very slow and difficult. It also passes superb rainforest scenery.

I am sure my trip on the line is typical: it involved interminable queues and struggling through a scrum to get a ticket; a mission to find the sleeping car and then being turfed out by the guard, despite the sleeping car cabin (couchette) being reserved in my name; crisp white sheets and an immaculate basin yet no water emanating from the taps in the couchette I was eventually given after a lengthy protest; and a ceiling fan that did not work and a train that arrived a couple of hours late. Still, it was a great experience.

The route is via Belabo and Ngaoundal (for road travel to the Central African Republic). In theory it leaves Yaoundé at 18.00 and Ngaoundéré at 18.20, arriving the next morning at around 08.30. If you have time to kill at Yaoundé, there is a row of wooden shacks serving beer and food, such as grilled fish and plantain, for CFA500 (53p/94c).

Tickets are only available on the day of departure and cost CFA18,000 (£19/US$34) in a first-class couchette sleeping two or four, CFA9,000 (£10/US$17) in a first-class seat and CFA6,000 (£6/US$11) in second class. Only the couchettes can be recommended because theft can be a problem with the cheaper options. Meals are available on the train, such as fish, rice and pawpaw for CFA2,500 (£2.67/US$4.72), and an omelette with tea/coffee for CFA1,000 (£1.07/US$1.89).

As far as safety goes, the railway has a good record. Remember to take drinking water. Street vendors will usually offer food such as boiled eggs, oranges, lemons, brochettes and bread rolls through the windows whenever the train stops. There is also a restaurant car.

Taking photographs can attract unwanted attention in Cameroon, and this is especially so on the trains. Also beware of thieves and keep your baggage buried well away from the windows and door. Close windows at night and do not store luggage in the overhead racks.

As for the other routes, the 305km Douala to Yaoundé service typically takes around four or five hours and therefore going by road is a quicker option. This service leaves Douala and Yaoundé at approximately 07.00 and 13.30 daily and first class costs CFA6,700 (£7.18/US$12.66), second class CFA3,000 (£3.21/US$5.67).

The service between Douala and Nkongsamba in the west, passing Yaoundé, has deteriorated in recent years with delays more common. This 170km route can take over eight hours.

The short branch line on this route from Mbanga to Kumba can often be a good travel option compared with going by road, as the road conditions can be bad, especially in the rainy season.

As schedules often change, enquire in advance by calling the train operator, Camrail (BP 304, Douala; tel: 340 60 45/340 30 80) for up-to-date information.

Disabled travellers

Facilities are very few and far between for disabled travellers in Cameroon, and private transport arrangements may be required. Many streets are unpaved or pot-holed, wheelchair ramps are very rare, and accommodation is likely to have few facilities such as a lift, except in the most expensive hotels.

General advice is available from **Tripscope** (tel: 0845 7585 641; web: www.justmobility.co.uk/tripscope) in the UK; the **Irish Wheelchair Association** (tel: 01 818 6400; web: www.iwa.ie) in the Republic of Ireland; the **Australian Council for the Rehabilitation of the Disabled** (tel: 02 6282 4333; web: www.acrod.org.au) in Australia; and the **Society for the Advancement of Travelers with Handicaps** (tel: 212 447 7284; web: www.sath.org) in America.

ACCOMMODATION
Hotels

In Douala and Yaoundé and generally in other big cities there are hotels of an international standard. The luxury hotels are not expensive when compared with Europe, Australia or North America but are compared with other Cameroonian hotels.

The better hotels in Cameroon are officially rated from one to five stars. All other accommodation is not officially rated, but tends to be better value. Often the price is negotiable at all levels of standard. There are almost no luxury wildlife lodges or tented camps of the kind you might find in southern or East Africa.

The best hotels will generally have clean rooms with air conditioning and a private bathroom. Lower-priced options may have fans rather than air conditioning, may or may not have a bathroom and will not necessarily have hot water, while the cheapest accommodation may be unclean, have few working facilities, shared bathrooms, a broken window and little or no security for your belongings.

Mid-range hotels, where they exist, are generally acceptable and good value, while the cheaper hotels often double as the local brothel and drinking den and can make for a disruptive night. *Auberges* (small hotels) are sometimes available at a wide range of standards, and in rural areas there are often *campements*, which are not campsites, but simple inns, lodges or motels with basic accommodation and shared facilities, although there are a few upmarket exceptions.

Generally, there is plenty of good-value accommodation in the cities, while in rural areas, and in the north especially, if an average hotel off the beaten track has a virtual monopoly on accommodation in the region, this is likely to be reflected in the prices.

Off the beaten track you may be able to stay in resthouses, in missions or with local people. Ask around when you arrive. Missions are an exception in the budget range, often providing clean and safe accommodation at a budget level, but priority goes to mission or aid workers and in recent years travellers have often been discouraged, and therefore obtaining a room can be more difficult.

When choosing a hotel, see the room beforehand and ask for a discount if the air conditioning cannot be used because there is no electricity, or the taps are not all working. Rates are often quoted per room rather than per person, but get this straight at the start.

If you pay under CFA5,000 (£5.35/US$9.45) per night for a room with two beds you can expect a basic hotel or *auberge* with basic amenities. For CFA5,000–10,000 (£5.35–10.70/US$9.45–18.90) you may get a self-contained room with a bathroom and more facilities, such as a fan. For CFA10,000–20,000 (£10.70–21.40/US$18.90–37.80) expect the hotel to be of a better standard, perhaps with a restaurant and bar. For CFA20,000–40,000 (£21.40–42.87/US$37.80–75.61) expect a standard business- or tourist-class hotel, perhaps with extra amenities like a swimming pool, tennis court and secure parking. If you spend over CFA40,000 (£42.87/US$75.61) per night you are approaching luxury class and top international standards. Even so, some rooms in hotels in Yaoundé and Douala exceed CFA200,000 (£214/US$378) per night.

Camping
Campsites are almost non-existent in Cameroon, but away from the cities, towns and beaches of Limbé and Kribi, where theft could be a problem, there's plenty of wild countryside to pitch up in, and wildlife parks and game reserves often have their own camping facilities. Outside the parks, ask the village chief or local landowner for permission to camp on their land.

Avoid camping on anything resembling a path through the bush, however indistinct, as it could be a game trail. If a lightning storm is on the cards, ensure that there are higher things than your tent nearby (but not too nearby – you don't want a tree or branch falling on you in the night!). Don't camp too near water, which animals may visit to drink, but then again don't camp so far away that water is difficult to get to.

Staying with local people
Offers of accommodation in people's homes are unusual except in villages in the north that are used to travellers, such as Mokolo and Roumsiki, where there are often few accommodation options anyway. Agree prices and terms clearly at the outset.

Long-term rentals
Villas and houses are available for rent in most towns in Cameroon, while apartments are commonly available for rent in Douala and Yaoundé. Estate agents (*agents immobiliers*) may be able to help.

EATING AND DRINKING
Eating
Cameroon offers some of the best cuisine in the whole of West Africa. The country's great geographical differences influence the crops grown around the country. In the south the cuisine is dominated by starch staples like yam and cassava (or manioc, or *batons de manioc,* often appearing as *feuille* on menus) and plantain (a large, green, unsweet banana that requires cooking – it is normally boiled when unripe and sometimes mashed into an edible glob, or fried when yellow and black

and ripe). In the north meals are far more likely to feature maize and millet. Peanut (groundnut) sauces and palm oil sauces are commonly added to many dishes.

Douala and Yaoundé have a good choice of restaurants, serving a variety of cuisines, including Cameroonian, French, Chinese, Italian, Lebanese, Cambodian, Vietnamese, Indian and Japanese. The most expensive restaurants and hotels tend to serve French dishes, although quality can be quite poor despite the high prices.

You may occasionally find restaurants and cafés serving something substantially more exotic than that, such as snake, giant land snail, pangolin, antelope, gorilla, chimpanzee, elephant, cat or dog. Of course, the author advises you to keep well away from such establishments. The grasscutter (or agouti, or cane rat), a rodent of the porcupine family, is sometimes found in stews. Less likely to be found on menus are traditional Cameroonian dishes such as fried grasshoppers, ants and termites.

Yet menus are likely to adjust somewhat since the Cameroonian authorities announced in May 2003 that any restaurant owner caught serving meat from endangered animals could face up to three years in prison and a fine of more than CFA8,000/£8,500/US$16,000.

Less formal than restaurants, 'chicken' and 'fish' houses abound, especially in the main cities. They serve chicken, fish, plantains and chips. Most are good and more reasonably priced than full-service restaurants.

The smallest, simplest restaurants are called *chantiers* ('worksites') and serve inexpensive Cameroonian dishes. There are also chop houses (basic eating houses) serving 'chop' (simple local-style dishes) and simple eateries often just consisting of a couple of tables and benches. At a street café you could typically expect to buy an omelette, bread or chips and a drink for under CFA1,000 (£1.07/US$1.89).

Street food is very widely available, is typically served on a stick and wrapped in paper or a plastic bag, and is cheap, clean, freshly cooked and tasty. The most common snack is the *brochette* or *soya*, a CFA100 (10p/18c) stick of kebabed meat or fish, usually accompanied by a sauce flavoured with peanut or spices. Although the meat or fish may not have been up to strict hygiene standards when raw, it is normally very thoroughly barbecued and often a far better bet than the frequently reheated pots of food in many restaurants. Spicy Maggi sauce is often on hand as a dressing. In the south, grilled fish is often sold at street stalls with fried plantain and cassava.

Beware, though, that in some towns and villages off the beaten track a kebab may consist of less attractive animal parts: sinews and rubbery intestines, tripe and strips of hide.

For snacks, street vendors also sell doughnuts, and peanuts in plastic bags. In Cameroon 'doughnuts' are called *beignets*. Good breads, pastries and chocolate are also commonly available. Chestnut-sized dark red, white and pink kola nuts are widely popular. A mild stimulant that also suppresses hunger, they are chewed for their bitter juices rather than swallowed. Commonly exchanged between friends, they are useful when travelling to offer to other passengers, as well as to pep yourself up.

Coffee stalls are also common, but are often only open in the morning and typically serve instant coffee with a hunk of bread and butter or mayonnaise, and perhaps various fillings.

Fish is popular throughout the country. Mackerel, sole and prawns are common. Eggs and bread are easy to obtain, but cheese much less so. Fresh milk is rarely available and only dried and sterilised (UHT) long-life milk are easily obtained.

Along the coast you'll find coconuts, commonly covered in a green shell. Sweetcorn (or corn on the cob) is commonly sold roasted or boiled, and peanut butter is often sold at markets.

Cameroon's great differences in climate and altitude also ensure a wide variety of fruit and vegetables being available, such as avocado, onion, sweet grapefruit, cucumber, mango, guava, paw paw, oranges (often green, yet ripe), sugar cane, tomato, various varieties of banana (including red-skinned), pineapple and papaya. Many are commonly available at markets. When potatoes are on a menu, they usually refer to sweet potatoes rather than ordinary potatoes. Aubergine (eggplant) is quite common, and can be yellow, white or red.

Dishes like soups, casseroles and stews are accompanied by rice or a thick, stodgy, bland, mashed dough, which is either couscous or *fufu* (or *foufou* or *foutou*) made from cassava, rice, banana, yam, plantain or corn.

Cowpeas *(wake)* and black-eyed beans are often mashed and cooked as deep-fried balls called *akara*. Little brown and white beans known as pigeon peas are also widespread.

When ordering chips *(frites)* there is often a choice, such as potato, yam or plantain.

Vegetarianism

Vegetarianism is rare in Cameroon and vegetarian restaurants almost non-existent, although Indian and Chinese restaurants in the cities often have vegetarian dishes. Pizzas, omelettes and chips made from root crops like potatoes or yam are commonly available in towns and cities, and boiled eggs and bread are commonly sold on the street. You can stock up on vegetables, fruit and nuts at the markets.

Some Cameroonian dishes

Ndole (or *ndola*) is made from a slightly bitter leaf that is similar to spinach, which is shredded and made into a thick sauce with spices, groundnuts or melon seeds. It often accompanies meat, shrimp or fish, and is especially popular around Douala and in the south. *Mbongo* (or *bongo*) is a dish with a blackish sauce made from crushed and burnt spices and added to meat or fish, and is especially popular in Littoral Province. Popular in the northwest is *njama-njama* (or *ama jama*), made from the huckleberry leaf and commonly eaten with *corn chaff* (maize cooked with beans, tomatoes, spices and palm oil). *Mintumba* is a type of cassava-based bread. In the west another dish often seen is *condreh*, made from plantains cooked with palm oil, meat and spices. Another dish of this region is *khokki*, a maize pudding cooked with yam leaves and palm oil. A speciality of the East Province is *Ouinga*, a traditional dish of meat with a sauce made from local herbs and lots of pepper.

Popular in the extreme north, *folere* is a dish of sauce with meat or fish accompanied by *fufu* (couscous). Baobab leaves are also prepared with meat or fish and eaten with fufu in this region. In the north, goat is the most common meat used.

Bobolo, a southern dish, is baguette-shaped and made from cassava. Another southern dish, *ebandjea*, a dish prepared with fish, lemon, tomatoes and pepper, is common around the coast. Around Buéa *eru* is popular: it consists of ekok leaves cooked with smoked fish in palm oil and served with cassava fufu. In the coastal areas of the South Province, *ndomba*, a highly spiced fish cooked in banana leaves, is popular.

Kwem (or *nkwem*) is a dish that is especially common in the Centre Province – it contains pounded cassava leaves and groundnuts cooked in palm oil. It is generally eaten with yam, plantain or cassava tubers. *Ekok*, a finely chopped forest leaf, is often prepared in palm nut pulp and then grilled, and is also popular in the centre of the country. *Nbomba* is steamed meat or fish wrapped in banana leaves, popular in the Yaoundé region. *Charwarmas*, a Lebanese snack of grilled meat in bread with salad and sesame sauce, is also regularly available.

Drinking

Coffee is often of the instant variety, and green tea is far more popular.

When sealed bottles of mineral water are not available, you could opt for soft drinks like Coke, Sprite, Fanta and lemonade, and various similar local concoctions, although there is no guarantee that the water used is clean in the latter. (Make sure you take the glass bottles to the shop or stall as they are often returnable.)

Buvettes, small drinks stalls or simple bars, are common. Drinking beer is an extremely popular pastime in Cameroon; indeed bars, often no more than wooden shacks, spring up all over the place. Lagers are common, such as the ever-popular 'Le 33 Export'. Castel, Gold Harp and Beaufort are others. A strong version of Guinness is also popular.

A 50cl bottle of a common beer like '33', Castel or Beaufort will generally set you back around CFA400–CFA500 (42–53p/75–94c) in a typical Cameroonian bar, rising to CFA1,000 (£1.07/US$1.89) in a mid-range bar or restaurant and CFA1,500 (£1.60/US$2.83) in an expensive tourist hotel or restaurant. The prices are similar in the few places that sell draught beer *(pression)*. Maddeningly, many bars have televisions blasting out the likes of *Hawaii Five O* in French, so don't always count on a quiet drink.

You may get an opportunity to try a home-made beer, often made from maize, millet or sorghum, and usually strong and cloudy in appearance. The millet beer found in the north is called *bilibili*, while a popular corn beer of the region is called *kwatcha*.

Potent palm wine (*matango* or *white mimbo*) made from palm sap is also popular, especially in the south and west. It is often distilled into something resembling gin and known as *afofo*. Beware of the strong alcohol content, and also be aware that unpurified water is often added to the wine.

PUBLIC HOLIDAYS, SPECIAL EVENTS AND FESTIVALS

If you are lucky you may stumble upon a traditional event such as a wedding, naming ceremony, thanksgiving to a deity or celebration of the end of the harvest, and be invited to watch or take part. Many such events involve music, singing, dancing and colourful, striking costumes and are a truly memorable spectacle.

January 1	New Year's Day
Late January	The Mount Cameroon Race, a gruelling 27km (17 mile) race up and down the 3,000m (10,000ft) mountain
February 11	Youth Day
March/April	Easter
May 1	Labour Day
May 20	National Day, especially well celebrated in Maroua
May 21	Sheep Festival
August 15	Assumption Day
Mid-November	Nso Cultural Week, Kumbo, western Cameroon, where horses race through the streets
Mid-December	Ngoun Festival, Foumban
Mid/late December	Lela Festival, Bali
December 25	Christmas Day

Above Homestead in the
Mandara Mountains, Extreme
North Province (JK)

Left Woman spinning, Rhumsiki,
Extreme North Province (RQ)

Below A professional woman
from Yaoundé (BC)

Left Doorway in the audience hall, Chefferie de Bandjoun, West Province (RQ)

Below Items in the museum of the Chefferie de Bandjoun, West Province (RQ)

Islamic holidays

Northern Cameroon is broadly Islamic, whereas the south is basically Christian, and therefore Islamic holidays have significantly greater significance in the north. Islamic holidays depend upon local sightings of phases of the moon and therefore vary from year to year and region to region. Because the Islamic calendar is based upon 12 lunar months that total 354 or 355 days, these holidays are around 11 days earlier than the year before.

During the lunar month of **Ramadan**, which varies each year (but is predicted to start on October 16 in 2004, October 5 in 2005 and September 24 in 2006), Muslims fast during the day and feast at night and normal business hours may be interrupted. Restaurants often close during the day and there may be restrictions on smoking and drinking.

The end of Ramadam (**Djoulde Soumae/Eid al-Fitr/Id al-Sighir**) typically lasts from two to as many as ten days (and is estimated to begin on November 14 in 2004, November 4 in 2005 and October 23 in 2006). Celebrated all over Cameroon, the festival is perhaps most noticeable in Foumban, where there are horse races, processions and dances.

Muslims in northwestern and northern Cameroon also widely celebrate **Tabaski** (or Eid al-Kabir) near the start of the year. This is predicted to be on January 20 in 2005 and January 10 in 2006. The celebrations coincide with the end of the pilgrimage to Mecca and commemorate Abraham's willingness to sacrifice his son, as commanded by God. During the event a lamb is sacrificed instead. Celebrations typically include a parade of *marabouts* (Muslim holy men and fortune-tellers) and great feasts.

New Year's Day in the Muslim calendar is expected to be on February 10 in 2005 and January 31 in 2006, while **Ashoura**, celebrating the meeting of Adam and Eve after leaving Paradise, is predicted to be on February 20 in 2005 and February 9 in 2006.

Just over 12 weeks after Tabaski is a smaller celebration, **Eid al-Moulid**, commemorating the birth of the Prophet Mohammed. It is predicted to be around April 21 in 2005 and April 11 in 2006.

SHOPPING

Bigger towns often have a Centre d'Artisanat where arts and crafts goods can be purchased. The main market in the town will often not sell them.

Bafoussam, Foumban and Bamenda in the west are cities renowned for their masks, woodcarvings, embroidered costumes, miniature figures, thrones, pipes and statues made from earthenware, bronze or wood.

Maroua in the north is known for its multi-coloured market where colourful textiles and embroidered tablecloths are sold together with bracelets, swords, mats and other decorative objects.

The Bamoun/Bamiléké region in the West and North West provinces is rich in art, which includes bas-reliefs, masks and statues.

The distinctive, long tobacco pipes used by the Tikar are widely available to buy in the area. In the north of the country, Fulani jewellery and leather goods are widely available.

A good selection of Cameroon's arts and crafts are available to buy in Douala and at Yaoundé's Centre d'Artisanat, although quality can be very variable.

Government permission must be sought to remove certain artworks and antiques out of the country. If you are in doubt, check the position by contacting the Delegation Provinciale du Tourisme located in Douala (tel: 342 14 22) or Yaoundé (tel: 223 50 77).

PHOTOGRAPHY
Ariadne Van Zandbergen
Equipment
Although with some thought and an eye for composition you can make nice photos with a 'point and shoot' camera, you need an SLR camera with one or more lenses if you are at all serious about photography. If you carry only one lens in Cameroon, a 28-70mm or similar zoom should be ideal. For a second lens, a 80-200mm or 70-300mm or similar will be excellent for candid shots, for wildlife, and for varying your composition.

Film
Print film is the preference of most casual photographers, slide film of professionals and some dedicated amateurs. Slide film is more expensive than print film, but this is broadly compensated for by cheaper development costs. Most photographers working outdoors in Africa favour Fujichrome slide film, in particular Sensia 100, Provia 100 (the professional equivalent to Sensia) or Velvia 50. Slow films (ie: those with a low ASA (ISO) rating) produce less grainy and sharper images than fast films, but can be tricky without a tripod in low light. Velvia 50 is extremely fine-grained and shows stunning colour saturation; it is the film I normally use in soft, even light or overcast weather. Sensia or Provia may be preferable in low light, since 100 ASA allows you to work at a faster shutter speed than 50 ASA. Because 100 ASA is more tolerant of contrast, it is also preferable in harsh light.

For print photography, a combination of 100 or 200 ASA film should be ideal. For the best results it is advisable to stick to recognised brands. Fujicolor produces excellent print films, with the Superia 100 and 200 recommended.

Some basics
The automatic programmes provided with many cameras are limited in the sense that the camera cannot think, but only make calculations. A better investment than any amount of electronic wizardry would be to read a photographic manual for beginners and get to grips with such basics as the relationship between aperture and shutter speed.

Beginners should also note that a low shutter speed can result in camera shake and therefore a blurred image. For hand-held photographs of static subjects using a low magnification lens (eg: 28–70), select a shutter speed of at least 1/60th of a second. For lenses of higher magnification, the rule of thumb is that the shutter speed should be at least the inverse of the magnification (for instance, a speed of 1/300 or faster on a 300 magnification lens). You can use lower shutter speeds with a tripod.

Most modern cameras include a built-in light meter, and give users the choice of three types of metering: matrix, centre weighted or spot metering. You will need to understand how these different systems work to make proper use of them. Built-in light meters are reliable in most circumstances, but in

Although haggling is often expected when purchasing something, don't bargain too hard. Each penny you save is likely to be of far more consequence locally than to you, and a bargain may be obtained because of low wages paid to the producer. Don't of course purchase products made from local wildlife, particularly from endangered species.

uneven light, or where there is a lot of sky, you may want to take your metering selectively, for instance by taking a spot reading on the main subject. The meter will tend to under- or overexpose when pointed at an almost white or black subject. This can be countered by taking a reading against an 18% grey card, or a substitute such as grass or light grey rocks – basically anything that isn't almost black, almost white or highly reflective.

Dust and heat
Dust and heat are often a problem in Africa. Keep your equipment in a sealed bag, stow films in an airtight container (such as a small cooler bag), leave used films in your hotel room, and avoid changing film in dusty conditions. On rough roads, I always carry my camera equipment on my lap to protect against vibration and bumps. Never stow camera equipment or film in a car boot (it will bake), or let it stand in direct sunlight.

Light
The light in Africa is much harsher than in Europe or North America, for which reason the most striking outdoor photographs are often taken during the hour or two of 'golden light' after dawn and before sunset. Shooting in low light may enforce the use of very low shutter speeds, in which case a tripod (ideally) or monopod (lighter) will be required to avoid camera shake. Be alert to the long shadows cast by a low sun; these show up more on photographs than to the naked eye.

With careful handling, side lighting and backlighting can produce stunning effects, especially in soft light and at sunrise or sunset. Generally, however, it is best to shoot with the sun behind you. Because of this, most buildings and landscapes are essentially a 'morning shot' or 'afternoon shot', depending on the direction they face. When you spend a couple of nights in one place, you'll improve your results by planning the best time to take pictures of static subjects (a compass can come in handy).

When photographing people or animals in the harsh midday sun, images taken in light but even shade are likely to look nicer than those taken in direct sunlight or patchy shade, since the latter conditions create too much contrast. Fill-in flash is almost essential if you want to capture facial detail of dark-skinned people in harsh or contrasty light.

Serious photographers should avoid travelling during the *harmattan*, since the sky is perpetually grey and ugly during this period (see page 52).

Protocol
Except in general street or market scenes, it is unacceptable to photograph people without permission. Expect some people to refuse or to ask for a donation. Even the most willing subject will often pose stiffly when a camera is pointed at them; relax them by making a joke, and take a few shots in quick succession to improve the odds of capturing a natural pose.

PHOTOGRAPHY
Although in the past a photography permit was required in Cameroon, this is no longer the case, although it is worth visiting the Ministry of Information and Culture in one of the capitals of the ten regional provinces and requesting a slip with official confirmation that a permit is *not* required. Although this will incur

a small fee, it should lessen the chance of delays later on.

Buy film and camera batteries beforehand as in Cameroon these tend to be either expensive, damaged by the heat or hard to find. UV/skylight filters not only protect the lens but reduce haze. Keep your camera in a dust-proof bag. Local photo-processing services can be very variable in quality. For further photography tips, see pages 88–9.

Many Cameroonian people can be suspicious, resentful or hostile of you taking photographs or videos, because of taboos relating to their traditional beliefs and for other reasons. Alternatively, they may expect payment if they are to be photographed. Therefore it is always best to ask people first before photographing them. Offer to pay a small fee or to send them a copy of the photograph, or, if you plan to take a lot of photos, consider taking a Polaroid camera so that you can furnish your subject with an instant portrait as a thank you. Bear in mind that local people may not wish you to take pictures of their places of worship or of a natural feature that has religious significance to them.

To avoid attention from policemen on the make or senior security officials, avoid taking photographs or videoing anything that could even vaguely be considered governmental, military, strategic or official in any way. This includes things like airports, harbours, railway stations, army, police and prison buildings, policemen, soldiers, bridges, dams, ferries and members of the government. To complicate matters, many such public facilities are unmarked, and even photographing something as innocuous as a shopfront or field can spark problems with officials.

Indeed, it is best not to bring out your camera wherever there are police, soldiers or other officials. Photography of parades and festivals, photography in Douala and Yaoundé, and any photography an official could deem likely to harm the country's reputation are also not recommended. I learnt of the sensitivity towards photography the hard way: I was arrested for pointing a camera inadvertently at a policeman.

MEDIA AND COMMUNICATIONS
Media
Cameroon Radio and Television Centre (CRTV) broadcasts on one television channel and some programmes are in English. There is also one national radio station and a station geared to each of the ten provinces of the country (again with some programmes in English), and several commercial stations. Satellite television is increasingly common, especially in better hotels. Cameroonian television, radio and press can be very patchy in their coverage of international current affairs.

The country's only daily newspaper, the *Cameroon Tribune*, is published in both French and English, but is heavily influenced by the government, which owns it. It has a website, www.cameroon-tribune.cm. *The Herald*, published in English, is largely concerned with representing anglophone interests in the west of the country. There is a thrice-weekly independent newspaper in French, *Le Messager*, as well as a very variable number of privately owned newspapers, including *La Nouvelle Expression, La Voix du Paysan* and the *Cameroon Post*.

English-language newspapers can be difficult to obtain and a good alternative is to bring a small short-wave radio which will pick up Voice of America (web: www.voa.gov or www.voanews.com; MHz 15.58, 11.98, 6.035, 0.909), European stations and the BBC World Service (web: www.bbc.co.uk/worldservice; MHz 17.83, 15.40, 11.77, 7.160). The latter broadcasts programmes such as *Network Africa* and *Focus on Africa*.

Copies of British, European and North American newspapers and magazines may be available in the lobbies of the expensive hotels in Douala and Yaoundé, and some street vendors also sell international publications.

Mail

Many roads and streets in Cameroon do not have names or numbered addresses. Consequently, the majority of businesses, government offices and individuals do not have street addresses. Mail is generally sent to a 'boite postale' (BP) or post office box (PO Box).

Post office opening hours are Monday–Friday 08.00–15.30 and Saturday 08.00–13.00.

The central post offices in Douala and Yaoundé (PTT, standing for Postes, Télécommunications et Télédiffusion) operate a quite reliable post restante service. When you collect mail you will be required to show your passport and each letter collected costs CFA150 (16p/28c).

People sending you mail should address their letters to you in this way, with their address on the back:

Ben WEST
Poste Restante
PTT (Grande Poste)
Yaoundé
CAMEROON

International airmail letters typically take from 8 to 15 days to arrive from Europe or the US. Allow at least a week for airmail from Cameroon to reach Europe and two weeks elsewhere. International surface mail can take from three to six months.

Important correspondence and parcels should be sent using an express mail service such as Federal Express or DHL Worldwide Express.

Telephone

Telephoning abroad from Douala and Yaoundé is generally not a problem, but can be difficult elsewhere in the country. In the major town of Garoua, for example, telephones that can be used internationally are rare, even in hotels. In such circumstances it is often easier to ask someone locally, such as a member of hotel staff, whether you can top up their mobile with a card bought by you and then use some of the credit on the card yourself.

Most major towns have IntelCam offices at post offices which can provide international calls at a price, and there are shops and telephone booths throughout the country (*téléboutiques* or *cabines téléphoniques*) where you can telephone and send a fax, also at a high rate. You may be able to receive incoming calls or faxes for a small charge.

It is often cheaper and easier to correspond by fax if this is possible, and instead of calling collect or reverse charging calls (to do so ask for 'PCV', pronounced 'pay say vay') it is better to arrange in advance to receive calls at a certain time and number.

Dialling codes

The international direct dialling code for Cameroon is 237 followed by the seven-digit number. When phoning Cameroon from abroad, add 00 before this code.

To call from Cameroon, dial the international access number (usually 00) and then the country code followed by the area code (dropping the first 0 if there is one) and then the number.

Therefore, to dial the UK from Cameroon, dial 00 44 and then the area code and number, dropping the first 0 of the area code.

Other international access codes are: North America and Canada (00 1); Ireland (00 353); Australia (00 61); South Africa (00 27); and New Zealand (00 64).

Mobile telephone
There is mobile telephone coverage of variable quality in Cameroon, but it's often excellent around Douala, Ngaoundéré and Yaoundé. Currently the cost to make calls to the UK is around £1.30 per minute, but of course it depends upon the network and payment method.

Satellite telephone
If you need a telephone that will work in even the most remote areas of Cameroon, consider hiring an Inmarsat satellite phone. The price is not cheap (typically £75 per week or £225 per month, plus £3 per minute for calls) but you can rest assured you should be able to get the football results even if you're deep in the rainforest. Web addresses for satellite telephone rental companies include www.adam-phones.co.uk, www.phone-rentals.co.uk, www.cellhire.com and www.mobell.co.uk.

Emergency telephone numbers
Police: tel: 17; fire: tel: 18.

Email and internet
There are numerous cybercafés and shops with email and internet services in city centres, but far less so in towns. There are several on Boulevard de la Liberté in Douala, for example. The costs typically vary from around CFA500 to CFA1,000 (53p–£1.07/94c–US$1.89) per hour for internet access. Service is often slow and unreliable.

BUSINESS OPENING HOURS
Government offices, public services: 07.30–15.30
Banks: 07.30–15.30
Pharmacies: 08.00–20.00
Shops: vary from around 08.00–15.00 daily, or 09.00–12.30 and 15.30–19.30, or 08.00–12.00 and 14.30–17.30
Markets: approximately 07.00–18.00
Post offices: Monday–Friday 08.00–15.30 and Saturday 08.00–13.00

SPORTS AND ACTIVITIES
Many areas of Cameroon are excellent for hiking, often affording beautiful scenery and varied terrain. The northern area between the towns of Rhumsiki and Mora, home of the Mandara Mountains, and the area around the Ring Road north of Bamenda in the southwest of the country, are especially excellent areas for hiking.

Mount Cameroon also offers good opportunities for mountaineering and hiking and, for those with the required stamina, it hosts an international mountain race each February.

There is also good rock climbing in the Mindif area, about 35km south of the northern town of Maroua, where there is a huge, challenging rock known as 'La dent de Mindif' (Mindif's tooth) jutting up out of nowhere.

The beautiful white beaches by the southern coastal town of Kribi, and the volcanic black ones of Limbé are popular for swimming, although beware of the strong currents. The safety of swimming at a particular beach should always be sought locally from a reliable source.

Some beaches along the coastline of Cameroon slope steeply and waves can therefore cause a strong undertow. If safety is an issue, many of the better hotels have pools that non-guests can use for a small fee, and there are also public swimming pools in Yaoundé and Douala. Only swim or take a boat in waters that you are absolutely sure are safe – not only from hazards like hippos and crocodiles, but also from water-borne diseases like bilharzia as well.

Cycling is a good way to travel in rural areas, and encourages interaction with the locals. Possibly the best cycling is to be had in the western and northern provinces of the country. Football and basketball are very popular, and, if you bring your own ball, a game can be easy to initiate in many villages.

Jogging is popular with expatriates, spearheaded by the 'Hash House Harriers', a group founded by some beer-swilling Australians in Malaysia in 1939 that has been running around Cameroon for decades. Yaoundé, Douala, Bamenda and Garoua all have Hash groups, and the local expat communities should be able to advise on the starting point of the latest run.

There are many opportunities to fish in rivers and coastal areas, while golf lovers will find a spectacular 18-hole course in Yaoundé and another course at Tiko, near Douala.

Douala and Yaoundé both have equestrian clubs, and numerous tour operators and travel agents can organise horseriding and trekking trips.

Football

For many people, the word 'Cameroon' conjures up football. Cameroon enjoyed feverish and instant worldwide attention when it defeated World Cup holders Argentina in the first game of the 1990 World Cup. Despite this, they were knocked out of the competition in the quarter-finals when they lost 3-2 to England after extra time. The 1998 and 2002 championships were disappointing, conversely.

Cameroon has also done remarkably well in the African Cup of Nations. Cameroon won the cup in 1984, 1998, 2000 and 2002, a record shared only with Ghana and Egypt.

Roger Milla, born on May 20 1952, is undoubtedly Cameroon's most famous player, known and loved the world over. His achievements are astounding. Representing Cameroon internationally from 1972 to 1994, he won the accolade of African Footballer of the Year both in 1976 and 1990. He is the oldest player to appear in a World Cup, as well as being the oldest ever to score a goal, which happened when he was aged 42, during a game against Russia in 1994. Sadly, as a contrast, the unexpected death of Marc-Vivien Foe during an international match in 2003 captured worldwide headlines.

CULTURAL DOS AND DON'TS
Greetings and etiquette

In Cameroon, a long drawn-out greeting made up of a handshake and various polite enquiries is common, even if you've just dropped into a shop.

It is a good idea to try to lock into the local pace of life and thought patterns as soon as possible. Timekeeping is often far more relaxed in this part of the world, for instance, and it is best to accept this philosophically. Just because the bus timetable is routinely ignored or a meeting occurs at 13.45 instead of the agreed 13.00 doesn't suggest an inferior way of life, simply a different one.

It is not unusual for men to hold hands with each other; for example, if you are male and ask for directions and are then guided down the street by a stranger, he may do this.

Unlike in the West, beckoning with the palm upwards is considered obscene, so avoid this action. Beckon with your palm downwards instead.

To avoid the possibility of having to pay a bribe or even suffer arrest, if you hear the national anthem being played in public, or see a flag being raised or lowered, stand still; never urinate in public; do not destroy any banknote; do not criticise the president or government in public where others could hear; and remain stationary or leave the road if you see an official-looking convoy such as limousines and motorcycles approaching.

Public nudity, open displays of affection or anger, and criticism of the country or government can all cause offence, especially the further north you go.

In non-touristy rural areas, if you wish to visit a settlement or tribal lands (which you may need to do to visit some of the crater lakes and mountains, for example) it is polite to ask permission by introducing yourself to the local chief, who is known as the *lamido* by the Fulani in the north of the country, the *sultan* by the Bamoun, and the *fon* by the Bamiléké in the west. You are often expected to give a small present such as a bottle of whisky or the monetary equivalent.

Homosexuality among men in Cameroon is against the law and therefore public displays of affection between men, except the customary walking arm-in-arm or hand-in-hand, should be avoided.

Avoid political discussions in casual conversation with Cameroonian acquaintances. It is also generally impolite to enquire about a Cameroonian aquaintance's ethnic origins. Wait for them to bring the subject up. Do not point with a finger, as this is considered rude.

If you are ever in need of information or help, Cameroonians generally are very courteous in their willingness to assist. If they do not know the answer to your query, the chances are they will find someone who does.

Hissing is a common way to attract a stranger's attention and is not an aggressive action.

Sometimes, when buying from a stall or visiting a shop, you may receive no courtesy, and this can be disconcerting. Yet there should be no assumption of offence and a simple smile and a 'Bonjour, madame' at first and 'Merci' as you leave can change things dramatically.

Likewise, occasionally you may experience some hard-looking man staring at you threateningly. Again, in most cases a simple 'Bonjour, monsieur' will result in the most sincere smile in response.

Islamic customs
In the north, observe the following. If visiting a mosque, take off your shoes. Some mosques do not admit women, while others may have separate entrances for men and women.

Bear in mind that it is impolite to drink alcohol in a Muslim's presence unless he shows approval. If you're a woman, don't take offence if a Muslim man refuses to shake hands with you, as he is simply following the Koran.

If you have a taxi driver or guide for the day, he may have a prayer ritual, which occurs five times a day, including at midday, late afternoon and sunset. Drivers of public transport may also stop en route to carry out these rituals.

Tipping
Tipping is uncommon although Cameroonians often expect *cadeaux* (gifts) from foreign travellers, who tend to look rich to locals. Plan to tip 5–10% or so at better restaurants unless service has been included in the bill, which is likely at establishments geared to tourists or rich Cameroonians. Drivers, guides, porters, hotel staff and taxi drivers (not necessarily share-taxi drivers) will all greatly appreciate a small tip.

Begging

With no social security system or welfare state, the giving of even the smallest coin will always be appreciated. (Indeed, one night in Douala a friend of mine was mugged while I was left alone, and I'm convinced that I was ignored because I had just given some coins to a small boy with a begging bowl.) If in doubt, give to those beggars the locals give to. One sad development in recent years in Cameroon is the rise in children begging. It is quite easy to deduce the ones that are truly destitute, maybe supporting sick parents, from those that are simply trying their luck in places frequented by tourists.

For more lasting good, it is better to give a donation to a recognised local project like a school, charity, mission, aid agency or health centre than to indiscriminately hand out sweets, pens, toys and money to children, which further perpetuates the begging.

Bribery and corruption

Low and often overdue salaries help fuel the widespread system of bribery in this part of the world. That said, most dealings with government employees should be trouble-free, and indeed many officials will go out of their way to help.

If you do encounter bribery, this shouldn't cause undue alarm, and indeed it is better to approach the matter as if it is a game. Try to take the attitude of long-term residents, who are generally far more relaxed about the matter and see it simply as one of the inconveniences of day-to-day life.

Always remain polite, patient and in good humour if an official is clearly after a bribe, as tempers can fray alarmingly quickly if you become impatient or angry.

One long-term resident of the country gives the following advice: if the law the official is upholding has obviously been made up, you can enter into discussions about the matter in the hope that he will lose interest, or offer a 'small gift' or 'special fee' or a 'dash' (don't use the word 'bribe'), maybe the equivalent of a couple of pounds or dollars, to help you on your way. If you suspect that you are indeed in breach of a law, you could suggest coming to an agreement or paying the fine (*amende* in French).

If the difficulty persists, take the names and numbers of the policemen or soldiers that they carry on their badges. If they are acting incorrectly they are likely to try immediately to hide their badges as you start writing the details down, but insist that they give the details to you.

Always ask for a receipt for the transgression. You cannot be fined without being issued one. Since the official is not able to issue a receipt if the charge is trumped up, you cannot pay. You might then suggest going to see the inspector at the police station, at which time the official will probably propose a private settlement of say CFA5,000 (£5.35/US$9.45). In this case you'd be well advised to give it to them as a gesture of good will and go on your way.

Drugs

Obviously, don't even think of contact with hard drugs. In this part of the world, long prison sentences in the grimmest conditions or the death penalty are possible penalties. While discreet use of cannabis should not attract more than a fine, the fondness some members of the police have for extracting bribes means it might be pushing your luck to indulge in a marathon smoking session outside the Presidential Palace.

Dress

The dress code is rather conservative throughout the country but strictest in the Muslim north where women should cover up knees and shoulders. In many areas a Western man walking around bare-chested can cause offence or even anger. I was challenged to a fight once in Mora when I took my shirt off in the midday sun, as of course Englishmen are fond of doing.

Men with long hair and the wearing of tight trousers and shorts may not fare much better in some areas. Shorts are OK if you have a bike, are hiking or engaged in a sport. In general, the more conservatively you dress, the better you will be received. So if you are making a visa application, it is better to turn up in smart clothes than a pair of jeans. Avoid wearing anything at all in a military style as you could be mistaken for a soldier.

Responsible tourism

Always attempt to minimise the negative impact of your travels: recycle as much as possible, favour locally owned businesses, spend as much as possible with local communities and support local sustainable development initiatives. Use and save energy, water and other resources efficiently and in keeping with local practices. Avoid places that use limited resources like water and electricity to the detriment of local people.

You can further minimise your impact on the environment by leaving no litter, using biodegradable soaps and detergents and conserving water. Campfires are inappropriate in areas where wood is scarce.

Walk and cycle when you can, rather than opting for motorised transport. Not only is this more environmentally friendly, but it will give you far more chance to interact with locals and savour the country. Observe, but do not disturb, natural systems. Move cautiously and quietly in natural areas.

More information on the subject is available from **Tourism Concern** (Stapleton House, 277–281 Holloway Rd, London N7 8HN, tel: 020 7753 3330; web: www.tourismconcern.org.uk).

Bradt Travel Guides is a partner to the 'know before you go' campaign, masterminded by the UK Foreign and Commonwealth Office to promote the importance of finding out about a destination before you travel. By combining the up-to-date advice of the FCO with the in-depth knowledge of Bradt authors, you'll ensure that your trip will be as trouble-free as possible.

www.fco.gov.uk/knowbeforeyougo

Part Two

The Guide

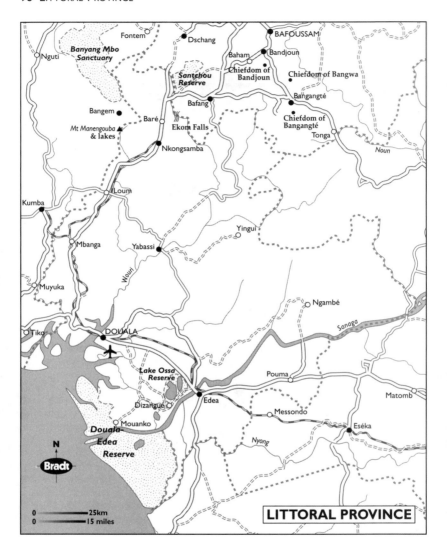

Littoral Province

About a third of Cameroon's economic activity occurs in this province, not least because its biggest city, Douala, is also the country's biggest city by far.

Dominated by Mount Cameroon (which you can see from the port), Douala is located 24km (15 miles) from the Atlantic coast on the southern shore of the Wouri River.

DOUALA

Yaoundé may be Cameroon's capital, but the considerably larger port city of Douala in Littoral Province is the economic centre of the country. Most visitors to Cameroon spend at least some time in this vibrant, colourful city with more than 1.8 million inhabitants, especially as Douala is Cameroon's main hub for air travel. It has a sizeable foreign community, with particularly large numbers of Nigerian and French nationals, as well as about 200 Americans.

The sprawling city has come a long way from its origins as a small fishing community that the Portuguese, the first Europeans to set foot on Cameroon, encountered in the 15th century. This triggered the start of a long tradition of trading between coastal rulers and passing European ships.

You either love or hate this city, often at the same time. Its pulsating atmosphere certainly excites, and it has a pleasant tropical ambience, with gradually decaying traditional colonial architecture (with verandas and louvred shutters) coexisting with modern buildings.

Yet its stifling humidity (it has often been dubbed the 'armpit of Africa') and its pushy inhabitants can be exhausting. Although it is guilty of having little traditional flavour and more than its fair share of dull architecture, as well as an alarming crime rate, considerable overpopulation, a woefully inadequate infrastructure and economic chaos, it is nevertheless a good base for some of Cameroon's most alluring destinations.

These include the white beaches of Kribi, the black sand beaches of Limbé at the foot of Mount Cameroon, and the energetic town of Kumba near picturesque Lake Barombi Mbo, en route to Korup National Park and the Nigerian border. Continue eastwards from Kumba and you come to Mount Kupé and the twin crater lakes of Manengouba, which is excellent hiking country. All are within a few hours' travel of Douala.

Douala is great for nightlife, being packed with lively bars and restaurants and live music venues. The Bonapriso district south of the centre, and Akwa just north of it, are especially vibrant at night.

Yet you have to be on your guard, especially at night, as crime has increased in recent years. The port area is especially to be avoided.

Douala also has its wealthy, extravagant side. Indeed, in the upmarket sections of the Boulevard de la Liberté, Douala's main street, you could almost be in Paris. Smartly dressed, glamorous-looking men and women smelling of expensive colognes talk animatedly in French, wave their hands and kiss each other theatrically and jump out of gleaming new cars into expensive restaurants.

But this does not disguise the largely characterless streets, concrete office blocks and overwhelming atmosphere of business. And the Parisian feel is fragile, as poverty and dilapidation are never far away.

This being Africa, it is not a long walk to where the tarmac ends and the muddy streets begin, the latter lined with haphazard shacks made of corrugated iron and scrap wood.

As Cameroon's principal port, Douala handles almost all of Cameroon's maritime traffic and is the major entry point for imports to Cameroon, the Central African Republic, Chad, Equatorial Guinea and the Republic of Congo.

The city has few distinct sights or attractions as such, and is best enjoyed as an experience in itself – a slice of vibrant, shambolic Africa, rather than a city with a programme of museums, churches and galleries to tick off.

Central Douala is divided into distinct neighbourhoods, mainly named after the original ruling families. These include the upmarket residential quarter, Bonapriso, industrial Bonaberi and administrative sector Bonanjo. At the centre of the city is Akwa, the principal commercial district, where lots of hotels, restaurants and shops can be found. The main centre of activity here is the Boulevard de la Liberté.

Getting there and away
By air
Most international flights to Cameroon land at Douala's relatively small airport. Cameroon Airlines operates flights from Douala to the main cities, including Yaoundé, Maroua and Garoua. More details can be found in *Chapter 3*.

By rail
The station, the Gare de Bessengue, is northeast of the centre in the Bessengue neighbourhood off Boulevard de l'Unité. Trains go to Yaoundé (where you can get an onward train to Ngaoundéré), Nkongsamba and Kumba, although trains to the latter two are painfully slow. More details can be found in *Chapter 3*.

By road
Yaoundé (for the north), Kribi and eastern destinations
Most *agences de voyage* operate along Boulevard du Président Ahmadou Ahidjo, near Place Ahmadou Ahidjo, just east of the centre.

Centrale Voyages BP 2789; 1460 Bd Ahmadou Ahidjo, Akwa; tel: 342 03 16/342 26 88. Centrale Voyages currently offers a 07.00, noon and 16.00 luxury service to Yaoundé for CFA8,000 (£8/US$15), with a less salubrious CFA3,500 (£3.75/US$6.61) service at other times. They are super-efficient and the journey takes around three hours.
Garanti Express BP 3222; Bd Ahmadou Ahidjo, Akwa; tel: 342 61 91. Garanti Express, whose office is almost opposite Centrale Voyages, offers a cheaper, less comfortable service to Yaoundé.

Also try **Confort Voyages** (tel: 983 95 27) and **Beauty Express** (Rue Congo Paraiso, Akwa; tel: 342 83 96).

Bamenda, Bafoussam, Kumba, Limbé and the southwest
Transport to Limbé, Bafoussam, Bamenda and other northern destinations is generally from the Bonaberi *gare routière* (motor park), next to the concrete tower,

about 6km northwest of the centre over the Wouri River bridge. There are plenty of share-taxis for various destinations operating from here.

Guaranti Express BP 3228; 5647 Gare Routière Nationale 3, Bonaberi; tel: 342 61 91
Binam Voyages BP 4293; Gare Routière Nationale 3, Bonaberi; tel: 344 57 17
Vatikan Express Tel: 783 95 27
Tchatcho Voyages Tel: 342 02 10. For Kumba and Mutengene, where you can obtain a share-taxi for Limbé.
Linda Voyages Tel: 340 39 57. For Nkongsamba.

Buses and share-taxis for Buéa, Limbé and Nkongsamba also terminate and depart from the Rond-point Deido near Wouri River bridge, 2km north of the centre.

Ebolowa and southern destinations
Buca Voyages Tel: 342 29 35

Where to stay
Douala, coupled with Yaoundé, has the costliest accommodation in the country, but there are still plenty of inexpensive options to choose from. The area around the Wouri Cinema in the centre is a good starting point for finding some of the less expensive hotels. Here are a selection.

German Seamen's Mission/Foyer du Marin BP 5194; Rue Galliéni, off Rue Joffre, Akwa; tel: 342 27 94; email: douala@seamannsmission.org. A great choice in Douala for its ambience, central location in the Akwa district, excellent standards and value for money. Near the Hôtel de Lido, it has very clean, recently refurbished rooms with AC and bathrooms. There's an inviting swimming pool in immaculate attractive gardens, a restaurant with good food (such as German sausage with cabbage salad) and a bar. It's a favourite haunt of expatriates and travellers, and a luggage room is available free of charge to guests. Because of its popularity it is best to book in advance. CFA15,000 (£16/US$28) single, CFA18,000 (£19/US$34) twin, CFA21,000 (£22/US$39) triple.
Hôtel de Lido Rue Joffre, Akwa; tel: 342 40 86. Just around the corner from the Foyer du Marin, though far less inviting, with double rooms with fan or AC for CFA8,000–10,000 (£8–10/US$15–18). There is also a restaurant/bar.
Hôtel Beauséjour Mirabel BP 5368; 337 Rue Joffre, Akwa; tel: 342 70 93/342 38 85. This upmarket mid-range hotel just down the road from the Hôtel de Lido has 135 rooms with satellite TV, a bar and a restaurant next door.
Residence Hoteliere la Falaise BP 5300; 503 Bd de la Liberté; tel: 342 46 46. Next to Jet Cam Tours, this smart but rather dull hotel with 133 rooms costs CFA37,500 (£40/US$70) for a single and CFA40,000 (£42/US$75) for a double. There is a restaurant, bar and swimming pool. Most rooms have a bathroom, AC and a satellite TV.
Hôtel Ibis BP 12086; Rue Pierre Loti, off Av de Gaulle, Bonanjo; tel: 342 58 00, email: hotel.ibis@camnet.cm; web: www.ibishotel.com. A reliable, secure, rather characterless hotel, ranked three-star by the government, popular with business people. There is a clean, pleasant pool. In the late afternoon hundreds of bats fly over it. The restaurant serves good European and African fare like Porc de Mbongo and Ndolé, but is relatively expensive, around CFA5,000–7,000 (£5.35–7.50/US$9.50–13.30) for main courses and a whopping CFA2,300 (£2.46/US$4.37) for a draught beer. The bar is nice and has live music each evening. Breakfast buffet including eggs, good, strong coffee and tea, fruit, bread, croissants, yoghurts and meats, is around CFA4,950 (£5.30/$9.50) per person. Free transport from the airport. Major credit cards accepted. Singles and doubles are both CFA49,500 (£53/US$95). A store opposite the hotel sells necessities like bottled water and snacks, which are much cheaper than the hotel prices. Says ex-Ibis resident Brian

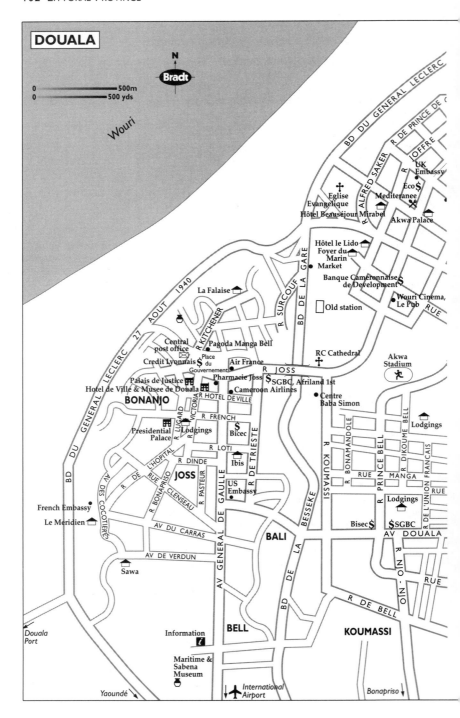

DOUALA

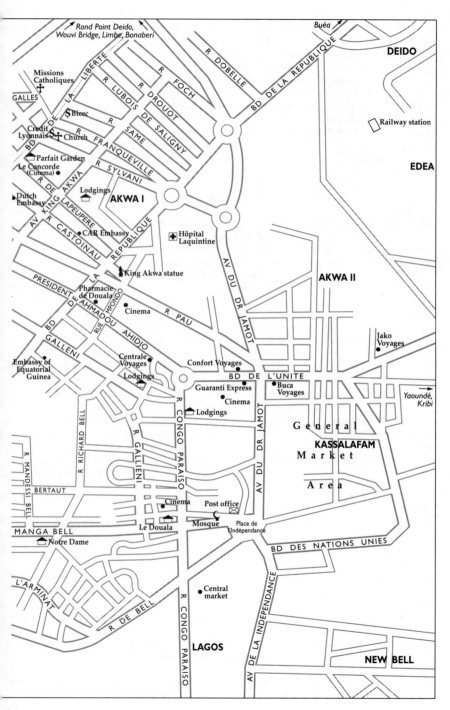

Rond Point Deido,
Wouvi Bridge, Limbe, Bonaberi

Buéa

DEIDO

Missions
Catholiques

GALLES

Brecc

Credit
Lyonnais
Church

Parfait Garden
Le Concorde
(Cinema)

Dutch
Embassy

Lodgings

AKWA I

CAR Embassy

Hôpital
Laquintine

King Akwa statue

Pharmacie
de Douala

Cinema

Embassy of
Equatorial
Guinea

Centrale
Voyages

Lodgings

Confort Voyages

BD DE L'UNITE

Guaranti Express

Cinema

Lodgings

Railway station

EDEA

AKWA II

Jako
Voyages

Buca
Voyages

Yaoundé,
Kribi

General

KASSALAFAM

Market

Area

Cinema

Post office

Le Douala

Mosque

Place de
l'Indépendance

MANGA BELL

Notre Dame

BD DES NATIONS UNIES

L'ARMINAT

Central
market

LAGOS

NEW BELL

R DOBELLE

BD DE LA REPUBLIQUE

R FOCH

R DROUOT

R LUBOIS DE SALIGNY

R SAME

FRANQUEVILLE

R SYLVANI

R DE KING AKWA

LAPEUPERE

R CASTOINAU

LA REPUBLIQUE

AV DU DR IAMOT

PRESIDENT

DE AHMADOU AHIDIO

RUE MPONDO

BD GALLENI

R PAU

R CONGO PARAISO

R RICHARD BELL

R GALLENI

R MANDESSI BELL

BERTAUT

R DE BELL

AV DE LA INDEPENDANCE

Cruickshank: 'At night, prostitutes gather just outside the hotel, which makes going outside rather annoying as they hiss at you to get your attention. Interestingly, condoms were available right in the hotel rooms – an admirable effort by the government to curb the AIDS problem. This is a trend I saw throughout the country.'

Hôtel Parfait Garden BP 5350; 1010 Bd de la Liberté, Akwa; tel: 342 63 57/342 83 98. A (government-ranked) three-star hotel by the Akwa Palace in a very lively part of town with 78 rooms, restaurant, bar and swimming pool. Around CFA40,000 (£42/US$75) for a double room. Credit cards accepted.

Hôtel Sawa BP 2345; 488 Rue de Verdun, Bonanjo; tel: 342 08 66/342 44 41; email: hotelsawa@camnet.cm. Despite being described as international class, rooms and food are variable in quality and the water supply can be unreliable during the dry season, although recent renovation may have cured this. The gardens are very pleasant, however. The good pool can also be used by non-guests, for a CFA3,000 (£3/US$5) fee. Most credit cards are accepted. The 291 rooms and six suites have satellite TV. CFA60,000 (£64/US$113) for a double room.

Hôtel Akwa Palace and **Hôtel Akwa Palace II Pullman** BP 4007; 52 Bd de la Liberté, Akwa; tel: 342 26 01/342 07 49; email: akwa-palace@camnet.cm. Located in the commercial heart of town a few hundred metres southeast of the shores of the Wouri River. The newer 124-room Pullman is ranked by the government as four star, while the original colonial Akwa Palace, with 60 rooms, is a more modest three star. Most credit cards are accepted and travellers' cheques are cashed in most major currencies. Rooms start at CFA35,000 (£37/US$66) per night in the older section and otherwise start at CFA65,000 (£69/US$122) per night, which is good value considering the general standards. The hotels feature a secluded garden area, a good restaurant (sandwiches CFA2,100–2,800/ £2–3/US$4–5, three-course meal of the day CFA12,000/£13/US$22), a bar and nightclub, satellite TV in rooms and a 25m pool at the rear (CFA4,000/£4/US$7 for non-guests).

Hôtel Le Méridien BP 3232; 35 Av de Cocotiers; tel: 342 50 00; web: www.lemeridien-hotels.com. Douala's most expensive hotel, in one of the city's most tranquil districts, it features attractive grounds overlooking the Wouri River, the harbour and a wooded park. It has good security, a pool (available to non-guests for a fee), gym, tennis courts, bookshop, casino, travel agent and golf course. The 144 rooms and eight suites have satellite TV and start at about CFA100,000 (£107/US$189). There is a free airport shuttle service. Credit cards are accepted.

La Procure Générale des Missions Catholiques BP 5280; Rue Franqueville, Akwa; tel: 342 27 97, email progemis.douala@camnet.cm. This Mission is good value but is often full. Facilities include a swimming pool. Rooms are clean and have AC and a shower room. Singles from CFA7,000 (£7/US$13), doubles from CFA12,000 (£12/US$22), quads from CFA20,000 (£21/US$37).

Hôtel Arcade BP 12120; Rue de Trieste, Bonanjo; tel: 342 40 25. A comfortable three-star hotel (199 rooms) with restaurant, bar, nightclub and swimming pool. Use of nearby tennis courts available. The hotel is next to a pleasant, inexpensive restaurant, Echo de Bonanjo. A single room is CFA38,000 (£40/US$71), doubles are CFA41,500 (£44/US$78).

Hôtel le Nde BP 12990; 105 Bd de la Liberté; tel: 342 70 34. Good standard hotel with 50 rooms, restaurant, nightclub/bar and pool. Double rooms CFA12,000–20,000 (£12–21/US$22–37).

La Solidarité Rue Bertaut, Bali; tel: 343 13 46. Clean air-conditioned rooms (CFA5,000/£5/US$9) and bar/restaurant.

Hôtel Royal Palace Bonaberi; tel: 339 34 26; web: www.royalpalace.fr.fm. This comfortable hotel just outside the city at Bonaberi, 8km from the airport, has 80 rooms with bathroom, satellite TV and telephone starting from CFA28,000 (£30/US$52).

Hôtel Lewat BP 12563; 2699 Bd de la République; tel: 340 00 24. A two-star hotel with 40 clean rooms and a good restaurant. Rooms CFA20,000–30,000 (£21–32/US$37–56).

Hôtel Sportif Av des Palmiers, Bonapriso; tel: 343 76 40/342 67 55. South of Bonanjo in Bonapriso. Rooms with shared facilities and fan start at CFA9,000 (£9/US$17), while an en-suite room with AC is CFA18,500 (£19/US$34).

Hôtel du Littoral BP 1389; 38 Av Douala Manga Bell, Bali; tel: 342 58 05. A bit tatty but in a very central location. 34 rooms from CFA5,000–10,000 (£5–10/US$9–18), plus bar and restaurant.

Hila Hotel BP 17497; 515 Bd de l'Unité; tel: 342 15 86. Not the best choice as it's on a busy street near the central market. Rooms are self-contained with bathrooms and are air conditioned with TV and telephone. There is also a bar and restaurant. Singles CFA9,000 (£9/US$17), doubles CFA13,000 (£13/US$24).

Hôtel Renom BP 17578; Av de Gaulle; tel: 342 34 52. Formerly the Hôtel de l'Air, this hotel near the airport has en-suite rooms with AC costing CFA5,000–10,000 (£5–10/US$9–18).

Where to eat and drink

There are a good number of restaurants at differing price levels, especially in the Bonapriso and Akwa neighbourhoods. Akwa has a good number of inexpensive food stalls, especially around Boulevard de la Liberté and Rue Joffre, but there are relatively few bars, apart from a couple by the Wouri Cinema, several basic shack-like establishments along Boulevard du Président Ahmadou Ahidjo, one or two in Rue Joffre and a few others scattered about elsewhere.

There are several Parisian-style cafés with good strong coffees and tempting pastries, especially in and around Boulevard de la Liberté.

Ets Edere Café Restaurant Bd de la Liberté, Akwa. Near the Pharmacie du Centre, this cheap and cheerful dive does a delicious roast chicken and plantain chips for CFA1,000/£1.10/US$1.89 and steak and chips for CFA1,500/£1.60/US$2.83. A big (.65 litre) bottle of beer is CFA600/64p/US$1.13. Where the locals eat. Take a taxi from here at night, even though it is centrally located.

Méditerranée Restaurant Bd de la Liberté, Akwa; tel: 342 30 69/342 92 34. Good-value Greek food (tzatziki/taramasalata CFA2,000/£2.14/US$3.78, salad CFA1,500/£1.60/US$2.83, moussaka CFA3,500/£3.75/US$6.61, white beans CFA2,500/£2.67/US$4.72, fillet steak CFA4,000/£4.28/US$7.56, beer CFA1,000/£1.07/US$1.89) at this outdoor restaurant opposite the Akwa Palace with a terrace looking out on to the busy street. A popular expat – and prostitute – hangout.

Echo de Bonanjo BP 11998; Rue de Trieste, Bonanjo; tel: 342 64 91. On the junction with Rue Joss, this pleasant, unpretentious restaurant has good but inexpensive dishes including Cameroonian speciality *ndole* (a spinach-like sauce) with meat or shrimps for CFA2,500–3,000/£2.67–3.21/US$4.72–5.67. Next to the Hôtel Arcade.

German Seamen's Mission/Foyer du Marin Rue Galliéni, off Rue Joffre, Akwa; tel: 342 27 94/91 54 52. Brochette or German sausage, bread roll, sauerkraut and chips for CFA1,500 (£1.60/US$2.83), grilled meats from CFA3,000 (£3.21/US$5.67), omelettes from CFA800 (85p/US$1.51) and continental breakfast for CFA1,300 (£1.39/US$2.45) by the pool.

Le Regal du Plateau Rue Joss, Bonanjo. Near Rue de Trieste and several banks and airline offices, this simple, inexpensive snack bar has a small terrace that's ideal for a drink after a typically lengthy banking transaction or flight booking.

Circuit Mado near Hôtel Akwa Palace, Akwa; tel: 342 99 69. Simple Cameroonian dishes, such as grilled fish or chicken in sauce, around CFA4,500 (£4.82/US$8.50).

4ème Protocol Snack Bar and Piano Restaurant Bd de la Liberté, Akwa. Inexpensive snacks by the Wouri Cinema, late-night opening. Next door is a 'pub' and a games room with slot machines, roulette, etc.

Le Dragon d'Or 771 Bd de la Liberté, Akwa. Opposite the Hôtel Akwa Palace, this offers Chinese and Vietnamese cuisine from around CFA4,000 (£4.28/US$7.56).

Café des Arts Pagoda Manga Bell, Pl du Gouvernement, Bonanjo; tel: 981 10 87. A clean, smart French restaurant with a pleasant little courtyard garden. Avocado vinaigrette CFA1,000 (£1.07/US$1.89), salad CFA1,500 (£1.60/US$2.83), beef fillet steak CFA4,000 (£4.28/US$7.56), mixed grill CFA7,000 (£7.50/US$13.23).

La Fourchette 317 Rue Franqueville, Akwa; tel: 343 26 11/42 14 88. Good-value centrally located French restaurant, around CFA15,000 (£16.07/US$28.35) per person.

Délicies Salon du Thé Bd de la Liberté, Akwa. Opposite the Hôtel Parfait Garden, this café specialises in ices, patisseries and cakes.

Chococho Rue Njo-njo, Bonapriso. A good bakery with croissants, pizzas, sandwiches and a good range of breads.

Le Tourne Broche Hôtel Akwa Palace, Akwa; tel: 342 26 01. The best French cooking served at the restaurant by the pool of the hotel. From CFA15,000 (£16/US$28) per head.

La Pacha Rue Njo-Njo, Bonapriso. Lebanese dishes.

Le Provençal 369 Av de Gaulle, Bonanjo; tel: 342 70 17. French cuisine at around CFA15,000 (£16.07/US$28.35) per person.

Le Glacier Modèrne Bd de la Liberté, Akwa. Paris-style café for pastries, snacks and ice-creams.

Chez Mich la Mbamoise Bd de la République, Bali. Tel: 342 22 40. Alfresco eating with Cameroonian cuisine at around CFA5,500 (£5.89/US$10.39) per head.

Phaco Club International BP 10063; 227 Rue Douala Mango Bell, near Rue Koumassi; tel: 342 68 81/955 30 08. African dishes, including a selection of exotic meats, with live music, dance and sometimes satirical comedy in the evening. From CFA10,000 (£10/US$18).

La Coupole 115 Av de Gaulle, Bonapriso; tel: 342 29 60. Lebanese food and pizzas from CFA4,500 (£4.82/US$8.50) per person.

La Paillote Bd de la Liberté, Akwa. Opposite the Hôtel Parfait Garden, this restaurant/club serves snacks and has a bar.

Le Beaujolais Rue Tokoto, Bonapriso; tel: 342 70 11. Rather pricey French food, around CFA15,000 (£16.07/US$28.35) per person.

Chez Wou 611 Av de Gaulle, Bonanjo; tel: 342 33 10. Douala's oldest Chinese restaurant serving decent food in an attractive environment. Main courses CFA5,000 (£5.35/US$9.45).

Oriental Garden 10 Rue Afcodi, Bonapriso; tel: 342 69 38. Pricey but good Chinese restaurant from around CFA18,000 (£19/US$34) per head.

Nightlife

Admission and opening times to nightclubs vary greatly and names often change. They usually get going from around 23.00 and generally close anywhere between 02.00 and 06.00.

Broadway Rue Toyota, Bonapriso. Live performances enliven the dancing.

Le Club 78 Rue Sylvani, Akwa. Swish, plays Western music and is popular with expats.

The Club Rue Batibois, Bonapriso; tel: 950 39 08/950 39 02; web: www.bar-the-club.com. On the junction with Av de Gaulle.

Le Byblos Rue Joffre, opposite the Hôtel Beauséjour, Akwa. Modern club, plays African and Western music. Admission is CFA3,000 (£3.21/US$5.67).

Orange Metallic Bonanjo; web: www.orange-mettalic.com. Popular with expatriates.

Saint Peres Rue Castelnau, near Hôtel Parfait Garden. A popular expatriate haunt which plays mostly Western music.

L'Elysée Nightclub Near Marché Deido, north of the centre, is popular with locals and few expats or tourists visit.

Le Sunset Av de Gaulle, Bonanjo; plays both Western and African music.
Kheops Nightclub Bd du Président Ahmadou Ahidjo, Akwa. Bd de la Liberté end: also
plays Western and African tunes.

Practical information
Air freight
DHL 224 Rue Joss, Bonanjo; tel: 342 98 82/342 36 36

Arts and crafts
Ali Baba Tel: 342 32 13
Coopérative des artisans et paysans Africains Tel: 342 19 81

Banks
There are several near the Hôtel Akwa Palace on Bd de la Liberté, including **Standard
Chartered Bank** (57 Bd de la Liberté, Akwa; tel: 342 36 12) and **Ecobank**. Banks are also
grouped together on Rue Joss in Bonanjo, just before Pl du Gouvernement, and include
Société Générale de Banques au Cameroun (SGBC) (78 Rue Joss; tel: 342 70 10)
which has an ATM; **Société Commercial de Banque-Crédit Lyonnais** (Rue Joss; tel:
342 65 01); and **Afriland First Bank**. **Banque Internationale du Cameroun Pour
l'Epargne et le Crédit (Bicec)** is at Av de Gaulle (tel: 342 84 31). **SCB-Crédit
Lyonnais** is at Rue Joss, Bonanjo (tel: 342 65 02).

Bookshops
Librairie Papétérie de Bonapriso 10 Rue Batibois, Bonapriso; tel: 342 63 67. Stocks
English-language publications.
Lipacam 27 Av Ahidjo; tel: 342 04 69
Afrique Papyrus Bd de la Liberté, Akwa. Good for English and French publications.
Hôtel Le Méridien Bookshop 35 Av de Cocotiers; tel: 342 50 00

Cinema
Films are usually in French.
Le Concorde Av King Akwa, near Rue Boue Lapeyrère, Akwa
Le Wouri Bd de la Liberté, Akwa; tel: 342 02 52. Occasionally has live theatre and music
events too.
Cinema Rex Bd du Président Ahmadou Ahidjo, Akwa
Bonapriso Av de l'Indépendance, Bonapriso

Cultural centres
British Council Bd de la Liberté, Akwa; tel: 342 51 45; email:
info.douala@britishcouncil.cm. For occasional events and language courses at its centre at
1.387 Rue Joffre. It has a cyber centre, and BBC programmes are shown.
Centre Culturel Français Bd de la Liberté; tel: 342 69 96. Occasional events like
concerts, films, theatre, music and talks.

Internet access
Cyberix Bd de la Liberté, Akwa; tel: 343 75 50
Cyber Bazaar Av de Gaulle, near Rue Pierre Loti, Bonanjo; tel: 342 60 36
Cyberbao Internet Café 1482 Bd de la Liberté, Akwa; tel: 342 29 16
Dot.com Bd de la Liberté, Akwa
Square Net Av de Gaulle, on junction with Av de l'Indépendance, Bonapriso
Global Net Tel: 341 02 72

Mail

Poste Centrale (main post office) Pl du Gouvernement, Bonanjo
Poste d'Akwa Bd de la Liberté, Akwa
Poste de Deido Rue Dibombe, Deido
Poste de New Bell Av Douala Manga Bell, by Pl de l'Indépendance, New Bell

Hospitals and clinics

Polyclinique de Bonanjo Av de Gaulle, Bonanjo; tel: 342 79 36/342 17 80. A private medical clinic situated by the Hôtel Ibis; highly rated by expatriates.
General Hospital Bassa; tel: 337 01 44/337 02 48/337 08 48
Clinique Bel Air 680 de la Rue Toyota (Rue no 1.239), Bonapriso; tel: 342 82 84/342 89 13. A small clinic with three beds for in-patients.
Laquintini Hospital Tel: 342 23 10

Dentists

Dr Bernard Zipfel 2ème étage, Immeuble Neuilly II, Av de Gaulle, Bonanjo; tel: 342 01 98/343 37 12. Appointments for temporary residents/travellers average around CFA25,000–30,000 (£26–32/US$47–56).
Dr Caroline Eyidi 1871 Bd de la Liberté, Akwa; tel: 343 49 51. Appointments start at around CFA6,000 (£6/US$11).
Dr Claudette Nouni Panka Bonanjo; tel: 342 22 03. Another centrally located dentist.

Pharmacies

Pharmacie Joss off Rue Joss, Bonanjo, next to Amity Bank and by Pl du Gouvernement. Open 24 hours.
Pharmacie de Douala 1017 Bd du Président Ahmadou Ahidjo, Akwa; tel: 342 74 80. Open 24 hours.
Pharmacie de l'Aeroport 1934 Bd des Nations Unies, Bassa; tel: 342 28 76
Pharmacie de Bonapriso Rue Tokoto, Bonapriso; tel: 343 48 61
Pharmacie de la Gare 1079 Bd de la Réunification, Deido; tel: 340 18 70
Pharmacie du Plateau 854 Rue Njo-Njo, Bonapriso; tel: 342 05 80. Open 24 hours.
Pharmacie de la République 668 Bd de la République, Akwa; tel: 342 09 98. Open 24 hours.

Photographic processing

Procolor Bd de la Liberté, Akwa. Developing and printing a 36-exposure colour negative film costs CFA7,500 (£8/US$14).
Photo Logona Tel: 343 92 34
Laboratoire Photo Prunet 545 Rue Pau, Akwa; tel: 342 08 67

Fitness and sports

Centre de Peche Sportive de Douala Tel: 343 02 93
Association Equestre de Douala BP 1157; tel: 342 03 84/981 94 15. Horseriding.
Golf Club de Likomba BP 156; tel: 35 11 73. Golf club located at Tiko, 40km from Douala.
Club PAD (Port Autonome de Douala) Bd de Gaulle, Bonanjo; tel: 342 51 21. Tennis, swimming and basketball.
KSA Fitness Centre Tel: 343 03 84
Atraf Fitness Clinic BP 84; tel: 343 70 23. Gym, aerobics, karate, Kung Fu, yoga, Tae Kwondo, table-tennis, basketball, sauna.
Centre de Remise en Form BP 15453; Rue Copseco, Bonapriso; tel: 342 70 20. Gym, step, karate, judo, Tae Kwondo.

Swimming The Hôtel Akwa Palace and Le Méridien Hotel have good swimming pools available to non-guests for a small fee.

Supermarkets
An extensive range that includes luxury – and pricey – foods imported from Europe is available south of the centre in Bonapriso from **Unimarché** on Rue Tokoto and from **Score Supermarché** nearby off Rue Tokoto. Cheaper options include **Mahima Supermarché** (BP 15430; tel. 343 44 87/342 73 38) on Bd du Président Ahmadou Ahidjo and **Onashi Supermarché** (BP 5527; tel: 342 6182/343 0190) at 421 Rue Alfred Saker, both in the Akwa district.

Tourist office
Delegation Provinciale du Tourisme Av de Gaulle, Bonanjo; tel: 342 11 71/342 14 22. Can provide some basic information about hotels, attractions and excursions.

What to see
Northwards along the Boulevard de la Liberté is the **Akwa Palace**, an old colonial hotel. An expensive place, it is nevertheless a good spot to have a coffee or a beer on the terrace. Northwards, at the junction with Rue Sylvani, is a baptist church built by the Germans in 1899. Lovers of churches will find more than ten in the maze of streets around the New Bell neighbourhood southeast of Akwa. The boulevard continues to the Deido district, which has a lively market. Cross the Wouri bridge for the principally industrial Bonaberi neighbourhood.

Parallel with the Boulevard de la Liberté is Rue Joffre, which is worth walking down as it immerses you into the vibrancy of a bustling market street cluttered with stalls. Curiously, an inordinate number sell stationery, but others sell cheap watches, clothing, fruit, vegetables and cola-nuts.

Near here, just before the port, is the **Temple du Centenaire** or **Eglise Evangelique**. The first European settlers in Douala were English missionaries in the 19th century; the best-known was Alfred Saker, who in 1845 set up a missionary community at the site of this church, which is off, appropriately, Rue Alfred Saker. It was built to commemorate the 100th anniversary of the arrival of Saker.

The missionaries were soon followed by German trading companies that in 1884 signed treaties with the Douala chiefs giving Germany legal rights under German law. The city was named Kamerunstadt and a German governor appointed. In 1907 Kamerunstadt was renamed Douala and became part of the French protectorate after World War I, when massive urban development and industrial growth set it on course to become the major economic centre that it is today.

Also near here, and also off the Boulevard de la Liberté, is the dusty, tree-lined Boulevard du Président Ahmadou Ahidjo, the main shopping street, with department stores and lots of stalls selling anything from football shirts to mattresses. **Boutique Cicam** (BP 4089; 712 Boulevard du Président Ahmadou Ahidjo; tel: 342 61 81; email: afric@camnet.cm) has a great selection of African textiles for sale, with beautiful, vibrant 6m cotton prints starting at CFA5,000 (£5.35/US$9.45). More choice is available at Congo market (Marché Congo) on Rue Congo Paraiso.

The Boulevard du Président Ahmadou Ahidjo becomes a heavily pot-holed mudbath, the Boulevard de l'Unité, where there is a sprawling **market** of seemingly endless stalls.

Move southwards along the wide, bustling Boulevard de la Liberté and you come to a neo-Romanesque, 1930s-built, pale green and cream building, the city's **Catholic Cathedral of Saints Peter and Paul**. You can't miss it.

The cathedral is open from 06.15 to 18.30 daily and on Sundays has a 06.30 choral mass, an 08.00 English mass, a 09.30 mass in the Douala language, an 11.00 mass in French and Latin and an 18.30 mass in French. The interior consists of red brickwork, a wood-panelled ceiling and vivid stained glass. Opposite the cathedral is a graveyard in the tropical style.

A little further on from here, as Rue Joss crosses a bridge over Boulevard de la Gare, there is a large expanse of lush greenery, a reminder of the huge amount of rainfall the city receives during the year.

South of the cathedral, the Boulevard de la Liberté leads into the Bonanjo district, the administrative sector of the city with a large square, the Place du Gouvernement, and various banks and offices.

The area around the **Place du Gouvernement** is like a sleepy provincial town when compared with Akwa, and the square itself is a sweet but rather tatty little scrap of a park. The main post office dominates the square and there is a World War II monument commemorating Général Leclerc. There is also a striking **pagoda**, built in 1904 and once the home of Prince Rudolph Manga Bell, and now housing a restaurant. Next to it is a surprisingly swish gallery with a small café housing modern African art, the **Espace doual'art** (tel: 342 32 59). Other art galleries in the city include Galerie Mam (tel: 342 28 63) and Les Galeries Continents (tel: 342 14 07).

Off the Place du Gouvernement is the **Musée de Douala** (open Monday–Friday 08.00–14.00, Saturday 08.00–12.00, CFA1,000/£1.07/US$1.89),

BIRDING SITE GUIDE
Keith Barnes

The Sanaga River runs near to the village of Edea and is an excellent place to see grey pratincole. It is possible to reach this site either from Douala or from Edea. The forest about 50km south of Douala is also excellent and warrants a few hours of birding.

Birding Sanaga River

Driving in the direction of Yaoundé from Douala, one finds excellent forest after about 50km. Here pied, piping, white-thighed and black-casqued wattled hornbills can be found. Red-vented and blue-billed malimbe, splendid glossy starling, bristle-nosed and yellow-spotted barbet and speckled tinkerbird may also be seen. Watch overhead for Sabine's spinetail and Bates' swift. The Sanaga River lies 60km east of Douala en route to Yaoundé (N3) near the town of Edea. Just before crossing the Sanaga River, turn right on the dirt road to Dizangue and drive for 10km until the road runs alongside the Sanaga River. From here follow the riverbank and check the sandbanks in the river for grey pratincole and African skimmer. The magical white-throated blue swallow can also occasionally be seen hawking up and down the river; check exposed rocks on the river as they sometimes perch on these. The sandbanks run for 5–6km depending on the water levels. It is possible to get fishermen to take you out on to the river, so that you can walk on the sandbanks. These also hold Senegal thick-knee and white-crowned lapwing. It is also worthwhile checking the bridge across the Sanaga River on the N3 near Edea; scan the telephone wires for Preuss' cliff swallows, and the reeds along the river for orange weaver.

located unobtrusively on the first floor of the Hôtel de Ville (the town hall). The museum is rather jumbled and erratic but is certainly worth a visit. Highlights include some clay Bamoun statues and a bronze cast, wooden Fang statues, colourful Douala pirogue decorations, a Fulani suit of mail with spears, Bamiléké thrones and Bamoun pictures.

Further south is the Joss district, which contains some German colonial buildings. Despite their general state of disrepair, UNESCO has classified the buildings as a World Heritage Site. Further west, towards the river, is the Presidential Palace, but this must not be photographed if you want to avoid trouble.

The arts and crafts market, the **Centre Artisanal de Douala**, has a good selection of artefacts and is situated at the Marché des Fleurs, 3km south of the centre off Avenue de Gaulle in the Bonapriso district, a main residential area of Douala.

East of the centre, the bustling Lagos and Kassalafam neighbourhoods offer lively markets including Cameroon's biggest, the **Marché Central** (or Marché de Lagos), south of Avenue Douala Manga Bell. Various ingredients for traditional African medicines are sold outside the mosque by the Place de l'Indépendance nearby and the market becomes the fruit and vegetable market, Marché de Kassalafam.

Around Douala
Maka Castle
North of Douala, about 8km from the town of Dibombari, is the German-built castle of Maka, which features a 30m-high tower and a 300m-long tunnel under the Djouki River.

EDEA
About 50km east of Douala on the main N3 road is the attractive town of Edea, home of the Bassa and Bakoko peoples. Edea has an impressive bridge spanning the Sanaga River, built by the Germans in 1903, which is 180m long. It also has plenty of shops, banks, a post office, a market and even a hydro-electric plant to admire.

Where to stay in Edea
Hostellerie La Sanaga BP 54; tel: 346 49 62/346 43 11. A comfortable hotel, with double rooms for around CFA25,000 (£26/US$47).
Carrefour Hotel BP 56; tel: 346 48 18. Government-rated one-star hotel with 22 rooms, satellite TV, restaurant and bar.
Hôtel Relais BP 239. Simple, inexpensive hotel with 18 rooms, satellite TV, bar, restaurant and nightclub.

Around Edea
Lake Ossa
Near Edea to the west, a few kilometres north of the town of Dizangue, is Lake Ossa, created by tectonic movements occurring within the Earth's crust. It is popular for fishing and various watersports and is surrounded by forest.

Douala-Edea Reserve
Southwest of Edea and sandwiched between Douala and Kribi is the Douala-Edea Reserve, which features a wide variety of fauna and flora as well as Lake Tissongo. Bordered on its northern edge by the Sanaga River and on its western edge by the Atlantic Ocean, it features a wide range of habitats.

NKONGSAMBA

Lying 135km from Douala, this sizeable town with a population of 110,000 is dominated by the 2,411m Mount Manengouba, which has two stunning crater lakes at its summit. Another local attraction is the Chutes d'Ekom, a magnificent waterfall.

Where to stay in Nkongsamba

Fere Hotel BP 368. A government-rated one-star hotel with 19 rooms, a bar and restaurant.

Hôtel Le Parisien BP 182; tel: 349 33 48. Basic accommodation for CFA6,000 (£6/US$11).

Hôtel du Moungo BP 18; tel: 349 12 17/349 14 57. Government-rated one-star hotel with 42 rooms, bar and restaurant.

Hôtel La Forêt Tel: 349 23 84. Small basic hotel.

Where to stay in Bangem

Prestige Inn Town Sq. Simple but acceptable accommodation, with shared facilities. CFA5,000 (£5.35/US$9.45) for a room.

CPDM Party House Melong Rd. Basic accommodation, CFA4,000 (£4.28/US$7.56) for a double room.

Chutes d'Ekom

Thirty kilometres down the road from Bafang are the impressive 80m-high Chutes d'Ekom on the Nkam River. To reach these you turn off the N5 road on to a track with a sign saying 'Chefferie de Bayong/Chutes'. The waterfall is another 12km or so from here and the last section is not accessible by car, and all of it may be impassable during the rainy season.

The Manengouba twin crater lakes

These stunning sacred lakes, the smaller, algae-green 'Man Lake' and the bigger, deep-blue 'Woman Lake', are situated within the large grass-covered volcanic depression at Manengouba, on the border with South West Province.

They are easily reached by walking from the pleasant town of Bangem, just over the provincial border in South West Province, which is about 40km north of Nyasoso (a three-hour drive on a good day) and home of the Bakossi people. May 2004 saw the launch of the Mount Manengouba Dream Race, a new national athletic competition.

Visitors to the lakes are required to register and pay CFA1,000 (£1.07/US$1.89) at the police station next to the CPDM Party House (which provides simple accommodation) on the Melong road in Bangem, leaving town. The lakes are a hilly three-hour walk from the town. Start by leaving town on 2nd Street, staying on the main track which becomes more and more feint and gradually climbs to the steep edge of the crater to reach the 2,411m/7,910ft summit of Mount Manengouba. You should now be able to see the level floor of the depression. If you continue across the crater towards the mountain tops on the other side of the crater you come to the Woman Lake. Take a short climb up the little hill on the right to reach the Man Lake, which is surrounded by steep wooded slopes.

Camping, fishing and swimming are only allowed at the Woman Lake. This is an especially good region for hiking. Numerous myths surround the area including the belief that years ago throwing a stone in the lake would cause it to bounce back and kill the thrower.

Southwest Province

This fertile region bordering Nigeria on its west side offers Mount Cameroon to marvel at, beaches to relax upon (at the old colonial town of Limbé), and beautiful crater lakes to explore. It's also home to the inviting Korup National Park.

The eastern edge of South West Province roughly follows a volcanic mountain range that stretches from Mount Cameroon on the coast to the Bamenda Highlands. The mountain range continues northwards, taking in the Adamawa Highlands, Atlantika Mountains and Mandara Mountains in the extreme north.

Inland, the region is often called the Grassfields. Popular crops here include the starchy root vegetable cassava, groundnuts (peanuts), cocoa and coffee. Bamenda and Bafoussam are prominent cities in this region.

LIMBE

The pretty little port of Limbé, 74km from Douala, 31km from Buéa and 96km from Kumba, is situated on a bay of the Gulf of Guinea at the foot of Mount Cameroon. The bay is sandwiched between the mass of Mount Cameroon on one side and Bioko (or Bioco) Island, which is part of Equatorial Guinea and is essentially another big volcano, rising out of the sea on the other.

This easy-going small-scale resort town with a population of about 50,000 is a welcome respite from overwhelming, chaotic Douala and boasts beautiful palm vistas, a lively, traditional market and British and German colonial architecture.

Limbé (which was known as Victoria until 1982) was founded in 1858 when the Baptist Missionary Society of London, needing a base, asked former naval engineer turned missionary Alfred Saker to buy land around Ambas Bay from King William of Bimbia, and this land became the town.

The town was largely populated by Bimbia peoples and slaves from nearby countries like Liberia and Ghana who had been freed. The initial church influence in the town was soon overshadowed by English and German commerce, but Victoria remained the responsibility of the missionaries rather than Britain or Germany.

Presbyterian missionaries from Switzerland bought the land from the Baptists in 1887, by which time Cameroon was a German colony, Kamerun. Victoria was central to this colony both economically and politically, until it became part of the British protectorate in 1915.

Cocoa, palm, rubber and banana plantations around Victoria increased and expanded significantly after World War II, and many remain today.

In recent years Limbé has been at the forefront of the anglophone opposition in the west of the country to the unfair degree of power and influence the francophone majority has over Cameroon.

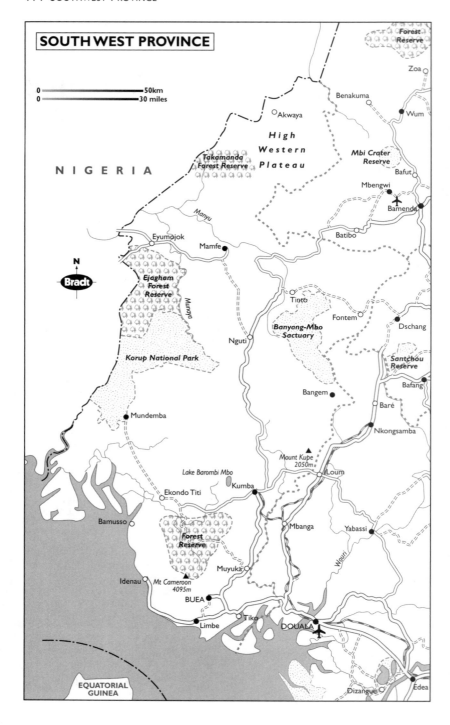

The town today retains little of its former importance. The principal economic activity appears to be based around accommodating weekend holidaymakers, especially expatriates from nearby Douala, who flock here outside the rainy season.

The attractive beaches of Ambas Bay (well, attractive at least in the dry season) are a short drive out of town, and are a popular weekend getaway from Douala. Beware of the oil that sometimes builds up in the sea.

A canoe race is held, usually between December and March each year, in the Atlantic waters around Limbé. The event features traditional dances and music from the nearby coastal villages of Wovia, Botaland, Bimbia and Idenao. There are also traditional Bakweiri wrestling tournaments during the dry season throughout the region.

As for the layout of the town, moving eastwards along Idenao Road by the Limbé River you come to the Atlantic Beach Hotel and the main street containing an old Presbyterian church, various banks and the Presbook bookstore and Prescraft centre, which sells local art. Further east are a fish market, a government school of the German colonial era and Down Beach.

Limbé is liveliest around Half Mile Junction, where Douala Road and Church Street intersect, at Limbé's only traffic lights. The long-running nearby Bakassi border dispute with Nigeria has in recent years caused there to be a good number of sailors in the town, which can certainly liven things up at night.

Eastwards, along Church Street, are a number of bars and stalls selling street food. Most of the population of the town live away from the shoreline, in shanty town suburbs in valleys hidden from the resort by the clefts and spurs of the mountain.

Getting there and away
Bus and taxi
If you are coming to Limbé from Douala, be sure to tell your driver, otherwise you may end up in Kumba instead, which is further north. Taxis cost CFA5,000 (£5.35/US$9.45). Make sure your driver is sober. You're likely to see lots of accidents at the side of the road from Douala to Limbé.

Coming from Douala, typically you will be dropped off at a roundabout of sorts, the motor park at Mile 4, about 5km north of the centre on the Buéa road, where you can await the next local bus for Limbé, which drops you outside the centre. A taxi to the centre costs around CFA500 (53p/94c). Share-taxis for Kumba, Buéa and Douala can also be picked up here.

The motor park has minibuses to Buéa (CFA400/42p/75c, 45 minutes, 30km), Douala (CFA1,000/£1.07/US$1.89, 90 minutes – compared with CFA15,000/£16/US$28 if you chartered a taxi – 75km) and Kumba (CFA1,500/£1.60/US$2.83, 150 minutes, 100km). All day departures are from Half Mile Junction in the centre of town.

Guaranti Express operates a service from Limbé at Mile 2 on the Buéa road to Douala, Yaoundé, Bamenda and Bafoussam, while Patience Express departs from the Buéa road about a kilometre from the centre, opposite the hospital. Yaoundé costs CFA5,000 (£5.35/9.45), while Bamenda and Bafoussam are CFA4,000 (£4.28/US$7.56).

Share-taxis for the beaches at Mile 11 and Batoké go from Idenao Road, near the stadium.

By boat
Weekly boats sail to Malabo, Equatorial Guinea. More details are available from Achouka, which is signposted on the Idenao road, a little under 2km after the Botanic Garden.

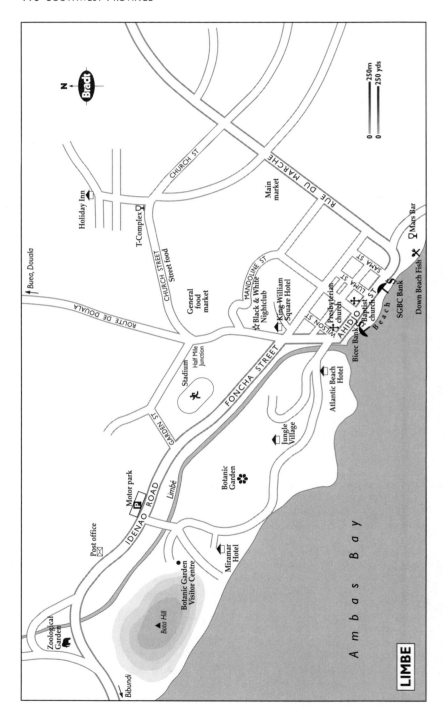

Seagrams Voyages (tel: 333 21 41), on the seafront, arranges a number of tours from Limbé from CFA10,000 (£10/US$18) per person for a minimum of two people. These include four-hour boat trips up the Ndian River to Mundemba and Korup National Park, costing around CFA30,000 (£32/US$56) per person. You're likely to see a good selection of wildlife, especially monkeys and birds, on this trip.

Ferries regularly depart from Limbé port to Calabar/Oron in Nigeria, but as you will be passing the Bakassi Peninsula, the focus of a long-standing Cameroon–Nigeria border dispute, check the situation locally before booking.

Where to stay

For security reasons, camping is not recommended on the beaches around Limbé.

Park Miramar Hotel BP 63; tel: 332 23 32/333 29 41. Run by the Atlantic Beach Hotel, this hotel 2km west of the centre of town is simple but clean and enjoys good views of Ambas Bay. Accommodation is in very clean and affordable *boukarous* (thatched huts) and some rooms have AC. There is also a restaurant and pool. Manager Moses is very welcoming and helpful. CFA10,000 (£10/US$18) single, CFA12,000–14,000 (£12–15/US$22–26) double.

Atlantic Beach Hotel BP 63; tel: 333 23 32/333 26 89. Originally the Botanic Garden research laboratory, this was once Limbé's best hotel but it is now distinctly shabby. There are 49 air-conditioned rooms and two suites, although increasingly showers/lights and other fittings are broken. There is a swimming pool, an expensive bar (CFA700/75p/US$1.32 for a small beer) and a good French/Cameroonian restaurant (king prawn and rice CFA4,000/£4.28/US$7.56) overlooking the sea. Rooms start at CFA16,500 (£17/US$31) for a single, and double rooms facing the sea are CFA23,500 (£25/US$44) and CFA19,500 (£20/US$36) facing the gardens, including a coffee and croissant breakfast. A more spacious garden apartment is CFA50,000 (£53/US$94). Non-guests can use the swimming pool for CFA1,000 (£1.07/US$1.89).

Bay Hotel BP 63; tel: 333 23 32/333 26 89. A colonial building near Limbé's main roundabout enjoying a good view of the bay. There are 23 en-suite rooms past their prime with fans or AC and a nearby restaurant. Co-owned by the Atlantic Beach Hotel, whose pool is available to guests. CFA6,500 (£6.96/US$12.28) single, CFA12,000 (£12.86/US$22.68) double.

Victoria Guest House BP 358; tel: 333 24 46. Next to the Bay Hotel. Simple but clean lodgings, with most of the 22 rooms air conditioned or having a fan and a bathroom. There is a restaurant and bar. From CFA6000 (£6.43/US$11.34) single, CFA10,000 (£10.70/US$18.90) double.

Botanic Garden Guest House BP 437; tel: 333 26 20. This colonial building in pretty surroundings offers shared dorms and a campsite. CFA1,000 (£1.07/US$1.89) per person for camping, CFA3,000 (£3.21/US$5.67) in the dorms.

King William Square Hotel Tel: 333 27 29/774 72 11. Off the main roundabout near the beach front, this hotel has basic but clean rooms with AC for around CFA9,000 (£9.64/US$17.01). The hotel can organise tours of the area.

Holiday Inn Resort Hotel BP 126; tel: 333 22 90. Northwards off Church St at the end of the road, this clean, comfortable hotel has 22 air-conditioned rooms with bathroom, TV and a good-value restaurant, bar and beer garden. Single CFA10,000 (£10/US$18), double CFA15,000 (£16/US$28).

Bevista Hotel BP 227; tel: 333 26 35. About 1.5km west of the centre, the hotel has simple en-suite rooms with AC or fan and a swimming pool. Rooms are CFA5,000–10,000/£5–10/US$18–36.

Tabai Park Hotel BP 10; tel: 333 26 22. Mid-range hotel with 36 rooms, bar, restaurant and swimming pool.

Tiko, outside Limbé on the Douala Road, has a couple of inexpensive hotels, the **Airport Hotel** and the **Park Hotel**, with basic rooms.

Where to eat and drink

There are lots of alternatives to the more expensive fare offered at the hotel restaurants. Each evening down the Bimbia road, by the fish market at Down Beach, grilled fish with grilled plantain are on offer. In the evenings street food vendors also appear around Half Mile Junction, Douala Road and Church Street. Church Street has a number of cheap restaurants and bars too.

Xplanade Bar On the beach and near the Atlantic Beach Hotel and the old church, this is a great spot to watch the fishermen. Food stalls either side of the bar offer grilled king prawns for CFA1,000 (£1.07/US$1.89) or sea bass with cassava or plantain for CFA1,500 (£1.60/US$2.83).
The Bella Restaurant Tel: 333 26 40. Just off Idenao Rd west of the stadium. Offers both good Cameroonian and European food for around CFA2,500–4,000 (£2.67/US$4.72).
Lady L Restaurant Church St. Has a sign stating 'where beauty merges with class'. If beauty is a rutted car park, OK, but the menu is interesting, with gizzard stew and fufu and stockfish soup and fufu, all CFA2,000 (£2.14/US$3.78).
Anepps Burger Off the road to Down Beach, for a fix of Western fast food, such as the omnipresent burger and chips.
T-Complex Bar Church St. A good spot for a drink and also offers burgers, chicken and chips, and similar fare, as well as more exotic choices.
A good spot for a sunset drink, chicken and chips or seafood (shrimps and rice CFA2,500/£2.67/US$4.72) is the comparatively upmarket **Mars Bar** with its perspex cage at the sea wall on Down Beach.

Nightlife

The Limbé Palace Nightclub One of the best clubs in Limbé, playing both Western and Cameroonian music. Entrance CFA2,000–5,000 (£2.14–5.35/US$3.78–9.45) and drinks typically CFA2,000.
The Black and White Night Club Next door to the Limbé Palace; has similar prices but is slightly shabbier.

Practical information

Banks
Bicec, **SGBC**, **Amity** and **Crédit Lyonnais** are on the main road on the waterfront. Surprisingly rarely for Cameroon (outside Douala and Yaoundé), euros, dollars and sterling can be changed.

Hospital
Limbé Provincial Hospital Tel: 333 23 53

Internet access
Web Center Tel: 333 23 76

Mail
Post office Idenao Rd. Past the entrance to the Botanical Garden, leaving the centre of town.

Tourist office
Fako Tourist Office Tel: 333 25 36; email: ftb@camnet.cm. Opposite the Crédit Lyonnais Bank on the waterfront, they can organise boat trips to the nearby islands.

What to see
The islands
The bay is dotted with fishing boats, numerous ships and a variety of small uninhabited islands, known as the Bota Islands, some of which have the remnants of buildings. They are still used for traditional ceremonies and the largest island has carved stone steps that can be climbed. You can ask one of the fishermen to take you to the nearby islands (ask on the beach) or your hotel or the tourist office (details below) can fix up a trip. Either way. the cost is around CFA20,000–30,000 (£21–32/US$37–56). Pirogues can also be hired for considerably less.

Limbé Botanical Gardens
PO Box 437, Idenao Rd; tel: 343 18 83/343 18 72; email: info@mcbcclimbe.org; web: www.mcbcclimbe.org. Admission CFA1,000/£1.07/US$1.89, open 06.00–18.00 daily.

Adjacent to the centre of the town and just to the west, are the impressive Limbé Botanical Gardens, founded a century ago by German horticulturists to introduce new economic and medicinal crops to Cameroon such as quinine, coffee, cocoa, rubber, tea and bananas. The shady gardens served as a training centre in agriculture, horticulture and forestry and are now an international research centre. The gardens were neglected for many years but recently they have been restored and are connected to the Mount Cameroon Project, which promotes ecological preservation. Guided tours of the gardens are available.

The gardens are ideal for a tranquil stroll and feature a so-called 'jungle village', with cultural activities for visitors, and there are various walks including a coastal trail, a biodiversity trail, a riverside trail (where many impressive trees, creepers and other plants can be seen), and an adventure trail, which features some wild animals. The Hot Spot bar/restaurant overlooking the bay is ideally placed for a meal or a drink while visiting the gardens.

Limbé Zoological Garden
Limbé is also home to one of the world's only (there are fewer than 20) primate sanctuaries, which has been established at the site of the town's old and neglected zoo by the Botanical Gardens. The centre is internationally renowned and houses chimpanzees, gorillas, drills, mandrills, red-capped mangabeys, guenon, crocodiles, snakes and duikers, and often houses the orphans of apes killed for bushmeat. Admission is CFA1,000 (£1.07/US$1.89) plus CFA1,000 per camera and it is open from 09.00 to 17.00 daily.

AROUND LIMBE
The beaches west of Limbé
To the west of town, with Mount Cameroon towering above them, are a number of beautiful beaches bordered by tropical vegetation. Some of the beaches feature in the film *Chocolat*. Rarely for the region, the waters are generally suitable for bathing although the currents can at times be strong. The fine sand is dark brown, created from ancient lava flows from Mount Cameroon.

To get to the beaches, taxis and share-taxis are available from the Batoké motor park by the sports stadium near Half Mile Junction in Limbé.

At Mile 6 on the Idenao road there is a signpost to a popular public beach of grey volcanic sands, by an oil refinery, which costs CFA500 (50p/92c) to enter. It has some monkeys that may pester you and a snack bar open during weekends.

At Mile 8 is Batoké fishing village, a better option, with a beautiful beach bordered by mountains where lava flows from a few years ago can be seen on the slopes. It is usually free, but the nearby hotel, the Etisah, sometimes charges a small fee.

Moving further west, you come to the guarded and remote tree-lined beach at Mile 11 near the 1999 lava flows. A CFA1,000 fee is payable at the Seme New Beach Resort Hotel here. You are not allowed to bring your own food and drinks.

The metalled road to Ideano passes further good beaches and at Mile 17 it reaches Cape Debundscha, which is notable for being the second-wettest place on Earth, with more than 10,000mm rainfall per year. The wettest place, according to the *Guinness Book of Records*, is currently Mawsynvan in Maghalaya State, India, with 11,873mm/467in annually.

Where to stay
Coastal Beach Hotel Mile 6; tel: 333 29 27. The good-standard rooms here have AC and bathroom and satellite TV for CFA16,000 (£17/US$30).
Etisah Hotel Batoké, Mile 8; tel: 997 49 98/998 32 39; email: etisah.beach@yahoo.fr. Signposted from the main road and about 350m from the beach, this hotel has simple rooms with fans or better ones with AC for around CFA10,000–18,000 (£10–19/ US$18–34), and a restaurant serving meals from about CFA3,500 (£3.75/US$6.61).
Seme New Beach Hotel Mile 11; tel: 333 27 69; email: camrevtour@camnet.cm. The comfortable air-conditioned rooms here have either a shower- or bathroom and are around CFA20,000 (£21/US$37). There is also a quite pricey restaurant, and a small beer at the bar will set you back CFA1,200 (£1.28/US$2.26). There is a natural swimming/rock pool with ice-cold spring water from Mount Cameroon, a private beach, nightclub, secure parking and tennis courts.
First International Inn Sonara Rd; tel: 333 26 97; email: dgi.pise@camnet.cm. There are 18 rooms here from around CFA10,000–22,000 (£10–20/US$18–36), plus bungalows, and a restaurant serving fish, African and European dishes.

West of Limbé
Cape Debundscha and the Boana Falls
The visitor centre at the Botanical Gardens in Limbé can provide a guide to take you to Cape Debundscha's crater lake, the old German lighthouse and also to the Bomana Falls (you can charter a taxi or take a share-taxi the 48km to Idenao for the latter), which are reached by trekking through thick forest.

North of Limbé
Engelbert Church
To the north of Limbé it is a pleasant uphill walk from the market of about 6km to reach Bonjongo and Engelbert Church, a splendid German Palatine Mission Church built in 1894. The hill, known as 'the Hill of Angels', boasts an impressive view of Ambas Bay.

Small Mount Cameroon (Mount Etinde)
From Bonjongo you can spend a day trekking up a sub-peak of Mount Cameroon, Mount Etinde (1,713m), which is also known as Small Mount Cameroon. An extinct volcano, it can be reached on foot from Limbé, which makes for a very long day by the time you return (the climb, via Ekonjo, takes an afternoon or so). Alternatively, take a share-taxi to Batoké village and then a further taxi to one of the villages at the base of the mountain, Etome (also known as Etumba) or Ekonjo.

Guides for the trek (from CFA7,000/£7.50/US$13.23 per day) are available from Cameroon Rev'Tours (tel: 342 10 05; email: camrevtours@camnet.cm) based at the Seme New Beach Hotel or from the visitor centre at the Limbé Botanical Gardens through the Mount Cameroon Ecotourism Organisation, which also has an office in Buéa. There is also a CFA3,000 (£3.21/US$5.67) fee per person plus a small fee for the local chief. Make sure you are clear about all fees beforehand, and whether you are providing food and drink for the guide on top, and ensure you have adequate food and drink for your party.

South of Limbé
Going southwards from Limbé, towards Mabeta, takes you past an army camp at Man O'War Bay after about 10km, and then the village of Bimbia, where the missionaries first arrived in Cameroon in the 1840s. There's a Baptist church here and some inexpensive bungalows that are bookable through the Saker Baptist Mission in Limbé (BP29; tel: 333 23 23).

Another 2km further on from Bimbia is the Mabeta Moliwe Reserve, with lowland rainforest and mangrove, and a two/three-hour nature trail that goes from Bimbia to Bonadikombo along a river towards the sea. Guides are obtainable at Bimbia or from the Botanical Gardens.

BUEA
Seventy kilometres and just an hour's drive northwest of Douala (and a regular *agences de voyage* route at just CFA1,000/£1.07/US$1.89), Buéa (pronounced 'boyah') is the most popular gateway to an invigorating yet perfectly possible climb up Mount Cameroon – but little else.

Being more than 1,000m above the sea (and a half-hour drive from the coast), located on the lower slopes of the mountain amid beautiful scenery, it is relatively cool, generally offering a refreshingly comfortable climate, especially during the dry season, from late November to February. Its trim tea gardens make it almost an African version of Darjeeling. After increasing cloud and rain in March and April, rain falls nearly every day from May onwards, and the town loses its charm somewhat.

Buéa was the German colonial capital from 1901, but only until 1909. During British rule, the town was under the authority of the Southern Provinces of Nigeria and the population greatly reduced. Soon after independence, Buéa's importance increased again when it became the capital of the anglophone Western Cameroon in 1961, but again this distinction was short-lived, as 11 years later the post-independence federation became a republic, and Buéa reverted to being the capital of South West Province only when Yaoundé was made the country's sole capital.

The sleepy town, now with around 60,000 inhabitants, many of them Bakweiris, boasts some interesting German colonial architecture, including a school, various administrative and commercial buildings, and homes and a palace built for German colonial governor Jesco von Puttkamer. It is now used by the president, so don't take photos.

Buéa has various facilities, including a post office and petrol station. The hospital (tel: 332 32 29) is located near the Mermoz Hotel.

Getting there and away
The motor park for transport to Douala, Limbé and Kumba is about 5km from the centre at Mile 17 along the Limbé road.

It is possible to walk to Limbé (around 22km) down the main roads going south from the Mermoz Hotel.

If you are thinking of moving on to Nigeria, Buéa has a Nigerian consulate (tel: 332 25 28), although it can be difficult for foreigners to obtain visas here and the consulate may require that you visit the high commission in Yaoundé for this.

If you are planning to visit Korup National Park, Buéa is 256km from Mamfé and 184km from Mundemba.

Where to stay

Mount Cameroon Ecotourism Organisation Guesthouse PO Box 60; tel: 332 20 38; email: mountceo@iccnet2000.cm. The organisation has very good-value, clean and spacious rooms in Buéa at CFA3,000 per person, although it can only accommodate four people, in two doubles.

Hôtel Mermoz BP 13, Long St; tel: 332 23 49. Quite newly renovated, but a recent guest reports that the hotel was dirty and had 'a really bad vibe'. The slightly better rooms are on the second floor and cost from CFA7,000 (£7.50/US$13.23), while those on the ground floor cost from CFA5,000 (£5.35/9.45). Both come with a shower and a TV. There is a restaurant and bar. It's a bit noisy.

Presbyterian Mission BP 19; tel: 332 23 36. Set in gardens, with very clean rooms with shared or separate facilities from CFA5,000 (£5.35/US$9.45) per person. It is past the police station roundabout and up the hill, about 800m southwest of Buéa market. There is a communal kitchen for which there is a small charge. You can also camp in the grounds for CFA1,000 (£1.07/US$1.89) per person.

Parliamentarian Flats Hotel BP 20; tel: 332 24 59. A short walk south of the police station roundabout, this government-owned hotel has good, clean, self-contained rooms, a restaurant, bar and a good view of the mountain. Singles CFA7,500 (£8.03/US$14.17), doubles CFA10,000 (£10.70/US$18.90).

Paramount Hotel Tel: 332 20 74. A hotel that has recently opened, with good, clean rooms from CFA8,000 (£8.57/US$15.12) and a bar and restaurant.

Miss Bright Guesthouse Tel: 995 17 44. Basic accommodation after Mile 17 along the Limbé road, 6km out of town.

Mountain Hotel BP 71; tel: 332 22 35/332 22 51. A short walk south of the police station roundabout and graded a three-star hotel by the government, this hotel seems like a tranquil hunting lodge with its aged trophied saloon, complete with carved wooden fireplace. It has an old English-style charm and is a good spot for a drink. There is a swimming pool available to non-guests for a small fee, a garden restaurant, nightclub and 63 clean double rooms. Singles are CFA9,000 (£9.64/US$17.01), doubles CFA15,000 (£16.07/US$28.35).

MOUNT CAMEROON

Mount Cameroon, 180 miles west of the capital of Yaoundé, is one of the country's main tourist attractions. An occasionally active volcano, with its base directly at the ocean floor and its summit nudging the clouds, it covers 1,280km². At 13,500ft high (4,095m), it is also the highest mountain in West Africa and the sixth-highest on the continent. In spite of its height, the mountain is relatively easy to climb, if somewhat arduous, and no particular climbing skills, climbing equipment or experience are needed, only a reasonable level of fitness and determination. The climb is much less strenuous than, say, ascents of Mount Kilimanjaro or Mount Kenya.

The mountain sides are covered in rainforest except for a few swathes of black rock formed by the cooling of recent lava flows. A series of fine beaches line the foot of the mountain, the sand a deep chocolate brown colour from the igneous rock. The lower sections of the mountain are a lush tropical wilderness extending right to the edge of the beach.

Its rugged peak, Great Cameroon, is the crown jewel of a succession of volcanic mountains that are strung like a giant necklace from the southwest to the extreme north of the country. A second distinct summit is the densely forested, 5,820ft

Small Mount Cameroon (1,713m). The entire massif is known locally as Mongo-mo-Ndemi, or Mountain of Greatness.

Mount Cameroon itself is known locally as Mount Fako or as Mongo-ma-Lobo, the Mountain of Thunder. It was described as long ago as 1472 by Portuguese navigator Fernando Po as the seat or the chariot of the gods. It has erupted seven times in the last 100 years, once during the filming of *Greystoke: The Legend of Tarzan*, in 1982, in 1999, and most recently in the spring of 2000, when the eruption lasted about three weeks, causing no casualties. Locals of the Bakweiri ethnic group attribute the recent eruptions to the influences of ancestral spirits because of the recent death of Monono Otto, a Bakweiri traditional chief.

Mount Cameroon is the closest African mountain to any sea coast. It rises from the waters of the Gulf of Guinea, making it a spectacular sight when viewed from the sea. The offshore island of Malabo, the capital of Equatorial Guinea, is south of the mountain. On this island, another volcano, Pico de Santa Isabel, rises to 9,868ft (3,008m).

Mount Cameroon was the site of one of the earliest recorded volcanic eruptions, in 5BC, which was observed by a Carthaginian ship while sailing down the Atlantic coast of Africa.

There are a number of local myths and legends about the mountain. For example, powerful ancestral spirits are said to inhabit the mountain's inner core. A mountain god called Epassa Moto (which when translated means 'half human') is considered the owner and protector of the mountain and permits people to live on and visit it as long as nothing is removed. It is believed that when he gets angry he shakes the ground and spits fire into the air.

Several aircraft on approach to Douala have crashed into the mountain, the last being in 1963 when a DC6 hit the mountain, resulting in 44 deaths.

Its very varied climatic conditions give the mountain its great biodiversity. Despite its equatorial latitude, snow, strong winds and freezing rain can often lash the summit.

The ascent

There are numerous trails, and various route options are possible, passing through a variety of terrains including sub-alpine meadows and dense high-altitude tropical rainforest where no sun filters through. Giant parasitic plants carpet the floor and trees are so big their roots are as thick as small trees. Typically a climb passes habitats of elephants, antelopes, primates and many tropical birds. Hiking here will uncover ever-changing vegetation – there are more than 42 plant species that are strictly endemic and another 50 species that are near-endemic to the mountain – as well as volcanic lava and even, at times, volcanic smoke coming out of the ground under your feet.

To climb the mountain, a permit obtainable from the local tourist office and a guide are compulsory. Many of the guides and porters are ex-hunters.

For the trip the Mount Cameroon Ecotourism Organisation (details below) asks you to bring food for yourself, but you could ask your guide and porter to provide and cook food, which is recommended as long as you like Cameroonian food, since it's a lot easier than planning your own menu. Your guide and porter may expect you to have hired sleeping bags and tents on their behalf, especially since it can get very cold on the mountain, so check beforehand. These and other items like mats and raingear can be hired from the Project office.

The round trip usually takes between one and six days, depending on the trail chosen and your level of fitness. Apart from being gruelling, to do the trip in a day would be so rushed there'd be little time to appreciate the climb or the mountain.

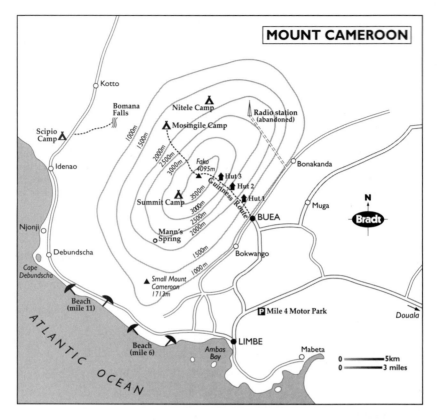

It is possible to shorten some routes by arranging to have a vehicle collect you on the descent. However you do it, it is going to be easier than it was for intrepid Victorian explorer Mary Kingsley, whose famous ascent in 1895 was plagued by camps being washed away by the rains, a string of tropical disease casualties and attacks by swarms of bees.

New trails up the mountain have been introduced in recent years to complement the original, steep and direct so-called Guinness Trail starting at Buéa, which has been neglected and is therefore not the best option. These newer trails are on the southeast face of the mountain because of the regular heavy rainfall and storms afflicting the other sides of the mountain. The southwestern side has an almost continuous rainy season with rainfall of around 10,000mm per year, compared with around 2,000mm at the summit and 3,500mm as an average in the region.

The tourist office on the main road in Buéa (**The Provincial Delegation of Tourism for the South West** BP 20; tel: 332 26 56/332 25 34. Open Monday–Friday 08.00–15.30) organises climbs up the Guinness Trail at a cost of CFA9,000 (£9.64/US$17.01) per person per day.

Climbs using better trails are organised through the **Mount Cameroon Ecotourism Organisation** (PO Box 60; tel: 332 20 38; email: mountceo@iccnet2000.cm. Open Monday–Friday 08.00–17.00, Saturday, Sunday, bank holidays 07.00–13.00), which supports the conservation of the biodiversity of the mountain. Its office is near the Mobil petrol station and the market, which taxi drivers are likely to know.

A trip up Mount Cameroon organised through the Mount Cameroon Ecotourism Organisation costs around CFA14,000 (£15/US$26) per person per day but costs can vary depending upon the size of the party and whether you are climbing to the summit. The costs are made up of fees per day of CFA6,000 (£6.43/US$11.34) for the guide, CFA5,000 (£5.35/US$9.45) for porters and a community fund per person of CFA3,000 (£3.21/US$5.67).

You can typically arrive at the office in Buéa, meet your guide and start your hike up the mountain the same morning, although most people find the preparation for the climb entails an overnight stay in Buéa. There used to be a requirement to buy a bottle of whisky and visit the chief of Bonakanda before going up the mountain, but this is no longer necessary.

The best time to attempt the climb is during the drier months, between November and May. Be prepared for the extremes of temperature: while it can be over 20°C (68°F) at the foot of the mountain, it can be below freezing at the summit, so you will need warm, waterproof clothes and a good sleeping bag if you are staying overnight. Humidity commonly reaches 96% in the summer. Although many climbers wear trainers, waterproof hiking boots with good ankle support are the ideal. Watch out for grass fires during the dry season.

Guinness Trail

On the Guinness Trail there are three very basic mountain huts en route, originally built by the Germans. The first is at 1,850m (about a two-hour walk). Another hour's walk gets you clear of the rainforest. Hut 2 is at an altitude of 2,800m (about three/four hours' walk from hut 1) and hut 3 is at 3,600m, about three/four hours' walk from hut 2. From hut 3 to the summit at Fako Peak (4,100m) you can reckon on a further 90 minutes or so.

Apart from at hut 1, there are very few opportunities to get water on the mountain (which is surprising in one of the wettest regions on earth), so ensure you bring plenty. There may be rainwater collected at hut 2 (the climb from hut 1 to 2 is the toughest section), but don't count on it.

On a good day at hut 2 you can see Buéa, Small Mount Cameroon, Douala, Limbé, the ocean and even Bioko Island (Equatorial Guinea). From hut 2, climbing to the summit is relatively easy, but beware of repeatedly believing you are almost there, as you will constantly see false summits.

Hunters' trails from Bokwango or Mapanja

If instead you follow one of the old hunters' trails from Bokwango or Mapanja, which are south of Buéa, you go through savanna, montane forest and grasslands, and pass lava flows from the 2000 eruption. Again there are good views of Small Mount Cameroon, Bioko Island and the ocean. There are two basic campsites on these routes at clearings in the forest, the first being Mann's Spring, where drinking water is available, and Summit Camp, where you're nearing the peak.

Radio station route

Another newer route starts at the village of Bonakanda, where you follow a so-called 'radio station track' which leads from the village (at around 900m) to about 2,600m before gradually descending to reach an abandoned radio station, now classified as an industrial monument, at 2,500m. The walk is about 15km, but it is not the easiest hike since you gain 1,700m in altitude fairly steeply from the village.

The forest and scrub above Bonakanda varies but logging has resulted in there

BIRDING SITE GUIDE
Keith Barnes

Although large sectors of Mount Cameroon have been deforested, the remaining natural vegetation supports Mount Cameroon francolin and Cameroon speriop, which are found nowhere else in the world, as well as brown-backed cisticola, Cameroon pipit and Bates' weaver, which are Cameroon endemics. Other special species on the mountain are Cameroon olive pigeon, western green tinkerbird, yellow-breasted boubou, green-breasted bush shrike, mountain robin-chat, mountain saw-wing, Cameroon mountain and grey-headed greenbul, green longtail, Cameroon scrub warbler, white-tailed warbler, yellow longbill, black-capped woodland warbler, Fernando Po oliveback, and Cameroon and Ursula's sunbird.

Birding Buéa
Approximately 70km west of Douala, the mountain is accessible from the town of Buéa. It is possible to walk up to 2,000m above sea level, where one can search for Cameroon pipit and Cameroon speriop. Visitors need a permit from the Tourism Office in Buéa.

Birding Limbé
The Botanical Gardens at Limbé can be very rewarding, and interesting species to be seen here include the blue-headed wood-dove, African blue-flycatcher, rufous-vented paradise-flycatcher, Mackinnon's shrike, brown-throated wattle-eye, Cassin's flycatcher, grey-headed nigrita, slender-billed weaver, Vieillot's black weaver, western bluebill, Reichenbach's sunbird, green-headed sunbird and Carmelite sunbird. Tracks up the mountain can be reached from Mapanja, a village just above Limbé.

being little primary forest left. Unfortunately, this is common on the mountain. The forests of the mountain are not currently protected under formal park status. On the eastern side of the mountain, for example, it has been estimated that as much as half of the forest cover has so far been lost.

From about 1,750m to the radio station is grassland. From the radio station you can descend down the northwest slope of the mountain to Nitele, a hunters' camp at an altitude of 1,870m, consisting of three small huts with straw beds. This is around another 7km from the radio station. Here there is some primary forest, starting as high as 2,300m, although much of the forest has been burnt, apparently as a result of fires spreading from the savanna above. Lower down, at about 2,000m, the trail passes through some tall, intact, primary montane forest, then emerges again into an open area of savanna just above Nitele.

The dense vegetation extends as far as the ocean and there are an increasing number of coffee, rubber tree, oil palm and banana plantations here, where the forest has been cleared.

From Nitele, to reach the peak you follow the mountain around, via another basic campsite near Mosingile village.

Descent of the mountain
There are several options for descending the mountain, the quickest and most straightforward simply following the Guinness Trail, which can be done in about

six hours, or following the hunters' trails via Mann's Spring. It is also possible to go down the west face of the mountain from Mosingile village to the village of Kotto, where you can join the road going to Idenao and Limbé. In good weather, this latter route in reverse acts as another alternative for ascending the mountain.

Shorter treks
Instead of tackling the summit, one-day treks going halfway to Mann's Spring are popular, and you can also take a short hike from Scipio Camp, 3km north of Idenao, which leads to the Bomana Waterfall.

The Race of Hope
A tortuous 40km foot race or marathon up the mountain, also known as the Mount Cameroon Race and the Guinness Mountain Marathon, has been held on the mountain since 1973. Usually held on the last weekend in January or the first weekend in February, it attracts nearly 400 runners from all over the world and is watched by more than 50,000 spectators.

The race starts from the stadium in Buéa, and the men's winner typically completes the ascent and descent of the steep and stony slopes in around four-and-a-half hours (meaning an average of a vertical 2,000ft/610m ascended or descended every hour) and the women's winner in little more, which represents an incredible feat, considering the rigorous climb, problems of altitude and heat, and the fact that most people take a few days.

In 2002 athlete Ngeve Zache Etutu made history by completing the race despite losing a leg in 2000 in a motorcycle accident. It took him 14 hours to get to the peak and another one hour and 43 minutes to descend.

Further details of the race are available from the Fédération Camerounaise d'Athlétisme (BP 353, Yaoundé; tel: 222 47 44) and the Provincial Delegation of Youth and Sports in Buéa (tel: 332 21 52).

KUMBA
Head for Kumba, the largest town of the South West Province (population about 125,000), 138km north of Douala and 160km south of Mamfé, to explore one of Cameroon's most beautiful regions, boasting among other things Barombi Mbo, a stunning crater lake with crystal clear waters, and the tectonic Lake Dissoni.

Kumba is situated on the edge of a forest, and therefore many buildings are made from wood. The numerous elevated wooden verandahs of these buildings, coupled with the wide, dusty streets and badly pot-holed roads give the place the look and feel of the American Wild West.

Kumba doesn't really have a centre as such, but to the east of the market (one of the country's biggest) is the principal motor park and further on are hotels, banks, the post office and *agences de voyage* offices for Douala and Mamfé. There is also a general hospital (tel: 335 41 39).

Kumba has a sizeable Igbo (or Ibo) immigrant community from southeastern Nigeria. They are Nigeria's third-largest ethnic group and predominantly Christian. There is also a significant mix of Bassa, Ewondo, Hausa, Bamiléké and other ethnic groups.

Getting there and away
You can reach Kumba by train from both Douala and Nkongsamba.

The road to the train station, northeast of the stadium, also leads to the Three Corners motor park in Fiango on the northeastern edge of the town. This has share-taxis for Bangem, Bafoussam, Tombel and Bamenda.

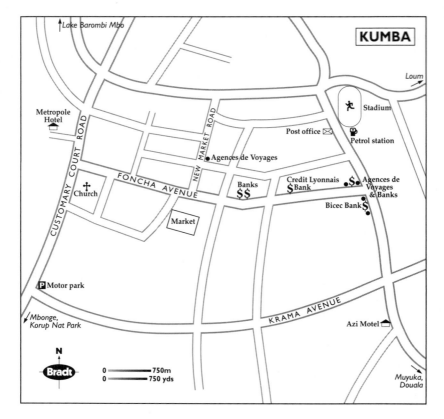

Southwest of the market on Ekondo Titi Road is the Mbanga motor park with share-taxis to Mundemba (for Korup) and Ekondo Titi.

Share-taxis for Buéa, Muyuka, Douala and Limbé are available at the Buéa motor park on the Buéa road, southeast of town. As a guide to prices, Buéa is typically CFA1,000/£1.07/US$1.89, while Limbé costs CFA1,200/£1.28/US$2.26.

Agences de voyage for Douala, Bamenda, Bafoussam and Mamfé are in the centre of town in the vicinity of Foncha Avenue. They include Tonton Express, Symbol of Unity, Guaranti Express and Tchatcho Voyages. Bafoussam is typically CFA1,200/£1.28/US$2.26, while Bamenda costs CFA1,500/£1.60/US$2.83.

Where to stay

Hôtel Metropole Tel: 335 40 64. West of the market off Mundemba Rd, this hotel is popular, with rooms with en-suite facilities, fans or AC. Rooms are CFA5,000–10,000 (£5.35–10.70/US$9.45–18.90).

Azi Motel BP 304; Buéa Rd; tel: 335 42 91. Possibly Kumba's best hotel, with 34 good rooms with bathroom and AC. Facilities include a restaurant and bar. Rooms are CFA5,000–10,000 (£5.35–10.70/US$9.45–18.90).

Tavern Cross Junction Hotel Buéa Rd; tel: 335 43 39. Near Azi Motel and the centre, this hotel has simple rooms with fans, and a bar and restaurant (probably the most popular in town) serving inexpensive Cameroonian food. Rooms are CFA5,000–10,000 (£5.35–10.70/US$9.45–18.90).

Bridge Inn BP 385; Mundemba Rd. Basic rooms with fans or AC for CFA5,000 (£5.35/US$9.45). Camping in the grounds is CFA2,000 (£2.14/US$3.78) per person. There is an inexpensive restaurant.
Hôtel Authentique BP 236; tel: 335 41 60. Government-graded one-star hotel with 21 rooms, bar and restaurant.

What to see
Barombi Mbo Crater Lake
Lake Barombi Mbo is about 5km north of Kumba, which is a CFA500 (53p/94c) taxi ride or a walk of little more than an hour down Lake Road, northwest of the centre. Take the road going off to the left when you pass the Senior Divisional Officer's office at little more than halfway.

Beautifully lush, thick, pristine rainforest with massive ancient tropical trees grows right inside the crater to the lake edge. Measuring 2.5km across and over 100m deep, Barombi Mbo is one of the largest crater lakes in Cameroon. It is overwhelmingly peaceful.

For hundreds of years the lake has provided all the needs of the Barombi people, who catch the cichlids (mouth-breeders) and catfish unique to the lake. The villagers continue to make their own basket traps by hand, ensuring that only the larger fish are caught, so that the lake is not overfished.

If a fisherman is around, he may take you around the lake or to Barombi village on the other side of the lake, for a fee of about CFA800 (85p/US$1.51). Dugout canoes are also available for hire.

MOUNT KUPE
Mount Kupé (2,064m), northeast of Kumba, is one of a semi-circle of mountains – the others being Mount Nlonako (1,825m) and the Manengouba Massif (2,411m) – combining to form a range which straddles the border between the South West and Littoral provinces and which combines to create the northern, southern and eastern borders of the Mamfé Depression, a region of low-lying, dense forest.

Mount Kupé, about 45km east of Kumba, is located at altitudes of between 450m and 2,064m above sea level and covers an area of about 30km², including 25km of primary montane forest. It dominates the town of Tombel (or Toumbel).

Along with the Ijim and Kilum forests at Mount Oku, near Kumbo, and the forests at Mount Cameroon, the forest of Mount Kupé represents a chain of montane forest with an exceptional degree of endemism. Mount Kupé is an area of great importance biologically as it is home to a number of endemic species of bird, reptile, amphibian, plant, insect and mammal, and a very rich variety of montane flora.

There is an exceptional range of birdlife here, with more than 320 species recorded, and the mountain is also home to chimpanzees and some species of rare primates, spectacular chameleons, pygmy crocodiles, golden cats and huge frogs. And *pentaphlebia stahli*, a large forest- and stream-dwelling damselfly, occurs commonly on Mount Kupé. The genus is found only in montane forest in Central Africa and its nearest relatives occur in a similar habitat in Venezuela, South America.

Mount Kupé is also of great importance to the dense local human population of around 150,000, who consider it home to their ancestral and forest spirits and the source of all wealth. The mountain has great subsistence value to these peoples, who are distributed within 16 villages and towns on both sides of the mountain. The population is English-speaking on the western side of the mountain, and is mainly made up of Bakossi (Akosse) peoples, while on the eastern side the population is composed of Bafun, Bakaka and Manehas and a high proportion of non-natives.

For hundreds of years the mountain has provided wood for building, carving and fuel, as well as bushmeat, plants and seeds for food, plants for medicines, and cane for baskets.

Getting to the mountain

To approach the mountain, head for the Bakossi village of Nyasoso, situated on the mountain slopes and surrounded by farmbush. It is around 12km north of Tombel (about a CFA15,000/£16/US$28 taxi ride from Tombel to Nyasoso), and share-taxis are regularly available from Kumba. Nyasoso takes around six hours from Douala by share-taxi via Loum and Tombel and it takes around four hours by car; a 4WD vehicle is recommended if you are travelling between June and October. The road is paved to Loum, but from Loum to Nyasoso it deteriorates rapidly. If you're stuck in Tombel, there is basic accommodation available at **Alison's Guesthouse**.

Climbing the mountain

BirdLife International established a conservation project on the mountain in 1991 and the Mount Kupé Forest Project (MKFP), which is part of the Worldwide Fund for Nature, manages the area. The WWF has an office in Nyasoso overseeing various conservation projects. It has no telephone – communication is by radio – but you can only contact WWF Cameroon's headquarters in Yaoundé (tel: 221 62 67) in advance.

MOUNT KUPE BUSH SHRIKE
The world's rarest shrike?
Christian Boix

Only discovered in 1949, at Mount Kupé near Nyasoso, the Mount Kupé bush shrike was only seen twice between 1949 and 1989 and was believed to be endemic to Mount Kupé. More recently, however, particularly since its highly distinctive vocalisations have been described, it has been recorded more frequently. This is not to suggest it is common, with an estimated seven pairs known to occur on the whole of Mount Kupé. However, two new localities have been discovered: Lake Edib (Bakossi Mountains), where the habitat available is eight times larger than that of Mount Kupé, and Banyang Mbo Wildlife Sanctuary, where a single bird was seen in 1999. The entire world population lives scattered in three apparent nuclei of less than 200km^2.

It is considered critically threatened by BirdLife International, with a global population of some 50–249 individuals. Its apparent scarcity is hard to explain and commonly attributed to habitat degradation. This is unlikely, given that its preferred habitat is well protected and the species generally occurs far from human settlements, using only primary forest with relatively open understorey at 950–1,450m above sea level at Mount Kupé, and 1,000–1,250m above sea level at Lake Edib. Despite this altitudinal isolation it seems to be a species that is naturally very scarce, and perhaps on the edge of natural extinction.

The French call it the 'Gladiator of Mount Kupé', and indeed this stunning gem has become a stalwart flagship species for forest conservation in Cameroon and it is unmistakable when sighted. The Mount Kupé bush shrike is a forest bush shrike with a green back, grey belly, yellow vent and unique head pattern, capped with a broad black mask that extends to its front, a slate-grey

Strictly, a permit from the Ministry of Environment, and, if you plan to take photos, a permit from the Ministry of Information (both in Yaoundé) are required, although in practice this may not be the case.

The project office in Nyasoso can provide good information on the ecology of the mountain as well as a list of mountain bird species and a guide to its Nature Trail, a short loop of 1km which passes through some fields into some forest near the village. It begins at the southern end of the school grounds.

To climb the mountain, there is a mandatory community forest fee of CFA2,000 (£2.14/US$3.78) per person per day spent in the forest, a mandatory guide costing CFA3,500 (£3.75/US$6.61) per day, plus optional porters at CFA2,500 (£2.67/US$4.72) per day. An allowance for meals for both you, your guide and porter/s is also required. The guides are generally very good, and the best ones will recognise the various wildlife calls and know the best places to spot them.

Camping is permitted on the mountain. If you plan to camp, you need to provide a tent for your guide. You don't need to provide cooking supplies, but can bring your own food. Alternatively, you can arrange for a porter to bring up food each day if you plan to stay a few days. You need some way of keeping your gear dry, as there can be heavy rains, even in the dry season.

The climb to the awesome view (on clear days) at the summit is steep but can be completed in around six to eight hours. The trails – Max's Trail and the Shrike Trail – are marked with altitude markers, and pass through beautiful forest with striking flowers, fruits and epiphytes. Both are steep and can be difficult to locate, which is why a guide is required.

crown and nape. A clear, pure-white throat rimmed by a narrow jet-black breast band, gives this bird away. Such a conspicuous throat appears to be used for advertising, although some of the adverts are poorly understood. For example, some adult individuals show a stylish maroon medallion in the center of the throat. Speculation has suggested it may be an age-related marking distinguishing breeding birds from non-breeders; or perhaps it's just a geographical morph or even a secondary sexual character? The only consensus seems to be that it is not sex specific. Furthermore, females during breeding appear to develop a yellow tinge surrounding the black patch; again, speculation suggests this may be a physiological consequence or an advert of receptiveness.

It's been confirmed as a monogamous territorial breeder, yet in the non-breeding season they are often sighted in trios, which could explain the need for distinctive throat markings to avoid aggression. But as with many other unstudied facets of this species, it still remains a mystery. Studies to understand what is limiting this species' total numbers or work to better understand the biology of this declining gem are needed urgently. Fortunately, the fact that the Cameroon government and Post Office have immortalised this species in the national stamp collection suggests that they are aware of the conservation significance of this species.

For those wishing to catch a glimpse of this highly enigmatic species, the best chances are along the Shrike Trail on Mount Kupé above Nyasoso and in the Bakossi forests near the village of Kodmin. Speak to the WWF project officers at Nyasoso to arrange a guide (and vehicle) for the day. But be warned that a libation ceremony at 06.00 in the morning, involving a fair amount of beer, whisky and cola-nuts at the chief's palace in Kodmin is an unavoidable prerequisite to the start of your hunt!

MOUNT KUPE NATIONAL PARK
Keith Barnes

An isolated massif, Mount Kupé is arguably the premier birding destination in Cameroon, not least because of the good infrastructure and excellent guides and information available from the local WWF office. Although only 25km² of primary forest remains, a list of over 320 species, including some of Africa's rarest birds, such as the Mount Kupé bush shrike, tempt all manner of birders here. The forests are home to 27 Cameroon Mountain EBA birds, including many scarce or threatened species that, despite having an extensive range, are difficult to see elsewhere in Africa. Diversity is high: resident species include eight kingfishers, eight woodpeckers, three trogons, seven honeyguides, 21 greenbuls, 14 shrikes, five wattle-eyes and 17 sunbirds. The most sought-after species are Cameroon olive and white-naped pigeons, Sjostedt's owlet, bare-cheeked trogon, western green tinkerbird, Zenker's honeyguide, grey-headed broadbill, mountain boubou, green-breasted bush shrike, black-necked wattle-eye, Crossley's ground thrush, mountain and white-bellied robin-chats, forest swallow, Cameroon mountain and grey-headed greenbuls, green longtail, white-tailed warbler, black-capped woodland warbler, white-throated mountain babbler, grey-necked rockfowl, Fernando Po oliveback, and Cameroon and Ursula's sunbirds.

Birding Max's Trail

Max's Trail is arguably the best trail for birding on Mount Kupé. It starts at the WWF project leader's cottage adjacent to the school. It passes through farms and secondary forest (farmbush) for the first 2km, up to 1,050m, and then continues through primary forest right to the summit. Ignore the 2km of farmbush at your peril, as it provides diversity and good numbers of birds; it is possible to spend a day here without reaching the forest. The farmbush holds a number of 'lowland forest' species not found easily in the primary forest itself, including yellow-billed turaco, black bee-eater, many-coloured, fiery-breasted and grey-green bush shrikes, African and black-and-white shrike-flycatcher, yellow-footed and dusky-blue flycatchers, white-chinned prinia, green longtail, black-faced rufous warbler, black-throated, black-capped and buff-throated apalis, naked-faced barbet, rufous-crowned eremomela, violet-backed hyliota, Woodhouse's antpecker, and pale-fronted and grey-headed nigrita.

In the primary forest the trail is steep in places. The forests at 1,050m and at 1,550m are highly productive and good for mixed species flocks with yellow-bellied wattle-eye, dwarf kingfisher, grey-green bush shrike and many-coloured bush shrike commonly seen. Zenker's honeyguide was regularly seen at around 1,050–1,150m in the 1990s, although records are increasingly scarce now.

Shrike Trail

The Shrike Trail is very steep. It starts at the right-hand side of the pink building at the far end of the school grounds, behind the dam. This trail soon reaches primary forest and provides the best chance of seeing the rarest and most endangered bird on the mountain, the Mount Kupé bush shrike, first observed in 1952, then assumed extinct until spotted again in 1989. There is a campsite on the trail.

Max's Trail

Max's Trail begins at the WWF project leader's cottage next to the school, about 1.5km from the village, through bush and secondary forest. It has a campsite at

Other birds to be seen are black-necked wattle-eye, Bates' sunbird, bar-tailed and bare-cheeked trogons, black bee-eater, African piculet, Woodhouse's antpecker, grey-headed broadbill (1,350–1,450m), green-breasted bush shrike (1,400–1,600m), white-throated mountain-babbler (1,250–2,000m), black-headed batis and white-tailed warbler. At about 1,550m there is a clearing that has been used as a campsite: check this area, as red-thighed sparrowhawk, green-breasted bush shrike, African piculet, Fernando Po oliveback and red-faced crimsonwing have been recorded here.

Birding Shrike Trail
The Shrike Trail is very steep (not recommended to anyone who is either unfit or does not have sure footing) and very quickly reaches primary forest. It is located to the right-hand side of the pink building on the far side of the school campus, behind the dam. Most sightings of Mount Kupé bush shrike have been along this trail at an altitude of 950–1,350m. Grey-necked rockfowl have been seen a few times, although this is far from regular and much luck is required, and white-throated mountain-babbler are often seen above 1,200m. Other specials seen regularly here include all the trogons, Crossley's ground thrush, Tullberg's woodpecker, chestnut-capped flycatcher, white-spotted wattle-eye, Bates' paradise flycatcher, Bocage's akalat, white-bellied robin-chat and the elusive olive long-tailed cuckoo.

Birding Nature Trail
The shortest and easiest trail is the Nature Trail, which despite being less than 1km long and being right at the edge of the village supports many of the specials, including grey-necked rockfowl (not seen now for several years). The entrance is reached at the southern end of the school campus. Search for Bates' swift, grey-headed broadbill, forest swallow, green longtail and violet-backed hyliota here. In the evenings Fraser's eagle owl may be seen or heard here. The highly productive farmbush below the Nature Trail can be reached by going towards the Nature Trail, but continuing straight on over the stream instead of turning left at the small Mount Kupé signpost before the stream. A path goes up a hill, skirting the forest, and then curves round to the right through nearly 180 degrees, before dropping back down to the stream. The dead trees along here are exceptionally good for forest-edge hole-nesting species, particularly barbets and tinkerbirds, including the bristle-nosed barbet, western green tinkerbird, red-rumped tinkerbird, yellow-throated tinkerbird, yellow-spotted barbet, hairy-breasted barbet and double-toothed barbet. Other specialities to be found include blue-headed wood-dove, fiery-breasted bush shrike, swamp greenbul and green longtail.

1,500m (Nyasoso is at an altitude of about 800m) after a steep climb up primary forest, but is much easier going above the campsite.

Where to stay in Nyasoso
There are several guesthouses with basic accommodation including **Thekla's Guest House**, **Mrs Ekwoge's Guest House** and the **Women's Centre**, with rooms costing about CFA6,000 (£6.43/US$11.34) per night. **Lucy's Guest House** provides good, basic meals and a pleasant guests' sitting room. Bathrooms are shared.

The WWF's guesthouse has closed down, but the WWF office in the town may be able to recommend guesthouses or accommodation in private homes at CFA3,000 (£3.21/US$5.67) per person per night.

Bakossi Mountains

Head for the little-explored Bakossi Mountains, an area of lower montane forest northwest of Mount Kupé, if you want to experience real remoteness and endless dense forest. Access is quite difficult and facilities non-existent, but guides may be found in Nyasoso or in the villages of Ngomboko, 10km north of Nyasoso, or Edib, about 7km north of Baseng.

One route into the mountain forests goes from Ngomboko, then 4km west to Bangem. You then ford a river and walk northwards to Edib village (6km). Two kilometres west of here is Lake Edib, and you can then proceed to Masaka or Nyali, each about 6km from the lake. The route is completed by reaching Nyandung village, 3–4km from Masaka, which is near the Mamfé–Kumba road, accessible by a track road from Masaka village.

KORUP NATIONAL PARK

Korup is Africa's oldest remaining rainforest. Scientists estimate that this living museum is more than 60 million years old. An area of extensive primary lowland tropical rainforest on the border of Nigeria, it is the most accessible forest of its type in Cameroon. The park was officially created in 1986 and is joined to Nigeria's Cross River National Park.

With a surface area of 1,260km^2 (126,000ha), Korup featured in the British television screening of *Korup: The Story of an African Rainforest*, which did much to create awareness of the plight of rainforests worldwide.

Korup's dense primary tropical rainforest has the highest species and natural genetic richness recorded so far in Africa. Isolated by the surrounding river systems, the forest is home to more than 1,000 known species, with 60 occurring nowhere else and 170 considered endangered or vulnerable. One of these is the Cross River gorilla, which in 2000 the International Union for the Conservation of Nature (IUCN) put on the critically endangered list, as there are thought to be only 150 to 200 remaining.

There are more than 600 tree and shrub varieties and over 400 bird species, as well as more than 100 species of mammals. In addition, there are 950 butterfly species, 174 species of reptiles and amphibians, and 140 varieties of fish, with new discoveries being made yearly. Korup is also home to a quarter of Africa's primate species.

There are populations of forest elephant, buffalo, drill, antelope, sitatunga, leopard and chimpanzee, and more specifically the collared mangabey, russet-eared guenon, red-capped mangabey, Preuss's red colobus and the putty-nosed monkey.

Its rich flora and fauna result from Korup surviving the ice age. More than 90 plants in Korup have been and are used for medicinal purposes and one creeper (*ancistrocladus korupensis*) is believed to have constituents that may prove useful in the cure of some forms of cancer and HIV.

If you visit the park, you are likely to see few animals, although you would be unlucky not at least to encounter monkeys leaping through the trees. Animals or not, the experience will still be fascinating. There is a gigantic variety of plants and trees here, and a huge range of birds creating a cacophony overhead. The forest floor is typically rather dark, shaded by the many different levels of growth overhead, from huge trees to tiny saplings, all competing for light.

Brightly coloured exotic fruits and flowers hang from the trees and the smell of fermenting fruit is strong. When you come to a clearing, where a tree has fallen,

Left Bridge in Korup National Park, Southwest Province (RQ)

Below left Chimpanzee (KB)

Below right Lowland gorilla (TI)

Above Cranes in Kribi (APS)

Right View from Mount Cameroon (APS)

Below Violet turaco (KB)

the sunlight on the forest floor causes lush green undergrowth, flowers and butterflies to appear.

Korup National Park Project

The WWF's Korup National Park Project is one of the organisation's largest integrated conservation and development projects. The WWF has two offices in the Korup region, one at Mundemba in the south and another at Nguti in the north.

Designed to protect and manage the national park and integrate it into the local economy and regional development plans, the project links park development, environmental education, scientific research, rural and tourism development, sustainable natural resources utilisation and use of non-timber forest products. The Korup Project has undertaken a number of conservation and poverty-alleviation initiatives, including the building of bridges, access roads, community halls and schools, and supported income-generating activities like cassava-grinding mills, palm-oil presses, cocoa driers and sprayers, natural resource plantations, and goat, pig and cattle farming.

Getting to the park

Access to the park can be a bit of a struggle due to the poor roads, but the park itself is especially rewarding as there are more than 100km of marked trails here, and good anglophone guides are available.

It takes a full day's travelling from Douala to reach Mundemba, which is near the main entrance to the park. It is far easier to reach in the dry season, as the road from Kumba to Mundemba is untarred, and the 150km (93 miles) stretch can turn into a mudbath during the rainy season. Regular share-taxis travel from Douala to Mundemba, via Kumba and Ekondo Titi.

You can either walk the 8km to the park entrance, or the Korup Information Centre at Mundemba (see page 136) can provide a park vehicle accommodating eight at CFA8,000 (£8.57/US$15.12) per vehicle per return trip.

You can also enter the park further north at Baro, via Nguti on the road from Mamfé to Kumba. There are few share-taxis for the last stretch, the 35km from Nguti to Baro, although you may be able to hitch a lift at Nguti with WWF staff. At Baro you enter the forest by crossing the Bake River. There are fewer facilities and less infrastructure geared to this northern region of the park.

You can also reach Korup by boat, along the Mana River as far south as Idenao, although it is not cheap at around CFA250,000/£267/US$472 for a boat holding six, one way. This can be arranged by the Korup Tourist Information Centre. You can also charter a boat to visit nearby Pelican Island and the mangrove swamps, which costs CFA125,000 (£134/US$236) or so.

Boats also sail from Limbé through the Rio del Rey into the Ndian River to Mundemba, or, if you are approaching from Nigeria, via the creeks from Calabar and Ikang and down the River Ndian to Bula Beach near Mundemba, which takes around three hours. If you plan to sail from Nigeria, check the situation concerning the Bakassi Peninsula border dispute with Nigeria.

Where to stay in Mundemba

Vista Palace The cheapest option offering simple rooms with separate or shared facilities for CFA3,000 (£3.21/US$5.67) or CFA4,500 (£4.82/US$8.50) with bathroom. It has a good, inexpensive restaurant, and the Chez Controleur Tourist Café opposite also does good-value meals.

Korup Park Hotel Near the post office. Has en-suite rooms with fans for CFA5,000–7,500 (£5.35–8.03/US$9.45/14.17), as well as a restaurant and bar.

Hotel Iyaz Has become rather run down of late. The restaurant serves dishes like chicken, steak or fish and chips. En-suite rooms with fans are around CFA6,000 (£6.43/US$11.34) for a single, CFA8,000 (£8.57/US$15.12) for a double.

Where to stay in Nguti
Safariland Hotel, the **Green Castle** and, less centrally, the **Samba Inn** have basic accommodation at under CFA5,000 (£5.35/US$9.45).

The park
Arrangements for entering the park can be made through the Korup Information Centre (email: korup@wwf.cm) in the centre of Mundemba. The centre is open from November to May daily, 07.00–17.00, and from June to October Monday–Friday 08.00–15.30, Saturday/Sunday 07.30–08.30 and 16.30–17.30.

BIRDING SITE GUIDE
Keith Barnes

Korup supports 425 bird species. Many lowland forest birds are found at Korup, but the greatest prize is the grey-necked rockfowl. Other delights include black guineafowl and both black-eared and grey ground-thrush. Although the bushmeat market has taken its toll, many mammal populations are recovering here and the forests are home to forest elephant, buffalo, sitatunga, leopard, chimpanzee and the magnificent drill, as well as collared mangabey, greater white-nosed guenon, Preuss' red colobus, russet-eared guenon and the bizarre water chevrotain.

Birding Mundemba
Heading to Mundemba from Kumba, 30km before Mundemba there is some excellent forest that is worth birding. The secondary growth offers black-and-white-casqued and yellow-casqued wattled hornbill as well as flocks of noisy grey parrots. At Mundemba itself one must arrange permits, a compulsory guide and porters at the WWF office. The Hotel Iyaz is 1km beyond the WWF offices; the rare Bates' swift has been recorded over the hotel. The scrub around the hotel may produce western bluebill, Levaillant's cuckoo, chattering cisticola, white-breasted nigrita and olive-bellied sunbird. In the secondary growth around Mundemba both black bee-eater and black-bellied seed-cracker are also seen. After passing through Mundemba (en route to the park), check the roadside pools and lakes for Hartlaub's duck. As you approach the park, 10km from Mundemba, you cross the Mana River and its famous suspension bridge. This area is well worth birding: rock pratincole are regularly seen on exposed rocks in the river, and the surrounding trees are good for hornbills. Be there first thing in the morning to maximise your chances of seeing both black and yellow-casqued wattled hornbills.

To find Picathartes Knoll you will certainly need a guide, which is compulsory to enter the park anyway. Near the entrance to the park there are a number of well-maintained foot trails (120km) and four camps with shelters and latrines. To see the rockfowl, you will need to walk the 8km to the basic Rengo Rock Camp and spend at least one night there (more for determined rockfowlers). It is best to be at Picathartes Knoll, where you take up a position in or near the cave, before 15.30 and wait patiently for the birds.

There is a CFA5,000 (£5.35/US$9.45) park entrance fee payable per day plus CFA4,000 (£4.28/US$7.56) per day and CFA1,000 (£1.07/US$1.89) per night for a compulsory guide (most of whom are very enthusiastic and knowledgeable) and CFA2,000 (£2.14/US$3.78) per day and CFA1,000 per night for a porter (optional). The centre also hires out sleeping bags and camping equipment. You can arrange this, and accommodation, in advance by contacting the WWF headquarters in Yaoundé (tel: 221 62 67; email: www.wwfcameroon.org) or emailing korup@www.cm.

If you want to make an early start to the park, it is important to arrive before 16.30 the previous day to make arrangements in Mundemba.

Don't forget to take insect repellent for the multitude of bugs you'll encounter, including driver ants, bees and blackflies, the latter attracted by the water if you have a swim in the rivers. You should dress for the extreme wet, to cope with the 100% humidity and the fording of waist-high pools.

The birds frequently come to roost at the knoll, which is about 1.5km from Rengo Rock Camp and 180m north of Hunter's Trail. Sometimes the birds do not return to the knoll at all, and you may need several nights there to improve your chances of meeting these scarce creatures. (See *Finding Grey-necked Rockfowl*.)

The trails right near Rengo Rock Camp are excellent and red-billed dwarf hornbill, bare-cheeked trogon, blue-headed bee-eater, Latham's forest francolin, Nkulengu rail, grey-throated rail, vermiculated fishing owl, Sjostjedt's owlet and black guineafowl were all seen very near the camp in April 2003. The trails to and from Rengo Rock Camp hold 11 different species of greenbul, white-crested and piping hornbill, buff-spotted woodpecker, blue-headed crested-flycatcher, chestnut and white-spotted wattle-eye, red-tailed and white-tailed ant-thrush, fire-crested and brown-chested alethe, black-eared ground-thrush, forest flycatcher, black-capped and brown illadopsis and Gray's and Rachel's malimbes. Rengo Rock is reasonably reliable for Cassin's and Sabine's spinetails, chocolate-backed kingfisher, tit hylia and blue cuckooshrike. Between Iriba Irene Camp and the suspension bridge it is possible to encounter black-casqued wattled hornbill, rufous flycatcher-thrush, white-browed forest-flycatcher, spotted, Sjostedt's, Xavier's and icterine greenbul, yellow and grey longbill and little green sunbird. At Iriba Irene camp, listen and look for rufous-sided broadbill, blue cuckoo shrike, green hylia, red-vented malimbe and spot-breasted ibis, particularly in the early mornings.

Birding Nguti

From Nguti, the road to the radio mast supports blue cuckooshrike and many-coloured bush shrike. To the west of Nguti, the village of Baro (30km) has barely been birded, but has already turned up some excellent birds, including black spinetail, chocolate-backed kingfisher, blue-headed bee-eater and Willcock's honeyguide. Once at Baro, bird the access road for long-tailed hawk and golden-crowned woodpecker. The track to Korup, reached by heading towards the church and following the track to the right after 1km, leads to a rope bridge over the river, which is good for blue-headed crested flycatcher and Kemp's longbill, and on to some good forest. The WWF may now have facilities in the park worth exploring.

At the approach to Korup, you pass regimented oil-palm plantations as the huge forest trees rise up in front of you, and the strange cries of birds and the hum of insects get louder and louder. You cross the Mana River, which borders the forest, on an awe-inspiring, 120m-long wooden suspension bridge (built in 1989 to allow year-round access) spanning the river. The forest then closes around you (although the bridge has recently been out of action and if this is still the case you will have to boat or walk across).

If time is short, and you can only visit for the day, follow the marked nature trail, which features information posts explaining points of interest such as the varied fauna and flora.

Further information on the park is available from the WWF Cameroon headquarters in Bastos, Yaoundé (tel: 221 62 67; web: www.wwfcameroon.org).

Where to stay in the park

Day trips are worthwhile, but there are three basic campsites with beds, insect-screened huts, drinking and bathing water, latrine toilets and simple kitchens with firewood. Mattresses and cooking equipment can be hired from the Korup Information Centre.

The basic Iriba Irene Camp is 1.7km from the park entrance on the nature trail.

Rengo Rock Camp is 8km in, past the Mana River Waterfall to the south and near some caves that are well worth exploring, and which lead to Mount Yuhan (1,079m). Rengo Rock Camp is situated next to a forest stream. There are four quite spacious wooden huts here (two with bunk beds).

There is also the larger Chimpanzee Camp, 10km from the entrance, where you may hear or see chimpanzees.

What to see
Rumpi Hills Forest Reserve

If you head in the opposite direction, ie: eastwards out of the park to Rumpi Hills Forest Reserve (which extends to 45,843ha or 458km²), you come to the Meta Waterfall (a good four-hour hike from Mundemba) and, 20km south of this, the Iyombo Waterfall. On the eastern border of the reserve, just west of Dikome Balue, is Mount Rata (1,770m).

Forest reserves

In the Korup region there are several forest reserves in addition to Rumpi Hills: Mawne River and Nta-ali (35,000ha or 350km²) east and southeast of Mamfé; Ejagham (74,851ha or 748km²), a continuation of Korup; and the Banyang Mbo Wildlife Sanctuary near Nguti. Many small villages are scattered around this area, and mainly belong to the five main tribes of the region, namely the Oroko, Ejagham, Balong, Korup and Isangele.

Kombone

This village near Kumba boasts a typically small coffee and cocoa farm where, if it is in use, it is possible to visit the drying house where the beans are prepared for shipment.

MAMFE

Anglophone Mamfé, north of Korup National Park, is the last sizeable town before the Nigerian border at Ekok and therefore the main southern entry point into Nigeria. The road to Mamfé can be impassable in the rainy season, when it is generally better to enter Nigeria from the north of the country. Yet the road enjoys some marvellous landscapes as it plunges through rainforest and around the mountains.

This rather unremarkable, remote town is somewhat livened up by the travellers and traders who perpetually descend upon the place, many of whom are selling goods smuggled from Nigeria. It is also known for the witchcraft practised in the area. Mamfé has a good spread of shops, a bank, a hospital and a petrol station.

Getting there and away

The motor park just southwest of the centre of the town has regular share-taxis to Kumba and Ekok (65km) on the Nigerian border, and sometimes into Nigeria.

There are also share-taxis to Bamenda (145km) and Dschang, but bear in mind that the admittedly beautiful mountain roads for these destinations are often quite treacherous and often impassable during the rainy season. Going south to Kumba and then on to Bamenda (180km and then 250km) is a more time-consuming route but significantly safer.

Agences de voyages Ali Baba, Tchatcho Voyages, Guaranti Express and Tonton Express all have regular services to Kumba, which average under CFA2,000 (£2.14/US$3.78) in the dry season to CFA4,000 (£4.28/US$7.56) when the rains make the roads very difficult to follow.

For Korup National Park, take a share-taxi on the N8 road to Nguti for the northern entrance or the far longer journey to Mundemba, via Kumba, for the southern, main entrance.

Where to stay in Mamfé

Data Club Hotel BP29; tel: 334 13 99. Just over a 1km walk northwest of the centre with a good restaurant and good views of the Cross River. Clean, air-conditioned en-suite rooms cost around CFA10,000 (£10/US$18).

Great Aim Hotel BP 69. North of and near the motor park, with a bar and restaurant and rooms for under CFA5,000 (£5.39/US$9.45) with shared facilities.

African City Hotel Near the motor park, with basic rooms for under CFA5,000 (£5.39/US$9.45).

Heritage Hotel Nguti Rd. Opposite the school, this has a variety of simple rooms from CFA8,000 (£8.57/US$15.12).

Abunwa Lodge Tel: 334 12 47. Basic accommodation for under CFA5,000 (£5.39/US$9.45).

What to see
Ekok

The 60km road from Mamfé to Ekok gets so bad during the rainy season that it is usually best to take a motorised pirogue. These ply the Cross River from Mamfé to Ekok, setting off from the old German bridge at Mamfé. In the dry season the journey can usually be covered in an afternoon.

The Nigerian border is continually open, but there are few very basic hotels and guesthouses in Ekok, which in the evening also offers rows of lively stalls and plenty of loud music.

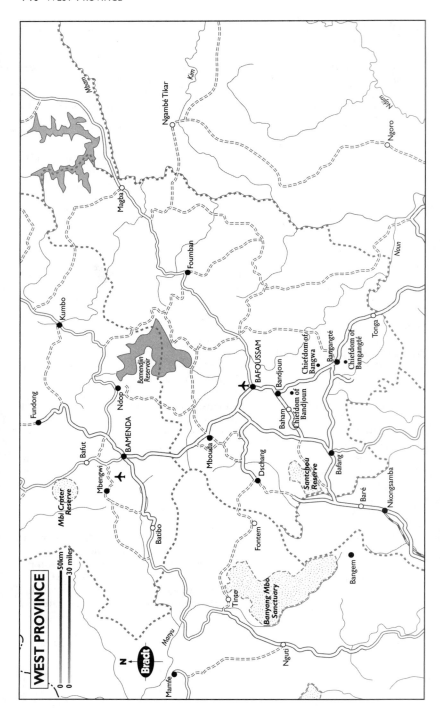

West Province

The northern sector of western Cameroon – the Central Highlands – provides the visitor with a stunning succession of landscapes, including volcanic crater lakes surrounded by dense vegetation, rolling hills and spectacular waterfalls. This region is also crammed with cultural distractions, and is rich in fascinating ancient chiefdoms.

It's also relatively easy to explore, as paved roads and a good selection of transport options connect the main towns.

Rich volcanic soils in the west have encouraged much higher rural population densities than elsewhere in the country. Coffee and cocoa are widely cultivated in the region.

The Bamiléké dominate francophone West Province, notably in the large town of Bafoussam. The Bamiléké originated from the north and probably settled in this region around the start of the 17th century. Bamiléké country also extends to towns such as Bandjoun, with its historic chiefdom, and the German colonial mountain resort town of Dschang.

The Cameroon Highlands are also populated to a lesser extent by other semi-Bantu peoples like the Tikar and Bamoun. The east of the province is home to the the latter, who are centred around Foumban, which has a number of sights of interest to visitors, including a splendid palace.

BAFOUSSAM

Rapidly enlarging, with a population of more than 200,000, this dusty, lively and loud regional commercial centre 285km from Douala is strongly dominated by the Bamiléké. It's the administrative capital of the Western Province, and its francophone nature contrasts strongly with neighbouring anglophone Bamenda.

There is a *chefferie*, or chief's compound, southeast of the centre off the road that goes to Bandjoun and Douala. The entrance fee is CFA2,000 (£2.14/US$3.78) and there is a further charge of CFA1,500 (£1.60/US$2.83) for photography. A better example of a traditional *chefferie* can be seen in Bandjoun, just under 20km further on down the road.

The Bamiléké, who dominate the town, built up Bafoussam through trading coffee, which is widely grown in the nearby fertile hills, and latterly through industry. It is also a major cocoa-producing area.

The town is split into an administrative quarter, the Tamja district, and the commercial neighbourhoods of Famla and Djeleng, in the middle of which a market is held every four days. The market is very dark and claustrophobic so beware of pickpockets.

Between the market, by the *gare routière*, and the Palais de Justice, is the main drag, Avenue Wanko, along which can be found several banks, as well as major

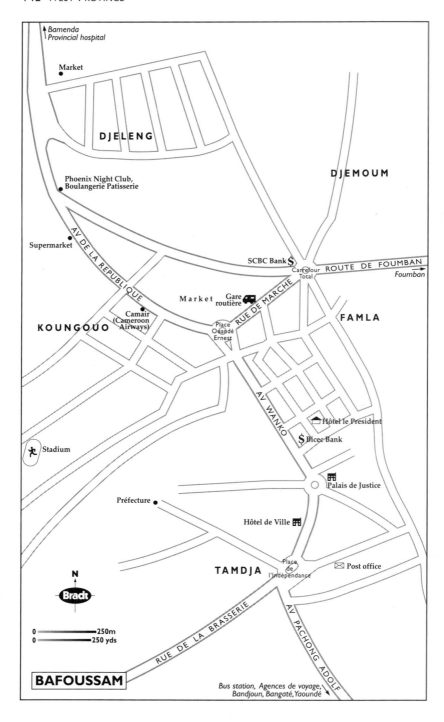

Bamenda
Provincial hospital

Market

DJELENG

DJEMOUM

Phoenix Night Club,
Boulangerie Patisserie

AV DE LA REPUBLIQUE

Supermarket

SCBC Bank $

Carrefour ROUTE DE FOUMBAN
Total
Foumban

Market Gare
routière

FAMLA

Camair
(Cameroon
Airways)

KOUNGOUO

Place
Ouandé
Ernest

RUE DE MARCHE

AV WANKO

Hôtel le President

$ Bicec Bank

Stadium

Palais de Justice

Préfecture

Hôtel de Ville

N

Bradt

Place
de
l'Indépendance

Post office

TAMDJA

0 ▬▬▬▬ 250m
0 ▬▬▬▬ 250 yds

RUE DE LA BRASSERIE

AV PACHONG ADOLF

BAFOUSSAM

Bus station, Agences de voyage,
Bandjoun, Bangaté, Yaoundé

shops. Craft goods such as carved wooden sculptures and furniture can be bought at the market and also at the workshops along Rue Nguetti Michel.

Getting there and away

The main *gare routière* by the market has share-taxis to destinations south of the town, such as Banjoun, Bafang and Kumba, as well as minibuses to Foumbot and Foumban.

Share taxis to Foumban and Foumbot can be taken from the Foumban *gare routière* opposite Crédit Lyonnais on the Carrefour Total roundabout.

Share taxis to Dschang and Bamenda leave from near the Shell station northwest of the centre. There are *agences de voyages* offices in this sector. Operators include Jeannot Express and Unity Express.

Agences de voyages offices, such as Binam, with services to Yaoundé (CFA2,000/£2.14/US$3.78), Douala (CFA1,000/£1.07/US$1.89) and Dschang, are located along the Rue du Marché by the market, and near the *chefferie* in the south of the town. For Bamenda (typically CFA800/85p/US$1.51, one hour), *agences de voyages* offices, such as Jeannot Express and Savannah Enterprises, are on Avenue République near the Hôtel de la Continental, 1km north of the centre. Other *agences de voyages* include Mayo-Banyo, Tonton Express, Paradise Travel and Vallance.

There is no direct transport to Limbé from Bafoussam, and therefore for Limbé you need to go to Douala first.

Where to stay

Hotel Le Continental BP 136; Av de la République; tel: 344 14 58. On the noisy main road, this government-rated one-star hotel has self-contained rooms with balcony and TV, a European restaurant of average standard (dishes CFA1,500–3,000/£1.60–3.20/US$2.83–5.67) and an extraordinary bar with eclectic decor that's worth seeing. Singles are CFA8,000 (£8.57/US$15.12) and doubles are CFA10,000 (£10.70/US$18.90).

Hôtel Jardin de Cooperates East of Av de la République. Basic clean rooms are CFA8,000 (£8.57/US$15.12) small, CFA10,000 (£10.70/US$18.90) medium and CFA12,000 (£12.86/US$22.68) large; there's also a bar and restaurant.

Ramada Motel Tel: 999 43 33. Off Carrefour Total, south of the Foumban *gare routière*, offering basic rooms with bathrooms for CFA10,000 (£10.70/US$18.90) and a bar.

Hôtel Le Président BP 78; Rue Nguetti Michel; tel: 344 11 36. A rather faded hotel, yet the 56 air-conditioned rooms, some with TV, are good value at around CFA8,000 (£8.57/US$15.12).

Hôtel Fédéral BP 136; Route Joumou; tel: 344 13 74/344 13 09. Recently renovated and close to the centre. The clean rooms with shower/bathrooms, balcony and TV are CFA9,000 (£9.64/US$17.01) for a double, and there is a good restaurant and a bar. There are slightly cheaper rooms at the front (CFA5,000/£5.35/US$9.45) but these are noisier.

Hôtel de l'Unité BP 99; tel: 344 15 16. 30 basic rooms, bar and restaurant.

Talotel BP 110; tel: 344 41 85. Off Av Wanko and by Le Ritz Palace nightclub, this very comfortable, central hotel has well-decorated and furnished en-suite rooms with satellite TV for CFA25,000 (£26/US$47) for a single to CFA30,000 (£32/US$56) for a family room, CFA54,000 (£57/US$102) for a small apartment and CFA77,000 (£82/US$145) for a large one. There is a good restaurant and bar.

Hotel Palace Garden BP 47; Route de Bamenda; tel: 344 16 96. On the outskirts of town with good air-conditioned rooms, a restaurant and bar. From CFA10,000 (£10.70/US$18.90).

Hôtel Le Saré BP 731; Route de Bamenda; tel: 344 25 99. Clean chalets with AC, and restaurant and bar. CFA15,000 (£16/US$28) for a room, CFA25,000 (£26/US$47) for an apartment.

Le Manoir Tel: 344 49 09. Bafoussam's top hotel, south of the centre opposite the Douala *gare routière*, offering good, clean rooms with bathrooms for CFA30,000 (£32/US$56), although this can often be negotiated. There is also a restaurant.

Airport Hotel BP 565; tel: 344 37 95. Government-graded two-star hotel with 16 plain rooms, a bar and a restaurant.

Where to eat and drink

There are numerous bars around the Avenue de la République, while around the Rou Joumou and the Foumban *gare routière* are some good, inexpensive eateries including **La Bauxite** for snacks and **La Refuge** for Cameroonian dishes. There are one or two patisseries in the centre, including **Boulangerie Patisserie** near the Hotel Le Continental, which has a large selection of cakes, pastries, croissants and French breads for CFA200–400 (21–42p/37–75c). There are various **UCCAO coffee** stalls that do a good coffee. The one set well above street level in Avenue Wanko is a great place to watch the world go by. Boys passing by selling cakes and doughnuts on the street below will happily climb the numerous steps to sell you one. Heading west along the Bamenda road, turn right after the Shell petrol station for a number of cheap food stalls. **Le Bonne Table de l'Ouest** on the Bandjoun–Douala road south of the centre is a popular, good eaterie serving both Cameroonian and European cuisine.

Nightlife

Phoenix Nightclub on Rue de la République boasts a live DJ on Saturdays (entrance CFA1,000/£1.07/US$1.89) and is recommended. **Le Ritz Palace** at the Talotel hotel, and **The Arcade**, off Avenue de la République, are further options.

Practical information
Cinema
Cine l'Empire Av de la République. Shows recent films in French and occasionally in English; four showings afternoon and evening, CFA800–1,200 (85p–£1.28/US$1.51–2.26).

Hospitals
Provincial Hospital Tel: 344 12 11
Dispensaire Urbain Tel: 344 13 46
Hôpital de Mbo Tel: 344 23 26

Internet
Cyber Espace Maflo Tel: 344 60 70
Cyber Café Premier Tel: 344 41 66

Pharmacies
Pharmacie Binam Tel: 344 25 55
Pharmacie du Benin SARL Tel: 344 15 57
Pharmacie Madelon Tel: 344 62 62
Pharmacie de l'Amitie Tel: 344 18 33
Pharmacie du Marché Tel: 344 66 11
Pharmacie des Montagnes Tel: 344 42 18
Pharmacie du Secours Tel: 344 13 27

Tourism
Tourist office Tel: 344 11 89/344 77 82. Near the Palais de Justice.

Tour operators and travel agents
Tandel Voyages BP 994; tel: 344 65 81/344 64 58
West Camtour BP 731; tel: 344 25 99
MTA Tel: 344 49 210

What to see
Within the rough triangle created by the Bamboutous Mountains to the west and the Noun River to the northeast there are a number of chiefdoms which have populations ranging from under 100 to over 25,000. There are also a number of crater lakes, including Lake Monoun, 3km east of the River Noun. The water depth of the lake remains a constant 96m, despite the season. Crater lakes are known to expel poisonous gases (the best-known incident being the tragedy at Lake Nyos in 1986, covered in the next chapter) and indeed poisonous gases at Lake Monoun asphyxiated 37 people on August 16 1984.

Baleng
In the Baleng region, just north of Bafoussam, is the crater lake of Baleng, as well as the *chefferie* of Baleng. The area is dotted with mud huts with tall 'witches' hat' roofs often made from corrugated iron. Other crater lakes in the area include ones at Banefo and Doupe, and near the town are the Metchie Falls.

Baleng also boasts a forestry reserve, created in 1935. Unfortunately, the reserve has suffered from a great deal of logging in recent years, triggered somewhat by the economic crisis in 1986.

BANDJOUN
This is the biggest of the Bamiléké chiefdoms and contains one of the most impressive traditionally built palaces in West and Central Africa.

Nearly 20km south of Bafoussam, Bandjoun is rich in the distinctive Bamiléké architecture, which typically consists of a square-shaped room made of mud and bamboo or palm leaves, with a thatched (although increasingly corrugated iron) conical roof and an exterior augmented by carved wooden panels.

The *chefferie* is about 3km south of the centre on the Route de Bangangté. Such compounds typically have a huge thatched reception hall, which traditionally would have been used as a court and for assemblies, a market square, and various huts for the chief and his wives. This one features tall, thin totem pole-like columns, bamboo walls decorated with geometric designs and elaborately carved doorways.

Under the chief, traditionally the judicial and religious leader and owner of all the land in the chiefdom, was a hierarchy of notables, freemen and slaves. Although this rigid social organisation has all but gone, various associations and secret societies relating to the chiefdom still remain today.

The *chefferie* at Bandjoun has a small museum (CFA1,000/£1.07/US$1.89 plus CFA1,500/£1.60/US$2.83 for photography) housed in the colonial-style treasury and featuring traditional items such as carved thrones, pipes and wooden carved panels. Today, the chief lives in a modern palace, located opposite the treasury.

Where to stay
Centre Climatique de Bandjoun Tel: 344 67 50. Outside town on the road to Bafoussam, this hotel has a restaurant and comfortable rooms with bathrooms and TV starting at CFA25,000 (£26/US$47).
Hôtel de Bandjoun Near the *gare routière*; simple rooms are from CFA5,000 (£5.35/US$9.45).

Where to eat and drink, and nightlife

The **Concorde Restaurant**, near the market, offers good-value food, and there are various food stalls around the market, with music and dance bars around the main square.

BAFANG

Bafang itself is nothing special, but the scenery around it is beautiful. There are various waterfalls, including the Chutes de la Mouenkeu, signposted from the Nkongsamba road a short walk out of town.

Another 30km down this road are the more impressive, 80m-high Chutes d'Ekom on the Nkam River. Details of how to reach these are in the *Littoral Province* chapter.

The town has various *agences de voyages* offering services to Yaoundé, Douala, Kumba and Bamenda.

Where to stay

Hôtel la Falaise BP 143; tel: 348 63 11/348 63 13. Opposite the Palais de Justice, this three-star hotel has 48 air-conditioned rooms, a restaurant and a bar. Rooms start at around CFA12,000 (£12.86/US$22.68).

Grand Lux Hotel BP 396; tel: 348 61 58. By the Palais de Justice; clean rooms with bathrooms and balconies start at CFA10,000 (£10/US$18). There is a good café/bar.

Hôtel le Samaritain BP 155; tel: 348 71 55. Has very basic rooms from CFA5,000 (£5.35/US$9.45).

Hôtel Le Calypso BP 211; tel: 348 62 11. A government-graded two-star hotel with 22 basic but comfortable rooms, bar and restaurant.

BANGANGTE

The pleasant town of Bangangté, a short drive south from Bandjoun, has a renovated traditional *chefferie*. Another, the Chefferie de Bana, is located off the road from Bangangté to Bafang, a route rich in spectacular scenery, not least the Col de Bana, or Bana Pass at 1,736m. Just north of Bangangté is another chiefdom, at Bangwa (or Bangoua).

Where to stay

Hôtel le Paysan BP 13; tel: 348 41 88. By the motor park, this hotel has rooms with bathrooms for CFA6,000 (£6.43/US$11.34) as well as an inexpensive restaurant.

Hôtel le Bazar BP 35; tel: 348 44 38. A couple of hundred metres east of the motor park along the main road, it's better than it looks, with clean en-suite rooms for under CFA8,000 (£8.57/US$15.12).

Jenyf Hotel BP 143. 30 comfortable rooms and six apartments, plus a bar and an inexpensive restaurant.

Hôtel Cristal BP 143; tel: 348 91 16. West of the motor park, with very comfortable and clean self-contained rooms for around CFA20,000 (£21/US$37) plus restaurant and bar.

DSCHANG

Established by the Germans in 1903, Dschang is a mountain resort, an old colonial and university town situated at an altitude of 1,400m (4,600ft), which makes the temperature pleasantly cool. Principally Bamiléké, it has a population of approximately 140,000.

Dschang can be reached by taking the paved road by share-taxi from Bafoussam (48km, which takes under an hour), the Bamenda road passing the Bamboutous Mountains which peak at 2,740m, and the paved road from Mbouda. The attractive but slow minor route through coffee and cocoa plantations from Melong, southwest of Bafang, was not possible at the time of writing because of bridges that had collapsed.

Apart from accommodation, there is not too much to distract in the town: a lively market, a municipal lake surrounded by banana, mango and pear trees, and a number of craft shops. Around 24km north of the town is Dsjutitsa, a beautiful, restful tea plantation with a lodge offering rooms for under CFA5,000 (£5.35/US$9.45).

Another excursion takes in two waterfalls: leave Dschang on the road from the Place de l'Indépendance heading for Fongo-Tongo, and the pretty hills and valleys lead to a signpost for a waterfall, the Cascade de Lingam, after about 10km. The same distance again leads you to another, bigger waterfall, the Chute de la Mamy Wata, accessible from a side road.

In 1942 Europeans in the area created the Centre Climatique as a holiday resort as, it being World War II, they were unable to go abroad for their holidays. The centre is still open today.

Facilities in Dschang include a hospital (tel: 345 13 66) and tourist office (tel: 345 21 25). There are minibuses and *agences de voyages* serving destinations that include Yaoundé, Douala, Bafoussam and Bamenda.

Where to stay
Centre Climatique BP 40; tel: 345 10 58. This holiday complex has bungalows in a range of price categories, from basic with shared facilities to luxurious with spacious balcony. There are landscaped gardens, an expensive but good restaurant, bars, a swimming pool (available to non-guests for a small fee), horseriding and tennis courts. Rooms are CFA10,000–35,000 (£10–37/US$18–66) and car hire can be arranged.
Hôtel Constellation BP 22; tel: 345 10 61. Centrally located near the *gare routière* and has 40 rooms for around CFA10,000 (£10.70/US$18.90). There is a bar and restaurant.
Hôtel Menoua Palace Tel: 345 16 93. Simple rooms for CFA3,500 (£3.75/US$6.61).

Where to eat and drink
The **Phoenix Restaurant** has interesting Cameroonian dishes and prices vary from around CFA1,000–4,500 (£1.07–4.82/US$1.89–8.50). The popular bar **La Maison Combatant de la Menoua** features traditional Cameroonian dancing and local dishes. If you've the energy to stay up late, there's also the **Conclusion** nightclub.

FOUMBAN
About 250km northwest of Yaoundé and 72km northeast of Bafoussam, the town of Foumban (or Fumban) is particularly history- and culture-rich. It is predominantly Muslim and the seat of the sultan of the Bamoun people. At 1,200m above sea level and located on the northeast edge of a mountain range, it sits by a vast plain. It is a bit touristy and you won't be short of children approaching you, asking to be your guide.

The Bamoun kingdom was founded here at the start of the 15th century by Nchare Yen, and therefore Foumban is one of the oldest towns in Cameroon.

Considered one of the art capitals of Africa, Foumban has a number of attractions, not least the outstanding Royal Palace of the Sultan, which the town is organised around. If you are lucky, you may be able to meet him. There are two good museums, a colourful market in the centre selling art objects, textiles, foodstuffs, etc (market days are Saturday and Wednesday) and plenty of opportunities to buy arts and crafts at a variety of shops and stalls. Foumban also has a number of traditional buildings dating from its period of German colonisation.

On the west side of town is the administrative quarter of Foumban, with such buildings as government offices, a hospital, the town hall and post office, while touristic sights are generally clustered around the Royal Palace at the centre.

Getting there and away

The motor park is by the market and has transport to Foumbot, Kumbo, Bamenda, Bafoussam and Nkongsamba. The journey to Bafoussam, for example, is typically CFA1,000 (£1.07/US$1.89) and takes an hour on the good roads.

Agences de voyages for Yaoundé, Douala (seven hours) and Bafoussam are generally west of the town.

Road conditions to Ngaoundéré and the north are very bad and there is no direct transport, so allow at least a couple of days to reach Ngaoundéré. It can take even more, and may be impossible in the rainy season. If you take this route, you can take a taxi to Banyo, stay overnight at the simple Auberge Pasada CFA2,500 (£2.67/US$4.72) or Auberge le Saré (under CFA5,000/£5.35/US$9.45) near the market and then get transport on to Tibati (a four-hour trip). From here you can take the crowded afternoon bus to Ngaoundéré, arriving at around midnight, or alternatively a taxi to Ngaoundal (under two hours) and then catch the train to Ngaoundéré. This should arrive in Ngaoundal at around 03.00 but can be delayed for some hours.

Where to stay

Relax des Princes Has basic rooms behind the bar for CFA2,000 (£2.14/US$3.78), but don't count on a restful night. It is to the left of where the Banyo bus stops.

Catholic Mission Rue de l'Hotel Beau Regard. In the centre near the church, it has an attractive garden and rooms with dormitory beds costing CFA2,500 (£2.67/US$4.72).

Hôtel Le Chalet Tel: 348 62 67/348 24 12. Down a side street off the road to Bafoussam, this hotel has good, quiet rooms, but is significantly west (3km) of the centre. CFA8,000 (£8.57/US$15.12).

Hôtel Beauregard BP 29; Rue de l'Hôtel Beau Regard; tel: 348 21 82/348 21 83. In the centre, it has a bar, and basic rooms from CFA4,000 (£4.28/US$7.56), some with bathrooms.

Hôtel Le Prunier Rouge BP 13; tel: 348 23 52. Off the Bafoussam road, this has simple rooms, pretty views and a restaurant. CFA4,00 (£4.28/US$7.56).

Hôtel le Zenith BP 122; off the Bafoussam road; tel: 348 24 25. Modern hotel offering clean rooms with en-suite facilities, some with TV. Double rooms are CFA6,000–9,000 (£6.43–9.64/US$11.34–17.01).

Residence Palace Baba BP 10; tel: 348 27 48. Away from the centre, with rooms costing CFA7,000 (£7.50/US$13.23).

Where to eat and drink

Street food is available just east of the *gare routière*. **Relax des Princes** is a very lively bar in the centre (see above) augmented by full-blast TV. The barbecues outside the bar can bring grilled fish, plantain, rice and cassava to your table for CFA250 (26p/47c). To the left of Relax des Princes a five-minute walk up the hill brings you to a square of sorts on the left, with numerous bars and food stalls and a great atmosphere.

Royal Café Route de Bamenda, near the market. Has Cameroonian/Western food from CFA2,000 (£2.14/US$3.78).

Restaurant de la Maturité Opposite the *gare routière*. Serves meals for around CFA500 (53p/94c).

What to see
The Royal Palace and the Sultan's Museum
The Bamoun can trace the lineage of their sultan back to 1394. Of the 17 kings in the present dynasty, the first, Nshare Yen, the son of a Tikar chief, proclaimed himself king with Foumban as his capital (then called Mfomben) after leading a group of rebels from the Tikar homelands. Another, Mbuembue, allegedly had a speaking voice that carried over a mile.

The old palace (the new one houses the present sultan) was completed in 1917 and designed by the king at that time, Ibrahim Njoya, inventor of the Bamoun alphabet. He converted to Islam and became a sultan.

The palace (tel: 348 22 27; grounds free, palace CFA2,000 (£2.14/US$3.78), CFA1,500 (£1.60/US$2.83) for photography, open daily 08.30–18.00) is architecturally unique and to an extent resembles a medieval chateau with German baroque and Romanesque styles thrown in. It was recently restored by UNESCO. Approached via a huge palm-fringed courtyard, the exterior of the palace features balconies of elaborately carved wood. The interior features a grand entrance and reception halls, a room of thrones, the sultan's, queen's and queen mother's residences, and an armoury.

The sultan appears in the foyer during the morning, and after prayers on Fridays, at around 13.00, musicians entertain him while subjects wearing strikingly flowing robes and with long brass trumpets meet with him. A traditional Bamoun dance, *mbansie*, is also performed.

Upstairs is the Sultan's Museum, and bilingual guides are available. It has artefacts of the Bamoun culture and history such as jewellery, shields, weapons, journals, dancing masks, carvings, royal gowns, arms and colourful bejewelled thrones carved in the shapes of the sultans who sat on them. There is also a demonstration of traditional musical instruments.

The Village of Artisans
Although there are a few art and craft shops by the palace entrance in the main square, the far more extensive Village of Artisans is approximately 1km away and reached by going west down the Bafoussam road, turning left before the post office and turning left again after passing the sports stadium. Each of the rows of houses on the short road to the village square contains a workshop, with craftspeople sculpting and carving, basket weaving, embroidering and beating metals.

Museum of Bamoun Arts and Traditions
Several hundred metres south of the palace and on the square near the Village of Artisans is the Museum of Bamoun Arts and Traditions (Musée des Arts et des Traditions Bamoun; tel: 348 25 86; free admission but donation expected, open daily 09.00–17.00), with an extensive collection relating to Bamoun history and art housed behind two elaborately carved doors. Exhibits include statues, masks, dyed textiles, clay and bronze pipes, spears, charms, carved furniture and carved wood panels depicting events in Bamoun history, as well as cooking implements, jugs and musical instruments, such as gongs and an ornately carved xylophone.

Every two years in December a colourful ceremony called the *Ngoun* takes place in Foumban. Representatives of all the villages in the chiefdom come to the palace, where the sultan is asked to explain his past activities. The representatives take care not to be seen by any women and children. The following day the sultan addresses his people at noon, problems are aired and the king is asked to suggest solutions. Problems posed often concern things like poverty, crime and degradation of the environment. Plenty of feasting follows.

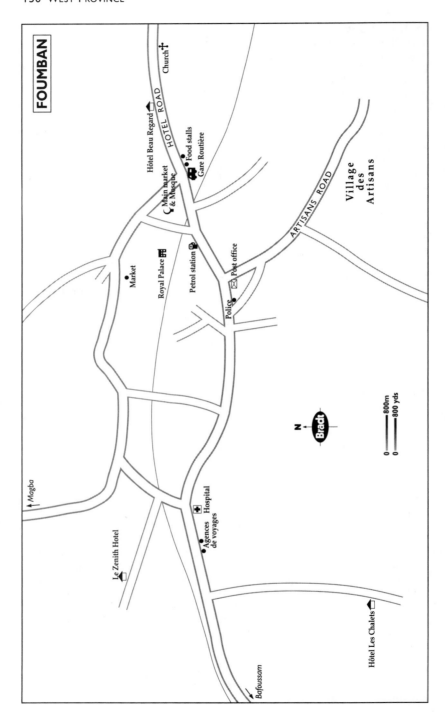

An excellent time to visit Foumban is at the end of Ramadan, when there are elaborate celebrations incorporating horse races, processions and dances. Seventy days later the town extravagantly celebrates Tabaski, marked by a parade of *marabouts* (fortune-tellers and wise men).

There are no banks in Foumban. The local hospitals are the District Hospital (tel: 348 21 23) and the Hôpital du Palais (tel: 348 24 47).

Around Foumban

If the touristic atmosphere of Foumban gets too much, an exploration of the surrounding villages can be richly rewarding.

Koutaba

Nearby Koutaba, for example, home of a monastery of Trappist monks and the Foumban Nkounja airport, has accommodation in the form of the Hotel Paradise Palace (BP 116; tel: 230 67 85/992 48 91). This hotel has air-conditioned rooms and suites with separate bathrooms and satellite TV, a restaurant and barbecue, and can provide guides for mountain walks, horseriding tours and visits to Foumban and other local sites. Koutaba has a meat and cattle market on Wednesdays.

Foumbot

On Sundays and Thursdays the nearby village of Foumbot holds a market known for its pottery, as well as for its vegetables, fruit, meat and other foods. Accommodation is available at the basic 16-room Hotel de Stade (BP 257; tel: 344 21 55), which has a bar.

Magba

This village northeast of Foumban holds a market on Sundays specialising in fresh and smoked fish.

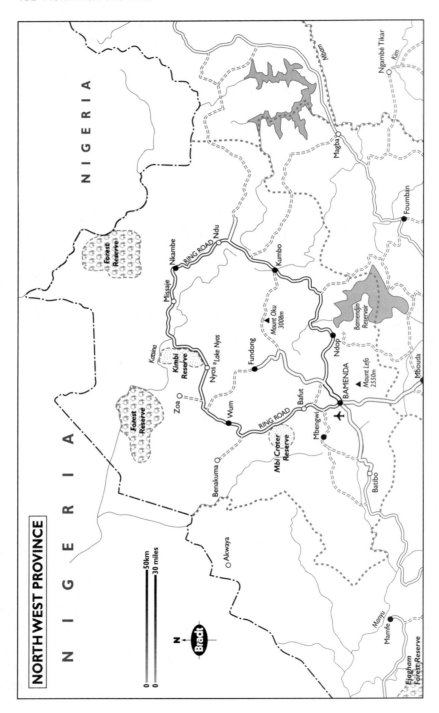

Northwest Province

This anglophone region has beautiful hilly scenery and enjoys a cool, comfortable climate. As with West Province, the rich volcanic soils in the area have permitted much higher rural population densities than elsewhere in the country, and coffee and cocoa are widely grown here.

Of most interest to travellers is probably the Ring Road, a beautiful red-earthed route which navigates the mountainous Grassfields and various Fulani settlements and Tikar chiefdoms. Bamenda, the capital of Northwest Province, is a good springboard for this.

BAMENDA

The capital of Northwest Province, anglophone Bamenda can be quite a contrast to francophone Bafoussam. It's been the heart of the English-speaking opposition movement against the French-speaking dominance within the country, and in recent years there have been various demonstrations and riots, although unrest has calmed down somewhat. An indication of this discord is the fact that many of the town's streets have both an official name given by the government and an established name used by the locals.

The gateway to the Fondom of Bali and Awing Crater Lake, the town, with a population of around 220,000, is located within pretty mountain scenery and has a pleasant climate, being at an altitude of more than 1,000m.

Resplendent with pine and banana trees, Bamenda has a museum and a craft market. Its administrative and commercial sectors are geographically separated by a steep drop.

Climb the snake-like road from Nkwen motor park and at 300m you come to one of the most prestigious neighbourhoods, Upper Station (or Upstation), which has a suburban flavour and contains government offices and much of the best residential property. Far more lively is the downtown area centred around the almost 2km-long Commercial Avenue. Noisy and bustling, this is where all the businesses and shops are, with lots of opportunities to buy local crafts.

For example, such crafts are available from the market behind the Ideal Park Hotel; from the Prescraft Centre, by the British Council Library on Commercial Street; and from the Handicraft Cooperative, east of town on the road climbing to Upper Station.

Getting there and away

Nkwen motor park, at the foot of Upper Station, has transport to Bamessing and Kumbo, while Bali motor park, about 1km southeast of the centre, serves Bali, Batibo and Mamfé. Ntarikon motor park, just southwest of the centre, has vehicles going to Bafut and Wum.

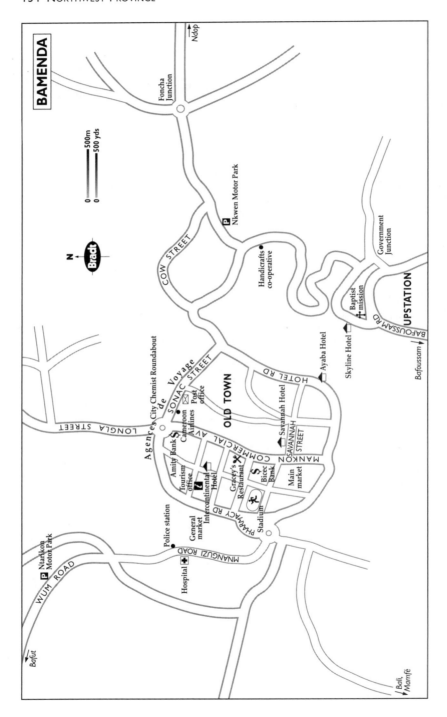

There are numerous *agences de voyages* in Bamenda, especially on the Sonac road and near Hospital Roundabout. Between them they go to a number of destinations including Douala, Yaoundé, Wum, Kumbo, Kumba, Buéa, Bafoussam and Dschang. It's best to ask around.

Where to stay

Nord-Ouest Ayaba Hotel BP 315; Hotel Rd, Bamenda; tel: 336 13 92/336 13 56; email: ayabahotel@refinedct.net. Once one of Bamenda's best hotels, now having seen better days. Graded by the government as a three-star hotel. There is a restaurant serving African and European dishes and Sunday lunch buffet, a snack bar, bar, weekend disco and swimming pool that can be used by non-guests for CFA1,500 (£1.60/US$2.83) per day. 100 self-contained, air-conditioned rooms with satellite TV, radio and video start at CFA18,000 (£19/US$34).

Presbyterian Church Centre Off Longlia Rd; tel: 336 40 70. Signposted 1km north of the centre, it has clean but basic dormitory rooms with beds at CFA2,000 (£2.14/US$3.78) and camping at CFA1,000 (£1.07/US$1.89) per tent.

New City Hotel Off Savanna St; tel: 336 24 67. Clean rooms with bathrooms for CFA3,000 (£3.21/US$5.67).

Holiday Hotel BP 7; tel: 336 13 82. Clean rooms, acceptable restaurant.

Baptist Mission Resthouse BP 1; tel: 336 12 85. At the start of the road leading to Upper Station, near the motor park. Clean rooms with shared facilities for CFA3,000 (£3.21/US$5.67).

Ideal Park Hotel BP 5; tel: 336 11 66. Off Commercial Av and right in the middle of the market area and therefore lively. Bamenda's oldest hotel, it is very good value, with a bar, a nightclub of sorts, and a good restaurant with very low prices. It has 16 clean, spacious rooms with bathrooms at under CFA6,500 (£6.96/US$12.28).

Tip Top Savannah Hotel BP 227; tel: 336 12 76. Off the southern end of Commercial Av in the town centre. 55 simple rooms, some with bathrooms, but noisy. Singles CFA3,500 (£3.75/US$6.61), doubles CFA5,000 (£5.35/US$9.45).

Ex Serviceman's Guest House Off Hotel Rd. A bit rough, with basic rooms from CFA3,500 (£3.75/US$6.61).

Hôtel Mondial BP 9; off Sonac St and Hotel Rd; tel: 336 18 32. This good hotel has 35 clean rooms with bathrooms and balconies overlooking town. There is a nightclub, a bar, a good restaurant and a path in the grounds leading to Upper Station. Singles CFA13,000 (£13.93/US$24.57), doubles CFA15,000 (£16.07/US$28.35), some basement rooms CFA8,000 (£8.57/US$15.12).

Unity Hotel BP 477; off the Wum road; tel: 336 37 82. Near the motor park for Wum and Bafut. As well as a lively restaurant/bar, there are clean rooms at under CFA5,000 (£5.35/US$9.45).

International Hotel BP 124; International St; tel: 336 25 27. 40 acceptable and spacious en-suite rooms in the centre of town from CFA6,000 (£6.43/US$11.34). There is also an inexpensive restaurant.

Hôtel le Bien BP 69; tel: 336 12 06. Basic hotel with 26 rooms, a bar and inexpensive restaurant.

Hôtel Skyline BP 111; Bafoussam Rd, Upper Station; tel: 336 12 89. A great view of downtown Bamenda. Good restaurant, bar, nightclub, swimming pool and rooms with AC for CFA16,000 (£17.14/US$30.24).

DEF Motel Nkwen St; tel: 336 37 48. Rooms vary from CFA6,000–12,000 (£6.43–12.86/US$11.34–22.68) and some have TV.

Hôtel le Bamboutos BP 110; south of Bamenda, at Mbouda; tel: 345 10 55. 49 basic rooms, a bar and a restaurant.

Where to eat and drink

There are plenty of places to eat in Bamenda, from the numerous roadside stalls and cheap eateries around Commercial Avenue, to better European and African cuisine at the more expensive hotels. For nightlife, again opt for the bigger hotels, such as the nightclubs at the Mondial and the International.

The Handicraft Cooperative Restaurant Station Rd, en-route for Upper Station. Offers good snacks, pizzas and other European and Cameroonian fare.

Gracey's Cafeteria and Restaurant Next to the Prescraft Centre on Commercial Av. Serves inexpensive European dishes, including good omelettes and steak and chips.

Mustard Seed Near Gracey's. Has a terrace on the street.

Sister Rose Last seen on the Wum road. An established Bamenda institution, but it tends to move a lot so ask around for its latest whereabouts. There is a choice of fish dishes and it also serves up huge helpings of chicken with plantains. Mains from CFA4,000 (£4.28/US$7.56), chicken CFA5,000 (£5.35/US$9.45).

Dallas International Quartier Metta; tel: 336 41 88. Grilled fish and half and whole chicken, pepper soup, from CFA2,000 (£2.14/US$3.78).

Tower Restaurant 4th Floor, Fru Ndi Bldg, Commercial Av; tel: 336 21 02. Western and African cuisine from CFA1,500 (£1.60/US$2.83).

Lisbon Snack Bar By the Holiday Hotel; tel: 336 13 82. Offers various grills and pepper soup. A whole chicken for two will set you back around CFA5,000 (£5.35/US$9.45).

St Denis Snack Bar Cow St, Nkwen; tel: 336 14 84. Hamburgers, grills and ice-cream. Meals average CFA2,000 (£2.14/US$3.78).

Practical information
Banks
Bicec, **Amity** and **SGBC** are on Commercial Av.

Cinema
Roxi cinema Just off Commercial Av.

Cultural organisations
British Council BP 622; Commercial Av; tel: 336 20 11; email: bc-bamenda.library@ camnet.cm. Library with more than 10,000 publications, videos, facility to show BBC television and internet access.

Medical facilities
Mezam Polyclinique Bali Rd; tel: 336 14 32

Tourist office
Commercial Av; tel: 336 13 95/794 99 93. Maps and details of excursions, such as the Ring Rd.

Travel agencies
ECO Travels and Tourism Tel: 336 16 16
Highlands Tourism Tel: 336 18 35

What to see
Surrounding Bamenda are beautiful mountains, crater lakes, waterfalls and traditional chiefdoms.

Lake Awing and Bafut-Nguemba Forest Reserve
This is easily reached from Bamenda, by driving south on the N6 main road and taking a left turn on to a dirt road about 18km from Bamenda, just before you

reach the town of Santa. A radio mast is on the right just before the turn. If you go by taxi from Bamenda, ask the driver to take you to Lake Awing. Walk from the two metal poles about 3km along the dirt track from the main road. Lake Awing, a peaceful crater lake surrounded by hills, is another 3km or so.

The reserve, which has been substantially destroyed, is mainly made up of eucalyptus plantations rather than forest, and is rich in birdlife.

Mount Lefo

Although 2,550m (8,364ft) high, this mountain can be climbed from Lake Awing in a day, although it is strenuous towards the summit. You are rewarded with fabulous views of various crater lakes and the Bamenda Plateau. The Fon of Awing (several kilometres down the road towards Mbouda) can provide a guide.

Bali

Bali, situated amid stunning scenery 20km west of Bamenda, is one of the principal chiefdoms in the area. It is an ideal day excursion from Bamenda.

Founded in around 1825, it has had numerous conflicts, not least with the neighbouring Bafut chiefdom. Its background is Chamba, which originates in the Adamawa region to the east.

Although the fon's (local chief's) palace is modern, it can provide information on local excursions. These include a cave containing the skulls of enemies of Bali. The palace can also provide guides, and if you are fortunate, you may be able to meet the fon himself. If so, you will be taken to his audience chamber where there are ancient thrones which are beaded all over or decorated with cowrie shells. Stylised handclapping begins, before the fon enters, dressed typically in embroidered robes and a fez-like cap.

The town has a German church built in 1903 and a Prescraft artisan centre, and its craftspeople can be seen working during the week.

Also in the area can be seen Forthung's Tower of Babel, a 70-room building that was never completed.

Bali puts on an end-of-year three-day festival, the *Leya*, towards the end of December, though not every year.

Where to stay in Bali

Bali Safari Lodge BP 19; book through the Atlantic Beach Hotel, Limbé; tel: 333 23 32. Outside town on the Bamenda road; comfortable en-suite rooms are around CFA20,000 (£21/US$37).
Mission House Rooms Bookable at Bamenda's Prescraft Centre (tel: 336 12 81); rooms here cost around CFA6,000 (£6.43/US$11.34).

Batibo

Batibo, some 40km from Bamenda, is the unofficial palm-wine capital of Cameroon. The villages in the region produce 7,000–10,000 litres of the highly alcoholic drink daily for sale across the country, and there are numerous palm-wine markets in the area.

BAMENDA HIGHLANDS RING ROAD

The 360km Ring Road passes through some wonderful scenery, the pasturelands of the Grassfields area of West Cameroon. There are terraced fields in the mountains, forests and meadows, with nomadic Fulani herders grazing cattle.

Much of the road consists of red-earthed dirt track, although some sections are paved. In the region are over 35 volcanic-crater lakes, several volcanic mountains (including the 3,000m-high Mount Oku), rolling hills, and waterfalls such as the impressive Menchum Falls.

The Ring Road encompasses many small villages located between the towns of Nkambé, Kumboi, Wum and Bamenda on the road. If time is scarce, there is the option of taking a shorter route, via Bamenda, Wum, Weh, Fundong, Belo and Bambui. An eventful trip is mentioned in Dervla Murphy's travelogue *Cameroon with Egbert*.

You can reach all the main towns on the routes by public transport, but having access to a car here (ideally a 4WD) is preferable as it allows you to reach interesting sites along the way, many of which are off the main road.

The condition of the road varies greatly from season to season and year to year, and recently the section between Nkambé and Wum could not be completed by vehicles because of collapsed bridges near Nyos and at Weh (or We), so check locally before setting off (for example at the tourist office in Bamenda).

When the road is in good condition, the longer Ring Road can be driven by car comfortably in a couple of days. It's also an ideal route for trekking and, in the dry season, mountain biking, a journey that takes about a week.

All the towns on the two routes have at least simple accommodation, and the region is ideal for camping too, but obtain permission first from the village chief if you are camping in a village compound.

Going clockwise from Bamenda, the first principal place of interest you come to on the route is Bafut, 18km from Bamenda.

Bafut

This traditional Tikar chiefdom was put on the map by a 1950s book by naturalist Gerald Durrell, *The Bafut Beagles*. An established 700-year-old kingdom, the town

---

BIRDING SITE GUIDE
Keith Barnes
Bamenda Highlands: Bafut-Nguemba Forest Reserve

This area comprises a mosaic of disjunct remnant montane and riverine forest within the Cameroon Mountains EBA. It is undoubtedly the best site to see two highly localised endemics – Bannerman's turaco and banded wattle-eye – and the near-endemic Bannerman's weaver. The best area for these birds is right next to Lake Awing. Other specialities that can be seen here include yellow-breasted and mountain boubou, brown-backed cisticola, bangwa scrub warbler, mountain robin chat, forest swallow, Cameroon mountain greenbul, green longtail and Cameroon sunbird, little grey flycatcher, grey-chested illadopsis, black-collared apalis, Congo serpent eagle and a mystery nightjar which was seen here in 2003. It is best to spend a night in Bamenda at the Hotel Skyline where both white-crowned cliff chat and Neumann's starling can be seen in the garden.

Birding Bafut-Nguemba

Leaving Bamenda, it is worthwhile checking the grounds of the Bali Safari Lodge, where Bamenda apalis has been recorded, particularly on the stretch of road towards Bamenda – check the first 500m. To get to Bafut-Nguemba, turn east off the N6 18km south of Bamenda, or 33km north of

has a large fon's palace (CFA1,000/£1.07/US$1.89 entry to the compound, CFA2,500/£2.67/US$4.72 museum entry, plus CFA1,500/£1.60/US$2.83 to take photographs or video), a complex of traditional buildings and courtyards, including many houses for the fon's numerous wives. The Achum, the palace of the last fon, features a striking, characteristic pyramidal thatched roof, and is the most sacred of these buildings and therefore cannot be viewed. Traditional dances can be performed at a cost of CFA10,000 to CFA15,000 (£10–15/US$18–27) per group, although this is negotiable.

The fon's wives guide visitors and the tour includes viewing the 'Nighaa Ni Bifh', a huge 300-year-old talking drum used to send messages around the Bafut Fondom, as well as ancient stones where prisoners of war and disloyal subjects were put to death. The palace also features carvings of animals, which are traditionally special protectors of the fon.

There are various colourful festivals in this region. Richly embroidered robes are usually worn for such ceremonial occasions, which include funeral ceremonies (known as 'cry dies') as well as the festivals of the various fons. There is much music and dancing, and visitors are often welcome.

There is an annual grass-cutting festival, featured in *The Bafut Beagles*, entailing the village venturing to the grassfields in April to collect bundles of grass for thatching buildings, followed by a feast in the company of the fon. A similar ceremony occurs just before Christmas most years, with four days of costumes and masks, dancing and music.

Bafut also has a market every eight days. One of Durrell's characters, Peter Shu, the King of the Snakes, puts on a show (CFA1,000/£1.07/US$1.89 plus CFA2,500/£2.67/US$4.72 for photography) in which he handles dangerous snakes such as pythons, vipers, cobras and mambas. It is well worth seeing if he is performing. It is best to telephone him in advance, on 336 38 15.

Mbouda, and drive a further 3km before reaching forested gullies among Eucalyptus plantations. Although all the rarest have been seen here, if you can, head straight up to Lake Awing, where most of the target birds are easy to spot. Bannerman's turaco, banded wattle-eye and Bannerman's weaver are all seen here with relative ease. Other excellent species one might notch up in this seemingly unimpressive forest patch include Cassin's hawk-eagle, yellow-breasted boubou, mountain boubou, forest swallow, Petit's sawwing, Cameroon mountain greenbul, Cameroon olive-greenbul, Cameroon sunbird, oriole finch, purple-throated cuckoo shrike, ruwenzori hill-babbler, Elliot's woodpecker, brown-capped weaver and Johanna's sunbird.

Birding Mount Oku

For Mount Oku head to Kumbo (aka Banso) and the village of Elak, where BirdLife International's Kilum Mountain Forest Project HQ is located. Green longtails have been recorded in the tiny patch of forest alongside the HQ, forest swallows breed here and oriole finches are found in the village. Opposite the HQ a trail leads through farmland (45 minutes) to the forest, which begins at 2,200m. Shortly after the school the trail splits into the gentle KA trail (right) and steeper KD trail (left) before reaching the forest. Bannerman's turaco, banded wattle-eye and Bannerman's weaver all occur here.

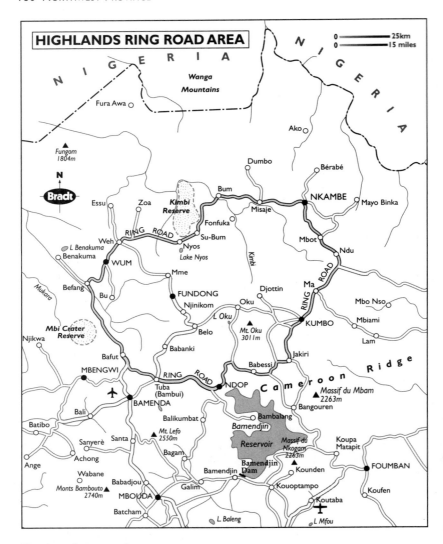

Getting there and away

There are regular share-taxis to and from Bamenda every day, with more on market day.

Where to stay in Bafut

You can stay in a century-old guesthouse which was Gerald Durrell's home when he wrote the book. It overlooks and is bookable through the fon's palace (tel: 796 83 05/336 38 18). Simple rooms with shared facilities are CFA4,000 (£4.28/US$7.56) and meals are available.

Savannah Botanic Gardens BP 2153; tel: 336 38 70. Out of the town on the Bamenda road, rooms with bathrooms start at around CFA7,000 (£7.50/US$13.23). There is a good restaurant and camping is permitted.

What to see
Menchum Falls
Moving northwards from Bafut on the west side of the Ring Road, the vegetation becomes thicker as the road gets worse. It can become impassable during the rainy season and taking the shorter route (details follow) to reach Wum, via Fundong and Weh, can be a better option.

The dramatic Menchum Falls, around 20km south of Wum and 30km north of Bafut, are away from the road on the west side, so listen out for the crashing sound of the water. The road may be churned up from tyre marks leading to the falls from the road. Beware of the so-called safety rails – people have fallen to their deaths here.

Lake Benakuma
An optional detour is the track road to Benakuma from Belifang, which leads to Lake Benakuma.

WUM
There is almost no public transport available beyond Wum, located 60km from Bamenda, and the recent collapse of bridges at Weh and Nyos has made moving on to Nkambé along the road – or rutted track, to be more precise – almost impossible, although the present situation may be improved. Hitching a lift in a lorry is not cheap: count on paying around CFA45,000 (£48/US$85) to reach Nkambé.

A couple of miles northwest of the town centre in the hills is Lake Wum, another beautiful crater lake. It is possible to swim in the deep waters, but bear in mind what happened at Lake Nyos (details follow) – there is some local as well as international concern about the safety of the crater lakes.

Where to stay in Wum
Morning Star Hotel Tel: 336 26 34. Rooms with bathrooms for CFA4,000 (£4.28/US$7.56) and a restaurant.

Shortening the route
Northeast of Wum, you have two choices when you get to Weh: either continue along the main Ring Road, or take the right turning going south back to Bamenda via Fundong, which constitutes a far shorter round trip. There is little public transport along this route.

After passing the village of Mme, you come to the Chimney Waterfalls at the town of Fundong. As an optional trek, a track road here to the village of Lara leads to Mount Oku (3,010m/9,864ft).

At Fundong you can stay at the **Tourist Home Hotel** where simple but clean rooms cost under CFA4,000 (£4.28/US$7.56).

From Fundong, this shorter route continues to the Chiefdom of Laikom to the left of the road and then to the village of Belo (or Befo), where there are a few cheap hotels and guesthouses, and where you can begin a morning's trek eastwards into the Ijim Forest, heading towards Mount Oku, Lake Oku and the Kilum Forest.

Wum to Nkambé: continuing on the Ring Road
If you do not deviate from the main Ring Road at Weh and instead continue east, you come to a collapsed bridge, which, until it is mended, stops you in your tracks unless you are prepared to hike. The region becomes much wilder, with beautiful landscapes and Fulani herders grazing their cattle, and a far thinner population generally.

LAKE NYOS

Travelling further along the Ring Road, and around 30km from Weh, you come to Nyos, site of a huge natural tragedy and now a dead village. It holds the dubious world record for being the deadliest lake. On August 21 1986 at Lake Nyos, a couple of kilometres south of the village, there was a mysterious natural gas eruption, with a massive cloud of suffocating carbon dioxide and other gases being expelled by the lake with such velocity that vegetation and some trees were levelled.

The cloud travelled northeast towards Su-bum, now the only substantial settlement in the area up to 25km from the site, and an estimated 1,800 people and countless animals lost their lives. Survivors were rehoused in infertile areas in two-roomed, concrete huts with tin roofs and mudbrick cooking huts. Their sense of being misplaced and forgotten has been high.

Scientists disagree about the source of the gas. Because the lake lies in the crater of a volcano, some believe that the gas was volcanic in origin. Other scientists argue that the decomposition of organic material at the base of the lake caused gases to build up naturally and that temperature changes at the surface of the lake, where there were warm waters, reacted with cold, gas-saturated deep waters, triggering the gas to be released. If either of these theories is true, presumably the same thing could happen again at any of the deep lakes in the area. Many locals are suspicious that the catastrophe was caused by Western scientific research. The lake is the subject of ongoing investigation.

KIMBI RIVER GAME RESERVE

Around 50km along the road from Wum is the Kimbi River Game Reserve. There is very basic accommodation available in the reserve (further details from the Bamenda tourist office) and you will need a vehicle to explore – which will be tricky while the bridges are in disrepair.

MISANJE – FOR HIKING INTO NIGERIA

Another 25km from the Kimbi River Game Reserve along the road eastwards (and 20km from Nkambé) is the village of Misanje, with barely acceptable rooms available for under CFA5,000 (£5.35/US$9.45).

From here you can head north for 18km on the track to Dumbo, for a fantastic two-day trek to Bissaula (or Bissuala) in Nigeria. The walk starts with a mild climb, followed by a level section, and then a steep descent into Nigeria takes in farmland, forest and rocky escarpments with fantastic views at their summits.

The hike is quite tough and it is also easy to get lost as the footpaths can be very faint in places, and it is therefore a good idea to obtain a guide at Misanje, at Bamenda Tourist Office, or failing that at Dumbo, which is also where immigration and customs formalities are processed. Or you could hire a Fulani herdsman in the vicinity.

There is a basic hotel (under CFA5,000/£5.35/US$9.45 per night) at Dumbo. Nigerian immigration and customs are at Bissaula, which has no accommodation.

Nkambé to Kumbo

This sparsely populated, almost infrastructure-free section of the Grassfields abruptly ends at the town of Nkambé, which has bars and restaurants, medical facilities, a post office, petrol stations and accommodation, including the **Divisional Hotel** (tel: 336 13 24; rooms under CFA5,000/£5.35/US$9.45). Here you could try to cadge a lift or take a share-taxi for the 35km to Abonshie on the Nigerian border, via Ako.

The Ring Road continues south towards Kumbo, passing the chiefdom of Mbot and its fon's palace, very near Ndu. Ndu has clean but basic rooms at the **Dallas Hotel** for under CFA5,000 (£5.35/US$9.45).

At Ndu you have the option of taking a track road going eastwards to the village of Sabongari, and then through the Mambila Mountains into Nigeria.

KUMBO

By Grassfields standards, Kumbo (or Banso, being home to the Banso people of the Nso linguistic group) is a large town and has a good range of restaurants, bars, banks and shops, petrol stations and a post office, plus a cathedral and two good hospitals, Banso Baptist Hospital and Shisong Catholic Hospital. It is at an altitude of over 2,000m, giving it a pleasant, cool climate. A large market is regularly held here, and one section is devoted to traditional medicine.

About 500m east of the town centre is a cave containing ancient skulls. Ask around for a guide to show you it.

As part of Nso Cultural Week, Guinness sponsors an annual horse race at Tobin Stadium, and horses also race through the streets. This is usually held in mid-November. Fulani and Banso riders compete in the exciting competition. Further details are available from the Bamenda Tourist Office or Guinness's headquarters in Kumbo (tel: 348 12 23).

Kumbo is the seat of a powerful chiefdom, and the fon's palace can be visited (admission free but a donation is expected).

Colonial times were particularly troubling for the Banso, who resisted the Germans and were defeated by them in 1906, at which time their fon was executed.

Getting there and away

Transport is available to Nkambé, Elak (or Oku-Elak or Oku), Bamenda and, except in the rainy season, Foumban.

Where to stay in Kumbo

Central Inn Hotel BP 47; tel: 348 10 15/348 16 80. By the *gare routière* in the centre; has simple rooms for around CFA3,000 (£3.21/US$5.67).

Fomo Hotel BP 46; tel: 348 16 16. North of the centre, offering good-value clean rooms with bathrooms at around CFA8,000 (£8.57/US$15.12).

Tourist Home Hotel BP 33; tel: 348 11 02. A government-graded one-star hotel with basic inexpensive accommodation, a bar and a restaurant.

OKU AND MOUNT OKU

From Kumbo you can take a track road heading west that deviates from the Ring Road and leads to the village of Oku (marked Elak on some maps) on the northern slopes of Mount Oku. At 3,011m (9,879ft), Mount Oku is the second-highest mountain in West Africa, after Mount Cameroon.

Oku is the settlement of the Oku Fondom. The Oku have a rich history and are known for their great knowledge of traditional medicines and practice of witchcraft. For a week each April various spectacles, such as masked dancing, can be seen, held at the fon's palace at the far end of town. There is basic accommodation in the village, including rooms at the **Elak Guesthouse**, and the **Touristic Hotel**, by the market.

If you want to climb the mountain or see its lake, take a gift of a bottle of whisky or something similar to the fon's palace. The palace can provide a guide, which should cost in the region of CFA4,000 (£4.28/US$7.56) but may be as much as CFA6,000 (£6.43/US$11.34).

Climbing the mountain takes about seven hours as a round trip. The climb is not particularly strenuous or challenging, and passes steep farmland which gives way to a large area of montane and riverine forest before becoming subalpine grassland. This forest, the Kilum Forest, adjoins the Ijim Forest, accessible from the smaller Ring Road at Belo (or Befo). The forest is rich in birdlife, including some Cameroon endemics. The Kilum Mountain Forest Project (tel: 336 32 93) in Elak, run by BirdLife International, can provide more information.

A trail begins on the opposite side of the road to the Project headquarters, taking in farmland (a walk of about 40 minutes) and then the forest, at an altitude of about 2,200m/7,218ft. The trail splits into two branches soon after the school, into the less steep and less challenging KA trail on the right, and the steeper KD trail to the left.

At 2,200m on the western slopes of Mount Oku is the beautiful, rich-green volcanic crater lake, Lake Oku, which is surrounded by dense forest. Like most of the crater lakes in the region, it is sacred, and therefore swimming and fishing are forbidden by locals.

Kumbo to Bamenda

This region is the most densely populated on the Ring Road. Moving south towards Jakiri and its superb range of hills, you get great views of the Ndop plains, a bed for the waters of the huge reservoir there, Bamendjing Lake. There is basic accommodation in Jakiri.

From Jakiri you can either carry on south towards Foumban or continue on the Ring Road heading west, past excellent landscapes, the village of Bamessi (or Bamessing) and the town of Ndop. The area is especially beautiful between Ndop and Bambui and well worth visiting if you have not had the time to explore the Ring Road.

BAMESSI, SAGBA AND NDOP

Bamessi, about 25km east of Bamenda, has an artisans' centre and a handicrafts training centre, where craftspeople can be seen at work and items like masks and pottery can be purchased. The village of Sagba can also be visited, 4km west on the Bamenda road; there is a hill half a kilometre after the village, which is very easy to climb, and which provides great views of the surrounding landscapes.

Further west towards Bamenda is Ndop, which has some facilities, including filling stations and basic accommodation, such as the **Green Valley Resort** (tel: 336 34 00) with a restaurant and simple rooms for CFA4,000 (£4.28/US$7.56).

At Ndop a branch road leads east to Bambalang, by Bamendjing Lake; otherwise you can complete the Ring Road by returning to Bamenda.

Centre Province

Of most interest to the majority of visitors to this province is the lush, climatically pleasant capital, Yaoundé, which has enough distractions to warrant a visit.

Virtually no roads penetrate the northern half of this province, and apart from a few exceptions, such as the impressive Nachtigal Falls near Ntui, north of Yaoundé, and the Sanaga Beaches around Monatele, most people enter this region to reach Yaoundé, en route for the chiefdoms and mountains of the west, the beaches of Kribi or Limbé, or, occasionally, the rainforests of the east. Yaoundé is also the departure point for the train to the north of the country, where further spectacular scenery and exotic villages wait to be discovered.

YAOUNDE

Yaoundé, the capital and the home of its government, is the political epicentre of Cameroon. Located in the southwestern corner of the country, Yaoundé is about 200km (124 miles) from both the Atlantic Ocean and the southern border.

'Yaoundé' comes from the word *Ewondo,* the name of the ethnic group who settled in the region during the German era. Commercial activity started here early in the last century and after World War I the French established Yaoundé as the capital of their new territory, with the British choosing Buéa as their capital. Despite being the capital of the country, Yaoundé's population, at around 1.2 million, is considerably smaller than Douala's.

Known as the city of seven hills, it expanded on to many other hills some years ago. Sprawled over these undulating hills, Yaoundé lacks a coherent street pattern and most streets are snake-like. It is characterised by a heady mixture of modern architecture and shanty towns.

Being at an altitude of about 700–1,000m (2,000–3,000ft), climatically it has a much cooler climate than one would expect in a city only five degrees north of the Equator, and it is certainly far more comfortable than Douala. Its sleepy reputation is gradually being lost, with more and more modern buildings sprouting up, especially in the administrative quarter.

One of the first things to strike many people driving from the airport, Nsimalen, is the greenery. Yaoundé, which stretches over an area of about 9km by 6km, is very fertile, and large trees abound throughout the city. The attractive range of peaks around the capital, such as Mount Fébé, add to the attraction of the place.

The River Mfoundi runs through the city, but along with the Municipal, Biyemassi and Ngoa-Ekelle city lakes, is suffering somewhat with pollution, from metals, household refuse and industrial waste. As a result, aquatic life has dwindled greatly.

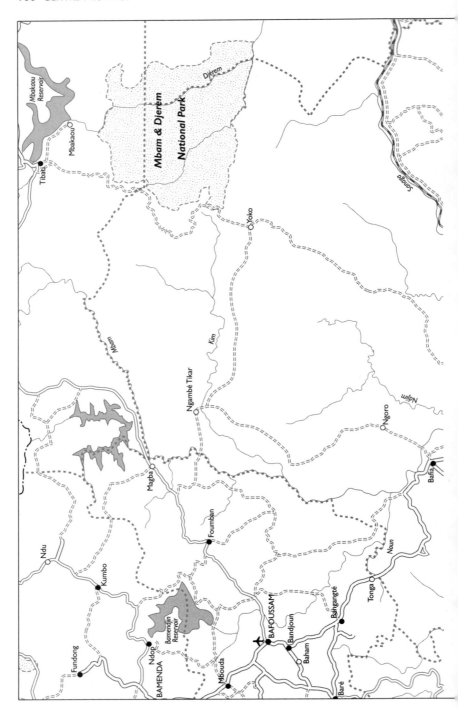

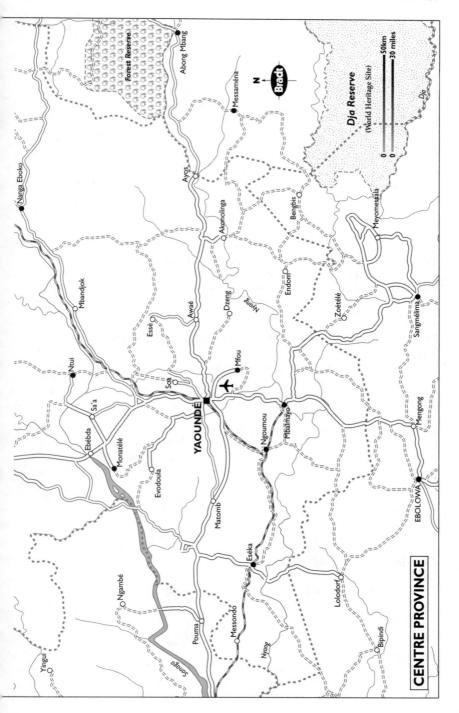

CENTRE PROVINCE

For a capital city, Yaoundé does not have a great number of specific attractions geared to the visitor; it is better simply to soak up the atmosphere, by people-watching at a café perhaps.

The centre

Yaoundé's centre is focused on the streets leading from the Place Ahmadou Ahidjo, a square which has a striking 1950s building with a large sloping roof, the Cathedral of Notre Dame. The cathedral is on Avenue Monseigneur Vogt, where a number of banks are located.

Also off the Place Ahmadou Ahidjo, and branching off from Avenue Ahidjo, is Avenue Kennedy, the main commercial corridor, with upmarket shops and terraced cafés and an unmistakably French air. At its northern end is another square, the Place Kennedy, which is home to the **Centre d'Artisanat**, containing Cameroonian and regional arts and crafts which are available to buy.

Also leading off the Place Ahmadou Ahidjo is the Avenue du Président El Hadj Ahidjo, and halfway up this is the busy *marché central* (**central market**), a massive market somewhat resembling a car-boot sale in a multi-storey car park.

Quartier du Lac and Melen neighbourhoods

The tranquil Lake Quarter and adjoining Melen Quarter, roughly to the west of Place Ahmadou Ahidjo between Boulevard du 20 Mai and Yaoundé's polluted and stagnant lake, contains many administrative offices and some interesting examples of modern building design.

Messa, Mokolo and Briqueterie neighbourhoods

The lively residential districts of Messa, Mokolo and Briqueterie, poor districts northwest of the centre, are hidden away in the hills. They all have numerous unlicensed chicken houses, which serve excellent grilled chicken, and Messa has a bustling market, the **Marché Mokolo**, selling foods, fabrics and clothes. Briqueterie houses Yaoundé's Grand Mosquee.

Bastos and other neighbourhoods

This quiet neighbourhood in the extreme north of the town has the most exclusive residential properties and restaurants, as well as the president's palace and various embassies. Weekly English-language services are held at the Bastos Presbyterian Church.

Other neighbourhoods include the residential quarters of Nkoldongo, Obili, Biyem Assi and Ngoa-Ekele south of the centre, and Nkolmesseng, Mimboman and Djoungolo to the east. Djoungolo features a temple built in 1937 by American William Caldell Johnston.

Getting there and away
By air

The international airport, Nsimalen, is approximately 19km south of the main square, Place Ahmadou Ahidjo, and is off Ebolowa Road. Taxi fares vary between CFA2,000 (£2.14/US$3.78) during the day and CFA3,000 (£3.21/US$5.67) at night.

By train

The train station, Gare Voyageurs (tel: 223 40 03), is by Place Elig Essono, which is 1km north of Place Ahmadou Ahidjo. The train to Ngaoundéré leaves at around 18.00 each day, and the Douala service at 07.40 and 13.30 daily.

By road

Many of the buses/*agences de voyages* are located on Boulevard de l'OCAM, about 3km south of the centre towards Quartier Mvan. Companies change frequently. A ticket to Douala (239km) typically costs around CFA2,000 (£2.14/US$3.78) in a minibus to CFA8,000 (£8.57/US$15.12) for a non-stop express service in a first-class bus.

Alliance Voyages Goes to Batouri and Bertoua (CFA6,000/£6.43/US$11.34, 8 hours).
Jeannot Express Goes to Buéa and Bamenda.
Guaranti Express Tel: 230 28 83. Goes to Douala, Buéa, Bamenda, Limbé and Bafoussam.
Buca Voyages Goes to Mbalmayo and Ebolowa.
Ocean Voyages Goes to Kribi.
Centrale Voyages BP 2789; south of the centre in Rue Andre Amougou, Mvog-Mbi; tel: 230 39 94/770 19 94. Provides a good 3hr service to Douala for CFA3,500 (£3.75/US$6.61) or CFA8,000 (£8.57/US$15.12) for a luxury, air-conditioned bus with waitress service. Centrale also goes to Bafoussam.
Confort Voyages BP 5029; tel: 221 57 16. For Bafoussam and Foumban, departing from *gare routière* d'Etoudi, 5km north of the centre.
Binam Voyages BP 4293; tel: 220 93 92. Goes to Bafoussam (CFA3,000/£3.21/US$5.67, 5 hours), again departing from *gare routière* d'Etoudi.

Where to stay

El Panaden BP 8457; Pl de l'Hôtel de Ville, Rue de l'Indépendance; tel: 222 27 65; email: elpanaden@yahoo.fr. In the commercial district; there's a garden restaurant and the 36 clean rooms (singles CFA10,500/£11.25/US$19.84, doubles CFA13,000/£13.93/US$24.57) have AC, TV, balcony and room service, but the en-suite shower rooms can be very basic and do not always have hot water.
Hôtel Prestige Messe des Officiers BP 2697; Av Charles Atangana; tel: 222 60 55/222 60 39. 32 double rooms and two apartments with balconies overlooking the centre of town. Rooms start from CFA12,000 (£12.86/£US$22.68) and have bathrooms, AC, TV and telephone. There is a snack bar, bar and restaurant serving both European and Cameroonian dishes.
Hôtel Prestige Plus BP 2697; Carrefour Biyemassi; tel: 231 82 52/231 89 60. 30 double rooms and two apartments with bathrooms, balconies, AC, TV and telephone, and a restaurant serving European, Asian and Cameroonian dishes.
Foyer Internationale de l'Eglise Presbytérienne (the Presbyterian Mission) Off Rue Onembele Nkou; tel: 985 23 76. Reached via the hill behind the four big concrete water towers on the hill above Carrefour Nlongkak. This popular, quiet guesthouse has clean dormitories with shared facilities at CFA2,000 (£2.14/US$3.78) and singles/twins with shared bathrooms from CFA4,000 (£4.28/US$7.56). There is also a shared kitchen.
Ideal Hotel Rond-point Nlongkak; tel: 220 98 52. In a rather noisy neighbourhood, the Ideal offers basic rooms with fans, bathrooms and sometimes a balcony. Double rooms from CFA7,000 (£7.50/US$13.23).
Hôtel Sipowa Tel: 221 95 71. In a pleasant area 450m northwest of Carrefour Bastos, opposite the Saudi embassy on the main road in the Bastos neighbourhood, this hotel has clean en-suite rooms with TV and AC for CFA17,000 (£18/US$32). Continental breakfast is available from CFA1,500 (£1.60/US$2.83), and the fresh bread is excellent.
Hôtel des Députés BP 24; Quartier du lac; tel: 223 15 55; email: hotel.deputes@iccnet.cm. This government-rated three-star hotel is located in the centre of the government district, away from the centre. Rather bland but comfortable; rear rooms have a pleasant view over a lake with the prime minister's residence and other exclusive homes in the background. There is a large restaurant, nightclub and lounge bar area. There

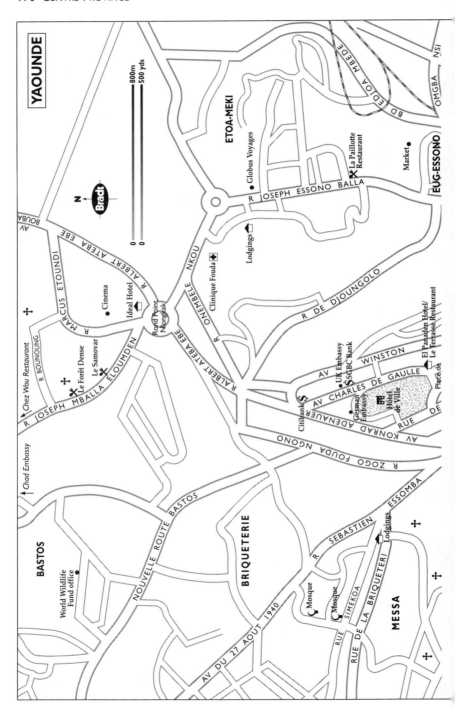

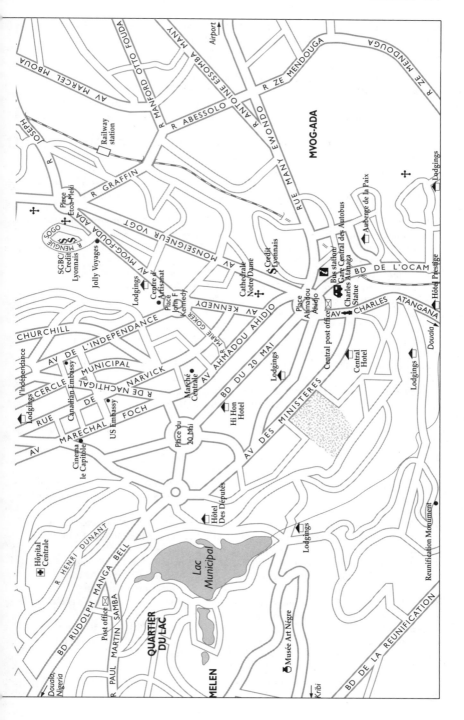

is a swimming pool and two tennis courts, all of which can be used by non-residents for a small fee. The 145 rooms and suites have satellite TV and AC, although some equipment may be faulty. There is a swimming pool and tennis courts. Security is good. The mini-suites at CFA40,000 (£42/US$75) are good value. Credit cards are accepted.

Sun Star Hotel tel: 951 33 27. In the Elig-Edjoa neighbourhood; clean, simple rooms are CFA8,000 (£8.57/US$15.12).

Le Caseba Catholic Mission Guesthouse Off Rue Joseph Essono Balla; tel: 221 30 13; email: casba@rctmail.net. Northeast of the centre; rooms are around CFA10,000 (£10.70/US$18.90).

Hôtel Grand Palmier BP 976; Rue Albert Atea Ebe, Bastos; tel: 220 45 93. Has 16 spacious if plain rooms for under CFA5,000 (£5.35/US$9.45) and a bar. Take a taxi during the night time in this neighbourhood.

Royal Hotel BP 446; tel: 222 44 28. A basic hotel with a reasonable restaurant, a bar and a nightclub. Located in the central business district; 42 rooms from about CFA16,000 (£17.14/US$30.24).

Hôtel Mansel BP 2060; Quartier Fouda; tel: 220 73 44/220 24 62. A government-rated two-star hotel in quite a noisy location, but the 80 rooms and three suites are comfortable and there is a restaurant and bar. CFA17,000–20,000 (£18.22–21.40/US$32.13–37.80).

Laginaque Hotel BP 1611; Carrefour Bastos; tel: 221 05 54. Ten comfortable rooms with AC and separate bathroom at CFA25,000 (£26.79/US$47.25) and upwards.

Hôtel Kaelly BP 4336; tel: 221 90 96. Near the Omnisport sports stadium about a mile northeast of Carrefour Nlongkak, this hotel has a bar and 22 clean rooms with AC for CFA13,500 (£14.46/US$25.51) per single.

Auberge de la Paix BP 106; off Bd de l'OCAM; tel: 223 65 02. Central and cheap, but very basic and small and therefore often full. CFA4,000 (£4.28/US$7.56).

Cablys Hotel BP 6478; tel: 222 61 09. A government-rated two-star hotel in the centre with 28 rooms from CFA15,000, plus a bar and a restaurant.

Hotel Grand Moulin BP 43 36; Rue Joseph Essono Balla; tel: 220 68 19. 58 en-suite rooms, suites and apartments at CFA10,000 (£10.70/US$18.70) and upwards. There is a restaurant and bar.

Hôtel Le Faubourg BP 1207; tel: 222 39 30. A government-rated one-star hotel with 41 plain rooms, bar and restaurant.

Hôtel Bellevue Tel: 221 10 96; email: hotelbellevue@caramail.com. AC, cable TV, telephone in rooms, bar, restaurant and terrace with panoramic view of Yaoundé.

Fraicheur Hotel BP 4707; tel: 222 86 05. Off the Bd de l'OCAM south of the bus station, this good-value hotel has a restaurant and a rooftop bar. Clean, air-conditioned rooms with bathrooms at CFA10,000 (£10.70/US$18.90).

Hôtel Indépendance BP 474; Av Winston Churchill; tel: 223 47 71. Now rather faded, this hotel has 40 comfortable rooms with bathrooms, AC and satellite TV for CFA15,000 (£16.07/US$28.35) and upwards. There's a bar and nightclub.

Central Hotel BP 06; off Rue Jezoiun; tel: 222 65 98. A no-frills hotel in the Lake Quarter, ranked by the government as a three-star, with rooms starting at CFA20,000 (£21/US$37) including continental breakfast, and better-quality suites starting at CFA30,000 (£32/US$57), including a fridge and separate lounge room. There is a good restaurant. Ideal if you have a vehicle, but few taxis visit.

Simm's 1 Hotel BP 4293; off Rue Joseph Mballa Eloumden; tel: 220 53 75. Bar, restaurant and 24 clean rooms for CFA13,000–25,000 (£13.93–26.79/US$24.57–47.25). It is in the Bastos neighbourhood; a sister hotel with the same name is in Ngousso.

Hôtel le Mercure BP 14304; Av Ahidjo; tel: 222 21 31, www.accorhotels.com. A very comfortable hotel in the centre of the city with 98 rooms starting at around CFA35,000 (£37/US$66), plus a bar, restaurant and tennis courts.

Hôtel Mont Fébé BP 711; tel: 221 40 02. Away from the city centre in the tranquil Presidential Palace district, situated on the upper slopes of Mount Fébé, this hotel enjoys magnificent views over Yaoundé. The 218 rooms, with all the trimmings like satellite TV, telephone and video, start at CFA56,000 (£60/US$105). Facilities include an 18-hole golf course, two tennis courts, a swimming pool (CFA2,000/£2.14/US$3.78 to non-residents) and a formal, expensive, but very good restaurant, Le Sommet, an open-air buffet restaurant by the pool, and a snack bar. There is also a bar, a casino and Le Balafon nightclub.

Yaoundé Hilton BP 11852; Bd du 20 Mai; tel: 223 36 46; email: info_yaoundé@hilton.com; web: www.yaoundé.hilton.com. Located in the heart of the government district and Yaoundé's top hotel, the Hilton's restaurants, coffee shop and bars (including a panoramic bar) are expensive and the 218 rooms (air-conditioned) start at CFA145,000 (£155/US$274), although rates may be negotiable. A steel band plays in the foyer every afternoon. Swissair and Cameroon Airlines have offices in the complex. There is also a health club, two floodlit tennis courts and a squash court. Other facilities include car hire, a casino, currency exchange, a playground, 24-hour room service, and direct dial in bedrooms, but of course you pay through the nose for all these. Credit cards are accepted, which is just as well.

Where to eat and drink

There are lots of restaurants and stalls on the streets selling cheap snacks, especially around Rond-point Nlongkak, on Rue Onembele, and on Rue Albert Ateba Ebe, and to a lesser extent in the Quartier du Lac during working hours. The Mvog-Ada neighbourhood is full of simple fish bars. Rue Joseph Essono Balla (the main road in Bastos) has a good selection of mid-range and more expensive establishments.

The cheapest cafés and restaurants are outside the centre, notably in the poorer suburbs like Briqueterie and Messa.

Bar Sintra Av Kennedy. This upmarket brasserie for 'business-types' with mobiles is good for people-watching. It has a French-based menu with dishes like steak, beef in red wine sauce and coq au vin for CFA2,500–5,000 (£2.67–5.35/US$4.72–9.45), with a '33'/Castel beer costing CFA400 (42p/75c) and a large Guinness costing CFA700 (75p/US$1.32).

Le Challenge Restaurant Av Kennedy; tel: 223 96 60. Going south down the Av de l'Indépendance and turning right you come to this self-service café purporting to be vegetarian; it instead offers many good-value meat and fish dishes such as fricassee chicken, pork roti, fish provençal, with rice and various stews for CFA2,500–3,500 (£2.67–3.75/US$4.72–6.61); beers are CFA400 (42p/75c).

Boulangerie Patisserie Av de l'Indépendance. About halfway down the avenue, this excellent patisserie sells freshly baked baguettes, pastries and probably one of the best croc monsieurs you will ever taste. Prices hover around CFA400–600 (42–64p/75c–US$1.13).

Boulangerie Calfatas Rue Nachtigal, opposite the American Embassy. Good cakes, pastries, ice-creams and croissants.

African Logik Rue Joseph Mballa Eloumden. Great atmosphere; grilled fish, chicken and chips and similar from about CFA2,000 (£2.14/US$3.78), with live music from 19.00 to 22.00 some nights.

Mont Blanc Rue Ateba Ebe, off Rond-point Nlongkak. Cameroonian and European cuisine from around CFA2,500 (£2.67/US$4.72), and a good bar.

Le Globus Rond-point Nlongkak. Meals not too pricey (CFA2,500/£2.67/US$4.72) and good for watching the city from the terrace with a cold beer.

La Maison Blanche Rue Rudolphe Abessolo. Wakes up at night, and a good place for grilled chicken, fish and plantain dishes. From CFA2,000 (£2.14/US$3.78).

L'Atlantique Rue Joseph Mballa Eloumden, Bastos, east of Carrefour Bastos; tel: 221 43 44. European dishes such as good pizza and grills in a pretty courtyard setting. Meals from CFA4,000 (£4.28/US$7.56) and upwards.

Terre Battue Rue Ebe, off Route de Obala. Good-value Cameroonian menu and excellent live music. Around CFA5,000 (£5.35/US$9.45) per head.

Chez Wu Rue Joseph Mballa Eloumden; tel: 220 46 79. Good Chinese food.

Restaurant Chinatown Rue Joseph Mballa Eloumden; tel: 221 45 14. Another Chinese restaurant in Bastos, but with cheaper fare. Around CFA9,000 (£9.64/US$17.01) per head.

La Terrasse Pl de l'Indépendance, adjacent to El Panaden Hotel; tel: 222 1262. Cameroonian and Italian cuisine with pizzas from around CFA3,500 (£3.75/US$6.61). Excellent steak with plantain chips CFA3,000 (£3.21/US$5.67).

La Forêt Dense Rue Joseph Mballa Eloumden; tel: 220 53 08. Exotic Cameroonian dishes generally ranging from CFA5,000–8,000 (£5.35–8.57/US$9.45–15.12), and simpler staples like *ndole* and chicken with plantains.

Le Gastrot Rue Joseph Mballa Eloumden, Bastos. A good mid-range menu. Next to La Forêt Dense.

L'Agora Rue Ateba Ebe, off Rond-point Nlongkak; tel: 222 35 96. Quite expensive but serves good Cameroonian food such as *ndole* with fish; even porcupine and pangolin are on the menu.

Le Samovar Rue Joseph Mballa Eloumden, Carrefour Bastos; tel: 222 55 28. Popular with expatriates, offering French and Russian meals from about CFA5,000 (£5.35/US$9.45). Adjacent to Le Forêt Dense and Le Gastrot.

La Marseillais Av Foch; tel: 223 46 88. Central restaurant with good-value fare. Other branches, including Rue Nachtigal.

Café Yaoundé Av Winston Churchill; tel: 222 85 94. An Italian-style restaurant resembling a Roman villa, perched on a hillside and surrounded by lush gardens. A live monkey guards the entrance.

Resto Thifany Rue Joseph Mballa Eloumden, Bastos. Breakfast from CFA1,000 (£1.07/US$1.89) and inexpensive European/Cameroonian dishes from around CFA2,000 (£2.14/US$3.78).

Campero Bar Corner of Av Kennedy. A rather rough and raucous bar with a video blaring in the corner. Lively and popular with the militia – so watch your step. Interestingly, the beer (CFA400/42p/75c for Castel, CFA700/75p/US$1.32 for Guinness) is served from behind a wire cage.

Nightlife

Compared with Douala, Yaoundé has a very subdued nightlife scene. The more expensive hotels such as the Hilton and Mount Fébé have discos and nightclubs, some restaurants and cafés also offer live music, and there are a handful of nightclubs and discos. The simple grilled fish bars around Mvog-Ada often feature traditional music and dance. Because of the increased security risk in recent years, use taxis to get about.

Le Caveau South of Pl Ahmadou Ahidjo, Mvog-Ada. Pulsating with African or Western music, there is sometimes live *bikutsi* music, the local speciality, here.

Bar Safari Near Pl de l'Indépendance. Popular with expats, this club, run by a Scotsman, attracts a young crowd and boasts a disco (playing loud Western music after 23.00), has video screens and a couple of pool tables. A beer is CFA1,500 (£1.60/US$2.83), rising to CFA2,000 (£2.14/US$3.78) after 23.00.

Katios Av Ahidjo by Rue Goker; tel: 223 14 91. Expensive but a good, lively nightspot.

Club Parallel Rue Ebe. Cameroonian and Western music plus a good menu.

La Paloma Mvog-Ada. For Assiko traditional dancing.
Super Paquita East of Pl Ahmadou Ahidjo, Mvog-Ada Quarter. Dance music and some live bands away from the centre.
Oxygen Off Av de l'Indépendance, by Royal Hotel; tel: 223 42 80. Disco with both African and Western music, popular with expatriates.
Arizona Bd du 20 Mai, opposite Hilton. Bar with live music.

Practical information
Airfreight
DHL tel: 223 13 58

Banks
Amity Bd du 20 Mai, near the Hilton Hotel
Citibank Av de Gaulle.
Bicec BP 5; just north of Pl Ahmadou Ahidjo; tel: 223 41 30
Crédit Lyonnais BP 700; just north of Pl Ahmadou Ahidjo; tel: 223 40 05
SGBC BP 244; Av de Gaulle, by the British Council; tel: 223 10 60 (it has an ATM)
Standard Chartered Av de l'Indépendance; tel: 222 38 80
Union Bank of Cameroon Pl Ahmadou Ahidjo

Books
Place Ahmadou Ahidjo has a number of street stalls selling books.

Cinemas
L'Abbia Rue Nachtigal; tel: 222 31 66. Mainly shows American films dubbed into French and costs around CFA2,500 per person. It also holds occasional live concerts.
Le Capitole Av Foch; tel: 22 49 77

Cultural centres
These have programmes of events like concerts, films, talks, etc.

British Council BP 818; Immeuble SGBC, Av de Gaulle; tel: 221 16 96/220 31 72; email: bc-yaoundé@britishcouncil.cm. Library, video club, cyber centre, BBC television showings, English-language teaching.
American Cultural Center Rue Narvick; tel: 223 16 33/223 14 37. Regular exhibitions and library. Americans can also get in touch with a sizeable community of fellow nationals at the American School of Yaoundé in the Quartier du Lac (tel: 222 9465/223 0421).
Centre Culturel Francais Av Ahidjo; tel: 222 09 44. Films are regularly shown in its new auditorium.
Goethe Institut BP 1067; Av Kennedy; tel: 221 44 09/222 35 77

Dentists
Polyclinic André Fouda Route de Ngousso; tel: 222 66 12/222 93 67
Clinique Dentaire Adventiste Route de Ngousso, Elig-Essono, near railway; tel: 222 11 10. Near the American Embassy and Adventist Church and operated by the Seventh-Day Adventists.

Internet services
Sidenet Av de l'independence; tel: 222 35 74
Cyber Espace Rue Eloumden
JDF Cybernet Rue de Narvick
Ureds Cyber Café Rue 1271, Essos; tel: 222 22 76; email: ureds@camnet.cm

Medical services

L'Hôpital Général de Yaoundé Tel: 220 11 22/220 22 44. Operates a 24-hour on-call emergency service and has medical and surgical specialists with US and European training, although the hospital is underfunded and has inadequate medical supplies.

Polyclinique André Fouda Route de Ngousso, Elig-Essono, near railway; tel: 222 66 12/222 93 67

Le Médecin Chef du Centre Médico-Social, Coopérant Française Tel: 223 01 39/223 01 37

Central Hospital Tel: 223 40 20/222 20 86

Cabinet Medical International Tel: 223 98 51

Polyclinique de la Grace Rue Nachtigal, near the Abbia Cinema; tel: 222 45 23

Hôpital Jamot Tel: 220 43 90

Fondation Chantal Biya: Centre Mère et Enfant Tel: 222 20 00

THE MABAM-MINKOM MASSIF

Colin Workman

Located approximately 40km northwest of Yaoundé is the Mabam-Minkom massif, a region of lowland mountain rainforest. Despite its proximity to the capital, the area, which has a population of around 3,000, is still farmed by the local people in the traditional way: clearing the forest to make an area to grow the staple diet of plantains, bananas and manioc (cassava), as well as other crops. The protein element of the diet has primarily been provided through hunting and trapping.

The area has a rich diversity of plant and animal life, including many endangered and unique species endemic to the region, which have adapted to their mountain environment and which are now in effect trapped, as the area is surrounded by lower, flatter terrain. It is this unique environment that makes the area so interesting for the nature lover; it is also an area of interest to science, with a number of studies taking place in the area, some of which are being funded by the British Foreign Office.

The birdlife is particularly diverse, and includes species such as the grey-necked picathartes (*picathartes oreas*), a beautiful ground-dwelling bird that is only found in this type of mountainous rainforest, as well as long-crested and Cassin's hawk eagles, African harrier hawks, turacos and parrots, to name just a few. The area is also home to a variety of primate species, and the villagers have stated that there are gorillas in the region.

The mountains are very steep and precipitous, with a high point of 1,295m. Although the whole of the area has been allocated to the local people, there is still primary rainforest here, as well as secondary forest, farmland and abandoned farms. The crop rotation cycle allows for two or three years of farming, followed by seven years of fallow.

The villagers are very interested in using their forest in non-destructive ways, with cash crops such as cacao being introduced in a small way, and they are hoping to start a bee-keeping collective and to have ecotourism. There is also the possibility of profiting from the medicinal properties of the many unique plants in the area.

Facilities for tourism are limited at present, with no accommodation, shops or restaurants. It is however possible to camp and buy produce off the locals, but this would need to be negotiated. Walking in the mountains, birdwatching and village life are the main attractions of the area.

Pharmacies

Pharmacie de l'Intendence 190 Pl Kennedy, Centre Ville; tel: 222 46 94
Pharmacie Française Av Kennedy; tel: 222 14 76
Pharmacie Bastos 1290 Rue Joseph Mballa Elounden, Bastos; tel: 220 6555
Pharmacie des Nations 437 Rue Albert Ateba Ebe, Nlongkak; tel: 220 93 56
Pharmacie Provinçale Av Adenauer; tel: 220 94 93
Pharmacie du Soleil 682 Av Ahidjo, Centre Ville; tel: 222 14 23

Post office

The main post office is on Pl Ahmadou Ahidjo, open Monday–Friday 07.30–15.30, Saturday/Sunday 07.30–noon. International telephone and fax, and post-restante service.

For walking trips in the forest it is necessary to arrange a guide (approximately CFA3,000/£3.21/US$5.67 per day), not only for navigation through the forest, but also to ensure that the correct etiquette is adhered to with the local villagers and their leaders.

A trip to this region is hugely rewarding. To fully appreciate the area and the local community it is essential to speak French if travelling independently, as there are currently no English speakers in the villages.

The way I travelled was with a trip organised through Earthwatch (web: www.earthwatch.org), an environmental charity that originated in the US but which also has offices in the UK. They are supporting a project run by the Cameroon Biodiversity Conservation Society (CBCS), investigating the habitat of the grey-necked picathartes and using this as an indicator species for the environment as a whole. I was part of a group of approximately 20 people: four westerners through Earthwatch, with the others being Cameroonian students, researchers and CBCS support staff.

The project was hugely rewarding and enlightening, giving participants the opportunity to contribute to the environment and giving them a real chance to meet and make friends and work with the local people and be a part of their team rather than just a spectator passing through. The CBCS have been working closely with the local people for a number of years and organised transport, guides, provision of water and the accommodation (the latter in tents, the campsite having been made in a clearing behind the village, with basic facilities – pit toilet, bucket shower, kitchen and a covered communal area).

The time the CBCS have invested in the area made it possible for the village etiquette to be understood, allowing us to have a better interaction with the villagers. When we arrived there was a welcome from the village chiefs, with dancing and drums, and before we left the locals put on a banquet of local foods and palm wine.

The local villagers have had very little interaction with Westerners/white people. One of the village leaders was discussing the project with us before we left and he commented on how well he felt our project had gone, as the villagers had been unsure how to treat us, as we were the first to come and visit and stay with them. The only other Westerners coming to the region, which is on average around two per month, tend to be either scientists or diplomats on a day away from Yaoundé.

Sport and fitness

Golf Club de Yaoundé BP 59; tel: 220 75 83. Located at the foot of Mount Fébé, this 18-hole golf course is one of the most spectacular in West Africa. There are sand greens, a practice range, and a clubhouse. Daily and weekend rates are available.

Tennis and swimming Hôtel des Députés and the Hôtel Mont Fébé both have tennis courts and swimming pools available to non-members.

Supermarkets

Tigre, Rue Joseph Essono Balla, north of the centre, is the biggest; **Score**, Pl Ahmadou Ahidjo; **Niki** has branches in Mvog-Mbi, Nlongkak and Messa.

What to see
The National Museum

Tel: 222 23 11. Open Monday–Saturday 09.00–16.00. Admission CFA1,000 (£1.07/US$1.89).

Off the Avenue des Ministères and southeast of the lake, the *Musée National* contains a whole range of items including thrones, masks, sculptures and tools, and has information on numerous aspects of Cameroonian tradition and culture, including art and rituals.

Monument de la Réunification

Boulevard de la Réunification

This spiral memorial was built in recognition of the uniting of the francophone and anglophone sectors of the country.

Petite Musée d'Art Camerounais

Mont Fébé; tel: 221 49 43. Open Thursday, Saturday, Sunday 15.00–18.00 and by arrangement. Entrance free, but donation expected.

Also known as the Cameroon Art Museum *(Petite Musée d'Arts Camerounais)*, the Petit Musée is near the foot of cool, lush-green Mount Fébé, 5km from the centre, and a CFA2,000 (£2.14/US$3.78) taxi ride from town. Housed in a Benedictine monastery (which holds a weekly English-language mass), it features steps leading to the museum from the main road that goes to Hôtel Mont Fébé. Although it is small, this is one of the region's best museums and has a very impressive collection, including much from the west of the country, such as carved wooden panels, ivory, terracotta, bronze and wooden pipes, various masks, bowls and other artefacts, all displayed against a plain white backdrop. The monastery's chapel, underneath the main church (mass 11.00 Sunday), is decorated with an array of local textiles and crafts. There is a guidebook in English and French at the entrance to the museum. Mount Fébé rises to an altitude of 1,000m (3,280ft) and you can wander up for great views of the city.

Musée Afhemi

Quartier Nsimeyong; tel: 231 54 16/231 90 38. Open Tuesday–Sunday 09.00–18.00; also open by appointment, and entrance can be combined with lunch if booked in advance. Admission CFA3,000 (£3.21/US$5.67).

South of the centre, this varied and extensive collection of regional art includes textiles, carvings and pictures.

Mvog-Betsi Zoo

Quartier Melen. Open daily 09.00–18.00. Admission CFA2,000 (£2.14/US$3.78), photography CFA5,000 (£5.35/US$9.45), video camera CFA10,000 (£10.70/US$18.90).

Jointly run by MINEF (the Cameroon Government's Ministry for the Environment and Forests) and CWAF (Cameroon Wildlife Aid Fund: www.cwaf.org), a UK-registered charity based at Bristol Zoological Gardens, this once-neglected zoo has been transformed in recent years into an impressive centre concerned with primate protection and conservation. The zoo is about 1km from Melen market and inhabitants include lions, a hyena, snakes, rodents, amphibians and reptiles, birds of prey and other forms of native fauna, as well as a collection of primates such as chimpanzees, gorillas, baboons, mandrills, mangabeys, guenons and drills, the latter a highly endangered species.

Paroisse de N'Djong Melen Catholic Church
Quartier N'Djong Melen
This church holds a fabulous, energetic mass each Sunday from 09.30 to noon. The open-air mass (inside the church during the rainy season) is spoken in Ewondo and blends Western and African culture, and is popular with tourists as it features drumming, singing and dancing, and everyone dresses up.

LUNA PARK
Two kilometres from Obala, a 45-minute drive from Yaoundé on the N2 Bamenda road, Luna Park is a sort of weekend holiday resort about 30km from the capital. It features a large swimming pool, volleyball court, accommodation in *boukarous* (thatched huts), a restaurant and greenery beside a river. The facilities can be enjoyed for free as long as you eat at the restaurant (around CFA2,500/£2.67/US$4.72 per meal). Luna Park used to keep monkeys and gorillas, until its animals were confiscated by the International Primate Protection League, In Defense of Animals, Yaoundé Zoo and Limbé Wildlife Centre due to inadequate care. Chimpanzees and other primates had been chained up for many years with insufficient food and water.

MFOU NATIONAL PARK
This park, at Mfou, southeast of Yaoundé, is run by Mvog-Betsi Zoo in Yaoundé, MINEF (the Cameroon Government's Ministry for the Environment and Forests) and CWAF (Cameroon Wildlife Aid Fund: www.cwaf.org), a UK-registered charity based at Bristol Zoological Gardens, concerned with primate protection and conservation. The park contains rescued primates such as monkeys and gorillas. For further details telephone 221 90 44/969 01 81.

NACHTIGAL FALLS AND MANGA EBOKO
A two-hour drive from Yaoundé on the N2 and then N1 roads leads you to this waterfall on the Sanaga River, northeast of Obala. It is about 20km further on from the small town of Batchenga. Guided tours of the Sanaga tobacco plantation in Batchenga are sometimes possible. Even further east along the N1 is the town of Manga Eboko, which has a crafts centre and basic accommodation in the form of the Etoile d'Or de Nanga (under CFA5,000/£5.35/US$9.45), although sometimes damaged bridges along this route make it impassable.

MBALMAYO
The good N2 road south from Yaoundé to Gabon passes forest and coffee and cocoa plantations, and after about 40km reaches the humid and hot town of Mbalmayo, a handy base with a good range of shops, a bank, a post office, a petrol station and a divisional hospital (tel: 228 15 79). It also contains the Mbalmayo Arts Institute, which can be visited.

Founded by the Germans and largely populated by the Ewondo, Mbalmayo stretches along both banks of the River Nyong. Timber extraction is a principal industry here. An excellent view of the town can be had from the top of Vimli Rock, 7km from the town.

There are regular minibuses and share-taxis from Yaoundé to Mbalmayo, as well as a service offered by *agence de voyage* Beauty Express. The rail network also has a branch line, although this is a slower option than travelling by road.

From here it is possible to visit the Mbalmayo Forest Reserve, about 10km out of town on the Ebolowa road. Accommodation is available at the Ebogo (or Eboko) Tourist Site (CFA5,000–8,000/£5.35–15.12/US$9.45–15.12), and there are trips where you can take a pirogue down the Nyong River from Mbalmayo, and possibly try your hand at fishing. The area is rich in several varieties of butterfly. There is a simple restaurant on the riverbank.

Also in this area is the village of Akono, which has one of the few Catholic cathedrals in black francophone Africa.

Where to stay in Mbalmayo
Hôtel de la Poste BP 226; tel: 228 11 57. Basic rooms at CFA5,000–8,000 (£5.35–15.12/US$9.45–15.12).
Jardin des Tropics Tel: 228 16 10. En-suite rooms with AC from CFA10,000 (£10.70/US$18.90).

South Province

This area offers lush vegetation and 'pygmy' villages nestled in the rainforest, but most visitors come here for the superb beaches.

Along the Atlantic coast, between the fishing village of Londji and the town of Campo on the border of Equatorial Guinea, there is a whole range of spectacular beaches, with Kribi in between, Cameroon's second port and a beach resort surrounded by gorgeous white beaches. It is often the first choice for weekenders like government officials and expatriates from Yaoundé and Douala looking for a holiday.

Much of the interior of the south of the country is thick rainforest, and the forest in the southwestern section, the Province du Sud, extends into Equatorial Guinea and Gabon. Much of this region, apart from along the coast, has few good roads and very little public transport or tourist facilities, and is therefore a challenge to explore.

So-called 'pygmies', Cameroon's oldest peoples, used to dominate in this region, but now those from the Bantu-language groups like the Bakoko and Batanga dominate, although some 'pygmies' remain.

THE COAST
Kribi

Its superb beaches, wide, white and sandy, and virtually deserted for much of the year, plus a good range of accommodation and good road access, combine to make Kribi the country's top beach resort. It is a drive of under three hours from Douala and four from Yaoundé.

Kribi is Cameroon's second port (after Douala), although the shallow waters prevent larger vessels from entering the German-built harbour.

Kribi has recently been transformed by the influx of industry and attention brought by the building of a controversial US$3.7 billion, 1,070km Chad–Cameroon oil pipeline to develop landlocked Chad's southern oilfields. This ends up at Kribi, despite pressure from environmental groups who say that the project threatens the 'pygmies' and other populations along the pipeline route.

The environmentalists also believe that construction of the pipeline has worsened deforestation and risks spillage and other damage to plants and animals. ExxonMobil, which constructed the pipeline, has admitted building stretches of the pipeline across three archaeological sites rather than bypassing them. In 2005 crude oil production should be at full capacity, in excess of 225,000 barrels per day.

The name Kribi is derived from the word *kiridi*, which translates as 'small men', a reference to the 'pygmies' who were the original inhabitants of this region. Bantu-speaking groups are the main inhabitants of Kribi today.

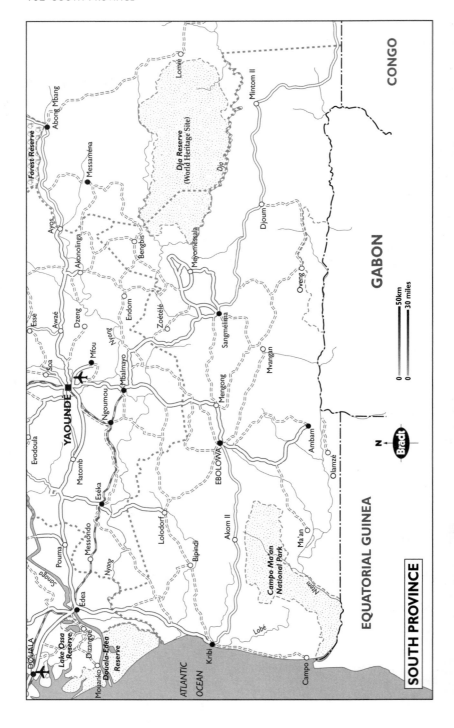

SOUTH PROVINCE

Above Houses in the palace of the Fon of Bafut, Northwest Province (RQ)

Left Participant in the Bafut Dances (TQ)

Below Dance in Northwest Province (RQ)

Above Children selling goods at Mora market, Extreme North Province (JK)

Below Buying a carpet at Mokolo, Extreme North Province (JK)

Below right A woman walks with her children in Ngaoundéré, Adamawa Province (BC)

An attractive town, though no longer the quiet backwater it once was, Kribi is located at the southernmost bridge over the Sanaga River, 177km from Douala and 112km from Edea. Kribi has numerous hotels, shops, a bank, a hospital and a post office, and a market.

Among Kribi's low-key sights are a colonial cathedral on the nearby hillside and some German administrative buildings along the northern beachfront. But Kribi's principal attraction is its gorgeous palm-fringed white beaches, a dramatic contrast to the volcanic, sometimes rocky, black ones of Limbé.

During the day the locals on the beach are very friendly and may offer to catch you fish and shrimps, scale the trees for coconuts and avocados, or let you try out the dug-out canoes they make on the beach. They often prefer to be paid in cigarettes rather than hard currency.

Check locally before swimming as currents can sometimes be strong. Also, don't walk along the beaches alone, especially at night. Kribi is best avoided during the heavy rains, from around June to mid-November, and is at its best from mid-November to February.

Getting there and away

From Douala, the journey time on the relatively new surfaced road is under three hours. The quickest route from Yaoundé is via Edea, but you can also go along tracks through the forests, passing the odd waterfall and 'pygmy' villages, at least in the dry season. If you take this far slower option, head for Ebolowa and then for Lolodorf and Bipindi, or Akom II.

The *agences de voyages* have offices on or near Rue du Marché in the centre, which is also where the main *gare routière* is, where non-agency vehicles and share-taxis depart from.

Central Voyages and La Kribienne go regularly each day to and from Yaoundé (CFA3,500/£3.75/US$6.61) and Douala (CFA2,300/£2.46/US$4.34) in under three hours. Other operators include Bon Pied la Route and Syd Voyage which go to Ebolowa, and Transcam which goes to Campo (CFA1,500/£1.60/US$2.83).

Where to stay

There is a good range of hotels in Kribi, but they tend to fill up quickly on weekends during the dry season, especially in December and January. It is increasingly possible to stay at people's homes, so ask around. Camping at campsites along the beach is popular, although it is increasingly not considered safe anymore, unfortunately.

Tara Plage BP 103; tel: 346 20 83. 3km south of the centre, signposted and 500m off the main road. On the beach, it is in an attractive setting, has a restaurant, and the air-conditioned en-suite rooms are CFA12,000 (£12.86/US$22.68) for a room sleeping two and CFA17,000 (£18.22/US$32.13) for rooms sleeping three and four people. Camping is CFA3,000 (£3.21/US$5.67) per tent.

Elabé-Marine Hotel Tel: 990 77 84. Relaxing, unpretentious beachside hotel north of the city beside the Residence Jully, with an excellent restaurant.

Auberge de Kribi BP 355; Lolodorf Rd; tel: 346 15 41. This is about 500m east of the *gare routière* and has simple but good-value rooms with fans and shared facilities for around CFA5,000 (£5.35/US$9.45).

Framotel BP 355; off Edea Rd; tel: 346 16 40. North of the centre, this government-rated three-star hotel has a restaurant, bar, pool, playground, gardens and a private beach nearby. The 24 double rooms are CFA17,000–22,000 (£18.22–23.57/US$32.13–41.58).

Auberge du Phare BP 319; tel: 346 11 06/346 11 08. South of the cathedral and with a pleasant setting overlooking the ocean; there is a good restaurant and good-value rooms with bathrooms – and with and without AC – from CFA12,000 (£12.86/US$22.68) and a suite for double that.

Hôtel Manapani le Nema Tel: 346 17 79. Beachside hotel with a nice little restaurant and clean rooms with bathrooms and AC or fans, from CFA9,000 (£9.64/US$17.01).

Residence Jully BP 195; tel: 346 19 62. North of the centre by the beach, about 3km off the Douala road, this three-star hotel has 40 very good quality rooms, three suites and two apartments with bathroom, TV and AC, and a popular beachfront restaurant. Singles CFA23,000 (£24.65/US$43.47), doubles CFA27,000 (£28.93/US$51.03), suites CFA32,000 (£34.29/US$60.49).

Thy-Breiz BP 35; tel: 346 14 99. On the beach, although many rooms do not face the sea. It is about 1km south of the bridge on the Campo road. Rooms have fans for CFA10,000 (£1.70/US$18.90) or there are better ones with AC for around CFA24,000 (£25.72/US$47.25).

Hôtel Coco Beach Tel: 346 15 84. Just southwest of the bridge on the beach, this small, popular, long-established hotel with a good restaurant has a few, very good, air-conditioned rooms from around CFA22,000 (£23.57/US$41.58).

Hôtel de l'Ocean Tel: 346 16 35. This beachside hotel with a good restaurant near Hotel Coco Beach has chalet rooms for CFA20,000 and upwards (£21.40/US$37.80).

Les Polygones d'Alice BP 97, Kribi; tel: 346 15 64. This three-star hotel has 17 comfortable rooms with en-suite bathroom and satellite TV, plus a bar and a restaurant.

Hotel Ni d'Or BP 186; tel: 346 14 35. Hotel near the market with a bar/restaurant and simple, self-contained rooms from CFA12,000 (£12.86/22.68).

Palm Beach Plus Hotel BP 351; tel: 346 14 47; email: hotelpb@iccnet.cm. On a paved side street off the road going to Campo, this new hotel has a good bar and restaurant and very comfortable rooms by the sea. Rooms are CFA32,000 (£34.29/US$60.49).

Hôtel Belle Hollandaise BP 128, Kribi; tel: 346 17 13; www.belle-hollandaise.com. 48 large air-conditioned rooms with satellite TV, plus a large pool, garden, nightclub, mini golf and jet-ski rental.

Hôtel Le Paradis BP 232; tel: 346 19 93; email: hotelleparadis-kribi@yahoo.com. Signposted north of the centre, this hotel that opened in 2001 has 53 comfortable rooms, suites and apartments, with en-suite facilities, AC, telephone and satellite TV, plus a good restaurant, bar, barbecue and swimming pool.

Where to eat and drink

A rather expensive but very attractive option for dining are the beachfront restaurants, which, unsurprisingly, specialise in seafood. The hotels by the beach have restaurants, which tend to get busy at weekends. A much cheaper (around CFA1,000/£1.07/US$1.89) yet excellent option is to visit the food stalls selling freshly grilled and barbecued fish, such as at Carrefour Kingue and on the beach south of the Hotel Framotel Grill, prepared by a group of women in daylight hours. Cheaper restaurants are near the market on the Rue du Marché.

Restaurant les Marseillais Route de la Poste; tel: 346 18 63. Good seafood at a price.
Le Forestier Restaurant Hotel Le Paradis; tel: 346 19 93. Well-rated hotel restaurant signposted north of the centre, with dishes from about CFA5,000 (£5.35/US$9.45).
Fleur Marine Tel: 346 20 11. French seafood restaurant near the school.
Le Cigare Route de Poste; tel: 346 19 28. Good seafood menu.

Nightlife

There are various late bars and nightclubs including the most established, **Le Big Ben** (tel: 346 19 28), **Geraldine** (tel: 346 82 29), and the **Palm Beach Plus Hotel**'s upmarket club playing African and Western sounds.

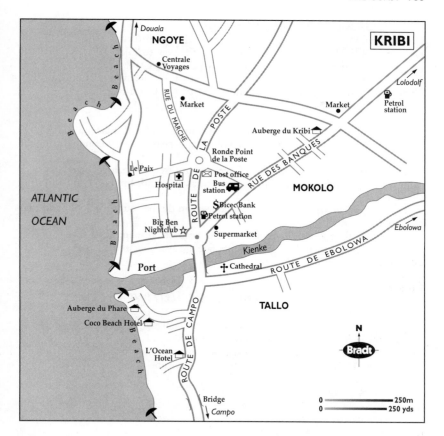

Practical information

Bank
Bicec Lolodorf Rd

Hospital
Central Hospital Tel: 346 11 31. West of the post office roundabout.

Internet access
Cyber@ljo Route de la Poste
Club Internet Lolodorf Rd

Post office
Route de la Poste, southwest of the post office roundabout

Supermarket
MCG Supermarket Rue des Banques

Tourism
Tourist office Tel: 346 10 80

THE COAST NORTH OF KRIBI

Beautiful white-sand beaches extend as far as the small fishing village of Londji, which is 24km (15 miles) north of Kribi on the way to Edea. It is a particularly picturesque section of coastline and passes Mpalla village and, after 15km, Cocotier Plage, an extremely attractive beach with very basic accommodation available. There is also quite a good beach 12km from Kribi, at Costa Blanca.

Londji

Londji is quite a sleepy, relaxing, but rather isolated place a CFA3,000 (£3.21/US$5.69), 24km taxi ride from Kribi; share-taxis also visit Londji during the day.

Londji's beach is spread around a huge coconut tree and palm-fringed bay with calm waters. It tends to get an influx of expats at weekends but is very quiet during the week.

The village fishermen take their canoes out on the bay after midnight and may take you for a small charge.

If your budget doesn't stretch to the seafood restaurant at the Auberge Jardiniere, grilled fish and rice and similar fare are available in the village, and there are one or two basic bars.

A SNAPSHOT OF CAMEROON'S SOUTHWEST COAST

Andrew Pape-Salmon

Campo-Ma'an National Park and the surrounding region provide a glimpse of the African wilds within easy access from Kribi. The park appears to offer something for all visitors, regardless of their adventure quotient, ranging from day trips to the three 'Chutes de Menve ele' outside of the eastern boundary of the park, to multi-day adventures hiking within the park and seeing a unique ecosystem with significant biodiversity.

Be warned that it is a relatively new tourist destination and there are still some bugs to iron out before it becomes a major destination – all the more reason for adventurous types to go now.

This hilly national park has several ecological zones with varied tree species, over 100 elephants, some large primates, lots of other mammals (we saw boars and white-nose monkeys) and numerous exotic birds. Its southern border is marked by the powerful Ntem River, which forms a biologically rich (and fish- and shrimp-filled) estuary at Campo. The southwest corner of the park between the Ntem and Bongola rivers is fabled to have an old German settlement that has not yet been 'discovered'.

Ebodjé is a gorgeous community on the road between Kribi and Campo that has declared itself an 'Eco-Tourism' village. You can easily spend three days there and enjoy a number of their organised activities through arrangements with the tourism office, currently managed by Alain Ngomi. In our one day in the community, arriving from Campo by boat, we enjoyed a traditional couscous (*fufu*) and peanut sauce lunch at Marie's clean beachside facilities (which include lodging for CFA2,000/£2.14/US$3.78 per night) and had a guided tour of the village to learn about its culture and history. The community was one of the most relaxing we experienced on our trip – and yet it was also stimulating to learn about how things work in rural Cameroon.

Ebodjé is famous for its sea turtles, which appear at night to lay their eggs. Tobie Mediko is managing the turtle project, which includes viewing

Where to stay

Camping on the beach is possible, with a small fee payable to the village chief. There are *boukarous* (thatched huts) on the beach at around CFA5,000 (£5.35/US$9.45).

Auberge Jardiniere BP 250; tel: 346 11 27; mobile: 991 72 69. On the beach, this is the most comfortable accommodation option, with rooms for around CFA10,000 (£10.70/US$18.90).

Elogbatindi

Continuing along the main road to Douala, away from the coast you come to the village of Elogbatindi, which has a number of pygmy camps.

THE COAST SOUTH OF KRIBI

Further beautiful white beaches extend as far as the town of Campo by the border with Equatorial Guinea.

Lobé Falls

About 7km south of Kribi, just before reaching the village of Grand Batanga, are the signposted Lobé Falls (Chutes de la Lobé), one of only a few waterfalls in the

opportunities at night, tagging, and sponsorship. The tourism office can arrange a cultural evening, hikes in the forest, and pirogue trips up the Likido River.

We began our trip by making contact with the co-ordinator of the Campo-Ma'an Project at the Worldwide Fund for Nature's Yaoundé office. Their approach to wilderness conservation is to provide a source of income for nearby populations through tourism – essentially converting hunters (or poachers) into wilderness guides, and creating economies around the lodging, feeding and entertaining of visitors. WWF also works cooperatively with neighbouring communities, forestry companies that harvest trees outside the park and maintain the road within the park, and the agricultural operations on the west side of the park.

In 2004, WWF are constructing facilities for researchers, tourists and dignitaries near Chutes de Menve ele, including lodging. WWF are also mapping the whole region. They can put visitors in touch with reliable guides in the area.

Although we were limited to one day in the park, we learned a lot from our guide named Innocent, who lives in the community of Nko'élon west of the park. We stayed at the WWF/MINEF house for a week on Campo Beach (facing Equatorial Guinea) and enjoyed a number of evening conversations with the WWF co-ordinator, Bertin Tchikangwa Nkanje, and the park ranger (Conservateur), Djogo Toumouksala. They share an office in front of the power plant, about 1km east of the centre of Campo town. You can telephone the ranger if you have no luck with WWF (tel: 955 0103/745 41 69/346 12 84).

You can also contact Ebodjé through their Kribi agent (tel: 977 32 36/959 10 16). The government of the Netherlands helped establish these operations through the 'Project Campo Man'an' initiative that was wound down in late 2002.

For me, the best things about Kribi include eating fresh barbecued fish on the beach; staying and eating at the beachside Elabé-Marine Hotel; heading downtown on Saturday night for some electric guitar music in classic Cameroon style, with mysterious Bassa dancers providing a visual spectacle; and walking for many kilometres along the beach.

world that fall directly into the sea. The River Lobé empties its waters into the ocean through a series of cascades more than 30m high, the force of the rapids producing a brown foam in the bay.

The nearby beaches are clean and good for swimming but the area is a bit touristy. Grilled fish dishes are available at a small restaurant at the foot of the falls. There may be guides available for hiking around the falls and you may be offered a half-day canoe trip (about CFA2,500/£2.67/US$4.72 per hour) up the river to see 'pygmy' villages. The villages are unconvincing but the boat trip is worthwhile.

A taxi from Kribi is around CFA2,000 (£2.14/US$3.78), but it is a good idea to pay extra for the driver to wait, as transport back to Kribi can be very infrequent.

Where to stay
Hotel Ilomba BP 305 tel: 346 17 44/991 29 23. Half a kilometre from the falls in a beachside setting, this hotel has *boukarous* of a high standard with AC, and a restaurant with meals from CFA5,000 (£5.35/US$9.45). Singles CFA25,000 (£26.79/US$47.25), doubles CFA30,000 (£32.15/US$56.71), 4-people suites CFA75,000 (£80.38/US$141.77), 8-people suites CFA100,000 (£107.18/US$189.00).

Grand Batanga and Eboundja
The village of Grand Batanga is 12km south of Kribi and has a good restaurant about 1km south of the centre called Auberge Mimado (tel: 997 79 17), although there's no accommodation as yet. There are also good, deserted beaches around the village.

Another 8km south is the fishing village of Eboundja where you can camp on the beach.

Loup Rock
A few kilometres further south is Loup Rock (Rocher du Loup), a supposedly wolf-like land formation rising from the ocean.

Ebodjé
Ebodjé is another fishing village situated on the shores of the Atlantic Ocean. Daily minibuses stop en route for Campo and Kribi. The beaches around here are beautiful, and sea tortoises usually come to the beaches from November to January to lay eggs. Excursions by canoe to the sea or to the Likodo River are offered locally.

Ebodjé was recently chosen as a site for the protection of sea tortoises by a very effective regional project organised jointly by the Cameroonian government and the Netherlands Development Organisation (SNV).

Accommodation is available in local homes for a nominal fee, and meals are CFA2,000 (£2.14/US$3.78).

The co-ordinator of the project, based at the World Wildlife Fund's Yaoundé office (tel: 221 62 67/221 70 83/221 70 84), can provide further information.

Campo
You are likely to come across customs and immigration checks at the border town of Campo, which has a large beach extending to the mouth of the Ntem River, the border with Equatorial Guinea.

Campo-Ma'an National Park
Campo is home to the 2,640km² Parc National de Campo Ma'an, consisting of dense unmanaged rainforest of extremely rich biodiversity.

The park contains more than 1,500 species of plants and over 300 species of birds, and a variety of rainforest vegetation, including coastal forest and sub-mountainous forest at an altitude of up to 800m.

It contains a wide range of wildlife, including buffalo, lion, leopard, hippo, mandrill, gorilla and forest elephants. There are more than 70 monkey species, including the red-capped mangabey, as well as pangolin, duiker and python. In the Ntem River region there are crocodiles and sea turtles.

The park is not particularly geared towards visitors – there is only very basic accommodation and no public transport to it – but the infrastructure is slowly being improved, and a track road cuts eastwards through the reserve from Campo to Ma'an, passing near to the Menve (or Menve ele) Falls halfway.

The forestry office (*poste forestier*) in Campo and Kribi's tourist office can both help with providing an obligatory guide (CFA3,000/£3.21/US$5.67 per day) and with the location of tracks in the forest. There is a CFA5,000 (£5.35/US$9.45) entry fee, payable to the forestry office in Campo. Obtain a receipt to show at the entrance. It is open daily from 08.00 to 18.00.

At the entrance to the park, the village of Nko'elon has guides who can take you to caves containing bats, as well as on a variety of forest walks.

Accommodation in Campo consists of the **Auberge Bon Course**, at Bon Course Supermarket at the main road junction: basic clean rooms are CFA5,000 (£5.35/US$9.45). Daily minibuses go to and from Kribi to Campo.

Ipono
Another 10km south of Campo at this small village you can take a pirogue the 10km journey up the Ntem River to Yengue in Equatorial Guinea, where you get your passport stamped. There is a track that leads to the road to the town of Bata. In Ipono there is simple accommodation available for under CFA5,000 (£5.35/US$9.45).

THE INTERIOR
Getting to Kribi via Lolodorf
If you are going the long, slow way from Yaoundé to Kribi, 75km on from Ebolowa you reach Lolodorf (the name, 'Lolo's village', originates from the German phase of Cameroon's history), where there is some basic accommodation. The 120km stretch from here to Kribi is slow, due to the condition of the forest tracks, which pass various 'pygmy' villages. At the village of Bidjoka, 35km on, are the Bidjoka Falls, and a further 10km on is the village of Bipindi, which has a rudimentary clinic as well as more 'pygmy' encampments.

Ebolowa
Ebolowa is the provincial capital, with a population of around 50,000, mainly made up of the Bulu people. Located in a valley surrounded by lush green hills, the town is 170km from Yaoundé and 120km from both Mbalmayo and Sangmélima.

It has an artificial lake and few specific attractions (other than, of all things, a dentist's chair used by Albert Schweitzer at the Hôpital Enongal), but facilities that include a bank, shops, a supermarket, a large market and a post office. It boasts two hospitals, the Provincial Hospital (tel: 228 32 20/228 33 33) and the Enongal (tel: 228 33 23). It is a cocoa-producing town and the majority of the population works in this sector.

Getting there and away
The main *gare routière* has regular share-taxis to Yaoundé, approximately a three-hour journey away, and some to Kribi, depending on the state of the roads. There

are also *agences de voyages* on the road to Yaoundé, including Buca Voyages and Jet Voyages.

Transport for Ebibiyin (Equatorial Guinea) and Bitam (Gabon) is available from Ambam, further south on the N2, which on the map looks like a primary road but soon becomes unsurfaced when you leave Ebolowa. The visa for Equatorial Guinea is currently CFA36,000 and for Gabon is CFA37,000.

Where to stay
Hôtel Ane Rouge BP 315; tel: 228 34 38. Near the main roundabout in town, this has simple, clean, shared and self-contained rooms for under CFA5,000 (£5.35/US$9.45).

La Cabane Bambou BP 144; tel: 788 88 85. Near the market; the en-suite rooms are clean and there is a bar/restaurant. From CFA5,000 (£5.35/US$9.45).

Hôtel le Ranch BP 690; tel: 228 40 37/228 35 17/28 35 32/28. By Mount Ebolowa, just southwest of the centre, this government-graded two-star hotel has 25 clean rooms with bathrooms for about CFA10,000 (£10.70/US$18.90). There is a bar and a restaurant.

Hôtel Porte Jaune BP 817; tel: 228 39 29. Ebolowa's most comfortable hotel. Rooms have bathrooms and either AC or a fan. From about CFA10,000 (£10.70/US$18.90).

Around Ebolowa
Ten kilometres east of the town is a natural tunnel, known as Phantom's Cave or Mbil Bekon ('hole of ghosts'), and 40km south on the road to Ambam are the magnificent Ako'akas Rocks.

Sangmélima
Sangmélima is southeast of Mbalmayo (Mbalmayo is covered in the chapter on *Centre Province*) on the N9 branch road. It has a hospital, bank, petrol stations and a post office. Sangmélima is a good base if you are planning a visit to the rather remote East Province.

Where to stay
Hôtel Afamba BP 423; tel: 228 84 27. Quite comfortable rooms with AC for around CFA10,000 (£10.70/US$18.90).

Hôtel Bel Air BP 499; tel: 228 81 42. A bar/restaurant and 18 basic en-suite rooms for around CFA10,000 (£10.70/US$18.90).

Hôtel Kono Refuge BP 654; Ndonkol; tel: 223 09 43. Restaurant, small gym and air-conditioned rooms, 35km from Sangmélima.

Jardin des Tropiques BP 537; Route de Mbalmayo; tel: 228 86 91. *Boukarous* right next to the rainforest for around CFA14,000 (£15/US$26).

Ambam
Thick forest gives way to this transit town with basic accommodation at several auberges.

Getting there and away
The motor park opposite the post office has share-taxis to Equatorial Guinea, which go via a ferry over the Ntem River and stop just before the border town of Ebebiyin. To reach Gabon, share-taxis depart from the market in the town, stopping for the market on Saturdays at Aban Minkoo.

East Province

The eastern region of southern Cameroon is part of the Central African belt of rainforest, the Congo Basin, which constitutes the largest stretch of unbroken forest in the world after the Amazon. This region has vast forests that continue into the Central African Republic, Gabon, Congo and Equatorial Guinea.

This area has changed dramatically in recent years due to poaching, metal/mineral prospecting and widespread, almost unrestricted, logging, yet much is still untouched wilderness with extensive populations of wildlife, including forest elephants, gorillas and chimpanzees, and an unparalleled biodiversity that remains largely unexplored. Thirty-metre mahogany trees sit side by side with Baka 'pygmies' still maintaining their traditional lifestyle.

This is the most difficult area of Cameroon to explore. There is a poor road network (the logging companies maintain many of the roads that head east from Yaoundé and these are often damaged by their heavy trucks) and there is a distinct lack of facilities, but if you are adventurous and have the time and determination there is much to experience in the rainforest.

TOWARDS BERTOUA

Bertoua, the capital of East Province, is 338km east of Yaoundé and can be reached via the N1 road following the railway track and Sanga River (where one can view the Nachtigal Falls on the Sanga, about 20km further on from the small town of Batchenga) via Nanga Eboko (which has a crafts centre and basic accommodation in the form of the Etoile d'Or de Nanga, from CFA4,000/£4.28/US$7.56), although sometimes damaged bridges and road surfaces along this route can make it impassable. An alternative route follows the Nyong River, taking the N10 road via Abong Mbang, which is surfaced as far as Ayos, 150km from Yaoundé. Abong Mbang has several examples of architecture of the German period, including a fortress, now the central prison.

About 18km south of Abong Mbang are the caves of Ntimbe: ask around Abong Mbang for a guide if you want to see them. The route also passes through the town of Doume, which was previously the capital of the eastern sector. It contains some interesting colonial buildings, including a fortress built by the Germans.

BERTOUA

Bertoua borders savanna and rainforest. Logging and other commercial activities have caused the population to grow to over 100,000, bringing a wide range of facilities such as hotels, cafés, bars and restaurants, shops, post office, hospital (tel: 224 18 29), bank, cinema and airstrip.

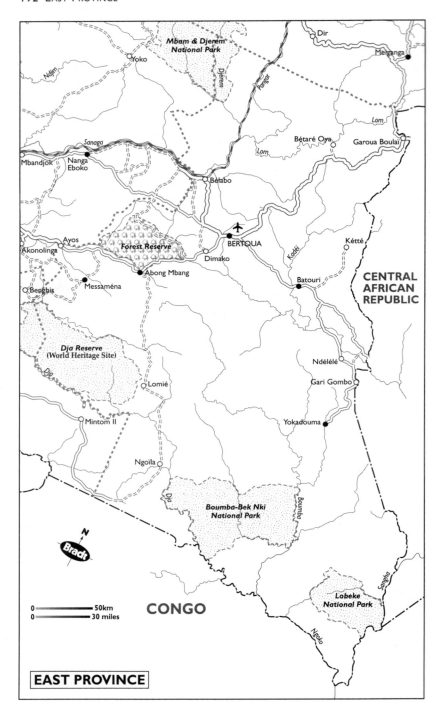

EAST PROVINCE

Botanists may note that the town of Nguelemendouka, southwest of Bertoua, is notable for having a two-headed palm tree.

Getting there and away

Transport for most destinations is available from the main *gare routière* in the centre of the town near the market. There are *agences de voyages* for destinations that include Yaoundé (CFA5,000/£5.35/US$9.45, around eight hours), Garoua-Boulai, Batouri, Yokadouma and Belabo (the last for joining the Yaoundé–Ngaoundéré train). By road Ngaoundéré typically costs CFA8,000 (£8.57/US$15.12) and takes around 12 hours.

Cameroon Airlines flies from Bertoua to Douala and Yaoundé.

Where to stay

Hotel Mansa BP 285; tel: 244 60 50/244 13 33. By an artificial lake, this newish single-storey motel with 48 rooms is the best in town, yet you should still save a bucket of water during the dry season as the town supply is poor. Good rooms with AC and satellite TV, CFA25,000 (£26.79/US$47.25). There is a restaurant, bar, swimming pool (available to non-guests for a small fee) and tennis court.

Phoenix Hotel BP 215; tel: 224 27 29. Near the motor park, with a good restaurant. Clean rooms with bathrooms are CFA10,000 (£10.70/US$18.90).

Complexe Hotel Tel: 224 11 04. Clean rooms for around CFA10,000 (£10.70/US$18.90).

Hôtel de l'Est Poste Centrale Rond-point; tel: 224 23 42/951 58 93. Rooms with AC and either shared or self-contained facilities cost CFA10,000 (£10.70/US$18.90).

Where to eat and drink, and nightlife

As well as hotel restaurants such as **Mansa's**, the **Café Moderne** at the *gare routière* has dishes from under CFA1,000 (£1.07/US$1.89), and other eateries worth trying include the **Savannah** (tel: 224 12 85) and **Grill la Ménagère** (tel: 224 16 82). Nightclubs include **Kristal** and **Espace Nkam Palace**.

BELABO

Tourists usually only head for Belabo, about 80km northwest of Bertoua, to catch the daily southbound train heading for Yaoundé and the northbound train for Ngaoundéré.

The trains stop at Belabo station any time between 22.30 and 01.00 in either direction. Security can be bad here, so take a taxi or moto (motorbike taxi) to your hotel. If you have a first-class ticket, you can wait in the first-class lounge rather than on the platform or street. There are several basic hotels in town.

About 23km west of Belabo on the Nanga Eboko road (take a taxi or moto) is the Sanaga Yong Chimpanzee Rescue Centre, which looks after 15–20 chimps.

GAROUA-BOULAI

Garoua-Boulai is little more than a rough and ready border town, and its highly transient population has contributed to its alarming incidence of HIV/AIDS. In terms of accommodation the town has a Catholic mission and inexpensive auberges.

Garoua-Boulai is on the border with the Central African Republic. The border is by Garoua-Boulai's motor park, and there is a customs point at Beloko on the other side.

The motor park has share-taxis and buses to Ngaoundéré via Meiganga. At Meiganga you can also take a share-taxi west to Ngaoundal to join the Yaoundé–Ngaoundéré train.

Southwest of Garoua-Boulai is a gold mine at Betare-Oya, and just south of this, 7km from Ndokayo, are the Mali Waterfalls.

The route from Bertoua to Garoua-Boulai has been much improved recently, and around the village of Ndokayo there are splendid mountain landscapes.

BATOURI

The 90km of road leading from Bertoua to Batouri is generally in poor condition. The landscape changes from forest to savanna, and is crossed by a network of rivers, including the Kadei and Koubou.

Batouri is a good base for exploring Mount Niong (or Nyong, 778m) and Mount Pandi, and also, in this gold-prospecting area, a mining village 3km away.

Getting there and away

There is daily transport to Yaoundé, Bertoua, Yokadouma and Kenzou, just west of Gamboula, the latter a transit point for the Central African Republic, 100km away.

If you are heading for the Central African Republic, the route is along difficult roads and tracks. Share-taxis usually leave for the border town of Kenzou at around 04.30 from the *gare routière*. Once inside the Central African Republic, share-taxis are usually available to take you the 100km to the town of Berberati. Ask about the current condition of the roads before setting off.

Where to stay

Auberge Cooperant Tel: 226 23 00. Acceptable rooms in the town centre for under CFA5,000 (£5.35/US$9.45).

Hôtel Belle Etoile Tel: 226 25 18. Clean simple rooms for under CFA10,000 (£10.70/US$18.90), plus a restaurant.

Hôtel Mont Pandi Tel: 226 25 77. Attractively located with en-suite rooms for CFA10,000 (£10.70/US$18.90), and there is a restaurant.

DJA RESERVE

The Reserve du Dja is an extensive area of primary rainforest that's part of the Congo rainforest, 243km southeast of Yaoundé, at an altitude of between 400m and 800m.

The reserve covers a surface area of 5,260km² (526,000ha) and the Dja River almost completely encircles it, forming its natural boundary. The reserve is remote and has few facilities for tourists. Only consider visiting Dja if you have ample time, patience and endurance.

The Dja comprises one of the largest and best-protected forests in Africa, and is particularly noted for its biodiversity and wide variety of primates. It is reported to have received some protection as early as 1932, with further laws protecting it in 1950 and 1973. It was internationally recognised by the United Nations Educational, Scientific and Cultural Organisation (UNESCO) as a UNESCO Biosphere Reserve in 1981 and declared a World Heritage Site in 1987 for its outstanding natural significance.

Except in the southeast, the reserve is fairly flat and is made up of a series of round-topped hills. Cliffs run along the course of the river in the south for 60km, and one section features rapids and waterfalls.

More than 1,500 plant species have been identified here, including 43 species of tree forming the canopy of the forest. The shrub layer alone contains over 53 species. Other main vegetation types are swamp vegetation and secondary forest around old villages, which were abandoned in the late 1940s, and recently abandoned cocoa and coffee plantations.

Although the reserve has been little surveyed, it is known to have more than 105 mammal species, notably forest elephants and chimpanzees. Dja also has western lowland gorillas and indeed is one of the few remaining gorilla sanctuaries in the world. Primate species include greater white-nosed guenon, moustached guenon, crowned guenon, talapoin, red-capped mangabey, white-cheeked mangabey, agile mangabey, drill, mandrill, potto, Demidorff's galago and black and white colobus monkeys.

Other mammals include bongo, sitatunga, buffalo, leopard, warthog, giant forest hog and pangolin. Reptiles include python, lizard and several species of crocodile.

Widespread hunting and the nature of the forest, which is so dense you can generally only see a short distance in front of you, means that many animals are difficult to see easily. Birdwatching, on the other hand, is far easier, and there are 320 bird species here, including hornbills.

Baka 'pygmies' live within the eastern part of the reserve in small, sporadic encampments, maintaining an essentially traditional lifestyle, although increasingly succumbing to a more modern one.

The reserve has an equatorial climate, with constant rain from August to November that peaks in September, and temperatures similar throughout the year, at around 23°C/73°F. August is the coolest month, and April the hottest. The best time to visit is between December and early March.

Accessing the reserve

Ecosystem Forestier d'Afrique Centrale (ECOFAC) (Avenue Adenauer, Yaoundé; tel: 222 42 71; email: ecofac@camnet.cm; web: www.ecofac.org) is in charge of conservation and tourism in the reserve and should be contacted before a visit.

ECOFAC can provide information as well as compulsory guides for Dja at CFA3,000 (£3.21/US$5.67) per day and porters at CFA2,000 (£2.14/US$3.78) per day, as well as basic accommodation at CFA5,000 (£5.35/US$9.45) at its training centre at Samalomo (or Somalomo) village on the northern border of the reserve. Samalomo also has a choice of simple accommodation.

Buses go to Samalomo from Mvog-Ada in Yaoundé and if you go independently the best route is Yaoundé–Mbama–Messamena–Samalomo. The 250km journey takes a full day. Public transport is available to Samalomo on Mondays, Tuesdays and Fridays and back to Yaoundé on Tuesdays, Wednesdays and Saturdays.

Samalomo is not the only access point to the park but is probably the best. From Samalomo you can trek for a day or so to Bouamir (around 35km) and camp at a disused research centre maintained as a tourist camp, and then go further into the seemingly endless primary forest. From Samalomo it is also possible to arrange trips along the River Dja.

Another alternative is to enter Dja from the east at Lomié, where guides are also available. Lomié has changed in recent years from an isolated, quiet town into a busy base for commercial forest activity. It is a good place to base yourself for exploration of the reserve, and Baka 'pygmy' guides are available via ECOFAC for trekking into the forest and for staying at their forest villages around the eastern boundary of the reserve.

In Lomié accommodation is available at the Auberge de Raffia, 2km out of the village, which has basic but clean rooms for CFA5,000 (£5.35/US$9.45).

A third option is to approach the reserve from Djoum, southeast of Sangmélima, although facilities here are patchy.

Further information on the reserve is available from the International Union for Conservation of Nature and Natural Resources (IUCN) (Route de Mont Fébé,

Bastos, Yaoundé, near the home of the Nigerian high commissioner; tel: 220 88 88) and the Co-ordinateur du Programme Dja, Ministère de l'Environment et des Fôrets, Yaoundé; tel: 223 92 32.

YOKADOUMA
Along with towns like Moloundou and Salapombe, Yokadouma has been transformed by the logging companies from an isolated village in the midst of untouched forest into a bustling hub of commercial activity with all the bars, brothels and boarding houses that go with it. Apart from logging, other intensive human activity that has grown up around it in recent years includes sport hunting, environmental development, gold prospecting and even missionary work, with religious relocation programmes aimed at settling Baka 'pygmies' in permanent roadside settlements in their objective of bringing God's words nearer to the people.

Unfortunately, bushmeat is another thriving business, with about a dozen vendors at the market selling wild animal carcasses, such as skinned antelope, chimpanzee, gorilla and elephant meat, chopped into big cubes. Dead monkeys, their tails tied around their necks as handles, hang for sale along all the roads around the town.

The WWF has an office here, and can assist with arranging a visit to the nearby Nki and Boumba-Bek forest reserves and Lobéké National Park.

Further information on the protected areas in the region and help with visiting the reserves are available from the WWF office to the north of the main centre or at the Cameroon headquarters at Bastos in Yaoundé (tel: 221 62 67; web: www.wwfcameroon.org).

Getting there and away
During the dry season at least, there are daily services to Moloundou, Batouri (195km) and Bertoua (279km). These can be quite torturous, especially as roads become very rutted and traffic jams are common. Check at the motor park about the condition of the roads before setting off.

Where to stay
La Cachette Tel: 224 28 63. Acceptable rooms in the centre with bathrooms for CFA8,000 (£8.57/US$15.12). There is a bar/restaurant.
L'Éléphant Tel: 224 20 77. Good air-conditioned rooms starting at about CFA10,000 (£10.70/US$18.90).

MOLOUNDOU
This border town that is about an eight-hour drive/bus journey from Yokadouma is en route for Ouesso in the Congo and the Nki Reserve.

Where to stay
La Forestière A small hotel with basic rooms for CFA3,000 (£3.21/US$5.67).
Jardin du Rose Simple rooms for CFA3,500 (£3.75/US$6.61).

NKI AND BOUMBA-BEK FOREST RESERVES AND LOBEKE NATIONAL PARK
The southeastern corner of Cameroon is part of the thick Republic of Congo basin rainforest, and extends into the nearby Central African Republic, the Republic of Congo and Gabon.

From Yokadouma the track road to the frontier town of Moloundou leads to Lobéké National Park and Boumba-Bek and Nki reserves. Lobéké and Boumba-Bek are accessible by 4WD vehicle, but Nki has to be approached by boat up the River Dja.

Reaching the three areas involves a lot of time and patience. Travel from Yaoundé takes a long two days each way in the dry season, so you will need to allow for a week in total as a bare minimum.

The region is rich in wildlife, yet the dense vegetation makes the wildlife here very difficult to spot. The best time to visit is when the region is at its driest, between December and early March.

These protected areas have suffered from logging and poaching, disturbing the lives of the Baka 'pygmies', other traditional local groups, and wildlife. Because the region is well known for its rich biodiversity in terms of various forest wildlife species and commercial timber trees, it has attracted many fortune seekers who over the last three decades have greatly exploited natural resources especially destined for European markets.

More than 283 bird species have been recorded in the region, including the rare Dja warbler, the Nkulengu rail and Bates' nightjar. More than 300 fish species have also been recorded, with at least three species new to science. The Nki Falls harbour significant populations of Nile crocodile.

The two main ethnic groups of people in this region are Bantu and Baka 'pygmies'. The Bantus in the region comprise more than 70% (20,000 inhabitants) of the population and are subdivided into nine tribal groups, including the Mbimo, Movongmvong, Konabembe, Djem-Dzimou, Bakwele and Bangandos.

Around a fifth of the population are Baka and the rest are outsiders such as Muslim traders and people from other West African countries.

The Bantus in this area are principally farmers and forest gatherers, their main cash crop being cocoa. Their hunting is mainly meant for domestic consumption, although they increasingly sell bushmeat.

The Baka remain more attached to traditional hunting and forest gathering, and many still hunt using primitive methods such as bows and poisoned arrows, and pit holes for larger game. In the forest they also harvest things like mangoes, honey and yams.

To the Baka the forest is mother, father and guardian, and they have a forest god, Jengi. The WWF, in the course of carrying out their conservation programme in the area (also called Jengi), found unexpected resistance from the Baka despite their efforts to help them. For example, one old Baka woman was against the formation of a protected area because she claimed the tomb of her forefathers was situated within it and it would prevent her from carrying out her ritual rites. And an eight-year-old girl went on hunger strike because her teeth had not been chiselled. She said that not only did chiselling her teeth make her more beautiful, but it also better adapted her to eat meat.

Conservation interest first manifested itself more than 20 years ago, when the first exploration missions to Boumba-Bek and Nki strongly highlighted the biological diversity of the area. By the mid-1980s, IUCN had classified the area as a critical site for conservation and since 1994 the WWF has been actively present and working in the region in collaboration with other conservation agencies and organisations, including the Ministry of Environment and Forests (MINEF) (tel: 224 28 99), to protect the forest and develop an ecotourist initiative that would provide local people with alternatives to the bushmeat and forestry industries. There are research camps in the three reserves, which can provide basic accommodation. More details are available from the WWF.

Nki and Boumba-Bek forest reserves

Boumba-Bek Forest Reserve is reached by heading westwards by vehicle and then on foot from Ngola, which is north of Mambele on the main Yokadouma road.

To reach Nki, from Moloundou take a boat westwards down the Dja River and then proceed on foot into the forest. The WWF project staff can help with obtaining a boat, which is likely to cost in the region of CFA30,000 (£32.15/US$56.71) per person for five people.

The Nki Reserve on the River Dja offers an opportunity to observe one of the most remote and relatively untouched parts of the Congo basin forest. It is hilly and devoid of human habitation. Unlike Lobéké and to some extent Boumba-Bek, it remains substantially intact and comparatively untouched by the chain-saws of the logging companies, its protection from logging imposed by nature rather than anything else. Developing the necessary infrastructure such as roads for logging operations, especially in the southern part of Nki, would be very costly.

Nki is a true wilderness, much of it still unexplored and with new discoveries still being made. It gives visitors the opportunity to view nature in its true and primitive form, and the wide variety of species in the region still goes through the basic rudimentary evolutionary processes, uninfluenced by man's alteration of habitats to meet his overwhelming needs.

Studies indicate the high biological diversity in the area of the reserves. The 600,000ha Boumba-Bek and Nki forest block harbours more than 5,000 elephants. Other important species include gorillas, chimpanzees, buffalo, bongo and a host of other forest antelopes. Various diurnal primate species, notably the highly threatened crested monkey, De Brazza monkey and the black colobus monkey, are also found in the Nki forest.

Lobéké National Park

Lobéké is the most accessible of the three areas and can be a fantastically rewarding – if strenuous – experience. It contains some of the highest densities of forest elephants and western lowland gorillas in all of Africa, as well as large numbers of chimpanzees and other primates, leopards, and ten species of forest ungulates. There are a few viewing platforms for observing the wildlife.

Except for the large concentrations of people around Moloundou (approximately 5,000), the Lobéké region is sparsely populated, with less than one person per square kilometre in most areas. These groups live almost exclusively along the main road running north–south from Yokadouma to Moloundou.

One recent study in the Lobéké found that the buffalo in this area feed in the night while the sitatunga (large antelope) feed in the same place during the day.

To visit Lobéké, first call in at the WWF office in Yokadouma to obtain information. A CFA5,000 (£5.35/US$9.45) entry fee per day and CFA3,000 (£3.21/US$5.67) guide fee per day are payable at the adjacent Ministry of Finance office, for which you should get a receipt. You will need to charter transport into the park.

Adamawa Province

Much of Adamawa (or Adamaoua) Province is made up of a huge area of savanna and forest which neatly separates northern and southern Cameroon. This region is very thinly populated and very hard to get around, as there are only a handful of very poor roads and the Yaoundé–Ngaoundéré railway line running through it. To travel through this region is far quicker by train (around 12 hours from Yaoundé) than it is by roads (around three days from Yaoundé).

Adamawa Province is cattle-raising country, thanks to its many water sources, including its beautiful lakes, waterfalls and pastures. Its peoples include the Fulani, Mousgoum, Mboum and Mambila.

NGAOUNDERE

When arriving from the south, Ngaoundéré, the capital of Adamawa Province, is the first sizeable town you come to in northern Cameroon. The town, the terminus of the solitary railway line from the south, is attractive, with tree-lined streets and a pleasingly mild climate, thanks to its 1,300m elevation. It has a university.

The town's first settlers, the Mboum, were defeated by the Muslim Fulani in the 1830s. The Fulani influence remains strong, from the architecture of the mosques and other buildings to the flowing robes of the people. The town changed little until the railway line was extended to Ngaoundéré in 1974, helping to trigger a boom in population from under 20,000 to over 150,000 now, and still rising rapidly.

The commercial centre, with banks, post office and various restaurants and shops, is focused around Rue Ahidjo and the Rue du Petit Marché. Rather confusingly, the town's *petit marché* on this latter street has become the principal, bigger market, rather than the town's walled *grande marché* on the Rue de la Grande Mosquée.

This latter market, down from the huge and magnificently gaudy grand mosque, sells bric-a-brac like plastic buckets and vegetables past their best. Some stalls are more useful, however: if you have any clothes needing repair, or want to have a shirt, dress or trousers made from some African fabric you may have picked up, there is an excellent tailor who will do such things for under CFA4,000 (£4.28/US$7.56). At last sighting he could be found by entering the market on the west side, turning left and heading straight into the corner.

Outside the market is a raised oval of ground, with a few hawkers but also with several Muslim barbers who will massage your face with oil and then meticulously and gently shave it with a cut-throat razor. A marvellous, soporific experience – well, for a man, anyway.

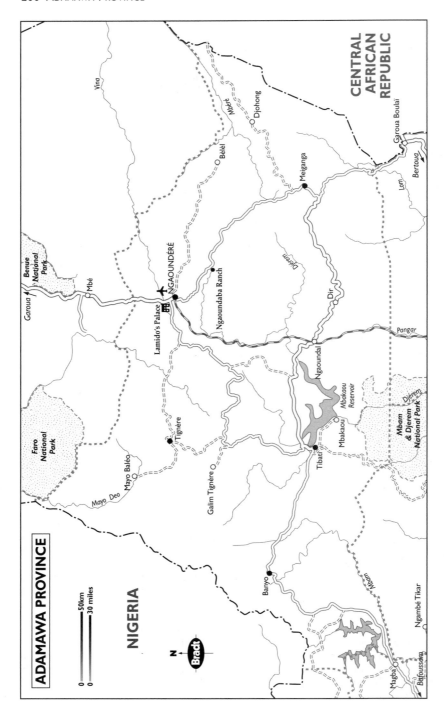

Getting there and away

Most visitors to Ngaoundéré arrive by train and upon arrival taxi drivers are likely to descend on you and attempt to take your baggage, to secure your custom. They will most probably demand CFA1,000 (£1.07/US$1.89) to take you into town but will almost certainly accept under CFA400 (42p/75c).

Roads heading south are bad, so travel in that direction is best done by train, although there are some minibuses to Garoua-Boulai and Bertoua.

The Yaoundé train departs from Ngaoundéré station (tel: 225 12 71/225 13 77) at around 18.00 daily to arrive at around 07.00 the following morning, although delays are common.

For northern destinations, *agences de voyages* Woila Voyages (BP 630; tel: 225 25 08/985 54 87), Joli Voyages (tel: 225 14 19) and Touristique Express (tel: 225 19 73) have services for the 300km route to Garoua and even further to Maroua (five hours, CFA6,000/£6.43/US$11.34).

For eastern Cameroon and the Central African Republic, take the train as far as Belabo and then take a taxi or minibus (currently Haut Nyong ply this route) to Bertoua.

At the *gare routière* next to the central market, share-taxis and minibuses are available going west via Tibati en route to Foumban. The road to Tibati is basically a dirt track and the torturous journey takes around eight hours – in the dry season.

Cameroon Airlines (tel: 225 12 95) operates flights to Yaoundé, Douala, Garoua and Maroua from Ngaoundéré's airport (tel: 225 12 84), 4km west of the centre.

Where to stay

Hôtel Relais BP 47; near the junction with Rue du Petit Marché and Rue de la Grande Mosquée; tel: 225 11 38. This hotel enjoys a perfect position in the centre of town and has friendly and helpful staff. The 34 rooms are clean and have a TV, but they have only very basic bathrooms, with missing fixtures and there is no hot water except on the first floor. There's a rather sad little bar, and although there is no restaurant, breakfast is available (omelette, bread and coffee for CFA1,500/£1.60/US$2.83). Singles CFA12,000 (£12.86/US$22.68), doubles CFA15,000 (£16.07/US$28.35).

Hôtel du Rail BP 319; Route de Garoua; tel: 225 10 13. A few minutes' walk from the train station, this long-established hotel has 18 good rooms, a bar, and a restaurant which does a good meat stew. Rooms from around CFA15,000 (£16.07/US$28.35). There's also a bar and a nightclub.

Auberge Possada Style BP 518; off Rue Ahidjo; tel: 225 17 03. Half a kilometre north of the cathedral off the main road; the rooms are acceptable and clean, with en-suite facilities. From CFA5,000 (£5.35/US$9.45).

Auberge de Château d'Adamaoua Off Rue du Petit Marché; tel: 225 20 42. Central hotel with very basic rooms for under CFA54,000 (£4.28/US$7.56).

Hôtel les Alizes BP 405; Plateau Mandock; tel: 225 16 89. Away from the centre, this pleasant option has an attractive garden, a good restaurant and bar, and balconied rooms with bathrooms. CFA10,000 (£10.70/US$18.90).

Auberge de la Gare BP 203; up the hill from the (striking) train station; tel: 225 22 17. A small hotel of an acceptable standard with a good-value restaurant and comfortable rooms with bathrooms. Around CFA7,000 (£7.50/US$13.23).

Hôtel Transcam BP 179; off Route de Garoua-Boulai; tel: 225 13 32/225 11 73/225 10 41. Located a kilometre or so southwest of the centre, this is the most comfortable option in Ngaoundéré. A government-rated three-star hotel with a bar, restaurant, nightclub, tennis courts, swimming pool and 43 good air-conditioned rooms with bathroom and satellite TV. From CFA24,000 (£25.72/US$45.36).

Where to eat and drink

The cheapest eateries are in the vicinity of the Rue de la Gare and the Rue de la Grande Mosquée and there are street stalls around the train station.

Adamaoua Losirs Rue Ahidjo. One of the best bars in town, the Adamaoua Losirs serves inexpensive simple meals and boasts a procession of hawkers selling anything from kebabs and nuts to belts and shoes.

Marhaba Near the cathedral. The place to go if you want unfriendly staff, little atmosphere and a blaring TV, although it has a disco at weekends and serves several fish and meat dishes.

Restaurant Au Feu de Bois Rue de la Grande Mosquée. Has Cameroonian options like *ndole* as well as Western fast food. Prices start at under CFA1,500 (£1.60/US$2.83).

Le Délice Rue de la Grande Mosquée. Good meals for under CFA2,000 (£2.14/US$3.78).

Santana Express Rue de la Grande Mosquée. Good-value food.

Bar Laitier Near the cathedral. For coffees, pastries and *dakkere*, a kind of yoghurt with rice.

L'Egi d'Or Near the cathedral on the main street. In the busy part of town, so great for people-watching. Reasonable prices, a good atmosphere, popular with expats at night. Draught '33' lager and excellent *chawarmas* (a Lebanese dish of grilled lamb slices served in pitta bread with a chickpea sauce), as well as good coffee, cakes and croissants, pizzas and burgers.

La Plazza Opposite Au Feu de Bois. A wide range of dishes and a good place to eat. You can change money here and they arrange tours.

Cafe Resteau Near Hôtel Relais. Turn right out of the hotel, and this great place for simple meals is on your right near the main road. Benches are enclosed in a blue tin shack with a white cloth door. The gregarious women who work here serve omelettes, rice, coffee, tea, soda, stews and a great avocado salad, and will even prepare vegetarian meals on request. Main meals are around CFA1,000 (£1.07/US1.89). You can't beat the cost or the ambience, plus you'll get to rub elbows with the locals.

Practical information

Banks
Bicec, Crédit Lyonnais Off Rue Ahidjo

Groceries
Commerce General Supermarket Behind Hôtel le Relais
Alissar Alimentation Near Au Feu de Bois restaurant

Hospital
Norwegian Protestant Mission Hospital BP 6; tel: 225 11 95. Southeast of the centre.

Internet access
Globalisation Rue du Petit Marché
Various internet cafés in the centre.

Moped hire
Outside Hotel le Relais

Tourism
Tourist office BP 527; Rue Ahidjo; tel: 225 24 63/225 25 89. The staff include a charming and knowledgeable man who speaks excellent English. They can advise on accommodation, restaurants and bars, and travel in the region.

Travel agents
Alto Tel: 225 15 24/225 11 29. By the *grand marché*, with various local excursions, including treks on horseback.

What to see
Lamido's Palace
The old town is dominated by the Palais du Lamido, near the market. Admission is CFA2,000 (£2.14/US$3.78); a guide (French-speaking) is CFA1,000 (£1.01/US$1.89); and there is a photography fee of CFA1,000. The *lamido* (chief) lives here with his wives. The palace and its courtyards, homes and public rooms are surrounded by a wall, in which people are buried. The palace is, in the Hausa language, a type of building known as a *sare*, with huts topped with large cone-shaped thatched roofs which nearly reach the ground, and which were used to hide children in times of war. You see such things as the lamido's ancient telephone installed next to his throne and are whisked around in about ten minutes.

There is a colourful Friday prayer service with the lamido leading a procession of notables, decked out in bright orange and red, to the mosque. There are also similar events on Saturdays and Sundays.

You can enter the complex by booking at the tourist office on Rue Ahidjo or alternatively at the lamido's secretariat office, the new concrete building by the entrance.

Around Ngaoundéré
This region is dotted with mud huts with tall 'witches' hat' thatched roofs, which almost seem to have grown out of the earth without the involvement of man. On the outskirts of Ngaoundéré is some beautiful forest with a number of types of conifer.

Lakes
Dang Lake, just north of the city by the main road to Garoua and near to the university, is a large, shallow lake that is a haven for birdlife, including moorhens, geese and ducks.

Lake Tison (Lake Tyson) is a circular volcanic crater lake 9km from Ngaoundéré, reached by taking the Garoua–Boulai/Meiganga road southwards for 5km, where there is a signpost for the lake, which is about 2km eastwards from here, through the woods.

Lake Mbalang is an irregular-shaped crater lake about 1km long with a little wooded islet in the middle. It is about 21km east of Ngaoundéré.

BIRDING SITE GUIDE
Keith Barnes

Dang Lake is a large shallow lake located just north of Ngaoundéré (near the university, alongside the road north to Garoua) and is visible from the main road. It is best to visit this lake in the early morning when the heat haze is greatly reduced.

Species at Dang Lake
This lake is good for waterbirds, and may prove to be under-birded and hold many more interesting species. Thus far the following have been recorded here: little grebe, long-tailed cormorant, white-faced whistling-duck, African pygmy-goose, yellow-billed duck, little egret, grey heron, great egret, squacco heron, black kite, hooded vulture, western marsh-harrier, lesser moorhen, African jacana, lesser jacana, wood and common sandpiper, spur-winged plover, pied kingfisher, woodchat shrike, sedge warbler and crested lark.

BIRDING SITE GUIDE

Keith Barnes

Surrounded by forest-savanna mosaic, the lake and the remnant patches of gallery forest here provide a perfect introduction to the birds of the Adamawa Plateau. Cool, forested gullies are interspersed with broadleaved woodlands. The gallery forests are in small valleys with banks that make viewing of the canopy easy. Ngaoundaba Ranch is situated 40km southeast of Ngaoundéré, the only place to stay, with chalets, a great restaurant and private facilities.

Birding Ngaoundaba

Over 200 bird species have been recorded at this ranch, although it undoubtedly holds more, among them a number of species difficult to see anywhere else in Africa, including Schlegel's francolin, brown-chested lapwing, Puvel's illadopsis, thrush babbler, white-collared starling, Bamenda apalis and Dybowski's twinspot. Some of the best birding is around the ranch buildings. The open woodland adjacent to the ranch supports brown-backed woodpecker, Senegal eremomela, white-shouldered black tit, white-collared starling, Emin's shrike, white-breasted cuckoo-shrike, black woodhoopoe, spotted creeper, grey-headed bush shrike, blue-bellied roller, marsh tchagra, gambaga flycatcher, white-shouldered black-tit, yellow penduline-tit, sun lark and bar-breasted firefinch. In burnt areas, watch for Heuglin's wheatear. The lake itself supports bittern, whistling cisticola and marsh tchagra. Brown twinspot is more easily found along the edge of the crater lake. Willcock's honeyguide and Bamenda apalis are seen regularly in the gallery forest in front of the chalets. The gallery forest near the ranch entrance is home to leaf-love, grey-winged robin-chat, grey-headed oliveback, red-faced pytilia, and thrush babbler, as well as two of Africa's star turacos, white-crested and Lady Ross's. Black-capped babbler, blue-breasted kingfisher, oriole warbler (moho), splendid glossy starling and white-crowned robin-chat are all residents here too. Night drives offer chances to see plain, black-shouldered, pennant-winged, standard-winged and long-tailed nightjars. The mammals are no less spectacular, with serval, civet and many others recorded.

Lake Myam is a lake of about 800ha surrounded by forest and home to hippos and crocodiles.

Waterfalls

Beni Falls is an impressive tabular waterfall at Mbang Mboum, 20km or so northeast of Ngaoundéré.

The spectacular **Vina Falls** are on the Garoua–Boulai/Meiganga road, soon after Wakwa village, 15km from Ngaoundéré. The water drops about 30m from a rocky table, and vast meadows form an impressive backdrop.

The equally impressive **Lancrennon Falls**, with a drop of around 100m, are situated in the extreme east of the country, by the border with the Central African Republic, about 80km from Djohong.

The **Tello Falls** are on the Addi road eastwards from Ngaoundéré, before the village of Tourningal, about 50km from the town. Endless streams of water tumble 50m down a great canyon into an emerald-green pool. There is a beach by a large red rock. A smaller waterfall sits beside the main one, and is perfect for a shower.

There are caves to explore behind both waterfalls. It is an isolated spot especially popular with expat families at weekends.

Nyem-Nyem Caves

The refuge of the Nyem Nyem peoples when they resisted the Germans, these caves are situated west of Ngaoundéré on the top of Mount Djim, about halfway between Tignere and Tibati, near Galim. Traditional festivities are held each January here.

Where to stay

Along the Meiganga road before the village of Bandal, 35km southeast of Ngaoundéré (about a 90-minute drive), is the mountain lodge of **Ngaoundaba Ranch** (BP 3; tel: 225 24 69/225 19 05/999 34 68; bookable through Alissar

---

DJOHONG
Brian Cruickshank

The drive through east-central Cameroon from Ngaoundéré along the twisting D22 road is rough, and is sometimes paved, sometimes not. It is very sparsely populated, save for the very small villages that occur every so often.

The scenery on the route is otherworldly. Few trees, and lots of small, mushroom-like ant-hills dot the roadside. The condition of the road can go from decent to bad rather quickly, so be prepared to swerve to miss giant holes in the road, or more likely, dried-up water channels where the rainy season waters have carved deep ruts across the track. The D22 road continues through Djohong and stops at the Central African Republic.

The village of Djohong is populated mostly by civil service workers, government officials, policemen, teachers and farmers. Others earn their living as labourers, builders, merchants, craft persons, tailors, farmers and cattle herders. There are smaller communities situated around Djohong, with populations of around 30 inhabitants. The nearest place for medical treatment is a Norwegian hospital at Belel, near the end of the D21 road.

The indigenous tribes of the area include the Gbaya and Mbéré. There are also, and have been for years, many Foulbé people in Djohong, and more recently, many Mbororo. A range of religions is represented through the diverse cultures in this area. Often the local religion is a mixture of animism along with other widely practised religions such as Islam and Christianity.

The region around Djohong is a savanna, with gently rolling terrain. It is mostly grassland with lots of small trees. Small wild animals are common, including monkeys and gazelle. Long-horn cattle also graze on the plateau, but during the dry season the semi-nomadic farmers take them to areas near the Ngou or Mbéré Rivers to graze.

Rains are hard and roads sometimes become temporary rivers during the summer months and into September. By the end of the rainy season, the grasses can grow as tall as a man, and certain varieties can then be used for thatching roofs, weaving fences or making mats, baskets and ropes. The dry season, from October to March, is dusty and windy and temperatures are generally cooler, going as low as 12°C/53°F. During December the Harmattan can be very strong here, making the area a dusty place indeed.

supermarket in Ngaoundéré; open November–May). A few kilometres from the main road, at a privately owned cattle ranch, it is nestled in the mountains 1,360m above sea level next to a beautiful volcanic crater lake. Here you can birdwatch, fish, swim and take a boat on the lake. The stone dining room is lined with animal trophies from hunting safaris of the past, and accommodation is in *boukarous* at CFA9,000 (£9.64/US$17.01) for singles, CFA12,000 (£12.86/US$22.68) for doubles, and CFA20,000 (£21.43/US$37.80) for suites, while camping is CFA1,000 (£1.07/US$1.89) per person. Breakfast and dinner are CFA6,000 (£6.43/US$11.34).

TIBATI

Tibati, 280km westwards by challenging road from Ngaoundéré, is a sleepy village by Mbakaou Lake with a slightly Wild West air. It's a good base for the Pangare Djerem Reserve. It is essentially a junction, with five roads joining the main one.

Where to stay
Auberge Kautang has a lively, loud bar, and the very basic rooms (behind the bar) are CFA2,000–3,000.

Alternatively take a moto to the **Auberge le Djerem**, an informal, family-run auberge with a public room with a blaring television, and another, far quieter, Buffalo Room named after the buffalo head on top of the now-defunct 1950s television. The auberge offers dishes like meat stew (CFA700/75p/US$1.32) and very basic rooms with a hole-in-the-floor loo and shower for CFA2,500–3,000 (£2.67–3.21/US$4.72–5.67).

Moving on from Tibati
Minibuses to Banyo (CFA3,800/£4.07/US$7.18) take around five hours thanks to the abysmal roads.

BANYO

The liveliest road in this sleepy corner is Rue Djouda, which has several bars, including the Spot Bar and the Club de Dandys, and the Restaurant de Pasta, which serves basic European meals for CFA1,500–3,000 (£1.60–3.20/US$2.83–5.67). Further down the road, Restaurant du Temps serves couscous, liver, tripe, bouillon and plantain chips for CFA600 (64p/US$1.13), and a good omelette breakfast for the same price.

Getting there and away
Take the bus to Banyo from Foumban. The bus for Foumban (CFA4,500/£4.82/US$8.50, five hours) can easily take two or three hours to fill up, but sweet tea is available opposite the bus station for a handsome CFA25 (2p/4c).

Where to stay
Banyo has two auberges, the **Auberge le Sare** and the better **Auberge Posada**. Turn right out of the bus station and walk until you hit the left fork at the Elf petrol station. Very basic rooms with a cold shower here are CFA2,500 (£2.67/US$4.72).

North Province

A trip to northern Cameroon offers a great change of scenery, climate and culture from the rest of the country. Its scantily vegetated savanna terrain, blistering, harsh temperatures, Islamic culture and archaic, primitive villages are a big contrast to the cooler, lushly vegetated, more developed, more densely populated and Christian parts of the country.

The north's principally Islamic culture is most noticeable in the larger towns, Maroua and Garoua, where flowing Islamic robes are often in abundance, in contrast to the omnipresent jeans and T-shirts typically worn in the south of Cameroon.

The southern border of North Province roughly follows the Adamawa Mountains, cutting across the centre of the country from east to west.

Whereas the south has been in contact with Europe for more than 500 years, until the 20th century the north was a part of a series of quasi-feudal Muslim Fulani (or Foulbé) kingdoms based in Nigeria.

Resistance to change and outside influence have meant that Western-style development has generally been limited. Despite this, this is one of the easiest regions of Cameroon to travel through, not least because there are good sealed roads stretching from Ngaoundéré all the way to Kousséri on the Chadian border.

GAROUA

Most people's first impression of Garoua, the capital of North Province and the principal economic and administrative centre of the north, isn't too inspiring: a tatty motor park with stalls selling anything from breakfasts of rice and beans to dodgy aspirins and toothpastes, and brochettes of meat doused in hot chilli sauce. Look around and there are also dreary modern office blocks and wooden and cement homes with tin roofs.

Garoua is 296km from Ngaoundéré, and 212km from Maroua. Its population has grown steadily in recent years and now exceeds 360,000, with many being Choa, Foulbé, Fali and Mandang. Its population is heavily Nigerian and Chadian, as well as Cameroonian.

Garoua evolved in the 18th century after the first peoples began to settle in the area, including the Bata and Fali. Then came nomadic Fulani herders in the 1800s, who built defences around the town to dispel invaders. Then other Muslim peoples settled at Garoua, including Hausa and Shua Arabs.

The town was colonised by the Germans in 1901 and they established a port, which helped forge links with Nigeria and Chad. It was also the birthplace of former president Ahidjo, who invested heavily in the town, and it now boasts a thriving range of industries.

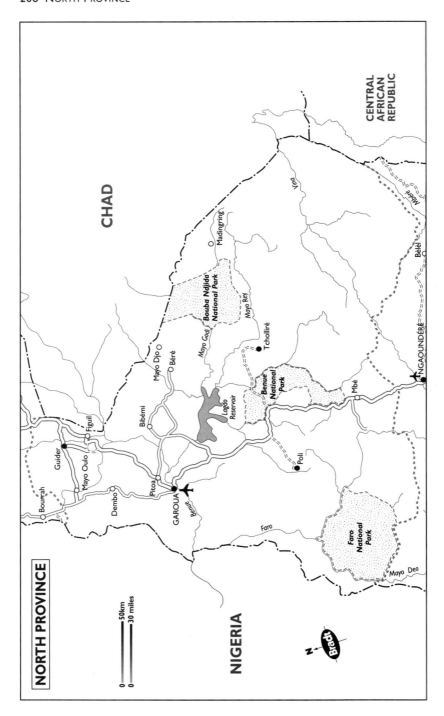

Despite being located well into the interior of Cameroon, Garoua has a large port, on the wide Bénoué River, although it is far less busy than in the past. It can only operate during the rainy season. A large bridge crosses the river.

Garoua has very few sights as such, apart from the huge Grande Mosque on Route de Maroua. Non-Muslims are not admitted. There is a good range of facilities, including banks, two hospitals, a post office, petrol stations, an airport and a range of hotels.

The central market is a lively destination, and is busiest at weekends, and there is a *petit marché* just southwest of the centre, near plenty of bars and simple restaurants. For purchasing arts and crafts, head for the group of traders under the neem trees just north of the market.

Getting there and away

Most *agences de voyages* are near the central market around Rue des Banques and Rue du Pont and go to and from Maroua (three hours) and Ngaoundéré (five hours), and include Lux Voyages (tel: 227 52 98); Super Voyages (tel: 227 12 03); Amy Voyages (tel: 227 33 05); Narral Voyages (tel: 227 11 16); Woila Voyages (tel: 227 30 82); and Star Voyages (tel: 227 14 85).

There are share-taxis bound for Nigeria at the *gare routière*, 5km north of the centre on the Maroua road.

Cameroon Airlines (tel: 227 10 55; airport: tel: 227 14 81) flies to Yaoundé, Douala and Maroua, and Ndjamena in Chad. The airport is 5km north of the centre.

Where to stay

Relais Saint Hubert BP 445; Rue du Novotel; tel: 227 22 34/227 30 33. This has an expensive bar, a restaurant serving Cameroonian and European fare (CFA3,500–4,500/ £3.75–4.82/US$6.61–8.50 for main dishes), and a reasonably extensive but expensive wine list (CFA5,000–15,000/£5.35–16.05/US$9.45–28.35), as well as a pool and gardens, and good, clean, comfortable air-conditioned rooms with TV, room service and en-suite facilities for CFA17,900 (£19.18/US$33.83) for a small room, CFA22,950 (£24.59/US$43.38) for a medium-sized room and CFA24,950 (£26.74/US$47.16) for a large room. Guides are likely to approach you for tours in the locality. Reckon on around CFA4,000–10,000 (£4.28–10.70/US$7.56–18.90) per day.

Auberge le Salam BP 496; tel: 27 24 26. Near the central market; there are basic rooms with fans and shared facilities around a courtyard; CFA2,500 (£2.67/US$4.72) single, CFA3,500 (£3.75/US$6.61) double.

Auberge Hiala Village BP 354; Rue Boumare; tel: 227 24 07. Good-value simple rooms with bathrooms, plus good restaurant and bar, located near the port.

Auberge de la Cité BP 14; Rue du Petit Marché; tel: 227 24 93. OK restaurant and self-contained rooms with fan or AC for CFA5,000–7,000 (£5.35–7.50/US$9.45–13.23).

Auberge Centrale BP 33; Rue Adamou Amar; tel: 227 33 49. Near the central market, this newer option has air-conditioned rooms, some with bathrooms. CFA5,000–7,000 (£5.35–7.50/US$9.45–13.23).

Hôtel la Bénoué BP 291; Rue du Mgr Yves Plumey; tel: 227 15 58. This upmarket hotel has a good restaurant, a nightclub, swimming pool, tennis court and 52 good rooms with showers/bathrooms and AC for CFA18,000–25,000 (£19–26/US$34–47).

Tourist Motel BP 1169; Rue de la Gendarmerie; tel: 227 32 44/997 92 41. Less than 2km northwest of the centre, this comfortable hotel has a swimming pool (non-guests can use it for a small fee) and 52 rooms with TV, AC and telephone. From CFA25,000 (£19/US$34).

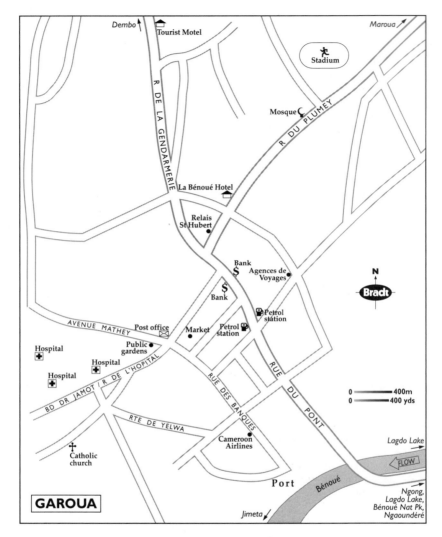

GAROUA

Where to eat and drink, and nightlife

Some inexpensive eateries are on Route de Maroua and around the *petit marché*.

Super Restaurant, opposite Star Voyages on Route de Maroua, offers reasonable prices, delicious fresh fruit drinks, a good avocado salad and various Sudanese dishes. It is in the busy section of the city and therefore great for people-watching.

In the northern section of town, off Rue de la Gendarmerie in the Roumde Adjia neighbourhood, are several bars, cafés and simple restaurants with cheap Cameroonian dishes, including **Chez Marie Bamiléké** and **Chez Lyna**. An expensive option, for French cuisine, would be **Le Nautic**, off Route Périphérique, southwest of the centre. Other options include **Le Baoba** and **Restaurant d'Afrique**.

Head for the Yelwa district just southwest of the centre for plenty of bars, cafés and cheap restaurants. Hotel la Bénoué on Rue du Mgr Yves Plumey has a pricey nightclub attached.

Practical information
Banks
Several banks are located on or around Rue des Banques (also known as Rue Centrale) including **Bicec, Crédit Lyonnais** and **SGBC**, which has an ATM.

Bookshops
Librarie Nouvelle Moderne Rue des Banques

Groceries
Supermarché Tigre Rue du Pont

Hospitals
Provincial Hospital Tel: 227 14 14
Southia Clinic Tel: 227 21 33
Centre Medico Social Tel: 227 16 08

Internet
Ets Bao Tel: 227 13 97

Pharmacies
Pharmacie du Grand Marché Tel: 227 20 95
Pharmacie du Nord Tel: 227 13 79

Photography
Photo FM Tel: 227 29 23

Tourism
Tourist office Off Rue des Banques; tel: 227 22 90

THE NATIONAL PARKS AND RESERVE
This region still has large mammal populations big enough to be considered of international importance, but among these are some of the world's most threatened species. The WWF has been involved in conservation projects here since the early 1990s, notably working on the dwindling rhino population, and inventory and management-related work on elephants.

The three parks in this region, Faro, Bénoué and Bouba Ndjida, are most popular for hunting, and Waza further north is a better bet for observing wildlife. All the parks are off the fast, good-quality paved Ngaoundéré–Garoua road. You need to arrange your own transport, hiring a vehicle at Ngaoundéré, Garoua or Maroua. Accommodation in the *campements* in the parks can be reserved through the Garoua tourist office (BP 50, Garoua; tel: 227 22 90). Accommodation tends to fill up quickly at weekends.

Faro Reserve
The 200,000-hectare Reserve de Faro, consisting of forested savanna, hills and mountains, extends to the border with Nigeria but has been badly affected by poaching in recent years, so Bénoué and Bouba Ndjida national parks are a far better bet for wildlife-watching. There are small populations of such animals as

BIRDING SITE GUIDE
Keith Barnes

The low rocky hills of the Bénoué National Park covered with orchard-like open forest support specials of this zone including Adamawa turtle-dove (drinking in river pools), white-throated francolin, Emin's shrike, rufous-rumped lark and white-fronted black chat. Some of the best birding is in the Campement du Bufflé Noir's garden along the Bénoué River. Prime specialities on the river are Egyptian plover (hippo pools) and three-banded and white-headed plover. At dusk check the terrace along the Bénoué River for bat hawk, northern white-faced owl and standard-winged nightjar. A walk along the river with a guard may be arranged in the morning, providing opportunities to see Bruce's green pigeon, grey kestrel, white-crested and violet turaco, giant kingfisher, bearded barbet, pearl-spotted owlet, white-breasted cuckoo shrike, sulphur-breasted bush shrike, spotted creeper, yellow penduline tit, swallow-tailed bee-eater, little and black-headed weaver and cinnamon-breasted bunting. Other Guinea savanna specials include blue-bellied roller, grasshopper buzzard, stone partridge, four-banded sandgrouse, Senegal parrot, Abyssinian roller, Abyssinian ground-hornbill, Hheuglin's wheatear, yellow-billed shrike, Senegal batis, Senegal eremomela, bush petronia, black-faced and black-bellied firefinch, red-winged pytilia and pygmy sunbird. The lucky may find brown-rumped bunting and West African (streaky-headed) seedeater.

rhinoceros, buffalo, elephant and harnessed guib, and the Atlantika Mountains, which the Cameroon/Nigeria border slices through the middle of, are to the north. Accommodation is available at the exclusive, very pricey Faro West camp above the Faro River, which is principally used by hunters. The luxury air-conditioned *boukarous* feature a living room, dining room, bar, balcony with panoramic view, and kitchen.

Bénoué National Park

The Parc National de la Bénoué, with the wettest climate of the three, is situated on the Bénoué Plains halfway between Garoua and Ngaoundéré in the northern Guinea savanna belt. It is about a three-hour drive from Ngaoundéré and covers 180,000 hectares, much being Guinea woodlands. It features a wide frontage to the Bénoué River. Inhabitants include lion, giraffe, hyena, panther, Nile crocodile, giant eland, antelope including kob, hartebeeste and waterbuck, as well as topi, black and white colobus, Guereza colobus, red-fronted (Thomson's) gazelle, green sun-squirrel, baboon and warthog, several hippopotamus colonies, and elephant and buffalo herds. It is popular with anglers.

Entry is at the small towns of Mayo Alim or Banda. It is best to arrive as early as possible since most of the large animals do not appear much in the sun. The park is open from December to May and there is an entrance fee of CFA5,000 (£5.35/$9.45), a vehicle charge of CFA2,000 (£2.14/US$3.78) and camera charge of CFA2,000 (£2.14/US$3.78) per day, and a guide is obligatory at CFA3,000 (£3.21/US$5.67) per day. The visitors' centre sells wood carvings for CFA8,000 to CFA10,000 (£8.57–10.71/US$15.12–18.90). Don't miss the waterfall at the far end of the visitors' centre. There you can have tea, coffee and peanuts while watching the African sunset.

Where to stay
Campement du Bufflé Noir BP 50, Garoua; tel: 227 22 90. Situated inside the park on the banks of the Bénoué River, this lodge is in a great setting. Although a bit run down, it has a restaurant (meals CFA6,000–9,000/£6.43–9.64/US$11.34–17.01), and rondavels with comfortable rooms (and separate bathrooms) sleeping four for CFA21,000 (£22.50/US$39.69). Camping is possible. The *campement* is supposed to be accessible from tracks leading from the entrances at both Banda and Mayo Alim, yet at time of going to press only the most direct route to the *campement*, leaving the main road at Banda, is negotiable, and even this is not in the best of shape. Allow 90 minutes or so to drive the 27km from the main road to the *campement*.

Campement Grand Capitaine tel: 227 22 90. On the main road from Tchollire to Guidjiba, this has more comfortable *boukarou* rooms for around CFA20,000 (£21.40/ US$37.80).

Bouba Ndjida National Park
The Parc National de Bouba Ndjida is a rugged reserve on the banks of the Mayo Lidi River and on the border with Chad. It covers around 220,000ha and is particularly remote and beautiful, with open wooded and bush savanna including elements of the landscape of the Sahelian zone. It contains most of Cameroon's population of the almost extinct West African black rhinoceros, as well as the rare Derby eland, the biggest antelope in the world.

A recent study by WWF found a population of between 1,000 and 3,500 Derby eland, and concluded that the total area of distribution of the species has drastically reduced over the years thanks to human pressure and habitat fragmentation. A 1990 IUCN report considers the Derby eland as a species threatened by extinction.

There are also buffalo, elephant, lion, leopard, wild dog and antelope here, and dinosaur fossils are also located in the park. Game can be difficult to see because of the size of the park and the more than 430km of tracks. It is open from November to May and the entrance fee is CFA5,000 (£5.35/US$9.45), with an obligatory guide costing CFA3,000 (£3.21/US$5.67) per day, payable to the conservator of Bouba Ndjida in Tchollire. The main entrance is at Koum, about 45km east of Tchollire.

Where to stay
Campement de Boubandjida BP 50, Garoua; tel: 227 22 90. Situated 42km inside the park by the River Mayo Lidi, this has 16 comfortable en-suite rooms at around CFA20,000 (£21.40/US$37.80). There is also a bar and a good restaurant.

What to see
Rey Bouba
The village of Rey Bouba, sandwiched between Bouba Ndjida and Bénoué parks, is a traditional Fulani *lamidat* (or principality), but the palace rarely receives visitors. There is a traditional, very basic resthouse here.

Lagdo Lake
It is possible to stay at an excellent retreat right on this huge lake about 30km southeast of Garoua. **Lagon Bleu** at Lagdo, near Ngong (tel: 946 89 83/985 53 53), offers ten rooms of comfortable self-contained *boukarous* accommodation with fans or air-conditioning all overlooking the lake. Rooms with a double and single bed are CFA20,000 (£21.43/US$37.80) and two-room suites sleeping four are CFA30,000 (£32.15/US$56.71). There is also a good restaurant, a pretty garden and a lakeside beach. A boat and pirogue are available for exploring the lake and its islands.

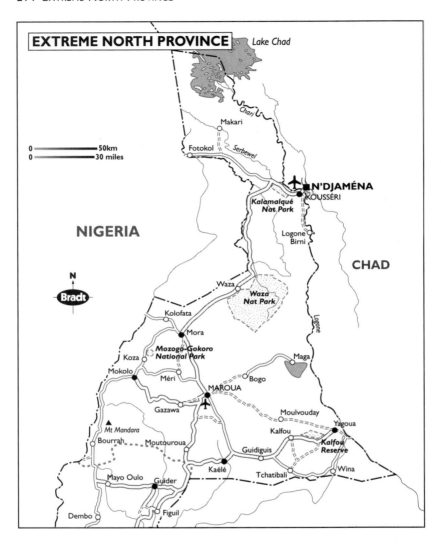

Extreme North Province

Along with the Western Highlands, the hot, dry north is certainly one of the most fascinating areas to visit in Cameroon. As well as containing the striking and spectacular harmattan-battered Mandara Mountains, exotic villages and Cameroon's best national park, Waza, it is home to a whole hotchpotch of peoples including Choa, Moundang, Toupouri, Mafa, Kapsiki and Mousgoum. The Fulani (or Foulbé) dominate and have strong traditional leadership structures. There is a high rate of immigration into the area from the Sahel.

North of here the country joins up with Lake Chad, which rises with the floods from the Chari and Logone Rivers during the brief rains each year, and dries out at other times.

MAROUA

Maroua, capital of the Extreme North Province, is 812km (503 miles) northwest of Yaoundé and 210km north of Garoua. It is Cameroon's second-biggest northern city (latest estimates suggest a population of over 200,000), and was one of the few cities that existed before colonial times.

The Mayo Kaliao River (which dries up during the dry season) cuts through its centre, separating its north and south. Neem trees line and shade its sleepy streets.

Located at the border of Sahelian Africa, Maroua is particularly ethnically diverse and is where the dominant Muslim peoples of the plains, particularly the Fulani and Mandara (or Wandala), meet the Kirdi (or mountain peoples) who live in perched villages in the highlands.

In the 18th century Maroua was controlled by a powerful Fulani leader, the Sokoto Caliphate, until the Germans came along in 1902. It was then occupied by the French in September 1914, after which it became part of French Cameroon, remaining so until Cameroonian independence in 1960.

There is a daily large and lively market, which is busiest on Mondays, when Kirdi peoples come from the mountains to trade. Everything from fruit, meat and vegetables to textiles, traditional medicines and Japanese electronic goods is sold. The city is a centre for traditional crafts and is known for its jewellery, leatherwork, silverwork, baskets, swords, bangles, painted ostrich eggs, dyes and perfumes. It has a big handicraft centre/*Centre Artisanal* next to the market.

Its location in the foothills of the eastern edge of the Mandara Mountains make Maroua popular with travellers as a base for trips to these mountains as well as to Waza National Park (125km away) and nearby picturesque villages like Mora (60km away) and Mokolo (75km).

Places worth visiting include the little-attended Diamare Museum (open Monday–Saturday 08.00–13.30, 14.30–18.00; free, but CFA500 donation expected). It contains items from the Sao civilisation, the Toupouri, Massa and Mousgoum peoples and the Fulani culture. There are musical instruments, carved calabashes, pottery, jewellery, shields, a lamido's gown and other treasures dating back as far as the 1100s.

The building also contains a craft market selling such things as jewellery, hand-woven cloth and leather goods, some made locally, others from further afield in Africa.

Getting there and away
By road
Regular transport for Kousséri and other destinations in the extreme north is available at the *gare routière* east of the centre.

For Garoua and Ngaoundéré, there are various *agences de voyages* on Boulevard de Diarenga and around the *marché centrale*, including Amy Voyages (tel: 229 16 99), Jolis Voyages (tel: 229 31 31) and Woila Voyages (tel: 229 17 57).

Star Voyages on Boulevard de la Renouveau (tel: 229 25 22) goes to Mokolo, and Yagua and Kaele on the Chadian border.

Non-agency transport to Rhumsiki, Mokolo and other southern destinations leave from Carrefour Parrah, about 3km southwest of the centre.

By air
Cameroon Airlines (tel: 229 15 15/229 20 19) flies to Yaoundé, Douala, Garoua, Ngaoundéré and Ndjamena (Chad) from Maroua's chaotic airport (tel: 229 10 21) located south of the centre, about 20km down the Garoua road.

Where to stay
Fety Hotel Bd de Diarenga; tel: 229 29 13. Relatively new, this small hotel near most of the *agences de voyages* has a restaurant and bar, clean rooms with AC and bathrooms from CFA6,500 (£6.96/US$12.28).

Relais Ferngo BP 112; tel: 229 21 53. Basic *boukarous* with AC/fans and bathrooms, CFA6,000 (£6.43/US$11.34). Also camping at CFA1,000 (£1.07/US$1.89) per person. Restaurant.

Matos Hotel Off Bd de Renouveau, Quartier Harde; tel: 229 29 13/990 19 01. Good rooms with bathrooms and AC for CFA7,000 (£7.50/US$13.23).

Maroua Palace BP 381; tel: 229 32 52/229 12 00. 1km north of the centre, this very comfortable hotel has a good restaurant, bars, tennis and swimming pool (CFA1,500/£1.60/US$2.83 to non-guests). The 50 smart rooms have TV, telephone and bathrooms. Singles are CFA20,000 (£21.40/US$37.80), doubles are CFA22,000 (£23.57/US$41.58) and suites CFA34,000 (£36.44/US$64.27). Also offers car hire, and credit cards are accepted.

Le Relais de la Porte Mayo BP 112; tel: 229 33 56/229 26 92. Very good-value 22-room hotel with air-conditioned, self-contained *boukarous*, a courtyard restaurant and bar with a pleasant terrace that is popular with Europeans, and a craft shop. The hotel has a chauffeur, 4WD transport and a guide available. Singles are CFA12,000 (£12.86/US$22.68), twins are CFA14,000 (£15.00/US$26.46).

Hôtel Le Sahel BP 853, Bd de Diarenga; tel: 229 29 60. Acceptable rooms, restaurant. CFA14,000 (£15.00/US$26.46) single, CFA18,000 (£19.29/US$34.02) double, CFA25,000 (£26.70/47.25) suite.

Motel le Sare BP 11; tel: 229 12 94. Good-value upmarket hotel set in pleasant gardens with swimming pool, tennis court, good restaurant and bar. Clean, comfortable rooms with AC, CFA22,000 (£23.57/US$41.58).

Campement Boussou Off Bd de Diarenga. Basic *boukarous* with fans and shared facilities. CFA3,000 (£3.21/US$5.67).

Auberge des Voyageurs Tel: 229 27 00. Just west of the market, this auberge has basic rooms, some with AC, for CFA5,000 (£5.35/US$9.45) and upwards.

Hotel Mizao BP 381; tel: 229 13 00. Comfortable but rather dull international-standard hotel with facilities like a swimming pool (CFA1,500/£1.60/US$2.83 to non-guests), tennis courts, a nightclub and a restaurant (CFA5,000/£5.35/US$9.45). The 53 rooms are CFA22,000 (£23.57/41.58) single, CFA27,000 (£28.93/US$51.03) double, CFA38,000 (£40.72/US$71.83) for an apartment. The hotel also offers car rental.

Where to eat and drink

There are numerous options, from cheap street food upwards. There are a number of clubs and bars along Boulevard de la Renouveau and some cheaper bars serving simple dishes like grilled fish on a street off this road, L'Avion Me Laisse.

Restaurant de l'Artisanat Opposite the market entrance, this serves filling Cameroonian dishes from around CFA900 (96p/US$1.70).

Le Baobab Restaurant Tel: 229 19 03/756 64 50. This *boukarous* located east of the market serves good-value Cameroonian cuisine. There are outdoor tables and meals cost from CFA2,000 (£2.14/US$3.78).

Chez Moussa East of the market, offering inexpensive fare, from brochettes for CFA100 (10p/18c) to substantial meals for over CFA3,000 (£3.21/US$5.67).

Chez Emmanuel (Bimarva Snack Bar) Just east of the market; tel: 229 19 95. A variety of dishes from CFA2,000 (£2.14/US$3.78), outdoor seating and satellite TV.

Practical information
Banks
Several are near the market, including **Bicec** and **Crédit Lyonnais**.

Cinema
The Diamare By the Cameroon Airlines office

Groceries
CGD Supermarché East of the market
Nziko East of the market

Hospitals
Hôpital Meskine Southwest of the centre off the Garoua Rd; tel: 229 25 79
CNPS Hospital Tel: 229 12 74
Provincial Hospital About 500m west of the lamido's palace; tel: 229 11 75
Pette Hospital Tel: 229 11 84

Pharmacy
Pharmacie du Centre Tel: 229 12 09/229 31 20

Post office
At the west end of Av du Kakatare

Tourist office
Provincial Delegation of Tourism Far North BP 675; tel: 229 22 98

What to see
The Maroua region
As well as its ethnic diversity – with its hotchpotch of Shua Arabs, Choa, Fulani, Kirdi and others – the Mandara Plateau is also one of the most environmentally

and agriculturally diverse regions of West Africa. Its forests, savannas, mountains and rivers contain many species, from colourful geckos to large mammals, although these are increasingly threatened by overgrazing and burning.

Mindif
La dent de Mindif (Mindif's tooth) juts up from nowhere 25km (16 miles) southeast of Maroua near the town of Mindif. It is one of the most challenging peaks to climb in Africa. Also on the road to Mindif is a tannery, which is worth a visit. Admission is CFA1,000 (£1.07/US$1.89).

The villages around the Mandara Mountains
The scenery of this region is stunning, at turns both beautiful and desolate, with the volcanic plugs of the Mandara Mountains rising up strikingly to the west of Maroua.

The most popular towns and villages visited by travellers include the rather touristy Rhumsiki, and Oudjilla, which has a traditional chief's compound and a surrounding wall that is reputedly over three centuries old. Mokolo is a charming, sleepy village and Mora has a great market. Other villages include pretty Djingliya, Mabas and Koza, Tourou, Maga and Bogo, and Mogode, north of Rhumsiki.

The region has limited facilities for travellers: no banks, few shops, and cafés, restaurants and most hotels are of a basic standard. Make sure you have adequate food and water as opportunities for obtaining these can be infrequent. Petrol is sold in Maroua and Mokolo, and is commonly also sold on the road.

MOKOLO
About 75km west of Maroua, the small, sleepy town of Mokolo, situated in a rugged, rocky setting, is the capital of the Mafa mountain peoples. It is little more than some round stone houses with thatched roofs and a motor park. It has a huge lively market on Wednesdays and a small museum near the motor park, which has a small collection of local crafts.

Before you leave Mokolo be sure to visit the post office on the main street, if only to experience a post office with no telephones, no airmail letters and, on occasion, no stamps either.

Getting there and away
If you are taking a minibus from Garoua to Mokolo, ensure you tell the driver your destination. You will usually be deposited at a crossroads at Carrefore Gakle (four hours, CFA3,800/£4.07/US$7.18) from where another minibus should take you the further stretch to Mokolo (two hours, CFA1,000/£1.07/US$1.89).

The departure point for most destinations, including Maroua and Koza, is the market in the town centre. Transport for Rhumsiki usually leaves before 08.00, west of the centre, where the covered road ends. Transport is most frequent on market day, Wednesday.

Where to stay
For the cheapest option, ask around to see if anyone will put you up in their home. They are used to this.

Bar Mecheme (see opposite) Has several small, reasonably clean and comfortable rooms with fans and a cold shower for CFA3,000 (£3.21/US$5.67).

Campement de Flamboyant BP 22; tel: 229 51 16/229 55 63. 22 comfortable air-conditioned rooms with bathrooms, singles CFA10,000 (£10.70/US$18.90), doubles

CFA15,000 (£16.07/US$28.35). The restaurant's menu is extensive but in reality steak, chicken or kebab and chips for CFA2,500 (£2.67/US$4.72) is generally all that is on offer. There is also a bar.

Where to eat and drink
As well as the Flamboyant, another option is **Café Fait-Tous**, with dishes starting at around CFA1,000 (£1.07/US$1.89).

Around the corner from the Campement de Flamboyant is the **Bar Mecheme**, a rather grubby, loud and entertaining bar run by the convivial Mr Francis. The people serving barbecues near the bar will happily bring you a plateful of fish, liver, beef, chicken or tripe and plantain for CFA1,000–2,500.

What to see and do
Try the local brew
If you are the adventurous sort and want to sample the local millet-based brew, 'bili-bili', go to the water tower to the left of Mokolo's market and enter the double iron green doors with 'La Maison de Commandant' painted on them. The CFA100 (10p/18c) brew is served by several women in an earthenware jug, with which you are given a wooden bowl to drink out of.

Trekking in the mountains
The Mandara Mountains are just southwest of Mokolo and offer great opportunities for trekking. Ask around for a guide, who typically cost from around CFA3,500 to CFA6,000 per day (£3.75–6.43/US$6.61–11.34). You can also organise a donkey for your luggage, or a horse if you wish to ride in the surrounding countryside.

Djingliya
This pretty village located on a hill 15km north of Mokolo on the way to Koza has basic accommodation from CFA3,000 (£3.21/US$5.67) at the Société Co-operative Artisanale de Djingliya (BP 94, Mokolo), which also has local crafts for sale, a restaurant and a bar.

Koza
This pleasant hillside village, located 20km from Mokolo and 30km from Mora at an altitude of 1,100m/3,600ft, has a few basic places to eat but no accommodation, unless you can find a villager to put you up. Market day is Sunday and there are vehicles going to and from Mokolo daily.

RHUMSIKI (OR ROUMSIKI)
Approximately 55km (34 miles) from Mokolo and 120km from Maroua, nestling deep in the mountains, is the small village of Rhumsiki. It is the most touristic place in northern Cameroon, but since the country has so little tourism, that should not put you off. Although a rather nondescript village itself, it is set in a spectacular, almost lunar landscape of extraordinary volcanic plugs and basalt outcrops surrounded by a series of imposing peaks, the highest being Kapsiki Mountain or Peak at 1,224m. André Gide, writer and explorer, found the area so attractive he considered it was 'one of the most beautiful landscapes in the world'.

The mountains are dotted with little thatched houses huddling against the rocks and looking almost as if they had simply grown rather than been constructed.

You are likely to be mobbed by village children urging you to follow their tour of sights of the village. These include the *feticheur*, or crab sorcerer (a fortune-teller who tells your future by watching the moves of a crab), traditional dancers, and crafts and tradespeople like potters and blacksmiths.

Hikes can be taken in the surrounding mountains (accompanied, these vary between under a day to several days and start at around CFA10,000/£10.70/US$18.90 per day, including camping with your own tent or staying in a local home) or up a hill at dawn or dusk to gaze over the beautiful landscape. You can cross into Nigeria from here, which is about 3km away. Tours are offered by most hotels.

This whole region is a genuine crossroads of races, tribes and religions, and their customs, clothes, hairstyles and physical characteristics are fascinating to compare.

Getting there and away
There is regular transport to Mokolo and Maroua, with the most choice on market day (Sunday in Rhumsiki, Monday in Maroua and Wednesday in Mokolo).

Where to stay
The cheapest option is to stay in a village home. Ask around.

Most other options are along the main road and can arrange trekking.

Auberge Le Kapsiki Tel: 229 33 56. A bar and restaurant and basic *boukarous*, with fans and shared facilities. Trekking and horse trekking can be arranged.
La Maison de l'Amitie Tel: 229 21 13. Good *boukarous* accommodation for CFA9,500 (£10.18/US$17.95), a restaurant, and trekking arranged.
Campement de Rhumsiki BP 27 Mokolo; tel: 227 16 46/229 16 46. Attractive *boukarous* facing the mountains with air-conditioned rooms for CFA7,000 (£7.50/US$13.23) single, CFA12,000 (£12.86/US$22.68) double and CFA17,000 (£18.22/US$32.13) triple. There are tennis courts and a restaurant with meals for under CFA5,000 (£5.35/US$9.45).

MORA
Capital of the Wandala (or Mandara) people, the attractive little village of Mora, 60km from Maroua, has one of the best markets in Cameroon, held each Sunday. Share-taxis take a 67km route from Mokolo via Koza to Mora on this day, which is prettier than the alternative route via Maroua. It is 30km or 19 miles from the Nigerian border. Minibuses from Ngaoundéré take the better part of a day.

The market attracts a curious mixture of people, including Muslim Fulani women clothed from head to foot, the bare-breasted Kirdi mountain women, the Podoko and Mofou, as well as the Wandala, and Shua Arabs, all coming from Chad and Nigeria, as well as Cameroon.

Foodstuffs, like grains, vegetables, fruit and slaughtered animals, cauldrons of maizemeal gruel, roasted corn and rice are typically sold, as are bright, colourful textiles, intricate carvings, painted gourds, leather goods, jewellery and *gris-gris* (necklace charms). There are open-air barber shops, blacksmiths with hand bellows, local doctors selling traditional medicines, and a separate section for trading animals, particularly donkeys, goats and cattle. There are few of the garish cheap plastic goods so often seen in the south.

Getting there and away
There is daily transport to and from Maroua.

Where to stay
Auberge Mora Massif 400m west of the main junction/two blocks east of the motor park. Has a bar/restaurant and simple, clean rooms and better *boukarous* for CFA3,000 (£3.21/US$5.67). Camping is CFA1,000 (£1.07/US$1.89) per person.

Auberge le Podoko Off the main road to Maroua. Has *boukarous* with fans and separate bathrooms, and a good restaurant.

TOUROU

This is another village in the area set in pretty countryside. The women of this Kirdi mountain village wear distinctive red wooden calabashes on their heads that look rather like army helmets and which indicate things like their marital status. There is little public transport available, but market day is Thursday, which offers the best chance of hitching a lift, although recently the Rhumsiki–Mabas–Tourou road has been impassable.

MAGA

This picturesque village has domed homes that have been made completely from clay. Basic accommodation is available. There is a market nearby on Tuesdays in the village of Pouss, northeast of Maga. Maga itself is 80km northeast of Mora on the Logone River and has excellent white beaches.

OUDJILLA

A popular destination for tourists in this region (although there is no accommodation), the Podoko hilltop village of Oudjilla is about 12km from Mora. The distinctive round thatched mudhuts you see from the road are a striking sight.

Parts of the village, which provides glorious views of the region, date back 400 years. You can visit the chief's walled compound (*sare*) (CFA1,000/ £1.07/US$1.89 per person) and meet the chief, who lives here in his palace with more than 50 wives and many children. Each wife has a hut and a kitchen and the compound includes other buildings, including a court house, huts with the tombs of the chief's father and grandfather, and a prayer hall. The walls are made from earth and the roofs of woven straw. A dance may be performed when you visit at a cost of around CFA10,000 (£10.70/US$18.90) per group of visitors, and market day is Sunday. At a ceremony in April, the Podokwo feast, a sacred bull is sacrificed.

MABAS

This small Kirdi village very near the border with Nigeria is notable for its *chefferie* (chiefdom) that enjoys uninterrupted, breathtaking views across the large Bornou plains of Nigeria. One can still see primitive blast furnaces here.

AMSA

At Amsa village blacksmiths can be seen at work, making vases and statuettes.

MOZOGO-GOKORO NATIONAL PARK

This relatively small (1,400ha) protected area south of Waza has only 10km of paths and is not open to the public, although this policy may change. It has not suffered from burning of the vegetation for over four decades and therefore it has become thickly forested. Warthog, bushbuck, grey duiker, python, vervet monkey, patas monkey and olive baboon have all been recorded here in recent years.

WAZA NATIONAL PARK

The Parc National du Waza is located in the flat plains of the far north of the country, 334km north of Garoua, 122km north of Maroua, and nudging the borders of both Chad and Nigeria. Not only is this Cameroon's most accessible, well-known and most-visited national park, but it also contains some of West and Central Africa's most impressive wildlife. It can be visited on a day trip from Maroua provided you start out early in the day.

Covering more than 170,000ha (1,700km²), Waza is home to the 'big five' animals of Africa. The large expanses of flat acacia savanna, seasonal marshes and grassland make viewing of game, especially herds of elephant, giraffe, hippo and antelope, relatively easy. The variety of landscapes, including forested areas and a huge expanse of grassland dotted with inselbergs and seasonal marshes, support a wide range of wildlife. The waters of the rainy season bring endless waterbirds, usually peaking in September.

Although the flat scrubland does not make for a striking landscape, one major attraction is the hundreds of elephants that gather at the Mare aux Eléphants, the main watering hole. Huge numbers of elephants can also be seen at other watering holes in the park, especially in the dry season. It is not unusual to see herds of over 100. The Mare aux Eléphants takes three or four hours to reach from the northwest entrance of the park. You also have a good chance of spotting lion, many species of antelope, hippo, warthog, cheetah, waterbuck, topi, red-fronted gazelle, sable roan, domilesque, hartebeest, kob, baboon, monkey, giraffe (these tend to be near the entrance) and buffalo.

Birdlife at the park is prolific and includes eagle, hornbill, crested crane, maribou, pelican, duck, goose, ostrich, heron, stork and guinea-fowl.

Waza is Cameroon's wildlife park that's most geared to visitors. Camping is not permitted in the park, but you can camp at the entrance and accommodation is available. The best time of year to see animals is from late March to early May, which unfortunately is also the hottest season. When the rains come, from May to October, not all areas of the park are accessible.

The park is open daily from November 15 to June 15, 06.00–18.00. The entrance fee is CFA5,000 (£5.35/US$9.45) plus CFA2,000 (£2.14/US$3.78) per vehicle and CFA2,000 for photography, and an obligatory guide per vehicle costs CFA3,000 (£3.21/US$5.67) per day. Walking in the park is not permitted. The main entrance, marked by two huts, is just outside the village of Waza.

Further information on the park is available from the International Union for Conservation of Nature and Natural Resources (IUCN), Route de Mount Fébé, Bastos, Yaoundé, near the home of the Nigerian high commissioner (tel: 220 88 88; Maroua: 229 22 68).

Getting there and away

The entrance to the park is signposted and around 500m from the main road. There are no vehicles for hire at the park, but buses run from Maroua and you can also hire vehicles in Maroua. Some roads around the park can be impassable during the rainy season.

Where to stay

Campement de Waza BP 13, Maroua; tel: 229 16 46/229 10 07 in Maroua; tel: 765 77 17/765 75 58 in Waza. On a hill 600m from the park entrance. *Boukarous* with AC, clean rooms and private bathrooms are built around a swimming pool (CFA1,000/£1.07/US$1.89 for non-residents). The restaurant (meals are expensive, with dinner averaging CFA6,000/£6.43/US$11.34 for soup, main course and fruit, but French fries and omelettes are a cheaper option) has great views of the park. A four-bed air-conditioned room costs CFA25,800 (£27.65/US$48.77), triples cost CFA20,000 (£21.40/US$37.80), doubles cost CFA16,000 (£17.14/US$30.24) and singles are CFA12,500 (£13.39/US$23.62).

BIRDING SITE GUIDE
Keith Barnes
Birding Waza-Mora
This area holds the richest birdlife in the entire Sahelian band, where the recorded list seems endless. The many small waterholes here teem with waterbirds, and also attract many dry-country species desperate for water in this harsh environment. The best birds at Waza include the highly sought-after Arabian bustard. Waterholes about 8–10km south of the park entrance on the road to Mora support river prinia and sennar penduline-tit. About 30km north of Mora there are flocks of Sudan golden-sparrow, and anywhere where the feathery golden grass can be found is good for quail plover and is an excellent habitat for the recently discovered golden nightjar. The entire district could also yield scissor-tailed kite. Other range-restricted birds that are best looked for in the Waza-Mora area include Clapperton's francolin, black-crowned crane, black scimitar-bill, chestnut-bellied starling and black scrub-robin.

The park is open from mid-November to mid-June, and it is only possible to enter with a vehicle and in the company of a guide. In the dry season nearly all of the roads are navigable in a 2WD, although birding by 4WD is much easier. There are three main areas to bird around Waza: Waza National Park, the pools along the main road south of Waza and the area around the village. Waza National Park is also one of the best parks in West Africa for observing mammals.

Centre d'Accueil de Waza Near the main entrance to the park; tel: 229 22 07. *Boukarous* for two with fans and shared facilities are around CFA10,000 (£10.70/US$18.90). There is a kitchen available to residents and meals can also be provided, costing about CFA2,000 (£2.14/US$3.78). Camping per tent is CFA2,500 (£2.67/US$4.72).
GIC-FAC Café Restaurant du Ilme Millenaire On the access road to the park just off the main road. Basic accommodation from CFA4,000 (£4.28/US$7.56).

KOUSSERI AND AROUND
The paved road (currently particularly damaged between Maroua and Mora) continues northwards from Waza as far as the port town of Kousséri, at the confluence of the Chari and Logone rivers. It sits next to the capital of Chad, Ndjamena, which is reached by either crossing a bridge over the border or taking a boat or pirogue. Kousséri has a market on Thursdays.

Where to stay
Auberge Le Confort Tel: 229 46 36. A restaurant, bar and clean rooms for under CFA10,000 (£10.70/US$18.90).
Campement du Relais de Logone Tel: 229 41 57. Outside the centre, with clean rooms for under CFA10,000 (£10.70/US$18.90).

North of Kousséri
Apart from at the Kalamaloué National Reserve, there is no accommodation north of Kousséri on the way to huge Lake Chad. Check the current local security situation in this region before setting out, as it has suffered from a number of incidents involving armed bandits in recent years.

Lake Chad

To reach Lake Chad, take a share-taxi on the picturesque route to Makari and then another to Blangoua by the river. When the river is not dry, motorised pirogues can take you to the lake from here for around CFA5,000 (£5.35/US$9.45).

Kalamaloué National Reserve

Just northwest of Kousséri is the relatively small (4,500ha) Kalamaloué National Reserve. Created to protect animals crossing to and from Nigeria and Chad, it offers opportunities for viewing wildlife that includes antelope, giraffe, monkey and warthog, although animal populations have greatly declined in recent years due to illegal hunting. There are guided walks to view hippo and crocodile in the Chari River. Basic accommodation may be available at the Campement de Kalamaloué, although this was closed at the time of writing.

Moving on to Chad

From Kousséri take a taxi across the bridge to Ndjamena.

Moving on to Nigeria

Head for Fotokol to cross the border to Gambouru in Nigeria.

Moving on to Niger

You can cross Lake Chad to reach Nguigmi in Niger, but it is better to make the journey from Ndjamena rather than from the northern extremities of Cameroon, where there may not be any border facilities.

Appendix 1

LANGUAGE
French and Cameroonian French, and common Cameroonian terms

aeroplane	*avion*
after	*après*
air conditioned	*climatisé*
a lot	*beaucoup*
at what time?	*à quelle heure?*
bad	*mauvais*
bank	*la banque*
bakery	*la boulangerie*
beach	*la plage*
bed	*le lit*
before	*avant*
behind	*derrière*
big	*grand*
Biro	*le bic*
boat	*le bateau*
BP (post office box)	*la Boîte Postale*
breakfast	*le petit déjeuner*
bribe, tip	*le cadeau, dash*
bridge	*le pont*
bus	*l'autobus*
bus (large)	*le car*
bush taxi	*le taxi brousse* (also *cinq-cent quatre/brake/sept-place* – for Peugeot 504) or *bache*, a covered pick-up
bus/taxi station/bush taxi park	*la gare routière/l'autogare/le garage/la gare voiture*/motor park/lorry park
café/inexpensive restaurant	*la gargote*
campsite	*le camping*
canoe (dugout or larger narrow fishing boat)	*le pirogue*
car	*la voiture*
car breakdown service	*le dépannage*
charm or amulet	*le gris-gris*
checkpoint	*le controle*
chemist	*la pharmacie*
chief or boss	*le chef, patron*
chief or king (northern Cameroon)	*le lamido*
chief or king (western Cameroon)	*le fon*
closed	*fermé*

cold	*froid*
countryside, the bush	*la brousse*
crossroads or meeting place	*le carrefour*
currency or money	*le devises, fric, sous, l'argent*
details or information	*les renseignements*
discuss	*discuter*
doctor	*le médecin*
document	*la fiche*
do you have rooms available?	*avez-vous des chambres libres?*
do you speak English?	*vous parlez anglais?*
drink	*boire*
dugout canoe	*le pirogue*
eat	*manger*
enjoyable	*intéressant*
entrance	*entrée*
estate car	*le break*
excuse me	*pardon*
exit	*la sortie*
expensive	*cher*
far	*loin*
festival	*fête*
fine or penalty	*l'amende*
food shop/grocery	*l'alimentation*
four-wheel-drive (4WD/4x4)	*quatre-quatre*
go away	*va t'en*
good	*bon*
goodbye	*au revoir*
go straight ahead	*continuez tout droit*
headache	*j'ai mal a la tête*
hello	*bonjour*
here	*ici*
hot	*chaud*
hotel (inexpensive)	*l'auberge*
hotel (hut with thatched roof)	*le boukarou*
hotel-cum-brothel	*la maison de passage*
how/what?	*comment?*
how many/much?	*combien?*
hut	*la case*
I am looking for the market	*je cherche le marché*
identity card	*carte d'identité*
identity papers	*les pièces*
I'd like a one-way ticket	*je voudrais un billet aller simple*
I'd like a return ticket	*je voudrais un billet aller retour*
I don't understand	*je ne comprends pas*
inexpensive	*bon marché*
in front of	*devant*
inn or boarding house	*le gîte*
in the afternoon	*l'après-midi*
in the evening	*le soir*
in the morning	*le matin*
I understand	*je comprends*
I want to change money	*je voudrais changer de l'argent*

kerosene	*le pétrole*
key	*le clef*
later	*plus tard*
left	*à gauche*
less	*moins*
little	*un peu*
lorry/truck	*le camion*
malaria	*le palu/paludisme*
man	*un homme*
market	*le marché*
may I see the room?	*puis-je voir la chambre?*
medicines/medical supplies	*médicaments*
meeting place	*la palava*
midday	*à midi*
minibus	*le petit car*
month	*le mois*
moped	*la mobylette*
more	*plus*
mosquito net	*la moustiquaire*
motor park	*stationnement*
my name is...	*je m'appelle...*
near	*près/pas loin*
next to	*à côté de*
no	*non*
now	*maintenant*
OK	*d'accord*
open	*ouvert*
out of order	*en panne*
pain	*la douleur*
petrol/gas	*l'essence*
pick-up truck or van	*la bâche*
please	*s'il vous plaît*
policeman	*le flic*
police station	*la préfecture*
post office	*la poste/PTT*
prohibited	*interdit*
railway station	*la gare ferroviaire*
rainy season	*l'hivernage*
refreshments stall (at station)	*la buvette*
required or demanded	*exigé*
right	*à droite*
roadblock or barrier	*le barrage*
road map	*la carte routière*
room (with a fan)	*la chambre (ventilée)*
roundabout	*le rond-point*
rural guesthouse	*le campement*
saloon car	*la berline*
shared-taxi	*le taxi-course*
shop	*le magasin*
shower	*la douche*
slum	*le bidonville*
small	*petit*

small hotel or guesthouse	*l'auberge*
sterling (pounds)	*les livres sterling*
stomach ache	*mal à l'estomac*
straight on	*tout droit*
street food stall	*le chantier/circuit*
supermarket	*le supermarché*
surfaced road	*la route bitumée/goudronée*
thank you	*merci*
there	*là*
ticket office	*la vente de billets/la billeterie*
today	*aujourd'hui*
tomorrow	*demain*
town hall	*la mairie, l'hôtel de ville*
track, trail or dirt road	*la piste*
traditional entertainer (eg musician, storyteller)	*le griot*
travellers' cheques	*des chèques de voyage*
turn left	*tournez à gauche*
turn right	*tournez à droite*
two o'clock	*à deux heures*
under	*sous*
water suitable for drinking	*l'eau potable*
week	*la semaine*
what is your name?	*comment vous appelez-vous?*
when?	*quand?*
when does it arrive?	*il arrive à quelle heure?*
when does it leave?	*il part à quelle heure?*
where?	*où?*
where can I rent a bicycle?	*où est-ce que je peux louer un vélo?*
where is the airport?	*où est l'aéroport?*
where is the hospital?	*où est l'hôpital?*
why?	*pourquoi?*
witch-doctor or magic man	*féticheur*
with	*avec*
without	*sans*
woman	*la femme*
year	*l'an*
yes	*oui*
yesterday	*hier*

The use of 'tu' and 'vous'

- Adults use *tu* to children.
- Children use *vous* to all adults.
- Adults use *vous* to other adults whether they are business or social contacts, unless invited to do otherwise.
- Cameroonian acquaintances, office employees, workers, etc should be given the *vous* greeting.
- Women should use *vous* when talking to Cameroonian men. If a friendship develops, a Cameroonian will sense when to shift to *tu*, and you can follow.
- Always use *vous* with anyone with an official position – especially in the police or military etc.

Appendix 2

CHARITABLE ORGANISATIONS

WWF Tel: 221 62 67; web: www.wwfcameroon.org. The Worldwide Fund for Nature's Cameroon headquarters are in Yaoundé behind the BAT factory in the Bastos district. They have numerous current projects around the country and protect various sites.

Survival International 6 Charterhouse Blds, London EC1M 7ET; tel: 020 7687 8700; email: info@survival-international.org; www.survival-international.org. Survival International is currently lobbying the Cameroonian government to recognise the rights of the 'pygmy' peoples, who see their rainforest homes threatened by logging, and are driven out by settlers. In some places they have been evicted and their land has been designated as national parks. In Cameroon, the life of the Bagyeli has been disrupted by the World Bank-sponsored Chad–Cameroon oil pipeline. Survival opposed the building of the pipeline, and lobbied governments, oil companies and the World Bank to that end.

ECOsystemes Forestiers d'Afrique Centrale (ECOFAC) Tel: 222 42 71/220 94 72; email: ecofac@camnet.cm; web: www.ecofac.org. ECOFAC is the European Union's organisation set up to help protect Central Africa's forest ecosystems and the forest-dwelling peoples. Cameroon is one of the six countries covered by the programme (the others being Congo, the Central African Republic, Equatorial Guinea, Gabon and São Tomé e Principe, all with a combined population of 20 million, which is growing by 3.2% yearly). Tropical rainforest stretches over about 670,000km² of these countries' territory but is being lost at a rate of almost 1% each year.

VSO (Voluntary Services Overseas) Tel: 020 8780 7200; web: www.vso.org.uk. A long-established charity that sends teachers, health workers and other qualified people to projects in developing countries, including Cameroon.

Peace Corps Tel: 1-800 424 8580; web: www.peacecorps.gov. Peace Corps volunteers have done two-year fieldwork stints in Cameroon for many years. Applicants have to be US citizens aged over 18.

Earthwatch Institute Tel: UK: 01865 318 838, US and Canada: 1-800 776 0188, Australia: 03 9682 6828; web: www.uk.earthwatch.org. Earthwatch Institute is a non-profit organisation matching members of the public with scientists all over the world. Cameroon is one of the countries with projects where volunteers can participate. There are two current projects. One is helping to save the rock fowl, a threatened species, where volunteers join ornithologists to assess the population status and determine ecological requirements of the bird. It involves camping in the forest and trekking long distances and the share of costs is £895. Another project involves documenting endemic plants in the rainforest. There are also occasional fellowships for students and teachers available. The website www.volunteerabroad.com has details of Earthwatch and other expeditions.

Cameroon Education Corporation Suite A, 333 Cedarcreek Dr, Nashville, TN 37211; tel: 615 833 1740; email: mlantum@excite.com. The Children's Reading Corner Remedial Nursery & Primary School in Buéa was formed by the Cameroon Education Corporation, a recognised non-profit organisation in Nashville, TN. It provides pre-nursery, nursery, and primary remedial education to over 180 children aged 3 to 14.

Greenpeace International Keizersgracht 176, 1016 DW Amsterdam, The Netherlands; tel: 20 626 1877; web: www.greenpeace.org. Among its activities in Cameroon is the investigation of illegal timber extraction. For example, in 2002 Greenpeace released information about the illegal logging activities in southeast Cameroon of Dutch logging and timber trading company Wijma.

Forests Monitor 69a Lensfield Rd, Cambridge CB2 1EN; tel: 01223 360975; web: www.forestsmonitor.org. Monitors activities like illegal logging.

Centre pour l'Environment et le Developpement (CED) BP 3430, Yaoundé; tel: 222 38 57; web: www.cedcameroun.org. The centre researches potential threats to the environment such as illegal timber extraction.

Cameroon Biodiversity Conservation Society BP 3055; Messa, Yaoundé; tel: 221 16 58/772 66 08; email: cbcs@iccnet.cm. This organisation, an affiliate of BirdLife International, works in the field of rural development and poverty alleviation, encouraging the conservation of Cameroon's biological diversity through the protection of natural habitats, as well as the promotion of study and enjoyment of wildlife for the benefit of people. It implements research, conservation, awareness-raising and education projects, as well as community-based natural resource management projects. One of its recent projects concerned bee-keeping in the Mbam-Minkom region near Yaoundé, encouraging villagers to create alternative income sources to allow them to benefit from their forest without the destructive effects of clearing for farming or timber. Colin Workman writes about this in the chapter on the *Centre Province*.

The Bushmeat Project Web: www.bushmeat.net. The Bushmeat Project develops and supports community-based partnerships to benefit local people and develop alternatives to unsustainable bushmeat commerce. The programme works to provide economic and social incentives to people to protect endangered wildlife.

The Bushmeat Crisis Taskforce 8403 Coleville Rd, Suite 710, Silver Spring, MD 20910-3314, USA; email: info@bushmeat.org; web: www.bushmeat.org. The Bushmeat Crisis Taskforce is a consortium of conservation organisations and professionals working throughout Africa, including Cameroon, and is dedicated to the conservation of wildlife populations threatened by illegal commercial hunting of wildlife for sale as meat.

The International Primate Protection League PO Box 766, Summerville, SC 29484, USA; tel: 843 871 2280; email: info@ippl.org; web: www.ippl.org. The International Primate Protection League has field representatives in Cameroon working towards creating and preserving national parks and sanctuaries, strictly controlling primate hunting, trapping and sale.

Rainforest Foundation Suite A5, City Cloisters, 196 Old St, London EC1V 9FR; tel: 020 7251 6345; web: www.rainforestfoundationuk.org. This charity was set up by rock star Sting in 1989 to support the indigenous people and traditional habitats of several countries including Cameroon. In Cameroon it is encouraging greater autonomy for Baka people, and the protection of some of the undamaged rainforest that remains in the south and east.

International Fund for Animal Welfare (IFAW) 87–90 Albert Embankment, London SE1 9UD; tel: 020 7587 6700; email: info@ifaw.org; web: www.ifaw.org. The International Fund for Animal Welfare (IFAW) works towards improving the welfare of wild and domestic animals throughout the world by reducing commercial exploitation of animals, protecting wildlife habitats, and assisting animals in distress. They seek to promote animal welfare and conservation policies that advance the well-being of both animals and people. Founded in 1969, IFAW has grown to become one of the largest international animal welfare organisations in the world.

The International Union for the Conservation of Nature (IUCN) Rue Mauverney 28, Gland, 1196, Switzerland; tel: 999 0000; in Cameroon: BP 5506, Yaoundé; tel: 221 6496; web: www.iucn.org. The International Union for the Conservation of Nature works in Cameroon to prevent the bushmeat trade.

In Defense of Animals – Africa (IDA-A) 700 SW 126th Av, Beaverton, OR 97005, USA; tel: 503 643 8302; web: ida-africa.org. Supporting Africa's chimpanzees, this joint project of In Defense of Animals and a non-governmental organisation in Cameroon provides a sanctuary for captive chimpanzees in Cameroon and wages a conservation campaign aimed at saving the country's remaining wild chimpanzees. The sanctuary, the Sanaga-Yong Chimpanzee Rescue Center (SYCRC), was founded in August 1999 in a forest within the Centre Province of Cameroon. This primate care facility is dedicated to the rescue and rehabilitation of threatened adult chimpanzees, occupies over 2km², and is currently home to around 24 chimpanzees. The sanctuary accepts animals that are commonly rejected at other facilities due to their overpowering size, strength and level of psychological damage.

The Jane Goodall Institute 8700 Georgia Av, Suite 500, Silver Spring, MD 20910-3605, USA; tel: 301 565 0086; email: info@janegoodall.org; web: www.janegoodall.org. The Jane Goodall Institute promotes primate habitat conservation, non-invasive research programmes on chimpanzees and other primates, activities ensuring the well-being of chimpanzees, other primates and animal welfare activities in general. In Cameroon, the institute is focusing on the commercial bushmeat trade.

Rainforest Action Network Suite 500, 221 Pine St, San Francisco, CA 94104, USA; tel: 415 398 4404; web: www.ran.org. The Rainforest Action Network works in Cameroon and other countries in Africa, helping communities to protect their land by allowing their voices to be heard in the power institutions to which these local people have no access. RAN focuses on institutions and companies based in industrialised countries that profit from Africa's riches, often adversely. RAN has confronted the World Bank and its role in creating an economic framework that perpetuates exploitation of the land at the expense of sustainable development.

The Wildlife Conservation Society 2300 Southern Bd, Bronx, New York, NY 10460, USA; tel: 718 220 5100; web: www.wcs.org. The Wildlife Conservation Society has headquarters at the Bronx Zoo in America and works towards saving wildlife and wild lands throughout the world. In Cameroon it is currently working on a conservation and community participation programme in Banyang-Mbo Forest Reserve, is looking into crop raiding and the economic losses faced by local communities, as well as compiling a biological inventory of the Banyang-Mbo Forest Reserve.

Cameroon Wildlife Aid Fund Web: www.cwaf.org. This British wildlife charity works in Cameroon on projects such as educational programmes aimed at encouraging schoolchildren to stop eating the meat of endangered species. The charity began work at Yaoundé Mvog-Betsi Zoo in the late 1990s as an initiative to look after primates orphaned as a result of the bushmeat trade. A UK-registered charity based at Bristol Zoological Gardens, it also operates from the forest of Mefou National Park on the outskirts of Yaoundé, where young gorillas and chimpanzees are looked after in spacious enclosures, rescued from threats such as poachers wanting them for bushmeat. It offers three-month placements for volunteers.

Global Witness PO Box 6042, London N19 5WP; tel: 020 7272 6731; web: www.globalwitness.org. Global Witness was launched in 1995 and works on forest issues, especially illegal logging and the problems intensive logging causes. It does this at an international policy level. In Cameroon it is the official independent monitor of the sector.

The World Parrot Trust Web: www.worldparrottrust.org. The World Parrot Trust works towards the survival of parrot species in the wild and the welfare of captive birds everywhere. They restore and protect populations of wild parrots and their native habitats, promote awareness of the threats to all parrots, captive and wild, oppose the trade in wild-caught parrots, educate the public on high standards for the care and breeding of parrots and encourage links between conservation and aviculture. In Cameroon, the Trust supports the protection of land that includes clearings which attract tens of thousands of African grey parrots.

The Elephants of Cameroon Web: www.www.nczooeletrack.org. Cameroon's elephant population stands at around 20,000 and faces considerable threats. A research team from the North Carolina Zoological Park, Cameroon's Ministry of Environment and Forests, and the Cameroon office of the WWF are studying elephant migration patterns by placing satellite tracking collars on animals and then analysing their movements over many months. The conservation research programme has produced maps that detail elephant locations, help predict where herds will be at specific times and highlight travel corridors that the herds use to move between territories. The programme's website provides the opportunity to interact with project researchers and post questions, read field diaries, see elephant location data and participate in online discussion forums.

Appendix

BIRD SPECIES
At Korup
Palm-nut vulture, Congo serpent-eagle, African green-pigeon, grey parrot, yellow-billed turaco, great blue turaco, Levaillant's and red-chested cuckoo, African emerald cuckoo, yellowbill, little swift, African pygmy and woodland kingfisher, white-throated bee-eater, blue-throated and broad-billed roller, African pied, piping, white-crested hornbill, speckled tinkerbird, yellow-spotted barbet, fire-bellied woodpecker, buff-spotted and golden-crowned woodpecker, forest woodhoopoe, black-headed paradise-flycatcher, square-tailed and shining drongo, common wattle-eye, forest robin, little, grey, Ansorge's, plain, slender-billed, simple, eastern bearded, yellow-whiskered, red-tailed and white-bearded greenbul, leaf-love, common and green-tailed bristlebill, yellow-spotted nicator, wood warbler, white-breasted and pale-fronted nigrita, black-headed waxbill, yellow and African pied wagtail, Vieillot's black weaver, Gray's malimbe, green, collared and olive sunbird.

Also present, but a lot less common, are white-crested tiger-bittern, afep pigeon, brown nightjar, white-bellied kingfisher, spotted and Willcock's honeyguide, olivaceous flycatcher, white-throated blue swallow, lemon-bellied crombec, Maxwell's black weaver, crested malimbe and Johanna's sunbird.

At Mount Oku
Western green tinkerbird, black-shouldered kite, short-toed eagle, gabar goshawk, red-necked buzzard, African hobby, African green-pigeon, speckled mousebird, African cuckoo, grey, green-backed, Tullberg's and Elliot's woodpecker, Mackinnon's shrike, bar-tailed trogon, blue-breasted and white-throated bee-eaters, white-headed woodhoopoe, African thrush, Waller's and chestnut-winged starling, common stonechat, black-throated and grey apalis, willow warbler, garden warbler, black-crowned waxbill, yellow wagtail, tree pipit, baglafecht, black-billed and Preuss' weaver, yellow bishop, orange-tufted sunbird, yellow-fronted canary, thick-billed seedeater and red-faced crimsonwing.

At Mount Kupé
Palm-nut vulture, African harrier-hawk, lizard buzzard, red-thighed sparrowhawk, long-tailed hawk, black goshawk, Ayres' hawk-eagle, scaly francolin, white-spotted flufftail, tambourine dove, African green-pigeon, speckled mousebird, guinea and yellow-billed turaco, Klaas', African, emerald and dideric cuckoo, yellowbill, blue-headed and Senegal coucal, black-shouldered nightjar, Sabine's and black spinetail, little swift, chocolate-backed kingfisher, white-crested hornbill, naked-faced and yellow-billed barbet, yellow-rumped tinkerbird, thick-billed and Cassin's honeyguide, cardinal woodpecker, African blue-flycatcher, white-bellied and blue-headed crested-flycatcher, black-headed and rufous-vented paradise-flycatcher, shining and velvet-mantled drongo, western black-headed and black-winged oriole, grey, blue and Petit's cuckoo-shrike, red-eyed, pink-footed and large-billed puffback, brown-throated, chestnut and white-spotted wattle-eye, African thrush, brown-chested and fire-crested alethe, narrow-tailed and chestnut-winged starling, purple-headed glossy-starling, white-bellied and

snowy-crowned robin-chat, barn swallow, lesser striped-swallow, common bulbul, Cameroon mountain, little, mountain, yellow-whiskered, honeyguide, Sjöstedt's, swamp, grey-headed, white-throated and icterine greenbul, Cameroon olive-greenbul, African yellow white-eye, chattering cisticola, white-chinned and banded prinia, grey-backed and olive-green camaroptera, white-tailed warbler, green hylia, black-capped woodland-warbler, yellow-bellied and violet-backed hyliota, grey-chested illadopsis, black-crowned waxbill, magpie mannikin, baglafecht, spectacled, black-billed, Vieillot's black and forest weaver, crested and redheaded malimbe, black-winged bishop, scarlet-tufted, green, collared, olive, Cameroon, green-headed, green-throated, Ursula's, northern double-collared, olive-bellied, Johanna's and superb sunbird, mountain robin-chat, tit-hylia, chestnut-breasted nigrita and green-backed twinspot.

At the Sanaga River
Grey and squacco heron, osprey, palm-nut vulture, common greenshank, common sandpiper, little stint, black-winged stilt, white-fronted plover, white-headed lapwing, black tern, palm and little swift, giant and pied kingfisher, little bee-eater, singing cisticola, tawny-flanked prinia, black-and-white mannikin, African pied wagtail, orange weaver, Vieillot's black weaver, black-winged bishop, olive-bellied sunbird.

At Ngaoundaba Ranch
Little grebe, long-tailed cormorant, African darter, spur-winged goose, little egret, grey and black-headed heron, great and cattle egret, squacco and striated heron, hamerkop, black-shouldered kite, black kite, palm-nut, hooded and white-backed vulture, brown snake-eagle, western marsh-harrier, Montagu's harrier, African harrier-hawk, gabar and red-chested goshawk, shikra, grasshopper and red-necked buzzard, Wahlberg's eagle, Eurasian and grey kestrel, red-necked falcon, double-spurred francolin, white-spotted flufftail, black crake, lesser moorhen, African jacana, common snipe, wood and common sandpiper, wattled lapwing, laughing, African mourning, vinaceous and red-eyed dove, blue-spotted wood-dove, Namaqua dove, Bruce's and African green-pigeon, Senegal parrot, red-headed lovebird, speckled mousebird, western grey plantain-eater, Klaas' cuckoo, yellowbill, Senegal coucal, African palm-swift, horus swift, African pygmy-kingfisher, malachite, grey-headed, blue-breasted, striped, giant and pied kingfisher, red-throated bee-eater, African grey hornbill, yellow-rumped and yellow-fronted tinkerbird, Vieillot's and double-toothed barbet, lesser honeyguide, green-backed, cardinal, grey and brown-backed woodpecker, African blue-flycatcher, African paradise-flycatcher, square-tailed and fork-tailed drongo, piapiac, pied crow, African golden-oriole, red-shouldered cuckoo-shrike, common fiscal, yellow-billed shrike, northern puffback, marsh and black-crowned tchagra, tropical boubou, sulphur-breasted and grey-headed bush shrike, white helmetshrike, brown-throated wattle-eye, African thrush, violet-backed and wattled starling, purple, bronze-tailed, greater blue-eared, lesser blue-eared and splendid glossy-starling, pale and European pied flycatcher, northern black-flycatcher, common nightingale, snowy-crowned and white-crowned robin-chat, whinchat, familiar chat, barn swallow, common bulbul, simple and yellow-throated greenbul, African yellow white-eye, whistling, croaking, siffling and zitting cisticola, tawny-flanked prinia, white-chinned prinia, red-winged grey warbler, yellow-breasted apalis, grey-backed camaroptera, moustached grass-warbler, sedge warbler, greater swamp-warbler, olivaceous warbler, Senegal eremomela, northern crombec, willow and wood warbler, yellow-bellied hyliota, greater whitethroat, brown babbler, bush petronia, red-billed, black-bellied and African firefinch, orange-cheeked, common and black-crowned waxbill, bronze mannikin, variable indigobird, yellow wagtail, yellow-throated longclaw, plain-backed and tree pipit, baglafecht, spectacled, black-necked and village weaver, red-headed weaver, yellow-shouldered widowbird, western violet-backed, green-headed, scarlet-chested, variable, olive-bellied, copper and splendid sunbird, yellow-fronted canary and bronze-winged courser.

At Bénoué National Park

Hadada ibis, African fish-eagle, white-headed vulture, brown snake-eagle, banded snake-eagle, bateleur, lizard buzzard, shikra, red-necked buzzard, Wahlberg's and booted eagle, Eurasian kestrel, red-footed, lanner and peregrine falcon, white-backed night-heron, Stanley bustard, Senegal thick-knee, bronze-winged courser, helmeted guineafowl, double-spurred francolin, green and wood sandpiper, laughing, African mourning, vinaceous and red-eyed dove, blue-spotted wood-dove, African green-pigeon, speckled mousebird, western grey plantain-eater, red-chested cuckoo, Senegal coucal, pearl-spotted owlet, African palm-swift, grey-headed, pied kingfisher, red-throated, white-throated and northern carmine bee-eater, rufous-crowned roller, African hoopoe, green woodhoopoe, African grey hornbill, Vieillot's barbet, greater honeyguide, fine-spotted and grey woodpecker, African blue-flycatcher, fork-tailed drongo, piapiac, pied crow, African golden-oriole, white-breasted cuckoo-shrike, brubru, northern puffback, black-crowned tchagra, tropical boubou, sulphur-breasted bush shrike, white helmetshrike, African thrush, purple, bronze-tailed and lesser blue-eared glossy-starling, swamp flycatcher, European pied flycatcher, northern black-flycatcher, whinchat, familiar chat, sooty chat, spotted creeper, grey-rumped, barn and wire-tailed swallow, common bulbul, croaking, siffling and rufous cisticola, tawny-flanked prinia, grey-backed camaroptera, olivaceous warbler, yellow-bellied eremomela, northern crombec, Bonelli's and willow warbler, yellow-bellied hyliota, brown babbler, white-shouldered black-tit, rufous-rumped lark, chestnut-backed sparrow-lark, black-bellied and red-billed firefinch, red-cheeked cordonblue, bronze mannikin, African pied and yellow wagtail, long-billed pipit, little and village weaver, western violet-backed, scarlet-chested, variable, olive-bellied and splendid sunbird, yellow-fronted canary, West African seedeater, cinnamon-breasted bunting, speckle-breasted woodpecker, black-headed gonolek and Cabanis' bunting.

At Waza

Ostrich, white-faced whistling-duck, comb duck, northern pintail, garganey, grey, black-headed and squacco heron, hamerkop, hadada and sacred ibis, yellow-billed, Abdim's, woolly-necked, white, saddle-billed and marabou stork, African openbill, bat hawk, black-shouldered kite, black kite, Egyptian, hooded, white-backed, lappet-faced and white-headed vulture, Rueppell's griffon, short-toed eagle, bateleur, pallid and Montagu's harrier, dark chanting-goshawk, grasshopper and red-necked buzzard, tawny and Wahlberg's eagle, Eurasian kestrel, helmeted guineafowl, African jacana, green, wood and common sandpiper, black-winged stilt, spur-winged plover, black-headed lapwing, chestnut-bellied sandgrouse, European turtle-dove, laughing, African mourning, vinaceous and red-eyed dove, African collared-dove, Namaqua dove, speckled mousebird, western grey plantain-eater, Senegal coucal, barn owl, spotted eagle-owl, African palm-swift, grey-headed kingfisher, green bee-eater, Abyssinian roller, African hoopoe, green woodhoopoe, red-billed and African grey hornbill, Abyssinian ground-hornbill, Vieillot's barbet, grey woodpecker, pied crow, woodchat and masked shrike, lesser blue-eared and long-tailed glossy-starling, yellow-billed oxpecker, whinchat, northern and Heuglin's wheatear, northern anteater-chat, sand and plain martin, barn, red-chested and Ethiopian swallow, red-pate and winding cisticola, tawny-flanked and river prinia, grey-backed camaroptera, melodious warbler, willow warbler, chestnut-backed sparrow-lark, grey-headed sparrow, bush petronia, red-billed firefinch, red-cheeked cordonblue, black-rumped waxbill, African silverbill, bronze mannikin, cut-throat, variable indigobird, northern paradise-whydah, yellow wagtail, white-billed buffalo-weaver, chestnut-crowned sparrow-weaver, little weaver, red-billed quelea, pygmy sunbird, white-rumped seedeater, cinnamon-breasted bunting, white-backed duck, secretary-bird, painted snipe, spotted thick-knee and lesser moorhen.

Appendix 4

FURTHER INFORMATION
Books
Background/general
Scarecrow Press, US, has a series of African Historical Dictionaries.

Hachette and Jeune Afrique publish guides in French to francophone African countries.

World Bibliographical Series from the Clio Press, Old Clarendon Ironworks, 35a Great Clarendon St, Oxford OX2 6AT; tel: 01865 311350.

Taussig, Louis *Resource Guide to Travel in Sub-Saharan Africa, vol. 1, East and West Africa* (Hans Zell 1994). Has very detailed information on Cameroon, including lists of organisations, societies and conservation projects, and reviews of travelogues, guidebooks and maps.

Caulfield, Catherine *In the Rainforest, Report from a Strange, Beautiful, Imperiled World* (University of Chicago Press 1984). Fact-filled tour by Caulfield of the ecology of the world's rainforests and the related thorny issues.

Reader, John *Africa, A Biography of the Continent* (Penguin 1998). An introduction to the history of Africa.

Martin, Phyllis and O'Meara, Patrick *Africa* (Indiana University Press 1979). Covers the history, culture, politics, religion, colonialism, arts and other aspects of the continent.

Beckwith, Carol and Fisher, Angela *African Ceremonies* (Harry N Abrahams Inc 2002). A visual guide to the diversity of ritual and ceremony in modern Africa.

Murray, Jocelyn (ed) *Cultural Atlas of Africa* (Facts on File 1988). A cultural portrait of African history and culture.

Davidson, Basil *The Black Man's Burden: Africa and the Curse of the Nation-State* (Times Books 1993). Tracing the origins of Africa's independence movement, this book places the continent's current political instability in a historical perspective.

Boyle, T C *Water Music* (Granta Books 1998, Viking Penguin 1983). Lengthy humourous fictionalised account of Mungo Park's explorations 200 years ago.

Journalism about Africa
Marnham, Patrick *Dispatches from Africa* (Penguin 1980). A very insightful, entertaining book.

West, Richard *The White Tribes of Africa* (Jonathan Cape 1965). Absorbing examination of how white people integrated in 14 sub-Saharan countries in Africa.

Lamb, David *The Africans* (Vintage Books 1987). Very readable and entertaining best-selling political and social survey of Africa in the early 1980s covering 46 countries, remaining relevant today.

Harden, Blaine *Africa: Dispatches from a Fragile Continent* (HarperCollins, UK 1992). Harden was the African bureau chief of the *Washington Post*, yet a disappointing read.

History of Africa
Hugon, Anne *Exploration of Africa, From Cairo to the Cape* (Thames and Hudson 1993). Concise chronicle of 19th-century exploration of Africa.

Fage, J D et al *History of Africa* and *A Short History of Africa* (Penguin 1990). Concisely written but comprehensive.

Pakenham, Thomas *The Scramble for Africa* (Abacus 1992). A very readable history of the Victorian land grab of Africa.

Oliver, Roland and Atmore, Anthony *Africa in the Iron Age, The African Middle Ages 1400–1800* and *Africa since 1800* (Cambridge University Press 1975). Detail of these important periods in African history.

Birkett, Dea *Mary Kingsley: Imperial Adventuress* (Macmillan 1992). Absorbing biography.

Afigbo, A E et al *The Making of Modern Africa, Vol 1 Nineteenth Century, Vol 2 Twentieth Century* (Longman 1986). A detailed history with illustrations.

Diop, Cheik Anta *Pre-Colonial Black Africa* (Africa World Press 1990). First published in the 1950s, Diop says that both African and Western civilisation started in Africa.

Davidson, Basil *Africa in History* (Scribner 1995). Readable history focusing on the 19th and 20th centuries.

Davidson, Basil et al *A History of West Africa 1000–1800* (Longman 1977). Readable historical account.

Webster, J B and Boahen, A *West Africa Since 1800* (Longman 1980). A follow-up to the above.

McEvedy, Colin *Penguin Atlas of African History* (Penguin 1995, 1980). Historical overview of the continent.

Hibbert, Christopher *Africa Explored: Europeans in the Dark Continent 1769–1889* (Cooper Square Publishers 2002)

Manning, Patrick *Francophone Sub-Saharan Africa 1880–1985* (Cambridge University Press 1988)

Davidson, Basil *The Story of Africa* (Mitchell Beasley 1984). A well-illustrated book that accompanied a TV history of Africa.

Davidson, Basil *Modern Africa* (Longman 1983). Looking at African history since 1900.

History of Cameroon
Catchpole, Brian and Akinjogbin, L A *A History of West Africa in Maps and Diagrams* (Collins Educational 1984)

Delancey, Mark W and Mokeba, H Mbella *Historical Dictionary of the Republic of Cameroon* (Scarecrow Press 1994). This book examines the many groups that make up Cameroon and focuses on individuals who have played a notable role, delving into political, economic, social, cultural and other aspects.

Njeuma, Martin *Introduction to the History of Cameroon; Nineteenth and Twentieth Centuries* (Macmillan Education 1989).

LeVine, Victor T *The Cameroon Federal Republic* (Cornell University Press: New York 1971).

Politics, culture, environment and society in Africa
O'Brien, Donal Cruise *Contemporary West African States* (Cambridge University Press 1990). Includes section on Cameroon.

Blakely, T D (ed) *Religion in Africa: Experience and expression* (Heinemann US 1994)

Church, R J Harrison *West Africa* (Longman 1980). Thorough, first published in 1957.

Rosenblium, Mort and Williamson, Doug *Squandering Eden* (Harcourt 1987). Proposals for stable African environments.

Caulfield, Catherine *Masters of Illusion: The World Bank and the Poverty of Nations* (Macmillan 1987). Exposing the huge inadequacies of this international development lending agency.

Timberlake, Lloyd *Africa in Crisis* (Earthscan 1985). Examines political and environmental factors contributing to drought and famine on the continent.

Cutrufelli, Maria Rose *Women of Africa: Roots of Oppression* (Zed Press 1983). Laborious study of women's position in contemporary Africa.

Politics, culture and society in Cameroon

Delancey, Mark *Cameroon: Dependence and Independence* (Dartmouth 1989). Very thorough survey of the economics, politics and history of Cameroon.

Takougang, Joseph and Krieger, Milton H *African State and Society in the 1990s: Cameroon's Political Crossroads* (Westview Press 2001).

Pool, Robert *Dialogue and the Interpretation of Illness: Conversations in a Cameroon Village.*

Bjornson, Richard *The African Quest for Freedom and Identity: Cameroonian Writing and the National Experience* (Indiana University Press 1991).

Ngwainmbi, Komben Emmanuel *Communication, Efficiency and Rural Development in Africa: The Case of Cameroon* (University Press of America 1994).

Austen, Ralph A and Derrick, Jonathan M *Middlemen of the Cameroon Rivers: The Duala and their Hinterland* (Cambridge University Press 1999). About the Duala 'middlemen', who functioned as intermediaries between Europeans and their own hinterland for over 300 years. Originally traders in ivory, slaves and palm products, they then became colonial-era cocoa planters, and finally took a leading role in anti-colonial politics.

Burnham, Philip *The Politics of Cultural Difference in Northern Cameroon* (Smithsonian Books 1996).

Alexander, Lloyd and Hyman, Trina Schart (illustrator) *The Fortune-Tellers* (Dutton Books 1992). This original folktale set in Cameroon is full of adventure and humour, telling of a young man becoming the village fortune-teller.

Herrera, Susana *Mango Elephants in the Sun: How Life in an African Village Let Me Be in My Skin* (Shambhala Publications 2000).

Bocquene, Henri *Memoirs of a Mbororo: The Life of Ndudi Umaru, Fulani Nomad of Cameroon* (Berghahn Books 2002). Recounting the life of a nomadic Fulani and subsequently effectively shedding light on Cameroonian pastoral society. Ostracised because of his leprosy and befriended by a missionary, Umaru becomes a field assistant and searches for a cure for his leprosy.

Books about Cameroon for children

Grifalconi, Ann *The Village of Round and Square Houses* (Little Brown 1986). For young children, the story of the village of Tos, where the women live in round houses and the men live in square ones.

Travel health guides

Dawood, Dr Richard *Travellers' Health* (OUP 2003). A very comprehensive yet readable book on the subject.

Schroeder, Dirk *Staying Healthy in Asia, Africa and Latin America* (Avalon Travel Publications 1995). A detailed, good all-round guide.

Werner, David *Where There is No Doctor* (Macmillan 1993). Geared to the longer-term visitor such as an expat or Peace Corps worker.

Arts

Bascom, William *African Art in Cultural Perspective* (W W Norton 1985). Covering African sculpture.

Laduke, Betty *Africa: Women's Art, Women's Lives* (Africa World Press 1997). Cameroonian pottery and bead-making are covered.

Caraway, Caren *African Designs of the Congo, Nigeria, The Cameroons and the Guinea Coast* (Stemmer 1986).

Denyer, Susan *African Traditional Architecture* (Holmes and Meier 1978). Includes many illustrations.

Blier, Suzanne *The Royal Arts of Africa: The Majesty of Form* (Prentice Hall Macmillan 1998). Includes a chapter on Cameroon.

Werner, Gillon *Short History of African Art* (Penguin 1991). Rather detailed instead of brief.

Willet, Frank *African Art* (Thames & Hudson 1994). A good in-depth overview of African art through the ages.

Picton, John and Mack, John *African Textiles* (Westview Press 1998). Includes numerous photographs.

Huet, Michael *The Dance, Art and Ritual of Africa* (Harry N Abrahams 1996). Engrossing photography.

Northern, Tamara *Art of Cameroon* (University of Washington Press 1986). Includes colour illustrations.

Fisher, Angela *Africa Adorned* (Harry N Abrahams Inc 1998). Includes coverage of West African jewellery.

Etienne-Nugue, Jocelyne *Crafts and the Art of Living in the Cameroon* (Louisiana State University Press 1982).

Northern, Tamara *Expressions of Cameroon Art: The Franklin Collection* (Rembrandt Press 1986).

Natural history and field guides

Wheatley, Nigel and Helm, Christopher *Where to Watch Birds in Africa* (A & C Black 1995). A comprehensive chapter on Cameroon.

Borrow, Nik et al *A Guide to the Birds of Western Africa: An Identification Guide* (Christopher Helm 2001). An illustrated comprehensive guide to the region. Although bulky and pricey, it is often recommended by birders as being the best.

Van Perlo, B *Birds of Western and Central Africa: an illustrated checklist* (Collins 2002). Useful, convenient pocket-sized birder's book.

Fishpool, L D C and Evans, M I (eds) *Important Bird Areas in Africa and Associated Islands: Priority Sites for Conservation* (Pisces Publications and BirdLife International 2002). Contains a chapter on Cameroon.

Serle, W and Morel, G *A Field Guide to the Birds of West Africa* (HarperCollins 1977).

Mackworth-Praed, C and Grant, C *Birds of West-central and Western Africa* (Longman 1970).

Urban, E K, Fry, C H and Keith, S *Birds of Africa* (Poyser 2004). A comprehensive six-volume set. *A Field Guide to the Butterflies of Africa* (Collins 1969).

Guide des Parc Nationaux d'Afrique: Afrique de l'Ouest (Delachaux, Lausanne 1992). Francophone coverage includes some Cameroonian parks.

Alden, Peter *Collins Photo Guide to African Wildlife* (Collins 1996). Covering the landforms, wild areas, mammals, birds, reptiles and insects of Africa.

Kingdon, Jonathan *The Kingdon Field Guide to African Mammals* (Christopher Helm 2003). A well-regarded comprehensive field guide to African mammals covering more than 1,000 species, with excellent illustrations, although not the most user-friendly.

Haltenorth, T and Diller, H *A Field Guide to the Mammals of Africa* (Collins 1981). A classic, if a bit dated.

Stuart, Chris and Tilde *Field Guide to the Larger Mammals of Africa* (Struik 1997). Excellently laid out, with over 400 photographs for easy identification.

Estes, Richard *The Safari Companion, A Guide to Watching African Mammals* (Chelsea Green Publishing 1999). An in-depth guide to the behaviour and habitats of large African mammals.

Lambertini, Marco and Venerella, John *A Naturalist's Guide to the Tropics* (University of Chicago Press 2000). Illustrated guide to the natural history of the tropics.

Giles-Vernick, Tamara *Cutting the Vines of the Past: Environmental Histories of the Central African Rain Forest* (University of Virginia Press 2002). The failure of conservation in Central Africa.

Lanting, Frans and Eckstrom, Christine *Jungles* (Taschen 2000). Stunning wildlife photographs.

Oakes, John F *Myth and Reality in the Rain Forest: How Conservation Strategies are Failing in West Africa* (University of California Press 1999). A study of national parks and conservation in West Africa.

African travel narrative/travelogues

Kingsley, Mary *Travels in West Africa* (National Geographic and other editions, including Everyman 1993). A travel classic first published in 1897, with Kingsley's cool, amused yet enthused account of her 1890s travels in the region, including a trek up Mount Cameroon. There is an imperial tone yet the book is intelligent and Kingsley has no faith in colonialism or missionaries.

Park, Mungo *Travels into the Interior of Africa* (Eland Books 1983). First published in 1799, this absorbing account remains a classic.

Daniels, Anthony *Zanzibar to Timbuktu* (John Murray 1988, Century 1989). A very absorbing, entertaining account of a trip from Zanzibar to Mali, including Cameroon, by train, lorry, boat and canoe.

Stevens, Stuart *Malaria Dreams: An African Adventure* (Atlantic Monthly Press 1989). Rather uninformative travelogue about a trip from Algeria to the Central African Republic, passing through Cameroon.

Gide, André *Travels in the Congo* (Penguin 1986). This classic of travel literature, which covers Cameroon and which was first published in 1927, shows Gide an angry witness to the injustices of French colonialism.

Turnbull, Colin *The Forest People* (Pimlico 1994). First published in 1961, a study of the Ituri forest Bambuti 'pygmies' in the Congo.

Turnbull, Colin *The Lonely African* (Chatto & Windus 1963). Turnbull's follow-up book examining the importance and meaning of the tribe in Africa.

Dickinson, Matt *Long Distance Walks in North Africa* (Crowood Press 1991). Despite the misleading title, this entertaining book has interesting accounts of a climb of Mount Cameroon and the Mandara Mountains.

Cahill, Tim *Hold the Enlightenment* (Black Swan 2003). Amusing romp through the Congo.

Biddlecombe, Peter *French Lessons in Africa* (Little Brown 1995). One of a series of quite amusing and occasionally insightful books by this travelling businessman.

Huxley, Elspeth *Four Guineas* (Chatto & Windus 1954). Huxley's trip through the four anglophone colonies on the eve of independence.

Watson, Pamela *Esprit de Battuta: Alone Across Africa on a Bicycle* (Aurum Press 1999). Recently published travelogue that includes Cameroon.

Matthiessen, Peter *African Silences* (Random House 1991). About the author's travels in Central and western Africa, with an ecological bias.

Naipaul, Shiva *North of South* (Penguin 1980). Compelling, entertaining, enlightening, disturbing account of Naipaul's travels through Kenya, Tanzania and Zambia.

Cameroon travel narrative/travelogues

Murphy, Dervla *Cameroon with Egbert* (John Murray 1989). Rather rambling and certainly not her best book, but the most popular travelogue by far about Cameroon in recent years.

Barley, Nigel *The Innocent Anthropologist: Notes from a Mud Hut* (British Museum Publications 1983, Penguin 1986). Absorbing, entertaining and insightful account of Barley's anthropological expeditions to a Cameroonian village populated by Dowayos, a pagan mountain tribe.

Barley, Nigel *A Plague of Caterpillars: A Return to the African Bush* (Viking 1986, Penguin 1987). Equally good follow-up.

Durrell, Gerald *The Overloaded Ark* (1953, Faber 2001), *The Bafut Beagles* (Faber 1954), *A Zoo in My Luggage* (Faber 1960). Entertaining 1950s accounts by the well-known naturalist of his searches for various animals, evoking a very English colonial Africa that has long gone.

Deane, Shirley *Talking Drums: From a Village in Cameroon* (John Murray 1985). An absorbing account of Yaoundé-based English teacher Deane's experiences spending weekends working with the women of the village of Etam.

Sheppherd, Joseph *Leaf of Honey* (Bahai 1988). An account by an American anthropologist about the Ntuumu peoples of Cameroon.

African literature

Strathern, Oona (ed) *Traveller's Literary Companion* (In Print Books 1994, Passport Books 1995). More than 250 examples of literature from around the continent.

Maja-Pearce, Adewale (ed) *Heinemann Book of African Poetry in English* (Heinemann). A good overview of poetry of the continent.

Moore, Beier (edited by Gerald Moore and Will Beier, Penguin 1991) *The Penguin Book of Modern African Poetry*.

Allen, Benedict *The Faber Book of Exploration* (Faber 2002). Collates the words of many travellers and explorers through the ages, including West Africa.

Naipaul, V S *A Bend in the River* (Random House 1989). Covers rural life in Central Africa.

Boyd, William *A Good Man in Africa* (Penguin 1982). A light-hearted look at West Africa as seen through expatriate eyes.

Cameroonian literature

Oyono, Ferdinand *Houseboy* (1956, translated from *Une Vie de Boy*, Heinemann 1990) and *The Old Man and the Medal* (1967, translated from *Le Vieux Negre et la Medaille*, Heinemann 1982). Striking criticism of colonialism.

Bebey, Francis *Agatha Moudio's Son* (translated from *Le fils d'Agatha Moudio*, Heinemann 1971). Musician Bebey's debut novel about human relationships within a village.

Beti, Mongo *The Poor Christ of Bomba* (Heinemann 1971), *Mission to Kala* (Heinemann 1964), *The Story of the Madman* (University of Virginia Press 2001), *King Lazarus* (Muller 1961) and other titles. Beti is probably Cameroon's best-known writer, covering social and political satire touching upon anything from dictatorship and democracy to basic human conflicts. *The Poor Christ of Bomba* cynically features the failure of a missionary to convert a village and missionaries are covered again in his novel *King Lazarus*, while inter-tribal conflict is a theme of *Mission to Kala*.

Makuchi *Your Madness, Not Mine: Stories of Cameroon* (Ohio University Press 1999). Short stories by this enduring Cameroonian writer.

Beyala, Calixthe *Your Name Shall Be Tanga* (Heinemann 1996), *The Sun Hath Looked Upon Me* (Heinemann 1996). Chronicling the injustices of women in a male-dominant society.

Mokoso, Ndeley *Man Pass Man!* (Addison Wesley 1998). Entertaining short stories.

Kenjo, Jumban *The White Men of God* (Heinemann 1980). Covers the country's colonial experience, where a Cameroonian village becomes divided when a white missionary arrives.

Asong, Linus Twongo *The Crown of Thorns* (Cosmos Educational Publishing 1990). Tribal society in the northwest.

Mbella Sonne Dipoko *Because of Women* (Heinemann 1975). A story about a river man quarrelling with his pregnant wife over another woman.

Guides

Hatt, John *The Tropical Traveller* (Penguin 1993). A well-written, absorbing and entertaining book full of advice on most aspects of travelling in the tropics, including everything from money to flying, health, culture shock, and animal and human hazards.

Magazines

Travel Africa 4 Rycote Lane Farm, Milton Common, Oxford OX9 2NZ; tel: 01844 278883; web: www.travelafricamag.com. An excellently designed and illustrated quarterly magazine with stimulating articles about all aspects of travel in Africa.

Specialist libraries and resource centres
Britain
Africa Centre 38 King St, London WC2E 8JT; tel: 020 7836 1973; web: www.africacentre.org.uk. Library, reading room, restaurant, bar, bookshop, live music, etc.
Commonwealth Institute Kensington High St, London W8 6NQ; tel: 020 7603 4535; web: www.commonwealth.org.uk. Library and exhibitions.
Royal Geographical Society 1 Kensington Gore, London SW7 2AR, tel: 020 7591 3030; web: www.rgs.org. The society has an expedition advisory service and lots of resource material. If you want a 150-page report on the plants of Mount Kupé, this is the place to come.
School of Oriental and African Studies Thornhaugh St, Russell Sq, London WC1H 0XG; tel: 020 7637 2388. Large library.

North America
Center for African Studies Florida University, 427 Grinter Hall, Gainesville, FL 32611; tel: 352 392 2183
Institute of African Studies Columbia University, 1103 School of International Affairs, 420 W 118th St, New York, NY 10027; tel: 212 280 4633; web: www.columbia.edu
Council on African Studies Yale University, 89 Trumbull St, New Haven, CT 06520; tel: 203 432 3436

Websites
Government travel advice
www.fco.gov.uk The British Foreign and Commonwealth Office
www.travel.state.gov US Department of State Travel Advisory Department
www.dfat.gov.au Australian Department of Foreign Affairs
www.dfait-maeci.gc.ca Canadian Department of Foreign Affairs

News
www.africanews.org
www.usafricaonline.com
www.allafrica.com
www.africaonline.com
www.africadaily.com
www.news.bbc.co.uk BBC World Service
www.panapress.com PanaPress

General
www.bbc.co.uk/worldservice/africa/features/storyofafrica Includes links concerning West Africa.
www.wwfcameroon.org Worldwide Fund for Nature (WWF) Cameroon site.
www.camnet.cm/mintour/tourisme Cameroon's Ministry of Tourism's site in French.
www.cameroun-plus.com Listings for hotels, restaurants, *agences de voyages*, touristic sites and other aspects of the country from a visitor's perspective.
www.irinnews.org Information on regional trouble spots and refugee issues.
www.africasounds.com information on Cameroonian music.
www.cafonline.com The African Cup of Nations (CAF, Confédération Africaine de Football) official website.
www.sas.upenn.edu/African_Studies/Home_Page/Country.html The University of Pennsylvania African Studies site includes information on Cameroon and links.
www.ecowas.int The website for the Economic Community of West African States (ECOWAS).

www.crawfurd.dk/photos/cameroon/htm Jacob Crawfurd's website has 100 excellent photos of Cameroon with informative captions.

www.africanbirdclub.org African Birdclub has information and links for those going to the region to birdwatch.

www.afrika.no Index on Africa is a Norwegian site containing information on cultural issues, language, etc.

www.nhbs.com Online natural history, environment and science bookstore has a number of specialist publications about Cameroon.

www.weather.com and **www.weather.yahoo.com** Daily weather reports on various towns and cities in Cameroon are available from a number of websites including these.

www.zyama.com The Online African Art Museum has examples of art from Cameroonian ethnic groups including the Bamiléké and Bamoun.

Online air ticket sellers

www.onetravel.com
www.sidestep.com
www.travelocity.com
www.travel.com.au For flights out of Australasia.

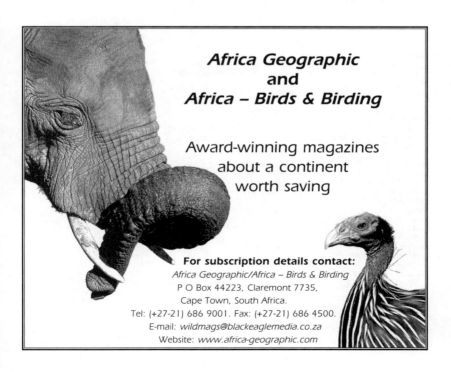

Index

Entries in italic indicate maps